"One must never confuse error and the person who errs, not even when there is question of error or inadequate knowledge of truth in the moral or religious field. The person who errs is always and above all a human being, and he retains in every case his dignity as a human person; and he must always be regarded and treated in accordance with that lofty dignity . . ."

—POPE JOHN XXIII, in
Pacem in Terris (Peace on Earth)

THE POPES' INTERPRETATION OF GOD'S LAW

This is the first book ever to summarize in one volume the teachings of the Catholic Church as expressed by the popes in their official letters. *The Papal Encyclicals* is of vital interest to readers of all faiths.

Ranging from the very beginning of the Catholic Church down to the present day, this significant collection covers the first epistle of St. Peter, the earliest letters from the succeeding Roman Bishops, and the voluminous directives of subsequent ages in which the popes have interpreted moral law in regard to the whole span of life, including belief in God, the Catholic Church and its doctrines, birth, marriage, death, political, social and economic events and theories.

Anne Fremantle, the noted writer and religious scholar, has provided historical introductions placing the time and contribution of each Pope and encyclical. Gustave Weigel, S.J., has provided the Introduction to this Mentor-Omega edition of *The Papal Encyclicals*.

Other MENTOR-OMEGA Books

THE
PAPAL
ENCYCLICALS
IN THEIR HISTORICAL CONTEXT

Anne Fremantle

With an Introduction by
Gustave Weigel, S. J.

A MENTOR·OMEGA BOOK

PUBLISHED BY
THE NEW AMERICAN LIBRARY

From twenty centuries of literature and scholarship, Mentor-Omega Books present a treasury of Catholic thought for the modern reader.

Grateful acknowledgment is made to the following for permission to quote from the works listed:

Ernest Benn Ltd. (T. Fisher Unwin Ltd.) (London) for *The Programme of Modernism* by A. Leslie Lilley (1908).

Benziger Brothers, Inc. for *The Great Encyclical Letters of LEO XIII* by Father John Wynne, S.J. (1903) and *Two Basic Social Encyclicals* (published by The Catholic University of America Press, 1943).

Burns, Oates & Washbourne, Ltd. (London) for *A Popular History of the Catholic Church* by Father Philip Hughes and *Church and State Through the Centuries* by Sidney Ehler and John B. Morrall (1954).

Carnegie Endowment for International Peace for *The Catholic Tradition of the Law of Nations* by John Eppstein; prepared under the auspices of, and published by, The Catholic Association for International Peace (Washington, D. C.) (1935); also published by Burns, Oates & Washbourne, Ltd. (London).

Catholic Truth Society (London) for *The Pope and the People* (1932).

Columbia University Press for *The See of Peter* by James T. Shotwell and Louise R. Loomis. Copyright 1927 by Columbia University Press.

The Devin-Adair Company for *Dogmatic Canons and Decrees* (1912).

Ginn & Company for *Readings in European History* by J. H. Robinson (1904).

Harvard University Press for *The Apostolic Fathers* edited by K. Lake (Loeb Classical Library).

The Macmillan Company (New York) for *Documents Illustrating Papal Authority* by Edward Giles, published in England by The Society for Promoting Christian Knowledge (1952) and *A Popular History of the Catholic Church* by Father Philip Hughes.

The Newman Press for *Church and State Through the Centuries* by Sidney Ehler and John B. Morrall (1954) and *All Things in Christ* by Vincent A. Yzermans.

The Paulist Press for *Mater et Magistra*, translated by William J. Gibbons, S.J., copyright 1961, 1962, by The Missionary Society of St. Paul the Apostle in the State of New York.

The Pope Speaks for *Fidei Donum* and *Princeps Pastorum*.

Sheed and Ward, Inc., for *New Testament* in the translation of Msgr. Ronald A. Knox, Copyright 1944 by Sheed and Ward, Inc., New York, and *The Church and Infallibility* by Dom B. C. Butler, Copyright 1954 by Sheed and Ward, Inc., New York.

The Tablet (London) for *Mit Brennender Sorge* (1937) and *Humani Generis* (1950).

Unitax (The Graymoor Press) for *Ad Sinarum Gentem* (Spring 1955 issue).

The Viking Press, Inc., for *A Treasury of Early Christianity* edited by Anne Fremantle, Copyright 1953 by Anne Fremantle.

Library of Congress Catalog Card Number 56-11328

MENTOR-OMEGA BOOKS are published *in the United States* by the New American Library of World Literature, Inc., 501 Madison Avenue, New York, New York 10022, *in Canada* by the New American Library of Canada Limited, 156 Front Street West, Toronto 1, Ontario, *in the United Kingdom* by the New English Library Limited, Barnard's Inn, Holborn, London, E.C. 1, England

PRINTED IN THE UNITED STATES OF AMERICA

Nihil obstat

JOHN A. GOODWINE, J.C.D.
CENSOR LIBRORUM

Imprimatur

✠ FRANCIS CARDINAL SPELLMAN
ARCHBISHOP OF NEW YORK

Acknowledgments

My warmest thanks are due to Father
Gustave Weigel, S.J., for his Introduction,
his notes on *Pascendi* and *Humani generis,* and for much general help and advice. Also to Father John Illich, of Incarnation Rectory, New York City.

Many encyclicals are quoted from Vatican
Polygot Press pamphlets, which can be obtained by writing to The Press, Vatican City.

Contents

INTRODUCTION: The Significance of Papal
   Pronouncements, *Gustave Weigel, S. J.*   9

1. What Is an Encyclical?   21
2. St. Peter and the Early Church   30
3. St. Leo to St. Gregory   51
4. The Church and the Holy Roman Empire   60
5. The Beginning of National States   71
6. The Church and the Reformation   82
7. Benedict XIV (1740-1758)   105
8. Clement XIII (1758-1769)   110
9. Clement XIV (1769-1774)   113
10. Pius VI (1775-1799)   116
11. Pius VII (1800-1823)   120
12. Leo XII (1823-1829)   122
13. Pius VIII (1829-1830)   123
14. Gregory XVI (1831-1846)   126
15. Pius IX (1846-1878)   129
16. Leo XIII (1878-1903)   156
17. Pius X (1903-1914)   196
18. Benedict XV (1914-1922)   214
19. Pius XI (1922-1939)   220
20. Pius XII (1939-1958)   263
21. John XXIII (1958-1963)   312

Complete List of Encyclicals Since 1740   425
Bibliography   442
Index   444

For Sister Mary Claudia Carlen

sine qua non

The Significance of Papal Pronouncements

A characteristic of our time is the absence of a predominant world vision guiding the peoples of the earth. Even our West is without a life-scheme to which the total community at least partially subscribes. All current philosophic blueprints for man and his habitat are minority opinions. As a result there is an openness of mind in our contemporaries to hear the theories of all the groups which make up our human family. It is not surprising, then, that so many thoughtful men are energetically curious to find out just how the Catholic Church considers life and society.

Of course many Catholics have offered their views, but they are expressions of the meditations of individuals. Many a non-Catholic wants to see something "official," and the nearest thing to an authentic synthesis of the Catholic view is to be found in the pronouncements of the Popes. Hence the need for an anthology of papal teaching has been felt by many.

Anne Fremantle has recognized this need and has been moved to meet it. For her zealous efforts the general reading community will be grateful. It is no easy thing to go through the papal records of almost two thousand years with the intention of extracting those documents which are peculiarly relevant to our situation.

Collectors of anthologies are perforce engaged in an ungrateful task. They must select individual items out of a *mare magnum* of material. No two persons will make the same selection, and every reader will wish to see a piece which interests him personally, though it may not interest others. As a result there is always a mild resentment in the reader because he does not find all that he wants and finds much that he doesn't want. There is no answer to this problem. Yet ours is the age of anthologies. We are impatient with a vast *corpus* of ideas, and we are sceptical of *summas*. The accepted compromise is the anthology. It is not the best way of achieving thought, but at least it is better than achieving no thought at all.

In any age an anthology is useful. It can act as an introduction to a whole field of theory and vision. When it does so, the reader is stimulated to read more of the source material. It is the hope of Anne Fremantle that this will be the fruit of her labors. She knows very well that a book of this size can do no more than offer samples of some of the wealth of papal teaching. She trusts that her offering of the samples will induce the reader to investigate the whole which can be found in other works.

9

In the light of these observations we can understand certain
omissions which might strike a casual reader as curious. For
example, the Leonine sociological encyclicals are not included,
except for *Rerum Novarum*. They were not ignored, but it was
necessary either to reproduce them in their entirety, which was
impossible in the compass of this work, or omit them entirely.
The omission is justifiable because these encyclicals are
gathered into volumes which are easily available.

Mrs. Fremantle planned this book for a large public. She
could not expect that such a public would possess even the
minimum knowledge which is a prerequisite for a Catholic
understanding of papal pronouncements. Hence she supplies
some elemental information without which much of her anthology would be mystifying to many readers. She has given
us a simple history of papal communications, introducing the
documents themselves into her story. The result is that there
is a continuity in her anthology which gives it the aspect of
narration rather than mere compilation.

Perhaps by way of introduction something more should be
done. A non-Catholic will read the papal message with interest,
and it will be evaluated in terms of its capacity to harmonize
with his beliefs. A Catholic, however, will approach the documents differently. For him the doctrine will be understood in
terms of Catholic faith and the Catholic theory of revelation.

Faith has different meanings for a Catholic and a Protestant.
To the Protestant, faith means a trusting self-surrender of the
complete man to the revealing God. For a Catholic, however,
this act of cordial surrender is called faith, hope, and charity.
To a Catholic, the word faith alone conveys the notion of an
intellectual assent to the content of revelation as true because
of the witnessing authority of God the Revealer.

Consequently the Catholic understands faith intellectually
and supernaturally. Faith is the Catholic's response to an intellectual message communicated by God. For the Catholic, God
reveals Himself through the medium of the teaching of the
living holy community called the Church. It is so important
for non-Catholics to appreciate this from the outset. A Christian of the Reform tradition believes that God makes Himself
and His truth known through a collection of books called the
Bible. This book is the teacher, and all other teaching is com-
mentary, good or bad. The divine message itself is restricted
to the Book.

In the light of these basic observations we can see the great
difference between the Catholic and Protestant conceptions of
the God-encounter. For the Catholic, the locus of meeting is
the Church, which for its task of bringing men to God uses
many means: the teaching of authorized masters, i.e., the bishops and their primate the Pope; the liturgy; books written by
men of the Church under divine inspiration, the Scriptures; the

common beliefs and practices of the Catholics stretched out over time and space. The inspired books, which have God as their author in consequence of their inspiration, are ecclesiastical instruments for teaching, guiding and exhorting. They are not over the Church, but rather a part of the Church's panoply to be used in her work of accomplishing the task of uniting man to God. It is the Church which teaches, the Church which sanctifies, the Church which builds and vitalizes. The Church is not a fruit of the Book but rather the Book is a fruit of the Church.

Hence it is that the Catholic does not say in the first instance, What does the Book say? Rather he asks, What does the teaching Church say? The Church and the Book say the same thing, and since the Book is in a peculiar sense God's Word, he will turn to the Book. However, this is not his ultimate recourse. He has only one ultimate recourse, the Church herself, and the Book is accepted from her hand and with her explanation. The Book is not the proof but only a divine expression in human language of the Church's teaching. Over the Book stands the Church, while according to the Reform conception, over the Church stands the Book.

This fundamental vision of the Church causes the Catholic to look to the episcopate for doctrine, because the bishops are the authentic exponents of God's message to the world. This is no idolatry of the bishops or their primate, the Bishop of Rome, but only a consequent of the Catholic theory of the Church. The Church is an organized visible fellowship theologically explained by the great scriptural symbols of the People of God, the Vine and Branches, the Body of Christ, the Temple of the Holy Ghost, the Marriage of Christ and his Spouse. Because it is a visible society, it has the social structure of such a union. Because it is divine in institution and dynamism, the Holy Spirit dwells in it, keeping it alive, keeping it true, making it grow. The Spirit is the source of the life of the Church, but that life is the life of a body. The body is made up of many members which are distinguished one from the other by functions for which they have a fixed structure. The hand is not the foot nor is the eye the ear, though all are in the Body and all live the one life of the Body. (I Cor. 12.)

In the Body, the bishops have the function of teaching and guiding, and this task they perform through the power of the Spirit who transfuses the whole Body, making each member effective in his function. The Body is one, and so the episcopate is one, as St. Cyprian said seventeen centuries ago. The unity of the episcopate is achieved through solidarity with the prime source of episcopal power, the Bishop of Rome, who is the successor of Simon changed into the Rock, on whom the Church was built and who received the keys of the Kingdom. In the primate dwells the fullness of episcopal power, and all bishops share it with him. Altogether they have no more than he has and he alone has all that they have.

Therefore, the Catholic sees in the Bishop of Rome the supreme source of teaching and guidance. In that man the episcopate is fully gathered; by means of the episcopate the Church teaches; through the indwelling power of the Holy Spirit the Church teaches because with the Spirit as the soul and the believers as the members, one living Body is formed and it is the Body of Christ himself, God's definitive legate to the world for redemption, sanctification and doctrine.

So it is that in the Catholic vision the pope teaches in the name of the episcopate and the episcopate teaches in the name of the Church and the Church teaches in the name of Christ, and Christ teaches in the name of God.

The above describes Catholic theory in blueprint fashion. It is the basic two-dimensional outline of a three-dimensional reality. In life the outline will lose its angularity, take on curves, deviate pleasingly from the rectilinear projection. In the hurly-burly of historical existence the severe fundamental outlines may not be noticed at first glance, and it will take much study to see them. This the Catholic knows as well as the non-Catholic. As a result one of the most important and most difficult tasks of the Catholic theologian is to keep in view the fundamental figure. To do so he will have to distinguish between the curves added by history to the plan established by God. The curves must be there, for otherwise it would not be a portrait of an historical thing. But the curves do not distort the basic lines; they only make them historically alive.

In consequence, the reading of the papal message over two millennia will give an historian a good index of the problems which vexed men in the Church in her contact with history. All of the pronouncements had some historical stimulus. In a period of perfect calm where there is no attacking storm, the popes do not speak, for there is no necessity. The struggles of the Christian in the concrete *mise en scène* of his moment call for guidance and light, and since it is the function of the episcopate to supply them, the popes will never fail to teach if the problems are more than local. The center of the episcopate will give the Christian message for the total Church.

Hence there is always an historical factor in papal teaching. The pope speaks for a definite moment of time, though he communicates a trans-historical message. The very language and forms of encyclicals show historical influences. The style is the so-called "curial style," set ages ago according to the norms of Roman rhetoric, for the papal language is usually Latin. This style is quite different from that of the vernaculars employed today, but the stability of the style is an eloquent witness to the Church's temporal continuity. The formalized style often succumbs to current needs: words like "typewriter," "motorcycle" and "airplane," for which the Romans had no counterpart, must be invented. That the communications are in Latin is due to the historical fact that the papacy is rooted in the ancient city of Rome with its language and style. That we see modern, invented words is due to the fact that the pronouncement deals with a contemporary situation.

When dealing with a contingent set of circumstances a question which seems merely abstract actually takes on very concrete meaning, and the total question is not a purely speculative one. Existentialist factors predominate. Into such a setting a question and its answer have burning facets which are far removed from abstract neutrality.

An analogy will serve to explain the point. Desegregation is an unemotional word in itself. In the light of such principles as the Christian brotherhod of man or Jacobin egalitarianism, the reality expressed by the word would be unassailable. Even in environments where the notion is not consciously related to principles, the label is not a fighting word. It may have this neutral quality in a place like Helsinki, Finland, but the situation in Biloxi, Mississippi, is altogether different. For Biloxians, something more than the simultaneous presence of Negro and white children in the same school is understood. In the minds of Southerners segregation is only one factor in a constellation of meaning, and an attack on the single factor is considered to be an attack on the total constellation. Segregation and desegregation have concrete meaning because of concrete circumstances. I doubt strenuously if even the abstract question of desegregation could have arisen in Finland.

Consequently papal directives face not only abstract problems but emotionally loaded concrete human situations. The hierarch must at one and the same time function as teacher and as director of communal coexistence. The direction is clearly for a concrete set of circumstances which will change with the movement of time. The doctrine is atemporal and always valid. Yet to divide the passing elements from the stable substance is not so easy.

Even an abstract proposition can produce communal nervousness by the very fact that its expression is an event in a community. The meaning of the abstract formula and its relevancy to the world vision of the group where the formula was launched may not be clear at a given moment, but the presence of the formula with all the acrid debates it arouses may be disturbing practically. The wise chairman of the meeting will shelve such a question and adroitly close the debate. The question is not answered because it seems inopportune to examine it in a heated environment. The question is not closed; only the debate.

Much of papal instruction shows this directional concern of the popes. They deal not only with speculative theory but with the very practical repercussions of such theory in a given community at a given time. Thus conflicting teaching seems to be given by the same or successive popes. It is easy to find papal affirmations in condemnation of democracy as well as papal praise of democracy. It is not wise to say that we have here a reversal of position. It is equally unwise to use one set of statements as indicative of the papal policy without referring to the other set. Jacobin anti-religious democracy was certainly condemned, but American democracy has been frequently lauded. Democracy is a chameleon word. The Soviet conception of democracy is not what the British understand by the term, and Mussolini said that Fascism was the most democratic society of all. When the pope speaks, he therefore must bear in mind to whom he is speaking and what the words can mean for his audience. The caution of papal communications can be seen in the subtitle of Pius XI's *Divini redemptoris* (1937), in which orthodox Marxist communism is rejected. The subtitle is: On *atheistic* communism. Whether or not a communism can be constructed in accord with Christian revelation is not being discussed. For many a student of the encyclicals, especially those in whom zeal outruns discretion, the cautious modifiers introduced into papal propositions are annoying. However, the popes realize full well the responsibility of their office, and they are always aware that after them there will come other popes who must not be embarrassed by previous solutions of concrete problems. The popes word their doctrine with extreme precision for a definite historical context, so that the doctrine will not necessarily take on meanings beyond those needed for the question to be treated here and now.

This qualification of papal communications, if overlooked, can lead to what the Germans call *Konsequenzmacherei*. The word means that conclusions are drawn out of given propositions with the aid of premises which the individual believes in, but which are not necessarily admitted by the original author of the propositions. The result will be that doctrine is attributed to the popes which they not only did not teach but which they reject. An example of this kind of procedure can be shown in the following form of reasoning which has often been foisted on the public. "The popes are opposed to Marxist Communism. But Marxist Communism is the betterment of the lot of the workers. Therefore the popes are opposed to the betterment of the lot of the workers." This is a mischievous presentation of papal doctrine. The popes have made it very clear over and over again that they seek the betterment of the situation of the workers. They have declared without ceasing this is one of the principal Christian tasks of our time. What they deny is that atheistic communism is the amelioration of the working-man's condition. To interpret the popes in the light of premises which they expressly repudiate is hardly an honest interpretation of their teaching.

At times Catholics themselves fall into the same trap. By projecting the papal message, they produce statements which are not the affirmations of the popes but which seem to the interpreters logically inevitable conclusions. However, the logic operates by the force of tacit or even unconscious assumptions which are not at all shared by the authors of the encyclicals. The interpreters then in bludgeon fashion brandish such extensions as valid papal teaching to beat down opponents who do not understand the Roman doctrine their way.

Another element in Catholic theory must always be borne in mind. It is what Cardinal Newman called the development of doctrine and others call the evolution of dogma. Catholicism insists that it teaches the preaching of Christ and only that. The Catholic believes that his beliefs are identical with those of the Apostolic Church, without a jot or tittle changed. However, he knows that the syntheses made in an earlier day are shorter and more meager than the syntheses made now. The affirmations of the Council of Nicaea (325 A.D.) are fuller affirmations concerning the constitutional structure of Jesus than the original New Testament statements. However, the Catholic insists that the doctrine of Nicaea is the identical doctrine of the New Testament. Nicaea detailed formally and clearly what was implicit in the scriptural formulas. According to Nicaea the scriptural title of Jesus, Christ the Lord, means and always meant that Jesus was God of God, Light of Light, true God of true God. The older phrase did not say it explicitly, but that is what is meant, and Nicaea made the implication explicit. The manner in which such explicitation is realized is generically the same in all ages. The serene faith of the total Church becomes agitated by some theologian who declares that the old and accepted formulas mean thus and so. When the theologian interprets the perennial expressions counter to the living consciousness of the Church, the *magisterium*, i.e. the teaching authorities, will reformulate the old expression so that the innovator's interpretations will be excluded. The new expression is obviously longer than the old one, but it is not a different one.

The way of development must be correctly understood. The drawing out of the implications from the older formula is not done mainly—much less exclusively—by a philological method. We can explain the philological method superficially by the example of the classical response of the oracle when asked by Pyrrhus if he could defeat the Romans: you will come out of the battle with the Romans victorious. The proposition is ambiguous. It can mean that the Romans will be victorious and it can just as readily mean that Pyrrhus will be the victor. It all depends on which word "victorious" modifies. Does it modify "Romans" or does it modify "you"? We cannot tell by mere literary analysis which meaning we are to take out of the statement. Two entirely different programs can be built for the guidance of Pyrrhus, and the builders of the different programs will quarrel among themselves, each insisting that he has the proper understanding of the prophecy. They must, however, ultimately use some principle of interpretation other than mere linguistic analysis. This other principle will then decide how we are to render the ambiguous answer of the oracle. The easiest solution would be to ask the oracle what she meant, but in the case of Pyrrhus this tactic was pointless, because the oracle on principle did not know what was meant. She repeated what the god inspired her to say. She was as much in the dark as Pyrrhus.

Yet in Catholic theory this easy solution is possible. The doctrine of Christ *lives* in the Catholic Church. At any moment, because of the abiding indwelling Spirit of God, the doctrine is known by the total Church, just as a man knows his total knowledge. If you quote to such a man a phrase he used on a former occasion, he can tell you what he meant by it and what he did not mean by it. If you argue with him that the words by linguistic analysis mean the opposite of what he is now saying, he will tell you that you misunderstand the meaning of the former phrase. This may not sound convincing to you, but the man is actually the only one who knows what he meant. He does not at all feel bound to understand his mind by your literary analysis of his words, because he knows what the words meant, even if it is not the meaning you derive from them. He may even explain to you why he used the particular words of his original statement by pointing to the concrete circumstances in which he was then talking, and he refuses to have you tear those words from their original context, which was a context of historical circumstances and not a mere context of words. There is a fluidity in verbal expression, because language is not a system of mathematical symbols with one and only one meaning attached to them.

The development of doctrine is the growth in awareness of the total content carried by ancient formulas. The result of such increased awareness will be new expression of old doctrine in the light of the impact of historical forces. The doctrine is the same but deeper and wider levels of its meaning are grasped and expressed.

The development of doctrine is a question of growth—the growth of the whole Church. The *magisterium* does not alone produce this development; it only formalizes it in due time. The episcopate with its center in Rome rejects invalid development and incorporates genuine reality into its teachings. The development, like all growth, is slow, almost imperceptible in short periods of time. The whole Church is involved in the process, for it is in the whole Church that the Spirit works. The first manifestations of growth will be in the meditations of the Church's theologians. They will formulate, often quite unconsciously, the living expansion. The theologians do not make the doctrine; they find it. The formulations of the theologians are not the authentic expression of the Church's teaching; only the *magisterium* can authentically express it. But the theologians are commissioned for their task by the directing *magisterium* and they work under its constant vigilance. They do more than merely repeat the authentic declarations; they compare them with the other sources of doctrine; they systematize their findings; they talk the language of their time and are very much under the influence of history. Hence it is that the consensus of the Church's theologians actually is the true echo of the teaching Church, for in the theologians we have the amplification of the authentic message so that it can be heard effectively by audiences gathered in many points of the ecumenical Church. Until the consensus is reached, there will be wranglings among the theologians and the famous *odium theologicum* will raise its ugly head, but time as the instrument of the Holy Spirit will bring about gradually and quietly the consensus which the *magisterium* will canonize when there is need to do so.

Many readers of this book will not be Catholics, and consequently will bring their own frameworks of discourse to their reading. Hence it is so urgent to point out the difference between the Catholic and non-Catholic conceptions of religious truth. The Reformers of the sixteenth century had as their intention the restoration of the genuine religious life of the early Apostolic Church. Actually this project was not restricted to the followers of Luther and Calvin. It was the goal of a great number of Catholics as well, and these men finally realized their ambition in the Council of Trent (1545-1563). What distinguished the Catholic reformers from the Protestants was their method. The Protestants thought that they had a way of knowing the doctrines and practices of the Apostolic Church without recourse to the Church's *magisterium*. They felt that the Scriptures without the episcopate could give any reader the portrait of the true Church and its doctrine. They had, therefore, recourse to philosophy and literary analysis. They also believed that the Spirit would enlighten the reading, not so much through His presence in the total Church but through His immediate action on the reader.

Consequently it is part of the Protestant tradition to suspend judgment on doctrine until the individual is satisfied that he can find it in the Scriptures, for "the whole counsel of God, concerning all things necessary for his own glory, man's salvation, faith and life is either expressly set down in Scripture, or by good and necessary consequence may be deduced from Scripture." (*Westminster Confession,* ch. 1, s. 6. 1647.) Hence it is that most Protestant Christians "test" all religious doctrine by the Bible. No religious teacher, not even the Church, deserves credence unless he teaches what the reader, enlightened by the Spirit, finds in the Scriptures. With the passing of centuries, Protestants do not understand the Scriptures so literally or subtly as their forefathers did, but the principle of personal judgment on religious doctrine is still proper to Protestant religion. Such personal judgment is, of course, largely determined by the tradition of the community to which the believer belongs. However, the principle is honored in all forms of Protestantism.

Consistently, therefore, the Protestant believer must see for himself that this or that doctrine is true. Before he accepts it, he weighs the doctrine in the balance of his own experience, of his own understanding of the Scriptures, of his own postulates concerning what God should be and say.

This is just the reverse of the Catholic's approach to belief. As the Catholic sees it, he must accept God on God's terms and not his own. It is not for him to "judge" the divine message but only to receive it. Since he receives it from a living teaching organ, he does not have to puzzle over the meaning of the revelation because the ever-present living *magisterium* can tell him exactly what the doctrine intends. The Catholic will be faced with the problem of reconciling one phase of the teaching with another, but that is essentially a theological enterprise which most people ignore. Theology, after all, is the pursuit of relatively few men.

If non-Catholics will bear this in mind, they will not be puzzled by the docility of the Catholic when he is given religious doctrine. The non-Catholic is so accustomed to work out his religious theory by his own efforts and convictions that it seems strange that the Catholics show no signs of doing what to him is the main task to be done. The basic difference between Catholic and non-Catholic approach to religious truth is that the non-Catholic *constructs* it in the light of his own experience and needs, while the Catholic *receives* it so that no reconstruction is called for or even in place. Both positions have their logic, but it is well to understand the logic of the Catholic position when confronted with Catholic pronouncements, for otherwise the Catholic position will not be understood. A non-Catholic will probably not like the Catholic way of achieving God's truth, but he should understand that way in order to deal with it intelligently.

This long introduction to Mrs. Anne Fremantle's anthology of papal doctrine is given in order to answer ultimate questions aroused by the reading of the contents of her book. However, there will be many readers who will not be interested in the ultimate questions. Nor does a profitable reading of the texts require such an interest. The popes propose their message not only in the light of the totality of revelation, but also with arguments intelligible to a non-religious man. The Catholic Church not only believes that its doctrine is revealed, but it also believes that such doctrine is reasonable. Hence it is that Church teaching always presents reasons for its positions. These reasons are not given for the ultimate motive of assent, but there is a firm conviction that reasons illuminate the revelation and that reason confirms and bolsters the tenets of faith.

Hence it is that readers of the encyclical literature will find much truth which they can assimilate without sharing the beliefs of Catholics, for whom the letters were primarily written. They will note that there is a calm tone of good sense in the affirmations, so that much light is given for the solution of the problems of our time.

There is even a richer good to be gained in the perusal of the papal documents. They are of history, in history, and for history. The Catholic Church is an old institution. Before the existence of many of the societies functioning in our time—the British Commonwealth, the Soviet Union, the Protestant Churches—she was ancient. The Church is not an ethnic group nor a culture, for she absorbs such things into herself. She is a society, strictly structured, dynamically united so that she speaks in a way superior to that of unorganized ethnic or cultural groupings. Her thought is not the spontaneous effusion of the *Zeitgeist,* but the reflective consideration of a moral person with a long maturity behind her. In her speech we note a familiarity with the great adventures of times past. She preserves a keen remembrance of her own critical moments, conditioned by vast or furious events in the story of mankind. She lived intensely in those moments, and she saw from the inside the events of our history. When we listen to her talk, we hear of "old, unhappy, far-off things, and battles long ago." We also hear of glorious things and triumphs more lasting and more solid than the strident din of arms. Whether history moves along the course of a dialectic is not so clear, but it is clear that it moves, and that the Church took an important part in that movement. The documents quoted in this book show that part and show up the movement. Our time, more than other periods of the past, shows a keen interest in the history of man, and Catholic doctrine is one of the most fascinating sources for an understanding of the evolution of humanity.

There is one last value which can be gotten from the reading of the papal message. We are in a time of crisis. A new period of history is aborning. Such a moment carries with it high responsibility for the men who live in it. Much which we know or knew will go, and new things will come. The new structure of things, in order to be highly satisfactory, should retain the solid values we have gained. Good men of every conviction should unite to conserve such achievements. We hear much today about ecumenical collaboration. Its first task is the understanding of one for the other. Papal doctrine is undoubtedly the most authentic expression of Catholic beliefs and positions. In the encyclicals the non-Catholic can see what the Church stands for, and knowing where she stands he can devise ways of collaboration. Whatever promotes mutual understanding, promotes mutual cooperation.

There is always danger of thundering in the index. Perhaps this little foreword has thundered too much. However, it is not important. The reader is enthusiastically urged to get into the book itself.

Woodstock College   Gustave Weigel, S.J.
Woodstock, Md.

Chapter 1

✝

What Is an Encyclical?

Just what is an encyclical? And why "papal"?

The word itself comes from two Greek ones, *en*, in, and *kyklos*, a circle. Thus *enkyklike* means a circular letter, a letter that is meant to "go the rounds." Originally, the term was applied to their pastoral letters by many bishops. Now it applies only to the letters of the bishop of Rome and successor of St. Peter, to his flock, all the Christians all over the world.

The "pastoral letters" of the popes have always been eagerly sought for, copied and preserved, and, as Sister Mary Claudia Carlen has put it, in *A Guide to the Encyclicals*, "the letters of the popes alone would suffice for a knowledge and understanding of the annals of the Church and its teaching."

The term "apostolic letters" has been given to certain specially important letters written by the popes. Of these, the first is the First Epistle of St. Peter, the genuineness of which was accepted in the second century A.D., after its use by Hermas, Papias and others.

When the pope today sends a solemn encyclical directed to the whole Church, he begins with the following words: "To our venerable brethren, Patriarchs, Primates, Archbishops, Bishops, and other local ordinaries, in peace and communion with the Holy See." The superscription contains the apostolic benediction and the date of signature, including the year of the pontificate.* The pope's name, followed by PP (for *papa*, the Latin word for pope) forms the signature. These documents are know as *litterae encyclicae* in general, and by their first words in the original Latin in particular; when they are addressed not to all bishops but just to some, they are called epistolae encyclicae. "Encyclicals," as the term is used today, are generally the *litterae*, addressed to all.

The "peace and communion" mentioned in the beginning of every encyclical are not merely words that occur frequently in classical Christian writing: they define a clear concept which, Dr. Hertling declares, in *Geschichte der katholischen*

---

* The popes used to date their year from March 25 (the feast of the Annunciation).

Kirche, "could almost be called a key to the understanding of the early Church."

The *communion* was understood by the early Christians to be the community of the faithful, that is, of the laity with their bishops, of the bishops among themselves, and of all with Christ. The outward and visible sign through which this community was, and is still today, constantly nourished and renewed, is the Eucharist. The Eucharist is the Communion, the reception by all Christians of the sacramental species of bread and wine, transubstantiated by the priest in the sacrifice of the Mass, into the Body and Blood of Jesus Christ, by saying over the bread and wine the same words used by Jesus Christ at the Last Supper on the evening before the Crucifixion. In the early Church, the sinner was excluded from the Eucharistic Communion, and therefore from the community of the Church. He was "excommunicated." If he repented, and did penance, he was readmitted into the *communion* of the faithful. The guest who came from a foreign church was admitted to the communion if he carried a certificate from his bishop that he belonged to the community of Christians. If he had no such "certificate," then the Eucharist and hospitality were both denied him.

In Rome, in the early days, when the different priests did not celebrate with their bishop, they said Mass on Sundays in the various churches. The custom grew up that the bishop said an earlier Mass, and had acolytes carry consecrated particles of the Host to the churches, which the priests then put into the chalice—the cup holding the wine—during his Mass. In the present Latin Mass, a prayer beginning with the words "this mixture and consecration" recalls this antique custom. Pope Innocent I (401-17) explained that this custom was "so that the priest may not feel he is separated from our *communion* on that day." Thus every priest, each Sunday, was publicly and demonstrably in *communion* with his bishop.

In Christian antiquity, to communicate with heretics meant to receive the Eucharist in their church. This was the reason why laymen who had to travel through places where there was no Catholic church, carried the Eucharist with them in order not to be forced to receive it in a heretical church, as this would have made them heretics, i.e., members of a heretical communion. Sometimes heretical bishops actually had Catholics who refused their Communion carried by force to the altar. This happened in the case of a heretical bishop of Constantinople, who forced the mouths of the Catholics open and obliged them to receive Communion, thinking they would thus be members of his communion, even though it was against their will.

In the fourth century, in Asia Minor, a small sect arose that did not believe in the Eucharist. They were called Messalians, and they were the only sect who allowed their members to receive Communion anywhere, either in Catholic churches or in heretical ones, because the Eucharist was not the source of the *community* for them.

When an early Christian started on a trip, he got a letter from his bishop, which served as a kind of passport. It made him welcome among Christians everywhere. This custom, which originated in apostolic times, was very useful not only to laymen, but also to their bishops. Without much expense, the bishops could in this way send mail and messengers throughout the whole Roman Empire. These letters were called "peace" or "communion" letters, because they served to prove that the bearer belonged to the communion and was allowed to receive the Eucharist. They were *encyclical* letters, for they were essentially letters directed from the center of the communion to the whole. This custom of giving a traveler a communion letter became such an extensive one that it was taken over into civil life. Julian the Apostate, when he was emperor (361-63), even introduced the practice among the pagans.

This habit was important, too, in the forging of church unity, for every bishop and every big church had a list of all the bishops belonging to the communion of the Church, and every change of bishop was communicated to the other churches. Thus, whenever a heresy or schism began, it was spotted; and the bishops sent around among themselves letters containing the list of those bishops and clergy remaining "in communion." The ultimate criterion in doubtful cases, then as now, was communion with Rome. And the encyclical letters were also, then as now, a means by which the whole communion of bishops and faithful were taught. They were a means to express the reality, the common teaching, and the interrelation among the members of the communion. This "peace" and "communion" set out at the beginning of every Christian letter was so important that it was also carved on tombstones: *Requiescat in pace* (often shown simply by the familiar initials, R.I.P.) implies that the sleeper died "in communion."

Indeed, every communication between the Christian churches, from the earliest days to the latest encyclical of the reigning pope, sends "grace and peace" in the very beginning.

In the fourth century, when the Christian religion and its hierarchies were given official recognition, papal documents were given different names according to their content, being called *decreta* or *statuta* or *decretalia constituta* according to whether they contained precise dispositions for organization, or appointments or instructions and exhortations on moral or religious doctrine. The names of these documents vary, but do not rigorously follow a system, so that they are sometimes called *sententiae,* sometimes *praecepta* or *auctoritates* when they are to settle disputes, lay down maxims, or solve some particular dogmatic question.

A complete index of the names given to these ecclesiastic documents would also include the *tomi, indiculi, commonitoria, epistolae tractoriae* or *tractatoriae.* Then at some point appeared the name of *epistolae synodicae,* which transmitted decisions of the episcopal synods. They should not be confused with the letters addressed by the bishops to the people at the time of their nomination, which were sometimes called by the same name in later times, having before been called simply "pastoral letters."

In the Middle Ages, the increasingly large and complex organization of the Church, which had become a great temporal and political power, produced a greater order and discipline even in the names of the apostolic letters, although the confusion in content remained, because often these documents, although they bore the same name, were of the most diverse nature. Sometimes they treated of strictly religious, and at others of exclusively temporal and political, matters. The papal letters, however, acquired a legislative aspect mandatory for all, so that no one could plead ignorance. The names of these documents were gradually clarified. It was established that papal letters and documents meant to solve problems of a general nature were *decreta* when emanating from papal decisions taken in consultation; and that, on the other hand, they should be called *constitutiones, edicta decretalia* and *sanctiones,* when they emanated exclusively from the pontiff's will. The solutions, however, of particular matters pronounced by the pontiff were given the name of *rescripta, responsa* and *mandata.* There appeared also some documents, most of which concerned political questions, that were given the name of *litterae curiales.*

Sixtus V, in his Bull *Immensa aeterni* (January 22, 1587), completely organized the offices of the Holy See, asking the congregations to fulfill specific functions, and the pontifical documents were given new names and were precisely defined.

Today, *Letters Apostolic* admit various classifications relative to their form. They consist of:

Papal Constitutions—which are ordinarily used for doctrinal or disciplinary pronouncements

Bulls—by which dignitaries are appointed, dioceses are erected, and saints canonized

Briefs—generally grants, the less important decrees, or privileges and concessions

Encyclicals—papal letters relating to doctrinal or moral matters; exhortations, warnings or commendations

Rescripts—regularly containing some grant or favor, some dispensation or privilege bestowed in consequence of some previous petition or request

Decrees—ordinarily issued by one of the Roman offices or congregations, to which the pope's approval is attached, either *in forma communi* (in the common form) or *in forma specifica* (in a special form)

Motu proprio—action taken on the pope's personal initiative

Chirographi (autograph letters)—letters in the pope's hand

Of all these documents, the *litterae encyclicae,* or encyclicals, are the most familiar. The term, used by popes from early days, was not common until the eighteenth century.

What is the authority of an encyclical?

The Church's authority derives from Jesus Christ, and is expressed in Scripture and through ecclesiastical tradition. From these come the Church's mandates to teach and guide the faithful through what is called the *magisterium ordinarium.* The Church teaches that there are four principal kinds of ecclesiastical matters subject to the sovereign power of the pope: faith, morals, discipline, and administration.

The pope ordains, as Cardinal Wiseman explained in his *History of the Last Four Popes,* "like an ordinary bishop; he recites his breviary like a common priest; he receives the Viaticum, 'for the journey' (Communion of the sick) under one species, and goes through the humble duty of confessing, generally to a simple priest like the everyday sinner of the world. In what is believed to be supernatural and belongs to the order of grace, he is on the level with his own children. He can give more than they, but he must receive the same." But when the pope defines truth concerning faith and morals, and he does so only when he himself states that he is talking in virtue of his full authority addressing himself to the whole Church and in order specifically to define, he is *infallible,* that is to say, he is preserved from error by God Himself. Even if the pope himself is a bad man, what he proclaims as truth to the Church cannot be anything but truthful; God Himself, who cannot save even the pope without his own concurrence, can, and does, protect His Church from untruth. For God is truth before even He is Love, and He promised mankind the Truth, and continues to provide it. The canons of the Vatican Council of 1870 put it clearly:[1]

On the Perpetuity of the Primacy of Blessed Peter in the Roman Pontiffs

That which the Prince of Shepherds and great shepherd of the sheep, Jesus Christ our Lord, established in the person of the Blessed Apostle Peter to secure the perpetual welfare and lasting good of the Church, must, by the same institution, necessarily remain unceasingly in the Church, which, being founded upon the Rock, will stand firm to the end of the world. For none can doubt, and it is known to all ages, that the holy and Blessed Peter, the Prince and chief of the Apostles, the pillar of the faith and foundation of the Catholic Church, received the keys of the kingdom from our Lord Jesus Christ, the Saviour and Redeemer of mankind, and lives, presides and judges to this day, always in his successors the Bishops of the Holy See of Rome, which was founded by Him and consecrated by His Blood. Whence, whosoever succeeds to Peter in this see does by the institution of Christ Himself obtain the primacy of Peter over the whole Church. The disposition made by Incarnate Truth (*dispositio veritatis*) therefore remains, and Blessed Peter, abiding in the rock's strength which he received (*in accepta fortitudine petrae perseverans*), has not abandoned the direction of the Church! . . .

Hence We teach and declare that by the appointment of our Lord the Roman Church possesses a sovereignty of ordinary power over all other Churches, and that this power of jurisdiction of the Roman pontiff, which is truly episcopal, is immediate; to which all, of whatsoever rite and dignity, both pastors and faithful, both individually and collectively, are bound, by their duty of hierarchical subordination and true obedience, to submit, not only in matters which belong to faith and morals, but also in those that appertain to the discipline and government of the Church throughout the world; so that the Church of Christ may be one flock under one supreme pastor, through the preservation of unity, both of communion and of profession of the same faith, with the Roman pontiff . . .[1]

And since, by the divine right of Apostolic primacy, one Roman pontiff is placed over the universal Church, We fur-

[1] *Dogmatic Canons and Decrees*. New York: The Devin-Adair Co., 1912, pp. 247-49.

ther teach and declare that he is the supreme judge of the faithful, and that in all causes the decision of which belongs to the Church recourse may be had to his tribunal, but that none may reopen the judgment of the Apostolic See, than whose authority there is no greater, nor can any lawfully review its judgment.

Therefore, faithfully adhering to the tradition received from the beginning of the Christian faith, for the glory of God our Saviour, the exaltation of the Catholic religion, and the salvation of Christian people, with the approval of the sacred council, we teach and define that it is a dogma divinely revealed: that the Roman pontiff, when he speaks *ex cathedra,** that is, when, in discharge of the office of pastor and teacher of all Christians, by virtue of his supreme Apostolic authority, he defines a doctrine regarding faith or morals to be held by the universal Church, is, by the divine assistance promised to him in Blessed Peter, possessed of that infallibility with which the divine Redeemer willed that His Church should be endowed in defining doctrine regarding faith or morals; and that, therefore, such definitions of the Roman pontiff are of themselves, and not from the consent of the Church, irreformable.

Thus the pope is *infallible* only when he defines a truth, or truths, that concerns faith and morals. And this definition is, in effect, a judgment; the pope distinguishes between a traditional truth, implicitly or explicitly known, and a new error. And in his definition, in the judgment he thus makes, the pope always defines by negation: the traditional phrase is, "if anyone denies that [such and such] is the truth . . . let him be anathema."

And the truth defined is always part of the tradition of the Church; it is to be found in the universal faith of one particular period, past or present; it is contained in the historic development of the Church. The pope, when defining, always does so in context, and always sets forth the truth he defines in, and with, its whole background.

According to the Vatican Council, the pope's authority in defining truths concerning faith and morals is exactly coextensive with that of the Church herself. The Church, and thus the pope, can teach infallibly by solemn judgment, or by the ordinary and universal *magisterium*.

As to the authority of papal encyclicals, Monsignor Joseph Fenton writes in the *American Ecclesiastical Review*:

It is quite probable that some of the teachings set forth on the authority of the various papal encyclicals are infallible

* *ex cathedra*—from the Chair (of St. Peter).

statements of the Holy Father. It is absolutely certain that all the teachings contained in these documents and dependent on their authority merit at least an internal religious assent from every Catholic.

Yet, as Father Thomas Peguès points out in *Revue Thomiste* XII, 1904, "the authority of the encyclicals is not at all the same as that of the solemn definitions *ex cathedra*. These demand an assent without reservations and make a formal act of faith obligatory." He insists, however, that the authority of the encyclicals is undoubtedly great: "It is, in a sense, sovereign. It is the teaching of the supreme pastor and teacher of the Church. Hence the faithful have a strict obligation to receive this teaching with infinite respect. A man must not be content simply not to contradict it openly . . . an internal mental assent is demanded. It should be received as the teaching of the sovereign authority within the Church." But in general "encyclicals do not contain solemn definitions like those of the Councils or solemn condemnations of heresy like those in the Constitutions."

There are some who may say that the prime value of an encyclical lies in the fact that it is an administrative instruction. Such an opinion, however, seems to weaken the doctrinal and dogmatic value of papal pronouncements.

In the *Summa Theologica,* in Part 2a 2ae (10th article), St. Thomas Aquinas asks whether the creed is subject to the authority of the pope, and concludes that it is, for two reasons: (a) because Jesus Christ prayed for Peter's faith, that it might not fail and because (b) the one Bread (of the Eucharist) "makes us one body" in one faith. Thus the pope is only infallible when he speaks *as* head of the Church, but then always and necessarily infallible. *Infallible* means he cannot speak anything but the truth about faith or morals, not that he cannot sin against either faith or morals. This infallibility is part of the primacy of Peter, and means that when the pope defines a doctrine he does not merely anathematize those who believe differently, nor only exclude error; he also determines and defines truth.

Encyclicals are thus not necessarily *ex cathedra* pronouncements. When they are, their matter must be of *faith* or *morals;* in method they must use the terms, formal or equivalent, *declare, define* or *pronounce,* and they must definitely state the "sanctions regarding the obligation to believe and the censures incurred." The encyclicals *Acerbo Nimis* (1905), on the teaching of Christian doctrine, and *Pascendi* (1907) are frequently given as examples of such *ex cathedra* pronouncements.

Those who follow the papal pronouncements, especially those of the last hundred years, will be impressed and astounded by the many and wide fields of thought in which they seem at home. The reader may even wonder how one man could amass such knowledge of so many subjects. Of course, it is well known that for all important pronouncements the pope makes use of preparatory commissions of experts, whose findings, and even formulations, are incorporated into the papal documents.

Since it would be difficult to choose from among the enormous bulk of papal documents accumulated during twenty centuries of Church history those communications of a doctrinal and universal nature having the form of an encyclical, and since such a choice would be arbitrary and unprecedented, and might not be feasible, it has been thought preferable for the purposes of this collection to give for the period from the earliest time until 1740, a brief history of, and examples from, what can be given the generic name of "apostolic letters." Only those have been included which were judgments—which influenced the history of their times or of all time. Most of those quoted in part, and all of the ones quoted in full, are not easily available. For several—*Unam Sanctam* and *Unigenitus* are examples—there is no good modern translation, and even the text is hard to come by. *Unigenitus* exists in English, as far as could be ascertained, only in an eighteenth-century Church of England translation of a Jansenist French version! The sequence of *encyclicals,* commonly so-called, begins with the *Ubi primum* of Benedict XIV (1740-58) published on December 3, 1740, and ends with the encyclical of Pius XII (1939–58) *Ad caeli reginam* of October 11, 1954. From 1740 on, all encyclicals are listed, together with their subject matter. Extracts are given whenever they bear on faith or morals, or have some particular religious significance. Since nine social encyclicals of Leo XIII (1878-1903) are published *in toto,* edited by Etienne Gilson (Image Books: *The Church Speaks to the Modern World*) less has been selected from them than from others. *Quanta Cura* and both syllabi, that of 1864 and that of 1907 *(Lamentabili),* are given, as these texts are not anywhere readily available.

Chapter 2

✠

St. Peter and the Early Church

The history of "apostolic letters" can be divided into three parts—early, medieval, and modern. Excerpts of the First Epistle (or Letter) of St. Peter are here given in the translation by Monsignor Ronald Knox.[1]

The First Epistle of the Blessed Apostle Peter

Chapter I

Peter, an apostle of Jesus Christ, to the elect who dwell as foreigners up and down Pontus, Galatia, Cappadocia, Asia, and Bithynia, chosen in the foreknowledge of God the Father, to be sanctified by the Spirit, to give their allegiance to Jesus Christ and be sprinkled with his blood; grace and peace be yours abundantly. Blessed be that God, that Father of our Lord Jesus Christ, who in his great mercy has begotten us anew, making hope live in us through the resurrection of Jesus Christ from the dead. We are to share an inheritance that is incorruptible, inviolable, unfading. It is stored up for you in heaven, and meanwhile, through your faith, the power of God affords you safe conduct till you reach it, this salvation which is waiting to be disclosed at the end of time. Then you will be triumphant. What if you have trials of many sorts to sadden your hearts in this brief interval? That must needs happen, so that you may give proof of your faith, a much more precious thing than the gold we test by fire; proof which will bring you praise, and glory, and honour when Jesus Christ is revealed. You never saw him, but you learned to love him; you may not see him even now, but you believe in him; and, if you continue to believe in him, how you will triumph! How ineffable your joy will be, and how sublime, when you reap the fruit of that faith of yours, the salvation of your souls! Salvation was the aim and quest of the prophets, and the grace of

[1] Msgr. Ronald A. Knox, *The New Testament*. New York: Sheed & Ward, 1944, pp. 505 ff.

which they prophesied has been reserved for you. The Spirit of Christ was in them, making known to them the sufferings which Christ's cause brings with it, and the glory that crowns them; when was it to be, and how was the time of it to be recognized? It was revealed to them that their errand was not to their own age, it was to you. And now the angels can satisfy their eager gaze; the Holy Spirit has been sent from heaven, and your evangelists have made the whole mystery plain to you.

Rid your minds, then, of every encumbrance, keep full mastery of your senses, and set your hopes on the gracious gift that is offered you when Jesus Christ appears. Obedience should be native to you now; you must not retain the mould of your former untutored appetites. No, it is a holy God who has called you, and you too must be holy in all the ordering of your lives: You must be holy, the scripture says, because I am holy. You appeal to God as your Father; yes, but he judges each man impartially by what he has done; look anxiously, then, to the ordering of your lives while your stay on earth lasts. What was the ransom that freed you from the vain observances of ancestral tradition? You know well enough that it was not paid in earthly currency, silver or gold; it was paid in the precious blood of Christ; no lamb was ever so pure, so spotless, a victim. Before the beginning of the world, God had foreknown him, but it was only in these last days that he was revealed, for your sakes; through him you have learned to be faithful to God, who raised him from the dead and endowed him with glory; your faith and your hope are to be centred in God. Purify your soul with the discipline of charity, and give constant proof of your affection for each other, loving unaffectedly as brethren should, since you have all been born anew with an immortal, imperishable birth, through the word of God who lives and abides for ever. Yes, all mortal things are like grass, and all their glory like the bloom of grass; the grass withers, and its bloom falls, but the word of the Lord lasts for ever. And this word is nothing other than the gospel which has been preached to you.

Chapter II

You must put aside, then, every trace of ill-will and deceitfulness, your affectations, the grudges you bore, and all the slanderous talk; you are children new-born, and all your craving must be for the soul's pure milk, that will nurture you into salvation, once you have tasted, as you have surely tasted, the goodness of the Lord. Draw near to him; he is the living antitype of that stone which men rejected, which God has chosen and prized; you too must be built up on him, stones that live and breathe, into a spiritual fabric; you must be a holy priesthood, to offer up that spiritual sacrifice which God accepts through Jesus Christ. So you will find in scripture the words, Behold, I am setting down in Sion a cornerstone, chosen out and precious; those who believe in him will not be disappointed. Prized, then, by you, the believers, he is something other to those who refuse belief; the stone which the builders rejected has become the chief stone at the corner, a stone to trip men's feet, a boulder they stumble against. They stumble over God's word, and refuse it belief; it is their destiny. Not so you; you are a chosen race, a royal priesthood, a consecrated nation, a people God means to have for himself; it is yours to proclaim the exploits of the God who has called you out of darkness into his marvelous light. Time was when you were not a people at all, now you are God's people; once you were unpitied, and now his pity is yours.

Beloved, I call upon you to be like strangers and exiles, to resist those natural appetites which besiege the soul. Your life amidst the Gentiles must be beyond reproach; decried as malefactors, you must let them see, from your honourable behaviour, what you are; they will praise God for you, when his time comes to have mercy on them. For love of the Lord, then, bow to every kind of human authority; to the king, who enjoys the chief power, and to the magistrates who hold his commission to punish criminals and encourage honest men. To silence, by honest living, the ignorant chatter of fools; that is what God expects of you. Free men, but the liberty you enjoy is not to be made a pretext for wrongdoing; it is to be used in God's service. Give all men their due; to the brethren, your love; to God your reverence; to the king, due honour.

You who are slaves must be submissive to your masters, and show all respect, not only to those who are kind and considerate, but to those who are hard to please. It does a man credit when he bears undeserved ill-treatment with the thought of God in his heart. If you do wrong and are punished for it, your patience is nothing to boast of; it is the patience of the innocent sufferer that wins credit in God's sight. Indeed, you are engaged to this by the call of Christ; he suffered for our sakes, and left you his own example; you were to follow in his footsteps. He did no wrong, no treachery was found on his lips; he was ill spoken of, and spoke no evil in return, suffered, and did not threaten vengeance, gave himself up into the hands of injustice. So, on the cross, his own body took the weight of our sins; we were to become dead to our sins, and live for holiness; it was his wounds that healed you. Till then, you had been like sheep going astray; now, you have been brought back to him, your shepherd, who keeps watch over your souls.

Chapter III

You, too, who are wives must be submissive to your husbands. Some of these still refuse credence to the word; it is for their wives to win them over, not by word but by example; by the modesty and reverence they observe in your demeanour. Your beauty must lie, not in braided hair, not in gold trinkets, not in the dress you wear, but in the hidden features of your hearts, in a possession you can never lose, that of a calm and tranquil spirit; to God's eyes, beyond price. It was thus that the holy women of old time adorned themselves, those women who had such trust in God, and paid their husbands such respect. Think how obedient Sara was to Abraham, how she called him her lord; if you would prove yourselves her children, live honestly, and let no anxious thoughts disturb you. You, too, who are husbands must use marriage considerately, paying homage to woman's sex as weaker than your own. The grace of eternal life belongs to both, and your prayers must not suffer interruption. . . .

Chapter IV

Christ's mortal nature, then, has been crucified, and you must arm yourselves with the same intention; he whose mortal nature has been crucified is quit, now, of sin. The rest of your mortal life must be ordered by God's will, not by human appetites. Time enough has been spent already in doing what the heathen would have you do, following a course of incontinence, passion, drunkenness, revelling, carousal, and shameful idolatry. They are surprised that you do not rush headlong into the same welter of debauch, and call you ill names accordingly; they will have to answer for it before him who is all in readiness to pass sentence on the living and the dead. That is why dead men, too, had the gospel message brought to them; though their mortal natures had paid the penalty in men's eyes, in the sight of God their spirits were to live on. . . .

Chapter V

And now I have a charge to give to the presbyters in your company; I, who am a presbyter like themselves, I, who bear

witness of Christ's sufferings, I, who have my part in that
glory which will one day be revealed. Be shepherds to the
flock God has given you. Carry out your charge as God
would have done it, cordially, not like drudges, generously,
not in the hope of sordid gain; not tyrannizing, each in his
own sphere, but setting an example, as best you may, to the
flock. So, when the Prince of shepherds makes himself
known, your prize will be that crown of glory which cannot
fade. And you, who are young, must defer to these, your sen-
iors. Deference to one another is the livery you must all wear;
God thwarts the proud, and keeps his grace for the
humble. . . .

I count on Silvanus as a faithful brother; and through him
I am sending you this brief letter for your encouragement;
to assure you that the grace in which you are so firmly
established is the true grace of God. The church here in
Babylon,* united with you by God's election, sends you her
greeting; so does my son, Mark. Greet one another with the
kiss of fellowship. Grace** be to all of you, friends in Christ
Jesus. Amen.

Of St. Linus, who succeeded St. Peter, no letter has survived. But the first epistle of St. Clement, the third successor
of St. Peter, "is perhaps the most famous document of primitive Christianity outside the New Testament."[2] It was probably
written about A.D. 95 or 96. The first manuscript of this
epistle brought to the West in modern times was sent by the
patriarch of Constantinople to King Charles I of England,
and was translated in 1633. The Church of Corinth was
founded by St. Paul, and, when St. Clement wrote, St. John
was probably still alive. But Rome, some 600 miles away,
intervened in a dispute about the authority of the Ministry.
And the Church of England Bishop of Oxford, Charles Gore,
commented that "the letter is written with a tone of considerable authority."

But to pass from the examples of ancient days, let us come
to those champions who lived very near to our time. Let us
set before us the noble examples of our own generation.
Through envy and malice, the greatest and most righteous
pillars of the Church were persecuted and contended even

---

* The word "church" is not expressed, but is evidently meant to be under-
stood, in the Greek. There can be little doubt that Babylon means Rome: cf.
Apocalypse xvii. 5. The Mark here mentioned, according to tradition, is the
Evangelist.
** For "grace" the Greek has "peace."
[2] James T. Shotwell and Louise Ropes Loomis, *The See of Peter.* New York:
Columbia University Press, 1927, p. 58.

unto death. Let us set before our eyes the good apostles. There was Peter, who by reason of unrighteous envy endured not one nor two but many trials, and so, having borne his testimony,* he passed to his appointed place of glory. Amid envy and strife, Paul pointed out the way to the prize of patient endurance. After he had been seven times in bonds, been driven into exile, been stoned, been a herald in the East and the West, he won noble renown for his faith, for he taught righteousness unto the whole world and reached the farthest bounds of the West and bore his testimony before the rulers; thus he departed from the world and passed unto the holy place, having set an illustrious pattern of patient endurance.

Unto these men of holy lives was gathered a vast multitude of the elect, who through many indignities and tortures endured envy and set a fair example among us.

. . . Receive our counsel and you will have no cause for regret.

. . . But if any disobey the words spoken by him through us, let them know that they will involve themselves in transgression and no small danger.

. . . For you will give us joy and gladness if, obedient to what we have written through the Holy Spirit, you root out the lawless anger of your jealousy, according to the prayer for peace and concord which we have made in this letter. We are sending faithful and discreet men, who have lived among us without blame from youth to old age. They will be witnesses between you and us. This we do that you may know that all our care has been, and still is, that you may be at peace.[3]

THE EARLY CHURCH AND HER PROBLEMS

All reality expresses itself in relationship. From the moment of her beginning, in the upper room at Jerusalem at Pentecost, when the Holy Spirit descended on the apostles in tongues of fire, the Church had to face one problem after another, one relationship after another. The early Christians first had to learn to live in two worlds: the pagan world all around them, and the small nucleus of the new world of the redeemed. The early church letters deal with concrete examples of these

---

* In Greek μαρτυρήσας "having been a martyr," that is, a witness. The word was not yet confined exclusively to its later Christian meaning of bearing testimony unto death. After the first two centuries, the term "confessor" gradually came into use for persons who testified to their faith under trial or persecution of any sort and "martyr" denoted those who sealed their profession by death.

[3]*The Apostolic Fathers*, ed. K. Lake. Loeb Classical Library 1913, (Harvard University Press) I, 16-18 (1st edition)

problems as they come up: What to do about Christians who
fall away under pagan torture and persecution? What to do
about Christians who disagree with one another? From earliest
times, the Church possessed one only source of authority, the
person of Jesus Christ her Lord. His mandate was clearly expressed in the two authentic sources of the knowledge she
has of her authority: the four Gospels and the traditions derived from the apostles and their successors. It was this
tradition that was constantly invoked in the various disputes
that arose.

For example, Irenaeus, bishop of Lyons from A.D. 178,
wrote in his book *Against the Heresies* about A.D. 180: "This
faith the Church, although scattered over the whole world,
observes diligently, as if it occupied but one house, and be-
haves as if it had but one mind, and preaches and teaches
as if it had but one mouth. And although there are many
dialects in the world, the force of the tradition is one and the
same. For the same faith is held and handed down by the
churches established in the Germanies, the Spains, among
the Celtic tribes, in the East, in Libya, and in the central
portions of the world."

The Roman primacy was already involved in the dispute
over Easter. The "communities of the whole of Asia, relying
on a tradition of great antiquity," as Eusebius (A.D. 311) put
it, thought the day should coincide with the Jewish passover,
whereas the "churches throughout the rest of the world"
thought the fast must end on the "day of the resurrection
of our Saviour." St. Victor I, the then pope (the thirteenth
after St. Peter), who reigned from *c.* 189 to *c.* 199, "denounced
in letters" the communities of the whole of Asia, and proclaimed that the brethren of those parts "were all wholly excommunicated" (Eusebius, Book 5, Chapter 23). Then St.
Irenaeus "wrote on behalf of the brethren in Gaul, whose
leader he was" and "did entreat and negotiate on behalf of the
peace of the churches—a man well named, for he was a peace-
maker both in name and character."

Another, far graver, problem now vexed the Church—the
problem of those Christians who had committed mortal sin
after baptism. Apostasy was the most obvious of such sins, as
it was the most serious, immediate issue. Many Christians,
under torture, or simply under strong political pressure of persecution, denied their faith. Then, when times improved, they
wished to be received back into the Church. The *Shepherd*,
"written quite recently in our own time by Hermas, while
his brother Pius, the bishop, was filling the chair of the church
of the city of Rome," as the Muratorian Fragment (written
170-80) has it (trans. J. C. Ayer, *Source Book for Ancient*

Church History), declared that by "repentance those who fall after baptism will be forgiven." The "lapsed," as they were called, could be reconciled again with the Church. (Of course, the same problem arose with adulterers, and other sinners, as with apostates.) St. Cyprian of Carthage, bishop during the Decian persecution (250-51) when the pope, St. Fabian (reigned 236-50), had been martyred and the see was vacant, notes that "upon one man He builds His Church," and insisted that "he who has not the Church for his mother has God no more for his Father. If a man could escape who was outside the ark of Noah, then he also may escape who is outside the Church." But, although St. Cyprian was indignant at "some of the lapsed who balked at penance and at making atonement to God" (many availed themselves of letters from their stauncher brethren who, before martyrdom, had interceded for the weaker), he yet agreed with St. Fabian that there was a "lawful way of salvation." But the proponents of easy reconciliation "offered peace who themselves have no peace. They who themselves have deserted the Church are preventing the Church from bringing back and recalling the lapsed. There is one God and one Christ and one Church and one seat of office established upon Peter by the word of the Lord. Another altar cannot be erected nor a new priesthood created beside the one altar and the one priesthood," as St. Cyprian wrote in his XLIII Letter in March 251.

It was in March 251 that St. Cornelius was elected pope by a majority of the clergy. But a few of the rigorists, who believed the Church should utterly reject the lapsed, withdrew from the assembly that elected Cornelius, and elected Novatian, sending one Maximus, with a whole delegation, to Carthage to try to persuade St. Cyprian to come over to their side. St. Cornelius merely sent a letter "regular in form," as Dr. Shotwell puts it, "and reported what professed to be a perfectly regular election. St. Cyprian then read it to his council. The lengthy communication from Novatian reported an admitted irregularity and was polemic in style. Cyprian did not read it to his clergy but merely stated the fact of the second election." This emphasizes the importance given to papal letters: that one from the true pope should be more valued than a whole personal embassy from the false antipope. Cornelius' brief reign of two years, which marks, as Dr. Shotwell says, "one of the crises in the history of ecclesiastical practice and dogma," is also memorable because three letters from Cornelius' own pen have been preserved, "the first indubitable utterances of a Roman bishop since the letter of Clement."[4]

4 Shotwell and Loomis, *op. cit.*, p. 352.

The text is to be found in Cyprian, *Epistolae*, XLIX, edited by W. Hartel, *Corpus Scriptorum Ecclesiasticorum Latinorum*, pp. 608-12.[5]

Cornelius, To His Brother Cyprian, Greeting.

The care and anxiety that we have endured over those confessors who were deluded and almost blinded and estranged from the Church by the guile and malice of an unscrupulous deceiver have been great but the joy which now relieves us is equally great and we give thanks to Almighty God and Christ our Lord that they have perceived their error and recognized the poisonous, serpentine wiles of the evildoer and by their own clear voice, as they themselves declare from their hearts, have returned to the Church which they had left. . . . When the whole affair had been reported to me, I decided that the presbyters should be called together. There were present also five bishops, who were with us on that day. For I wished that after thorough consultation it might be determined by general agreement what should be done with regard to these men. And in order that you may know the feeling of us all and each person's opinion I have thought best to notify you of our various judgments, which you may read enclosed with this. Then Maximus, Urbanus, Sidonius, and many brothers who had agreed with them, came into the presbytery and begged earnestly that the events now past might be forgotten and never again mentioned and that henceforth all their sins might be obliterated, whether of deed or word. . . .

The next step was to bring the entire performance to the knowledge of the people, so that they too might see them standing within the church, after they had so long beheld them wandering and astray. When this intention was made known, there was a huge gathering of the brotherhood. With one voice they all gave thanks to God, and showed by tears the joy in their bosoms, embracing the confessors as if it had been the day of their liberation from the pains of prison. I will give you the confessors' own declaration. "We," they said, "recognize Cornelius as bishop of the most holy Catholic Church, chosen by Almighty God and Christ our Lord. We confess our error; we have been victims of imposture; we have been deceived by perfidy and loquacity. Yet even though we seemed to hold a kind of communion with one who was a schismatic and a heretic, our heart was always in the Church. And we know that there is one God and one Christ the Lord whom we have confessed, and one Holy Spirit and that in a

[5] Translated in *ibid.*, p. 364.

catholic church there ought to be one bishop." Who would not have been moved by this profession? ... So we bade the priest Maximus resume his office. All the past errors of the others we committed by an overwhelming vote of the people to Almighty God, to Whose power all things are reserved.

St. Cyprian wrote to a brother bishop who was still hesitant whether to acknowledge Cornelius or Novatian, because Cornelius "was holding communion from time to time with persons who had offered sacrifice (to idols)." This, St. Cyprian says in Letter LV, "originated also in the tales invented by the apostates. . . . The bond of harmony stood firm, and the indivisible sacrament of the Catholic Church continued." And he goes on to say: "As to the character of Novatian, dearest brother, about whom you requested I should write you what heresy he has introduced, remember in the first place that we ought not even to be inquisitive as to what he teaches, so long as he teaches outside the Church. Whoever he is and whatever he is, he who is not in the Church of Christ is not a Christian."[6]

In his Letter LIX,[7] St. Cyprian wrote to St. Cornelius about the troubles in Africa,* where Felicissimus and a band of five heretics who had been excommunicated by the pope, had arrived and ordained one Fortunatus as rival bishop of Carthage.

. . . What sort of people do you think they are, those enemies of the priests and rebels against the Catholic Church, who are alarmed neither by the severe warning of the Lord, nor by the vengeance of future judgement? *For this has been the source from which heresies and schisms have arisen, that God's priest is not obeyed, nor do people reflect that there is for the time one priest in the Church, who for the time is judge instead of Christ,* and if the whole brotherhood would obey him, according to divine teaching, no one would stir up anything against the college of priests; no one after the divine judgement, after the votes of the people, after the consent of the fellow bishops, would make himself a judge, not now of the bishop but of God. . . .

. . . Peter, however, on whom the Church has been built by the same Lord, speaking one for all, and answering with the voice of the Church, says, "Lord to whom shall we go? . . ."

But I did not immediately write to you, dearest brother,

[6] *Ibid.,* pp. 373-74.
[7] *Ibid.,* p. 666.
* This passage was cited by Pope Leo XIII in *Satis Cogitum.*

about Fortunatus, that false bishop who was set up by a few inveterate heretics, because *the matter was not one which must at once and in haste be brought to your notice, as though it were great and serious;* especially as you already knew the name of Fortunatus well enough. . . .

For these too it was not enough to have departed from the gospel, to have deprived the lapsed of the hope of satisfaction and penance. . . . After all this, they yet in addition, having had a false bishop ordained for them by heretics, dare to set sail, and to carry letters from schismatic and profane persons *to the chair of Peter, and to the principal church, whence the unity of the priesthood took its rise.* They fail to reflect that those Romans are the same as those whose faith was publicly praised by the apostle, to whom unbelief cannot have access. . . .

THE CHURCH AND HER DEFINITIONS OF DOGMA

As the heretics increased, more and more definitions of dogma became necessary. The Church had to define the relationships of the persons of the Trinity One with Another; she had to define the nature of the humanity of Jesus Christ, and that of His divinity and their relation to each other; she had to define the relationship to His Godhead of Mary His mother. As the Christian faced the many problems of such definitions, the papal letters become more frequent.

Only a fragment of a letter by the Pope St. Felix I (269-74) survives, written to Bishop Maximus and the clergy of Alexandria, in which the pope pointed out the error of the Adoptionist position, which was that the man Jesus had achieved divinity, and of the Monarchian or Sabellian position, which was that Christ was a temporary manifestation in the flesh of the one, everlasting spirit of God "without permanent individuation distinct from the Father."[8] The pope stated the orthodox position. The text is from G. D. Mansi, *Amplissima Collectio* L, 1114, translated by Shotwell and Loomis.[9]

As regards the incarnation of the Word and our faith, we believe in our Lord Jesus Christ, born of the Virgin Mary, that he is himself the eternal Word of God and not man adopted by God to be another beside him. Nor did the Son of God adopt a man to be another beside himself, but being perfect God, he became at the same time also perfect man, incarnate from the Virgin.

[8] *Ibid.,* p. 441.
[9] *Ibid.,* p. 441.

Eusebius quotes a letter from the Emperor Constantine the Great to Pope St. Melchiades (311-14) about the Donatist heresy in Africa. Donatus was bishop of Casa Nigra in Numidia, and insisted that no ordination was valid unless conferred by a person in a state of grace—that is, free from mortal sin. The Church's position was, as it had been earlier in the case of baptism performed by heretics, that a sacrament rightly performed, with valid intention, is efficacious by its own virtue. Later, at the Council of Arles, convoked by Constantine shortly after the election of St. Sylvester (314-35) the bishops and clergy present wrote a "synodical letter" to St. Sylvester, and later Marinus and the assembly of bishops gathered in the city of Arles sent the canons or resolutions of the Council "to their most holy lord and brother Sylvester."

The persecutions had come to an end in 313, with the conversion of Constantine, but the Church was soon after faced with various Trinitarian heresies, most of which centered on the nature of Christ. The twofold problem was how to affirm the human nature of Christ without falling into idolatry by affirming there were three gods. The Gnostics and the Docetists said Christ was either a ghost wearing a body, or a pure deity in disguise; the Arians said He was created by the Father, not of the same substance as the Father, but only similar and essentially subordinate. The orthodox position as defined by the Council of Nicaea is that Jesus Christ is "very God of very God, of one substance with the Father," and, as the creed of St. Athanasius phrases it, "He is God, of the substance of the Father, begotten before the worlds; and Man, of the substance of his mother, born in the world; perfect God and perfect Man, of a reasonable soul and human flesh subsisting; equal to the Father, as touching His Godhead, and inferior to the Father, as touching his Manhood; who, although he be God and man, is not two, but one Christ; One, not by conversion of the Godhead into flesh, but by the taking of the Manhood into God." St. Athanasius was ordained bishop of Alexandria in 328, but in 390 certain heretical members of his diocese appealed against him to the then Pope, St. Julius I (337-52). Pope St. Julius wrote a long letter in reply, quoted in J. P. Migne, *Patrologia Graeca,* and quoted by Dom B. C. Butler,[10] in which he says:

I have read the letter which was brought by my presbyters Elipidius and Philoxenus, and I am surprised that whereas we wrote in charity and conscious sincerity, you have replied with contention and impropriety; for the pride and arrogance of the writers is exhibited in the letter. These things are alien

[10] Dom B. C. Butler, *The Church and Infallibility.* New York: Sheed & Ward, 1954, p. 161.

to the faith in Christ; for what was written in charity should also have a reply in charity. . . . But we are obliged to infer that the words by which you seem to honour us are transformed by irony. . . .

. . . I must inform you that although I alone wrote, yet the view I expressed is not only mine, but that of *all the bishops throughout Italy and in these parts.* Indeed I was unwilling to make them all write, lest they should have the pressure of numbers. Of course the bishops assembled on the day fixed, and agreed in these views which I again write to signify to you; so that, beloved, although I alone write, be sure that this is the opinion of all. So much then for the unreasonable, unjust, and suspicious excuses which some of you have devised.

Now when these things were so spoken, and there were so many witnesses for him [Athanasius], and so much in justification was advanced for him, what did it bind us to do? What did the ecclesiastical canon require, but that we should not condemn the man, but rather receive and treat him as a bishop, as we have done? And besides all this, he stayed here a year and six months, awaiting the arrival of you, or of those who wanted to come. His presence shamed everyone, for he would not have been here, if he had not had confidence; and he came not of his own accord, but *he was summoned by letter from us,* as we wrote to you. But after all this, you complain that we acted against the canons. Now consider: who are they that have done so? We who received the man after so many proofs, or they who, being at Antioch thirty-six halts away, appointed a stranger to be bishop, and sent him to Alexandria with a military force? . . .

Among the insurgents were several bishops (Eusebius of Constantinople and Flacillus of Antioch were two of these) and Julius not only chides them for their heresy, for they had reverted to Arianism, but also asks: "Why were we not written to especially about the church of the Alexandrians? Are you ignorant that the custom was first to write to us, and then for justice to be determined from here? If then the bishop [Athanasius] was at all suspect, it should have been reported in writing to the church here. . . . I beseech you," he concluded, "readily bear with me; what I write is for the common good. For what we have received from the blessed apostle Peter, that I point out to you."

The first letter to be called an *encyclical letter,* as such, is that written by the heretical eastern bishops at Sardica, and given in Hilary, *Fragmenta Historica,* Series IV. Pope St. Julius, however, triumphed at the Council, and wrote congratulating the "priest, and deacons and people of Alexandria" for having by their "saving letter furnished meat and drink to your shepherd who, so to speak, had hungered and thirsted for your devotion." And he concludes with:[11]

> It is right to close my letter with a prayer. May Almighty God and His son, our Lord and Saviour Jesus Christ, grant you His grace forever in recompense for your marvellous faith, which you displayed in glorious testimony for your bishop, that for you and those who come after you, here and hereafter, the better things may abide which eye hath not seen nor ear heard nor have they entered into the heart of man, which God hath prepared for them who love Him, through our Lord Jesus Christ, in whom to God Almighty be glory forever and ever, Amen. I bid you, beloved brethren, farewell.

The Arian controversy dragged on, and presently the emperors, who had moved to Constantinople in 330, became Arians, and persecuted the Catholics. Pope St. Damasus I (366-84), a Spaniard, wrote in A.D. 375 a letter to "his most beloved brother Paulinus."[12]

> . . . By my son Vitalis, I directed to you a letter, in which I left everything to your discretion. And through Petronius the presbyter, I briefly indicated that, just as he set out, I was rather upset. And so lest any scruple should remain in you, and lest your wise caution should deter those who would perhaps want to be joined to the Church, we are sending you a statement of faith, not so much for yourself, who share the communion of the same faith, as for those who, by subscribing to it, may wish to be joined to you, that is, to us through you, most beloved brother. Further, if my son Vitalis, mentioned above, and those with him, should desire to be brought into the flock, they ought first to subscribe to that exposition of faith which was affirmed by the pious will of the Nicene fathers.

St. Jerome, the translator of the Bible into Latin, was living at Bethlehem during part of the reign of Pope St. Damasus, and he wrote to him around 377 about the troubles of the Church in the East:[13]

> Because the East is shattered by the fierce antagonisms of its peoples and is rending into tiny fragments the undivided and woven tunic of the Lord . . . therefore I have

[11] Socrates, *Historia Ecclesiastica*, II, 23. Text is from J. P. Migne, *Patrologia Graeca*, LXVII, 249-56, translated in Shotwell and Loomis, *op. cit.*, p. 531.
[12] J. P. Migne, *Patrologia Latina*, 13:356, translated by E. Giles, p. 133. *Documents Illustrating Papal Authority*: London: The Society for Promoting Christian Knowledge, 1952, p. 2.
[13] C. T. G. Schoenemann, *Pontificorum Romanorum Epistolae Genuinae*, pp. 374-78; translated in Shotwell and Loomis, *op. cit.*, p. 659.

thought best to turn to the See of Peter and to the faith that was praised by the apostle's lips, to ask food for my soul from the source where once I received the raiment of Christ. . . . An evil posterity has squandered its patrimony. You alone preserve unspoiled the heritage of the Fathers. . . . A victim, I implore the priest for salvation; a sheep the shepherd for protection. Away with Jealousy of the Roman pre-eminence! away with ambition! I speak to the successor of the fisherman and to the disciple of the cross. I follow no one as chief save Christ but I am joined in communion with your blessedness, that is, with the See of Peter. Upon that rock I know the Church is built. Whoever eats the lamb outside that house is profane.

Pope Damasus' answer to St. Jerome has, alas, not survived. But his letter to the Eastern bishops, written in 378 and dealing with the heretical situation discussed by St. Jerome, is quoted in Theodoret, *Historia Ecclesiastica* V. 10.[14]

And when the renowned Damasus heard of the rise of this [Apollinarian] heresy, he announced the expulsion not only of Apollinarius but also of Timothy, his follower. And he informed the Eastern bishops of it by a letter which I have thought valuable to insert in my history.

The letter of Damasus, bishop of Rome:

"Since your love renders to the Apostolic See the reverence which is its due, do you, most honored sons, accept much for yourselves.

"Even though we are within that holy church in which the holy apostle sat and taught us how we ought to guide the rudder which we have received, we confess nevertheless that we are unworthy of our honor. But for this very reason we strive with all our might, if perchance we may attain to the glory of his blessedness. Be then hereby informed that we have sometime since condemned Timothy, the unhallowed disciple of the heretic Apollinarius, with his impious doctrine, and we believe that what remains of him will obtain no consideration whatever henceforth. But if that old serpent, who has once and again been smitten, revives for his own undoing and continues without the Church, ceaselessly endeavoring to overthrow the faithless with his deadly poisons, do you still avoid him like a pestilence and be mindful of the faith of the apostles, that is, of that which was set down in writing by the Fathers at Nicaea. Do you abide on firm ground, strong in the faith and immovable, and permit hereafter neither your clergy

14 J. P. Migne, *Patrologia Graeca*, LXXXII, translated in Shotwell and Loomis, *op. cit.*, p. 673.

nor your laity to listen to vain reasonings and idle speculations. For we have once for all furnished a pattern and
he who knows himself a Christian may keep it. . . . Why,
then, do you ask me again for my condemnation of Timothy?
Here, by judgment of the Apostolic See, in the presence of
Peter, bishop of the city of Alexandria, he has been condemned."

Pope St. Damasus died in December 384 and was succeeded
by St. Siricius, who was pope until his death in 398. Pope
St. Siricius's letter announcing his appointment to Himerius,
bishop of Tarragon in Spain, on February 11, 385, is the
first papal decretal that has come down to us.[15]

. . . In view of our office, we are not free to dissemble
or to keep silent, for our zeal for the Christian religion
ought to be greater than anyone's. We bear the burdens of
all who are heavy laden, or rather *the blessed apostle Peter
bears them in us, who in all things, as we trust, protects
and defends those who are heirs of his government.*
At the beginning of your page, you have observed that
many who were baptized by the wicked Arians are hastening to the Catholic faith, and that they wish to be rebap-
tized by one of our brethren: this is illegal, being forbidden
by the apostle, by the canons, and *in a general order sent to
the provinces by my predecessor Liberius* of revered memory, after the quashing of the Ariminum council. As has
been laid down in synod, we admit these persons, in common with Novatianists and other heretics, into the congregation of Catholics, only through the invocation of the
seven-fold Spirit, by the laying on of hands of a bishop.
All the East and West keep this rule; and in future it is by
no means fitting that you, either, should deviate from this
path, if you do not wish to be separated from our college
by sentence of the synod.
. . . Up to now there have been enough mistakes of this
kind. In future all priests must keep the above rule who
do not wish to be torn away from the solid apostolic rock
upon which Christ built the universal Church. . . .
We have explained, as I think, dearest brother, all the
matters of which you complained, and to every case which
you have referred, by our son Bassian the presbyter, to
the Roman Church, as to the head of your body, we have
I believe returned adequate replies. And now we urge the
mind of our brotherhood more and more to observe the
canons and keep the decretals which have been framed, so

[15] E. Giles, *op. cit.,* pp. 142-43.

that what we have replied to your inquiries you may bring
to the notice of all our fellow bishops, and not only of those
who are in your diocese: but let what we have profitably
ordained be sent, with your letters also, to all the Cartha-
ginians and Baeticans, Lusitanians and Gallicians, and to
those in the provinces adjoining your own. And though *no
priest of the Lord is free to be ignorant of the statutes of
the apostolic see,* or of the venerable provisions of the canons,
yet it would be more useful, and, on account of the senior-
ity of your priesthood, a very high honour for you, beloved,
if those things which have been written generally, and to
you especially by name, were brought by your care to the
notice of all our brethren; so that what has been profitably
drawn up by us, not without consideration, but with care
and great caution and deliberation, may remain inviolate,
and that the way may be stopped for all excuses in future,
which are now open to no one among us.[16]

In another letter, Pope St. Siricius wrote to the Church
of Milan in A.D. 390:[16]

Therefore in accordance with the apostolic precept (Gala-
tians 1:9) since they preached other than what was received,
it was the one sentence of us all, presbyters, deacons and all
the clergy that Jovinian, Auxentius, Genialis, Germinato,
Felix, Plotinus, Martian, Januarius and Ingaious, who were
found to be promoters of new heresy and blasphemy,
should be condemned by the divine sentence and our judgment, and remain permanently outside of the Church. I have
sent this letter, not doubting that your holiness [St. Ambrose,
bishop of Milan] will observe it.

St. Ambrose's reply to Siricius, paragraph 5, notes: "Let
them believe the apostles' creed which the Roman church
has always kept undefiled," and, paragraph 14, "and so you
are to know that Jovinian, Auxentius, etc., whom your holiness has condemned, have also been condemned by us, in
accordance with your judgment."

THE CHURCH AND THE CHRISTIAN EMPERORS

Many new problems arose for the Church when the emperors became Christian. The persecutions were over; the
state was no longer hostile. But the Church's relationship
with a Catholic ruler was far more complicated than with
pagan, or later, Saracen. For the emperors, in spite of their

[16] *Ibid.,* p. 146.

personal Christian faith, were also the inheritors of the Roman tradition, in which the state was paramount, and religion a department of that state. So that, from the outset, the Church had to cope with a problem that continues still to vex her today, the problem, as Father Philip Hughes puts it in *A Popular History of the Catholic Church:* "In its earliest form, as it presented itself to the Catholics of the third and fourth centuries, it was the problem of the place to be given to the personage who was the omnipotent master of the Roman world. How embarrassing, and indeed injurious, to the cause of truth the new imperial protection could be was to be shown with a terrible clarity. . . ."

But the pope had not only to deal with the menace of a bear-hugging emperor, but to struggle for dear life against the barbarians.

In the reign of Pope St. Innocent I (401-17), Rome was besieged by Alaric the Goth, and captured in 410. The pope wrote quietly on; the following extracts are from his letters.[17]

Epistle 25, to Decentius, bishop of Eugubium *(Si instituta).* 19 March 416.

Who does not know or observe that it [the church order] was delivered by Peter the chief of the apostles to the Roman church, and is kept until now, and ought to be retained by all, and that nothing ought to be imposed or introduced which has no authority, or seems to derive its precedents elsewhere?—especially since it is clear that in all Italy, the Gauls, Spain, Africa, Sicily and the adjacent islands, no one formed these churches except those whom the venerable apostle Peter or his successors made priests. Or let them discover that any other apostle be found to have been or to have taught in these provinces. If not, they ought to follow that which the Roman church keeps, from which they undoubtedly received them first; but while they are keen on foreign statements, they seem to neglect the head of their institution.

Epistle 29, to the Council of Carthage *(In requirendis).* 27 January 417.

In inquiring about those things which should be handled with all care by priests, and especially by a true, just, and catholic council, by preserving, as you have done, *the example of ancient tradition,* and by being mindful of the discipline of the Church, you have truly strengthened the vigour of our religion, no less now in consulting, than before

---

[17] This and the following letters are in E. Giles, *op. cit.,* pp. 194, 201-02.

in passing sentence. For you decided that *it was proper to refer to our judgment,* knowing what is due to the apostolic see, since all we who are set in this place desire to follow the very apostle from whom the very episcopate and whole authority of this name has emerged; following whom, we know how to condemn the evil and to approve the good. So also, you have by your priestly office preserved *the institutions of the fathers,* and have not spurned that which they decreed by a sentence not human but divine, that *Whatever is done, even though it be in distant provinces, should not be ended until it comes to the knowledge of this see,* that by its authority the whole just pronouncement should be strengthened, and that from there the other churches (like waters proceeding from their natal sources and flowing through the different regions of the world, the pure streams of an uncorrupt head) should take up what they ought to enjoin, whom they ought to wash, and whom that water, worthy of pure bodies, should avoid as defiled with uncleansable filth.

I congratulate you, therefore, dearest brothers, that you have directed a letter to us by our brother and fellow bishop Julius, and that while caring for the churches which you rule, you also show your concern for the advantage of all, and that *you ask for a decision which may benefit all the churches of the world together;* so that the Church, being established in her rules, and confirmed in this decree of just proclamation against such errors, may be unable to tolerate those men.

Epistle 30, to the Council of Mileve (*Inter caeteras*).
27 January 417.

It is therefore with due care and fitness that you consult *the chancery of the apostolic office* (that office, I mean, to which belongs, besides those things that are outside, the care of all the churches) as to what opinion should be held on doubtful matters, following the form of the ancient rule which, you and I know, has ever been kept in the whole world. But this I pass by, because I am sure your prudence is aware of it: for how could you by your actions have confirmed it, unless you knew that answers to questions always flow through all provinces from the apostolic spring? Especially as often as *questions of faith* are to be ventilated, I think all our brothers and fellow bishops ought to refer to *none but Peter,* that is to the author of their name and office, even as your affection has now referred [to us] a matter which may benefit all churches in common throughout the whole world. For they must needs be more cautious when they see the inventors of these evils, on the report of two synods, cut off by the decree of our sentence from ecclesiastical communion.

Therefore your charity will do a double good; for you will obtain the grace of having observed the canons, and *the whole world will share your benefit.* For who among Catholics will choose any longer to hold conversation with Christ's enemies? . . .

We declare that Pelagius and Celestius, that is the inventors of new doctrines which, as the apostle said, are wont to produce no edification, but rather utterly empty questionings, should by the authority of apostolic vigour be deprived of ecclesiastical communion, until they recover from the snares of the devil, by whom they are held prisoner by their own choice.

St. Boniface (418-22) intervened with a long letter of September 19, 419, in a disputed election in Thessalonica.[18]

As you have loyally said in your letter, the most blessed apostle Peter watches with his eyes in what manner you exercise the office of rector. He who was appointed shepherd of the Lord's sheep in perpetuity cannot but be very close to you, cannot but watch over any church, no matter where it is situated, in which we have laid a foundation stone of the universal Church.

On March 11, 422, Pope St. Boniface wrote to the bishops of Thessaly:

The universal ordering of the Church at its birth took its origin from the office of blessed Peter, in which is found both its directing power and its supreme authority. From him as from a source, at the time when our religion was in the stage of growth, all churches received their common order. . . . So it is clear that this church is to all churches throughout the world as the head is to the members, and that whoever separates himself from it becomes an exile from the Christian religion, since he ceases to belong to its fellowship.

To Rufus and the other bishops of Macedonia, Pope St. Boniface wrote on the same day *(Manet Beatum)* that "none has ever been so rash as to oppose the apostolic primacy, the judgment of which may not be revised; none rebels against it, unless he would be judged in his turn."

---

[18] This and the following letter are in E. Giles, *op. cit.,* pp. 230-31.

Pope St. Celestine I (422-32) wrote to Nestorius, bishop of Constantinople, on August 11, 430, in friendly warning because Nestorius did not believe that Mary was the mother of God, but only the mother of the humanity of Jesus Christ.[19]

Take heed that unless you teach, about Jesus Christ our God, what the Roman, Alexandrian and universal Church holds, and what up to your time was held by the holy church of Constantinople; and if within ten days after the receipt of this you do not openly and in writing condemn this impious novelty, which tends to undo what the ancient Scriptures join, you are excluded from the communion of the whole Catholic Church.

[19] E. Giles, *op. cit.*, p. 241.

Chapter 3

✠

St. Leo to St. Gregory

By the fifth century the Church had stabilized her relationship with the now Christian emperors. St. Leo the Great (440-61) was the first of the great papal letter writers. It was in St. Leo's reign that Nestorius and Eutyches were both condemned as heretics. Nestorius claimed Christ was wholly a man; Eutyches, a monk of Constantinople, denied two natures in Christ and made Him only God. The "brigand council" of Ephesus, attended by 130 bishops presided over by Dioscurus, patriarch of Alexandria, approved Eutyches and deposed his bishop, Flavian, who had excommunicated Dioscurus. Flavian, who was protected by the favor of the Emperor Theodosius II, appealed to Rome, and so did Theodoret of Cyprus, who had also been condemned by the "brigand council." Theodoret wrote to St. Leo: "I await the pleasure of your apostolic throne . . . if you pronounce that I must submit [to my deposition] I shall do so, and shall importune no one else in the world, putting myself in God's hands for the final word."

In the following letter St. Leo made it quite clear he was for Flavian against Dioscurus and why.[1]

> And so, dearest brothers, let all attempts to call in question the divinely inspired faith be entirely put down, and the vain unbelief of heretics be laid to rest, and do not let that be defaced which may not be believed, since in accordance with the evangelical decrees, the voices of the prophets, and the teaching of the apostles, with the greatest fullness and clearness in the letter which we sent to the late Bishop Flavian, it has been made clear what is the devout and genuine confession upon the mystery of the Incarnation, of our Lord Jesus Christ.

Pope St. Leo, as soon as the Emperor Theodosius was dead, called a new council, the Council of Chalcedon. This was the

[1] J. P. Migne, *Patrologia Latina*, 54.937, translation in *A Select Library of the Nicene and Post-Nicene Fathers of the Christian Church*, ed. Philip Schaff. New York: The Christian Literature Co., 1886-90, Series 2, Vol. 12, p. 70. (This, and other excerpts from the same book, have been slightly adapted.)

Fourth Ecumenical Council (meaning Council of all the Churches). Pope St. Leo did not go to it himself, but sent his legates, or deputies. When these legates saw that Bishop Dioscurus was present they announced they had "instructions from the blessed and apostolic bishop of the City of the Romans, who is the head of all the Churches, and these instructions prescribe that Dioscurus must not have a seat in the Council. . . . We must respect these instructions. . . . If you please, Dioscurus will go out, or we shall withdraw."[2] And Dioscurus went. An early example of the use of *veto* in an international assembly.

The members of the Council then wrote to Pope St. Leo the following letter:[3]

". . . Teaching them to observe all things whatever I commanded you" (Matthew 28:20). You have kept this command, which is like a golden cord leading down from its author to us. . . . We were delighted at the spiritual food which Christ supplied to us through your letter; we revelled in it as at an imperial banquet. . . .

The 187 bishops present then voted, and Dioscurus was informed of his deposition. But later, at the end of the council, "in the absence of the imperial officials and the papal legates"[4] the Twenty-eighth Canon was passed by less than half the full quota of bishops. This canon gave to Constantinople a presidency in the East comparable with that of Rome. "The papal legate protested at the next meeting, and reserved the right of the Apostolic See to revise this canon."

Those responsible for the Twenty-eighth Canon wrote to St. Leo: "You were for all the mouthpiece of the voice of the blessed Peter, and for all you procured the blessing of his faith. . . . We were about five hundred and twenty bishops, whom you led as the head leads the members." And they added they hoped he would "honor this decision by your confirmation, and just as we for the good have agreed with the head, that the head will agree with the children in what is fitting." But Leo, who ratified the doctrinal achievements of the Council, refused to ratify the Twenty-eighth Canon.

To the Empress Pulcheria St. Leo wrote on May 22, 452:[5]

. . . indeed resolutions of bishops which are repugnant to the rules of the holy canons composed at Nicaea, in conjunction with the loyalty of your faith, we dismiss as invalid, and by the authority of Peter, the blessed apostle, we absolutely disannul by a general decree in all ecclesiastical cases. . . .

[2] Batiffol, *Le Siège Apostolique*. Paris, 1898, p. 538.
[3] J. P. Migne, *Patrologia Latina*, 54.932, translation in Schaff, *op. cit.*, p. 72.
[4] Dom B. C. Butler, *op. cit.*, pp. 178 ff.
[5] J. P. Migne, *Patrologia Latina*, 34.998, translation in Schaff, *op. cit.*, p. 76.

In his letter of June 953, to Theodoret of Cyrus, he said:[6]

> On the return of our brothers and fellow priests whom the
> see of blessed Peter sent to the holy council, we ascertained,
> beloved, the victory you and we together had won, by help
> from above, over the blasphemy of Nestorius and the mad-
> ness of Eutyches. Wherefore we glory in the Lord ... who
> has ... corroborated, by the irrevocable assent of the whole
> brotherhood, what he had before defined by our ministry, to
> show that what had before been enacted by the first see of all,
> and received by the judgment of the whole Christian world,
> had truly proceeded from himself, and that in this too the
> members may agree with the head.[6]

Pope Gelasius I (492-96) wrote to the Byzantine Emperor
Anastasius I to deny the Emperor's right to interfere in Church
affairs, notably by supporting schismatic patriarchs in Constantinople. Pope St. Gelasius I stated the famous theory of
the two powers, which ever after was to be called the
Gelasian theory.[7]

> The Apostolic See's confession of faith is unassailable; it
> is impossible for it to be stained by any false doctrine or to be
> contaminated by error ... know that the world is ruled over
> by two great powers, that of the pontiffs and that of the
> kings, but the authority of the pontiffs is far greater, since
> they must, on the judgment day, give account to God of the
> souls of the kings. ... For you know, our very clement son,
> that although you have the chief place in dignity over the
> human race, yet you must submit yourself faithfully to
> those who have charge of Divine things, and look to them
> for the means of your salvation. You know that it behooves
> you, in matter concerning the reception and reverent ad-
> ministration of the sacraments, to be obedient to the
> ecclesiastical authority rather than to control it. So in these
> matters you should depend on ecclesiastical judgment, not
> seek to bend it to your own will. For if in matters belonging
> to the administration of public discipline, the bishops of the
> Church, knowing that the Empire has been conferred on you
> by Divine instrumentality, are obedient to your laws, lest in
> purely material matters there may seem to be dissension, I
> ask you, should you not willingly obey those to whom the
> administration of Divine mysteries is entrusted? So just as
> the danger is great for the Popes if they do not say what is
> needful in matters concerning the Divine honour, so there

[6] *Ibid.*, 1046, translation in *ibid.*, p. 87.
[7] J. H. Robinson, *Readings in European History*. Chicago: Ginn & Co.,
1904, I, 72.

is also no small peril for such as are obstinate in resistance at
the time when they should be obedient. . . .
. . . When the see of blessed Peter has decided, no one is
allowed to pass judgment on its decision; it may be appealed
to from all parts of the world, but from its decision no one
can appeal.

Pope St. Gregory the Great (born ?540 —died 604) belonged to
a rich and noble family, and became praetor at the age of
thirty. Gradually, however, he withdrew from the world, and
about 574 he sold his goods and with the proceeds built seven
monasteries, in one of which he became a monk. Pope
Benedict I made him a deacon, and in 578 sent him as
apocrisiarius, that is, as papal nuncio or ambassador, to Constantinople. On the death of Pope Pelagius II, the unanimous
choice of the senate, clergy and people fell on Gregory. His
papacy of fourteen years, from 590 to 604, fighting heresy,
enforcing ecclesiastical discipline, reforming official prayer,
organizing the liturgical chant, was also distinguished by the
evangelization of Anglo-Saxon Britain through St. Augustine,
whom he sent to England, and who became Archbishop of
Canterbury. His letters are witnesses to the saintliness and
ability of this successful pope.

Letter 99 to Sabinianus, nuncio at Constantinople:[8]

Thou art well acquainted with my ways, that I bear long;
but if once I have determined not to bear, I go gladly in the
face of all danger . . . I was before prepared to die rather
than that the Church of the blessed Apostle Peter should
degenerate in my day.

By an edict of 593, the Emperor Maurice forbade government officials or soldiers to become priests or monks. Gregory
wrote to the emperor:[9]

I am speaking not as a bishop nor as a subject, but simply
for the right which I find in my heart as a man. . . . Hearken,
O Emperor, to what Christ says to you through me, His
humble servant, and keep it in mind: "I raised you from
being a clerk to the post of a captain of the guards, and
from that post to the rank of Caesar, and from Caesar to
Emperor. I have confided my priests to you. And you seek
to ban soldiers from my service. . . ." In the name of that
terrible judge I implore that your piety find the means,
whether by a favorable interpretation or by a suitable moderation, to soften the rigor of this law. . . . I have now performed

8 *A Treasury of Early Christianity,* ed. Anne Fremantle. New York: The
Viking Press, 1953, pp. 155 ff.

my two-fold duty. I have paid to my emperor the tribute of my obedience, which is due to my emperor, and to God the testimony of my conscience, which belongs only to God.[9]

At the end of five years the emperor gave in; officials were allowed to become monks after they had turned in their reports, and soldiers after a three-year novitiate.

Further letters from Pope St. Gregory show the extent of his influence.[10]

To Theodelinda, queen of the Lombards

. . . For they say that in the times of Justinian of pious memory, some things were ordained contrary to the Council of Chalcedon; and, while they neither read themselves nor believe those who do, they remain in the same error which they themselves feigned to themselves concerning us. For we, our conscience bearing witness, declare that nothing was altered, nothing violated, with respect to the faith of this same holy Council of Chalcedon; but that whatever was done in the times of the aforesaid Justinian was so done that the faith of the Council of Chalcedon should in no respect be disturbed. Further, if anyone presumes to speak or think anything contrary to the faith of the said synod, we detest his opinion, with interposition of anathema. Since, then, you know the integrity of our faith under the attestation of our conscience, it remains that you should never separate yourself from the communion of the Catholic Church, lest all those tears of yours, and all those good works, should come to nothing, if they are found alien from the true faith. It therefore becomes your Glory to send a communication with all speed to my most reverend brother and fellow-bishop Constantius, of whose faith, as well as his life, I have long been well assured, and to signify by your letters addressed to him how kindly you have accepted his ordination, and that you are in no way separated from the communion of his Church; although I think that what I say on this subject is superfluous: for, though there has been some degree of doubtfulness in your mind, I think that it has been removed from your heart on the arrival of my son John the abbot, and Hippolytus the notary. . . .

. . . It has come to our knowledge from the report of certain persons that your Glory has been led on by some bishops even to the offence against holy Church of suspending yourself from the communion of Catholic unanimity. Now the more we sincerely love you, the more seriously are we distressed about you, that you believe unskilled and

9 *Ibid.*, p. 175.
10 *Ibid.*, p. 171.

foolish men, who not only do not know what they talk about, but can hardly understand what they have heard; who, while they neither read themselves, nor believe those who do, remain in the same error which they have themselves feigned to themselves concerning us. For we venerate the four holy synods; the Nicene, in which Arius, the Constantinopolitan, in which Macedonius, the first Ephesine, in which Nestorius, and the Chalcedonian, in which Eutyches and Dioscurus, were condemned; declaring that whosoever thinks otherwise than these four synods did is alien from the true faith. We also condemn whomsoever they condemn, and absolve whomsoever they absolve, smiting, with interposition of anathema, anyone who presumes to add to or take away from the faith of the same four synods, and especially that of Chalcedon, with respect to which doubt and occasion of superstition has arisen in the minds of certain unskilled men.

Seeing, then, that you know the integrity of our faith from my plain utterance and profession, it is right that you should have no further scruple of doubt with respect to the Church of the blessed Peter, Prince of the Apostles: but persist ye in the true faith, and make your life firm on the rock of the Church; that is on the confession of the blessed Peter, Prince of the Apostles, lest all those tears of yours and all those good works should come to nothing, if they are found alien from the true faith. For as branches dry up without the virtue of the root, so works, to whatsoever degree they may seem good, are nothing, if they are disjoined from the solidity of the faith. . . .

To Childebert, king of the Franks[11]

The letter of your Excellency has made us exceedingly glad, testifying as it does that you are careful with pious affection, of the honor and reverence due to priests. Whence also we have received with pleasure what you have written, and grant what you desire with willing mind. . . . But, inasmuch as some things have been reported to us which greatly offend Almighty God, and confound the honor and reverence due to the priesthood, we beg that they may be in every way amended with the support of the censure of your power, lest, while headstrong and perverse doings run counter to your devotion, your kingdom, or your soul (which God forbid) be burdened by the guilt of others.

Further, it has come to our knowledge that on the death of bishops some persons from being laymen are tonsured, and mount to the episcopate by a sudden leap. And thus one who has not been a disciple is in his inconsiderate ambition

[11] *Ibid.*, p. 176.

made a master. And, since he has not learned what to teach, he bears the office of priesthood only in name; for he continues to be a layman in speech and action as before. How, then, is he to intercede for the sins of others, not having in the first place bewailed his own? For such a shepherd does not defend, but deceives, the flock; since, while he cannot for very shame try to persuade others to do what he does not do himself, what else is it but that the Lord's people remains a prey to robbers, and catches destruction from the source whence it ought to have had a great support of wholesome protection? How bad and how perverse a proceeding this is let your Excellency's Highness consider even from your own administration of things. For it is certain that you do not put a leader over an army unless his work and his fidelity have first been apparent; unless the virtue and industry of his previous life have shown him to be a fit person. But, if the command of an army is not committed to any but men of this kind, it is easily gathered from this comparison of what sort a leader of souls ought to be. But it is a reproach to us, and we are ashamed to say it, that priests snatch at leadership who have not seen the very beginning of religious warfare.

But this also, a thing most execrable, has been reported to us as well: that sacred orders are conferred through simoniacal heresy, that is for bribes received. And, seeing that it is exceedingly pestiferous, and contrary to the Universal Church, that one be promoted to any sacred order not for merit but for a price, we exhort your Excellency to order so detestable a wickedness to be banished from your kingdom. For that man shows himself to be thoroughly unworthy of this office, who fears not to buy the gift of God with money, and presumes to try to get by payment what he deserves not to have through grace.

These things, then, most excellent son, I admonish you about for this reason, that I desire your soul to be saved. And I should have written about them before now, had not innumerable occupations stood in the way of my will. But now that a suitable time for answering your letter has offered itself, I have not omitted what it was my duty to do. Wherefore, greeting your Excellency with the affection of paternal charity, we beg that all things which we have enjoined on our above-named brother and fellow bishop to be done and observed, may be carried out under the protection of your favour, and that you allow them not to be in any way upset by the elation or pride of anyone. But, as they were observed by his predecessor under the reign of your glorious father, so let them be observed now also, by your aid, with zealous devotion. It is right, then, that we should thus have a return made to us; and that, as we have not deferred fulfilling your will, so you too, for the sake of God and the blessed Peter, Prince of the Apostles, should cause our ordinances to be observed in all respects; that so your Excellency's reputation, praiseworthy and well-pleasing to God, may extend itself all around.

To Brunichild, queen of the Franks[12]

The laudable and God-pleasing goodness of your Excellence is manifested both by your government of your kingdom and by your education of your son. To him you have not only with provident solicitude conserved intact the glory of temporal things, but have also seen to the rewards of eternal life, having planted his mind in the root of the true faith with maternal, as became you, and laudable care of his education. Whence not undeservedly it ensues that he should surpass all the kingdoms of the nations, in that he both worships purely and confesses truly the Creator of these nations. But that faith may shine forth in him the more laudably in his works, let the words of your exhortation kindle him, to the end that, as royal power shows him lofty among men, so goodness of conduct may make him great before God.

Now inasmuch as past experience in many instances gives us confidence in the Christianity of your Excellence, we beg of you, for the love of Peter, Prince of the Apostles, whom we know that you love with your whole heart, that you would cherish with the aid of your patronage our most beloved son the presbyter Candidus, who is the bearer of these presents, together with the little patrimony for the government of which we have sent him, to the end that, strengthened by the favour of your support, he may be able both to manage profitably this little patrimony, which is evidently beneficial towards the expenses of the poor, and also to recover into the possession of this little patrimony anything that may have been taken away from it. For it is not without increase of your praise that after so long a time a man belonging to Church has been sent for the management of this patrimony. Let your Excellency, then, deign so willingly to give your attention to what we request of you that the blessed Peter, Prince of the Apostles, to whom the power of binding and loosing has been given by the Lord Jesus Christ, may both grant to your Excellence to rejoice here in your offspring, and after courses of many years

---

[12] *Ibid.*, p. 180.

cause you to be found, absolved from all ills, before the face of the eternal Judge.

To the Brethren Going to England[13]

Since it had been better not to have begun what is good than to return back from it when begun, you must, most beloved sons, fulfil the good work which with the help of the Lord you have begun. Let, then, neither the toil of the journey nor the tongues of evil-speaking men deter you; but with all instancy and all fervour go on with what under God's guidance you have commenced, knowing that great toil is followed by the glory of an eternal reward. Obey in all things humbly Augustine your provost (*praeposito*), who is returning to you, whom we also appoint your abbot, knowing that whatever may be fulfilled in you through his admonition will in all ways profit your souls. May Almighty God protect you with His grace, and grant to me to see the fruit of your labour in the eternal country; that so, even though I cannot labour with you, I may be found together with you in the joy of the reward; for in truth I desire to labour. God keep you safe, most beloved sons.

During the truly "Dark Ages" between the death of St. Gregory and the Council of Sutri (1046) the waves of violence that passed over Europe also often threatened the Holy See. In the hundred years between the murder of Pope John VIII (882) and the Council, there were thirty-seven popes, of whom one, St. Nicholas I (858-67), was the third out of all the 260 popes to be called the Great. To the Council of the Bulgars, in November 866, St. Nicholas wrote, reiterating the Church's already age-old stand against rebaptism:[14]

You claim that in your country many have been baptised by a Jew and you don't know if he was a Christian or not and you asked what you should do. It is certain that they do not have to be rebaptised, if they were baptised in the name of the Holy Trinity or only in the name of Christ as we read in the Acts of the Apostles because both these forms are identical as St. Ambrose explains.

[13] *Ibid.*, p. 179.
[14] Latin text in C. Mirbt, *Quellen zur Geschichte des Papsttums*. Berlin, 1876.

Chapter 4

✠

The Church and the Holy Roman Empire

The pagan religion was, as has been earlier emphasized, totally subject to the state, indeed was a mere part of it, and when the emperors became Christian the government identified itself with Christianity. Indeed the emperors, western or Byzantine, assumed that the Church, though Christian, would be totally subject to the Christian state; that when the emperor was an Arian, or a Donatist, the Church and the state would meekly follow suit. Any discrepancy between what the emperor believed and what he permitted his subjects to practice was frowned upon as conducive to civil disorder—the Arian Byzantine emperor had the Catholic Boethius put to death *only* because he was a Catholic and a civil servant at the same time. The pope's refusal to accord equality to the see of Constantinople was based on the fact that from the time of St. Peter Rome had been the center of the whole Christian "communion," and had Constantinople or any other bishopric prevailed against Rome—that is, had one tried to separate the supreme spiritual authority from the traditional center of the "communion"—this authority would have foundered in the precarious sands of civil dominion, as Abbot Butler puts it, and the Church (could God have allowed such a thing) would have been completely identified with the Roman Empire.

When the Frankish emperor Charles the Great (Charlemagne) was crowned Holy Roman Emperor in St. Peter's on Christmas Day, 800, by Pope St. Leo III, "Charles was now, in some way, joint sovereign with the pope. . . . As he had already done in the East, Caesar was now obtaining a kind of suzerainty over the Church in the West."[1]

The conflict between Church and state in the West raged intermittently throughout the Middle Ages. Pope St. Gregory VII (1073-85) in a letter to Hermann, Bishop of Metz, dated March 15, 1081, states the pope's position in his struggle with the German Emperor Henry IV.

Following the procedure of the very earliest Christian days, the bishop of Rome first advised his fellow bishop as to who

---

[1] Father Philip Hughes, *A Popular History of the Church.* New York: The Macmillan Co., Doubleday Image Book 1954.

60

was not "in peace and communion." Next, the pope explains his views on the controversy with Henry IV, emperor. He emphasizes four points: (1) that the spiritual power is superior to the temporal power, being derived from God Himself, whereas the temporal power generally originates in despicable human passions; (2) that kings and emperors, like any other of the faithful, can be punished by ecclesiastical penalties including excommunication; (3) that the superiority of the spiritual to the temporal power implies the right of judging the rulers for their temporal activities; (4) that the papal right to bind and loose can be used against a guilty ruler and that it can absolve his subjects from their allegiance.[2]

Bishop Gregory, servant of the servants of God, to his beloved brother in Christ, Hermann, Bishop of Metz, greeting and apostolic benediction.

It is undoubtedly owing to the grace of God that you are ready, as we have learned, to go through trials and dangers in the defence of the truth. For such is His ineffable grace and immense mercy that He never permits that those chosen by Him go entirely astray and never allows them to fall or to be cast down completely. On the contrary, letting them pass through a time of persecution as a useful probation, He makes them stronger than before, even after some trepidation. And because among strong men he who acts bravely and goes forward with fervour inflames virile hearts—likewise among cowards fear induces one to flee more shamefully than the other—we wish to impress upon your Grace, with admonishing voice, the following: that you should be pleased to stand among the first in the army of the Christian religion if you do not doubt that they are nearest to God the Victorious, and that they are the most worthy ones.

It seems, however, hardly necessary to us to comply with your request, namely to be somewhat assisted by a letter from us and fortified against the madness of those who keep repeating with perverse mouth: that the Holy and Apostolic See has no authority to excommunicate Henry—a man who despises the Christian law, destroys the Churches and the Empire, sponsors and supports heretics—and to absolve any one from the oath of fealty to him. We hardly deem it necessary because so many and quite clear proofs of this can be found on the pages of Holy Scriptures. Nor do we believe that those who accumulate for themselves damnation by despising and opposing the truth, have added these views to the defence of their audacious standpoint either

[2] *Monumenta Gregoriana*, ed. Jaffe, p. 453, translated in *Church and State Through the Centuries*, by Sidney Ehler and John B. Morrall. Westminster, Maryland: The Newman Press, 1954, pp. 30 ff.

by ignorance or by madness and wretched desperation. And no wonder. For such is the habit of the wicked that looking for protection of their iniquity they defend those who are similar to themselves; and they attach no importance to the fact that they incur perdition for lying.

Now, to say only a few words out of many, who does not know the words of our Lord and Saviour Jesus Christ who says in the Gospel, "Thou art Peter and upon this rock will I build my Church, and the gates of hell shall not prevail against it; and I will give unto thee the keys of the kingdom of Heaven; and whatsoever thou shalt bind upon earth shall be bound also in Heaven, and whatsoever thou shalt loose upon earth shall be loosed also in Heaven"? Are the kings excepted here? Are they not among the sheep that the Son of God committed to St. Peter? Who, I ask, can consider himself as exempted from this universal power of binding and loosing, conferred upon St. Peter, unless such an unfortunate one who, unwilling to bear the yoke of the Lord, subjects himself to the burden of the devil and refuses to be among Christ's sheep? For such a one it will add very little to his wretched liberty if he shakes from his proud neck the power divinely granted to St. Peter; the more any one, out of his pride, refuses to bear it, the more heavily it shall press upon him and he shall carry it to his damnation at the Judgment.

The Holy Fathers, supporting and serving the Holy Roman Church with great veneration, called her the Universal Mother in Councils and also otherwise in their writings and acts. By this doing they supported and served this institution of Divine will, this pledge of a dispensation to the Church, this privilege handed over since the beginning to St. Peter, chief of the Apostles, and confirmed to him by a heavenly decree. And accepting the proofs of all this and including them in the confirmation of the faith and in the doctrine of the holy religion, they also accepted her judgments; consenting in this, they agreed as if with one spirit and one voice: that all major affairs and important matters, as well as jurisdiction over all churches, ought to be referred to her as to a mother and head; that from her there is no appeal; and that no one should or could retract or repudiate her sentences. Consequently, when the blessed Pope Gelasius wrote, armed with Divine authority, to the Emperor Anastasius, he instructed him what and how he should think in the matter of the primacy of the Holy and Apostolic See as follows: "Although the faithful should be obedient to all priests in general who duly fulfil the duties of religion, how much more must they give adherence to the ruler of that See which the Supreme God-head wished to preside over all priests and the subsequent piety of the whole Church has always honoured? So your prudence will perceive that by no human design of any sort whatever can any one set himself up as equal by privilege or acknowledgment to him whom the Voice of Christ has made supreme, and whom the venerable Church has always recognized and held in honour as her Primate. . . ."

Equipped, then, wth such enactments and authorities, many bishops have excommunicated, sometimes kings, sometimes Emperors. If special mention of the names of these princes is sought, it can be pointed out that the blessed Pope Innocent excommunicated the Emperor Arcadius, because he consented to drive out St. John Chrysostom from his See. Another Roman Pontiff, Zacharias, deposed the king of the Franks from his kingdom, not so much because of his crimes, as because he was not suitable to exercise such great authority; and he set up in his place Pippin, father of Charlemagne the Emperor, and absolved all the Franks from the oath of fidelity which they had taken to the previous king. Holy Church often does the same thing by virtue of its authority when it absolves vassals from the bond of an oath which has been taken to those bishops who have been deposed from pontifical rank by the Apostolic authority. Blessed Ambrose, though a saint, was not bishop over the Universal Church; yet he excommunicated and shut out from the Church the Emperor Theodosius the Great for a sin which was not looked upon as serious by other priests. He also shows in his writings that the priestly dignity is as high in comparison with the royal power as gold is in comparison with lead. He writes in this way near the beginning of his pastoral letter: "The episcopal honour and sublimity, brethren, can not be compared with any other. If you compare them to the splendour of kings and the diadem of princes it would be far worse than to compare the metal lead to the glitter of gold; so you may indeed see that the necks of kings and princes are bowed before the knees of priests and, after the monarchs have kissed the hands of the priests, they believe themselves to be strengthened by their prayers." Shortly afterwards he says: "You should know, brethren, that we have mentioned all these things to show that nothing may be found in this world more excellent than priests or more sublime than bishops."

You ought to have remembered, Brother, that greater power is granted to an exorcist, when he is made a spiritual emperor to drive away demons, than is obtained by any layman by reason of secular dominion. Indeed it is unfortunately true that demons rule over all the kings and princes of the earth who do not live a godly life and do not fear God in their deeds as they ought, and they torment them with a wretched captivity. For such men desire authority, not for the honour of God and the salvation of souls, as do religious priests who are led by Divine love; but in order that they may show their insupportable pride and the ambition of their mind, they desire to dominate others. Blessed Augustine spoke of them in the first book of his *De Doctrina Christiana*: "Indeed whoever strives to gain control over those who are naturally his equals, that is men, is intolerably proud in every way." Now exorcists, as we have said, have power from God over demons; therefore they have far greater power over those who are subject to, and in companionship with, demons. If, then, exorcists so far surpass the earthly rulers, how much more will priests surpass them!

Furthermore, every Christian king, when he comes to his end, seeks as a poor suppliant the aid of a priest, so that he may escape the prison of hell, make his way from darkness to light and appear absolved from the chains of his sins before the judgment of God. But who among laymen (leaving priests out of the question), when near to death, has begged the assistance of an earthly king for the salvation of his soul? And what earthly king or Emperor is able by the office committed to him to snatch any Christian from the devil's power by Holy Baptism, and to number him among the sons of God, and to strengthen him with the Holy Chrism? And which of them is able to make with his lips the Body and Blood of the Lord, which is the greatest deed in the Christian religion? Or to which of them has been given the power of binding and loosing on earth and in Heaven? From these considerations it is obvious that the authority of the priests is by far pre-eminent in power. To take another case, which of these earthly potentates can ordain any cleric in Holy Church? Much less can he depose a cleric for any fault. For in the ecclesiastical hierarchy the power of deposition is ranked as higher than that of ordination. For bishops can ordain other bishops, but can in no case depose them without the authority of the Apostolic See. What man of even mediocre intelligence is able to doubt, then, that priests are to take precedence of kings? But if kings should be judged for their sins by priests, by whom should they more rightly be judged than by the Roman Pontiff?

To sum up, it might be more fitting to consider any good Christians as kings than to consider bad princes to be such. The former, pursuing the glory of God, exercise strict control over themselves; but the latter, their own worst enemies, pursuing not the things of God but their own interests, oppress other men despotically. The former are the Body of Christ, the true King; the latter are the body of the devil. The former govern themselves so that they may reign eternally with the Supreme Emperor; but the authority of the latter has as its result that they perish in eternal damnation with the prince of darkness, who is king over all the sons of pride.

Nor indeed should it be a matter for great surprise that bad bishops ally themselves with a wicked king, whom they love and fear because of the honours which they have obtained from him by evil means; who, ordaining simoniacally whom they please, sell even God for a contemptible price. For, just as the elect are inseparably united to their head, so also the reprobates are joined together primarily against the good, with him who is the head of the malice. . . .

These remarks apply to kings and emperors who, puffed up with excessive worldly glory, reign not for God but for themselves. But because it is part of our office to distribute advice to each person according to the status and dignity which he enjoys, we make it our business, under the inspiration of God, to provide weapons of humility for Emperors, kings and other princes, so that they may be able to restrain the floods of their pride, rising, as it does, like the sea. For we are aware that worldly glory and secular anxiety usually do draw into pride, in particular those who rule; as a result, neglecting humility and pursuing their own glory, they perpetually yearn to dominate the brethren.

To Henry IV himself St. Gregory VII wrote in December 1075:[3]

Bishop Gregory, servant of the servants of God, to King Henry, greeting and apostolic benediction, that is, if he be obedient to the apostolic chair as becomes a Christian king. Considering and carefully weighing with what strict judgment we shall have to render account for the ministry entrusted to us by St. Peter, chief of the apostles, it is with hesitation that We have sent you the apostolic benediction. For you are said knowingly to exercise fellowship with those excommunicated by the judgments of the apostolic See and by sentence of the synod. If this is true, you yourself know that you may receive neither the favour of the divine nor the apostolic benediction unless—those who have been excommunicated being first separated from you and compelled to do penance—you do first, with condign re-

[3] *Ibid.*, p. 457, translation in *ibid.*

pentance and satisfaction, seek absolution and indulgence for your transgression.

Henry IV's abject submission, kneeling in the snow at Canossa, has often been taken as the supreme victory for pope over emperor. Actually, as it turned out, it was a defeat rather than a victory for the Holy See, for by making the papacy the nucleus of all anti-imperial activity, it prepared the way for the long French domination over the popes, which, in turn, led to the scandal of the Great Schism of the West, the papal exile at Avignon, the breakup of the empire and the Reformation itself. Canossa marked the end of an era of increasing harmony between Church and state that never reoccurred.

But St. Gregory VII was not only a great militant pope, fighting with the emperor. He was also one of the greatest reformers the Church has ever known, and his tremendous work among the clergy is attested by many hundreds of letters like the following,[4] which is one of the first to be called an encyclical by Mirbt.

To the faithful in Italy and Germany, 1709.

If there are priests or deacons or subdeacons who live in fornication forbid them in the name of God and by the authority of St. Peter to enter the church before they do penance and change their life. If they want to persevere in their sin none of you should dare to attend their services.

The Church is not only the ark of salvation. She is also, in history, a society, in fact *the* society *par excellence,* linking together the communion of saints, which is the Church triumphant in heaven; the communion of the suffering, who are the Church in Purgatory, and the communion of the faithful, the whole company of Christians, of saints and sinners who make up the Church militant here on earth. And here on earth the Church is in history, and every Christian is faced continually with human history and its problems, and no Christian more so than the "servant of the servants of God," the pope. . . .

When the pagans had been baptized, and the barbarians civilized, and the emperors taught their relationship to the Church, a new menace arose: Islam. Muhammad was the founder of the faith called Islam, or the Surrender (to God), and his followers were called Muslims, "those who have surrendered." Islam was, and is, a strictly monotheist faith: "There is no God but God, and Muhammad is his prophet" is its whole creed, and the Quran, the book written down at

[4] Text in C. Mirbt, *op. cit.*

Muhammad's dictation (he himself could neither read nor write) states specifically that God "begets not nor is begotten." The duties of a Muslim are to worship God by prayer five times daily; to fast from dawn to dusk one lunar month a year; to give a tenth of all he possesses in alms; and, once in his lifetime, to make a pilgrimage to Mecca. Jihad, or holy war, is an approved activity for Muslims, and before Muhammad had been dead a hundred years his followers had conquered the whole Near East, including the Holy Land, as well as North Africa and Spain.

Between the Concordat of Worms and the First General Council of the Lateran (1123-53) there was peace between pope and emperor. In 1095, at the Council of Clermont, Pope Urban II had launched the First Crusade, granting a plenary indulgence (remission of the penalties for sins committed, confessed and absolved) to all who pledged themselves to fight against the Muslims for the deliverance of the Holy Places, of which the chief were Jerusalem, Nazareth and Bethlehem. Jerusalem was taken by the Crusaders on July 14, 1099. Soon after, the Christians began to squabble among themselves; the Byzantine emperors resented the Crusaders and vice versa. These dissensions enabled the Muslims to make a counteroffensive, capturing Edessa in 1144. A year later the pope, Blessed Eugene III, issued a summons to a second crusade, on December 1, 1145.[5]

To all the faithful ones of God who are established throughout Gaul,—greeting and apostolic benediction.

How much our predecessors the Roman pontiffs did labour for the deliverance of the oriental church, we have learned from the accounts of the ancients and have found it written in their acts. For our predecessor of blessed memory, Pope Urban, did sound, as it were, a celestial trump and did take care to arouse for its deliverance the sons of the holy Roman church from the different parts of the earth. At his voice, indeed, those beyond the mountain and especially the bravest and strongest warriors of the French kingdom, and also those of Italy, inflamed by the ardour of love did come together, and, congregating a very great army, not without much shedding of their own blood, the divine aid being with them, did free from the filth of the pagans that city where our Saviour willed to suffer for us, and where He left His glorious sepulchre to us as a memorial of His passion,—and many others which, avoiding prolixity, we refrain from mentioning.

[5] Text in M. Doeberl, *Monumenta Germaniae*. München: J. Lindauersche, 1889-94, Vol. 4, p. 40.

Which, by the grace of God, and the zeal of your fathers, who at intervals of time have striven to the extent of their power to defend them and to spread the name of Christ in those parts, have been retained by the Christians up to this day; and other cities of the infidels have by them been manfully stormed. But now, our sins and those of the people themselves requiring it, a thing which we can not relate without great grief and wailing, the city of Edessa which in our tongue is called Rohais,—which also, as is said, once when the whole land in the east was held by the pagans, alone by herself served God under the power of the Christians—has been taken and many of the castles of the Christians occupied by them (the pagans). The archbishop, moreover, of this same city, together with his clergy and many other Christians, have there been slain, and the relics of the saints have been given over to the trampling under foot of the infidels, and dispersed. Whereby how great a danger threatens the church of God and the whole of Christianity, we both know ourselves and do not believe it to be hid from your prudence. For it is known that it will be the greatest proof of nobility and probity, if those things which the bravery of your fathers acquired be bravely defended by you the sons. But if it should happen otherwise, which God forbid, the valour of the fathers will be found to have diminished in the case of the sons.

We exhort therefore all of you in God, we ask and command, and, for the remission of sins enjoin: that those who are of God, and above all, the greater men and the nobles, do manfully gird themselves; and that you strive so to oppose the multitude of the infidels, who rejoice at the time in a victory gained over us, and so to defend the oriental church —freed from their tyranny by so great an outpouring of the blood of your fathers, as we have said,—and to snatch many thousands of your captive brothers from their hands,—that the dignity of the Christian name may be increased in your time, and that your valour which is praised throughout the whole world, may remain intact and unshaken. May that good Matthias be an example to you, who, to preserve the laws of his fathers, did not in the least doubt to expose himself with his sons and relations to death, and to leave whatever he possessed in the world; and who at length, by the help of the divine aid, after many labours however, did, as well as his progeny, manfully triumph over his enemies.

We, moreover, providing with paternal solicitude for your tranquillity and for the destitution of that same church, do grant and confirm by the authority conceded to us of God, to those who by the promptings of devotion do decide to undertake and to carry through so holy and so necessary a work and labour, that remission of sins which our aforesaid predecessor Pope Urban did institute; and do decree that their wives and sons, their goods also and possessions shall remain under the protection of ourselves and of the archbishops, bishops and other prelates of the church of God. By the apostolic authority, moreover, we forbid that, in the case of any thing which they possessed in peace when they took the cross, any suit be brought hereafter until most certain news has been obtained concerning their return or their death. Moreover since those who war for the Lord should by no means prepare themselves with precious garments, nor with provision for their personal appearance, nor with dogs nor hawks or other things which portend licentiousness, We exhort your prudence in the Lord that those who have undertaken such a work shall not strive after these things but shall show zeal and diligence with all their strength in the matter of arms, horses and other things with which they may fight the infidel. But those who are oppressed with debt and begin so holy a journey with a pure heart shall not pay interest for the time past, and if they, or others for them, are bound by an oath or pledge in the matter of interest, we absolve them by apostolic authority. It is allowed to them also, when their relations, being warned, or the lords to whose fee they belong, are either unable or unwilling to advance them the money, freely to pledge without any reclamation their lands or other possession to churches, or to ecclesiastical persons, or to any other of the faithful. According to the institution of our aforesaid predecessor, by the authority of almighty God and by that of St. Peter the chief of the apostles, conceded to us by God, we grant such remission and absolution of sins, that he who shall devoutly begin so sacred a journey and shall accomplish it, or shall die during it, shall obtain absolution for all his sins which with a humble and contrite heart he shall confess, and shall receive the fruit of eternal retribution from the Remunerator of all.

The problems of the Church in its moments of victory were no less great than its problems when in conflict, and the Christian, faced with a Christian world, had as much to learn and was involved with as many difficulties as when coping with pagan or paynim.

The Church reached the zenith of its earthly power with Pope Innocent III (1198-1216). Then it was a supranational world state, organized "with its judiciary and its law, its centralized bureaucracy, its financial system and its armies, prepared to coerce by force of arms, by the threat and the reality of a holy war, any rebellion against the standard doctrines of belief and conduct or against the papal policies."[6] A great number of documents remain from this time, of which *Sicut Universitatis conditor* is given here as expressing Innocent III's view on the relationship between the two powers of Church and state. It is addressed to the towns of Central Italy, which had formed a league to defend themselves against the bands of marauding German soldiers, remnants of Emperor Henry VI's army. The letter, dated November 3, 1198, is personally to the noble man Acerbus, Prefect, and to the other leaders of Tuscany and of the Duchy.[7]

Just as God, founder of the universe, has constituted two large luminaries in the firmament of Heaven, a major one to dominate the day and a minor one to dominate the night, so he has established in the firmament of the Universal Church, which is signified by the name of Heaven, two great dignities, a major one to preside—so to speak—over the days of the souls, and a minor one to preside over the nights of the bodies. They are the Pontifical authority and the royal power. Thus, as the moon receives its light from the sun and for this very reason is minor both in quantity and in quality, in its size and in its effect, so the royal power derives from the Pontifical authority the splendour of its dignity, the more of which is inherent in it, the less is the light with which it is adorned, whereas the more it is distant from its reach, the more it benefits in splendour. Both these powers or leaderships have had their seat established in Italy, which country consequently obtained the precedence over all provinces by Divine disposition. And therefore, as it is lawful that we should extend the watchfulness of our providence to all provinces, we must especially and with paternal solicitude provide for Italy where the foundation of the Christian religion has been set up and where the pre-eminence of the priesthood and kingship stands prominent through the primacy of the Apostolic See.

We therefore admonish and exhort you all in the Lord through this Apostolic letter, enjoining that since you receive a true and firm assurance from us who—as it is fitting for the Apostolic dignity—intend to do more for you than we want to promise, you should always endeavour to act in a way which would add to the honour and growth of the Roman Church so as to deserve and strengthen the pledge of her favour and friendship.

[6] Father Philip Hughes, *op. cit.*, p. 122.
[7] Translation in Sidney Ehler and John B. Morrall, *op. cit.*

Chapter 5

✠

The Beginning of National States

In its long fight with the emperors, the papacy had traditionally throughout the Middle Ages enjoyed the support of the French monarchy. But the French king Philip IV (1285-1314) started levying taxes on the clergy, and scared most of them into paying. The impoverished clergy appealed to Rome, and the pope, Boniface VIII (1294-1303) issued on February 25, 1296, a bull, *Clericis laicos,* which reiterated the Church's stand. No lay power, declared the pope, had any right to tax the Church without its consent. The French king's answer was to forbid the export of gold and silver from France, so the papal dues could not leave the country; Philip IV also arrested a bishop. The pope summoned all the remaining French bishops to Rome to discuss matters, and meanwhile Philip IV was badly beaten by the Flemish at Courtrai on July 11, 1302. The text of the bull, dated February 25, 1296, follows.[1]

The history of olden times teaches, and daily experience proves, that the laity have always felt hostile to the clergy and have constantly striven to overstep their bounds by wickedness and disobedience. They do not reflect that all power over the clergy, over the persons and property of the Church, is denied them. They lay heavy burdens on prelates, churchmen and both regular and secular clergy, crush them with taxes, taking sometimes half, at other times a tenth or a twentieth or some other portion of their revenues, trying to reduce them to slavery in a thousand ways. In the bitterness of our souls we must add that certain prelates and other ecclesiastical persons, fearful when there is nothing for them to fear, seek fugitive peace, and dread a temporal majesty more than the eternal. They may lend themselves to these abuses less through temerity than imprudence, but without obtaining due faculty and authorization from the

[1] J. H. Robinson, *Readings in European History.* Chicago: Ginn & Co., 1904, I, 448.

Holy See. . . . To cut short these abuses we, in accord with the cardinals and by virtue of our apostolic authority, ordain the following: all prelates and in general all persons belonging to the Church, monks, or secular clergy who, without the consent of the Apostolic See, pay or promise to pay to laymen any imports, taxes, tithes or half tithes or even a one-hundredth part or any portion whatsoever of their revenues or of the goods of their church by way of a subvention, loan, gift, subsidy, etc., as also emperors, kings, princes, barons, rectors, etc., who levy the same, who exact such taxes or receive them or who even put their hand on valuables placed in the church or who co-operate in this sort of act, all these persons *ipso facto* incur excommunication. We interdict anyone who preaches in defense of these condemned acts. Under the penalty of deposition, we order prelates and all Christians not to permit these taxes to be collected without the express consent of the Holy See.

This excommunication was automatically incurred in 1955 by the Argentine dictator, Juan Perón.

It was in the face of the defeat of Philip IV at Courtrai that Boniface VIII issued one of the most famous of all papal bulls, *Unam Sanctam,* in November 1302.[2]

We are compelled, our faith urging us, to believe and to hold—and we do firmly believe and simply confess—that there is one holy Catholic and apostolic Church, outside of which there is neither salvation nor remission of sins; her Spouse proclaiming it in the canticles: "My dove, my undefiled, is but one, she is the choice one of her that bare her"; which represents one mystic body, of which body the head is Christ; but of Christ, God. In this church there is one Lord, one faith and one baptism. There was one ark of Noah, indeed, at the time of the flood, symbolizing one church; and this being finished in one cubit had, namely, one Noah as helmsman and commander. And, with the exception of this ark, all things existing upon the earth were, as we read, destroyed. This church, moreover, we venerate as the only one, the Lord saying through His prophet: "Deliver my soul from the sword, my darling from the power of the dog." He prayed at the same time for His soul—that is, for Himself the Head—and for His body,—which body, namely, he called the one and only church on account of the unity of the faith promised, of the sacraments, and of the love of the church. She is that seamless garment of the Lord which was not cut but which fell by lot. Therefore of this one and only church

there is one body and one head—not two heads as if it were
a monster:—Christ, namely, and the vicar of Christ, St.
Peter, and the successor of Peter. For the Lord Himself said
to Peter, Feed my sheep. My sheep, He said, using a general
term, and not designating these or those particular sheep;
from which it is plain that He committed to Him *all* His
sheep. If, then, the Greeks or others say that they were not
committed to the care of Peter and his successors, they
necessarily confess that they are not of the sheep of Christ;
for the Lord says, in John, that there is one fold, one
shepherd and one only. We are told by the word of the gospel
that in this His fold there are two swords,—a spiritual,
namely, and a temporal. For when the apostles said "Behold
here are two swords"—when, namely, the apostles were
speaking in the church—the Lord did not reply that this was
too much, but enough. Surely he who denies that the
temporal sword is in the power of Peter wrongly interprets
the word of the Lord when He says: "Put up thy sword in
its scabbard." Both swords, the spiritual and the material,
therefore, are in the power of the church; the one, indeed, to
be wielded for the church, the other by the church; the one
by the hand of the priest, the other by the hand of kings and
knights, but at the will and sufferance of the priest. One
sword, moreover, ought to be under the other, and the
temporal authority to be subjected to the spiritual. For when
the apostle says "there is no power but of God," and the
powers that are of God are ordained, they would not be
ordained unless sword were under sword and the lesser one,
as it were, were led by the other to great deeds. For according to St. Dionysius the law of divinity is to lead the lowest
through the intermediate to the highest things. Not therefore
according to the law of the universe, are all things reduced
to order equally and immediately; but the lowest through the
intermediate, the intermediate through the higher. But that
the spiritual exceeds any earthly power in dignity and
nobility we ought the more openly to confess the more
spiritual things excel temporal ones. This also is made plain
to our eyes from the giving of tithes, and the benediction and
the sanctification; from the acceptation of this same power,
from the control over those same things. For, the truth bearing witness, the spiritual power has to establish the earthly
power, and to judge it if it be not good. Thus concerning the
church and the ecclesiastical power is verified the prophecy
of Jeremiah: "See, I have this day set thee over the nations
and over the kingdoms," and the other things which follow.
Therefore if the earthly power err it shall be judged by the
spiritual power; but if the lesser spiritual power err, by the

greater. But if the greatest, it can be judged by God alone not by man, the apostle bearing witness. A spiritual man judges all things, but he himself is judged by no one. This authority, moreover, even though it is given to man and exercised through man, is not human but rather divine, being given by divine lips to Peter, and founded on a rock for him and his successors through Christ himself whom he has confessed, the Lord himself, saying to Peter "Whatsoever thou shalt bind," etc. Whoever, therefore, resists this power thus ordained by God, resists the ordination of God, unless he makes believe, like the Manichaean, that there are two beginnings. This we consider false and heretical, since by the testimony of Moses not "in the beginnings" but "in the beginning" God created the Heavens and the earth. Indeed we declare, announce and define, that it is altogether necessary to salvation for every human creature to be subject to the Roman pontiff. *The Lateran, November 14, in our 8th year.* As a perpetual memorial of this matter.

King Philip IV's retort to this bull was to send a French force to Italy to arrest the pope and bring him back a prisoner. Boniface VIII would not budge, even when French soldiers broke into his palace. He was only saved when the local populace arose and drove out the foreign invaders. But the pope died of shock a month later, on October 11, 1303.

As the Church became increasingly involved in politics, the opposition to it grew, not only of those who were pro-emperor against the pope, but of those who sought to appeal from the policies or pronouncements of the current pope to that of a general council of the whole Church.

The king of Poland's representatives at the Council of Constance, which met in November 1414, asked Martin V, just elected, to condemn as heretical an anti-Polish book written by a German friar, John of Falkenberg. The pope refused, and the Polish delegates left the council, declaring they would appeal from this decision of the pope to a future general council.

When Aeneas Silvius Piccolomini was elected pope in 1458 (he took the name Pius II), he promulgated the bull *Execrabilis*, which forbade any such appeals to a future council.[3]

1. An execrable, and in former ages unheard-of abuse, has sprung up in our time, namely that some people, imbued with the spirit of rebellion, presume to appeal to a future Council

---

[3] *Magnum Bullarium Romanorum*, ed. Cherubini (2nd ed.) I, 386, translation in Sidney Ehler and John B. Morrall, *op. cit.*, p. 113.

from the Roman Pontiff, the Vicar of Jesus Christ, to whom it was said in the person of blessed Peter: "Feed my sheep" and "Whatsoever thou shalt bind on earth shall be bound also in Heaven"; they do not do so because they are anxious to obtain sounder judgment, but in order to escape the consequences of their sins, and anyone who is not ignorant of the laws can realize how contrary this is to the sacred canons and how detrimental to the Christian community. Because— passing over other things which are most manifestly opposed to this corruption—who would not find it ridiculous when appeals are made to what does not exist and the time of whose future existence nobody knows? The poor are oppressed in many ways by the stronger, crimes remain unpunished, freedom is conceded to delinquents, and all the ecclesiastical discipline and hierarchical order is confounded.

2. Wishing therefore to thrust away from Christ's Church this pestilent venom, to take care of the salvation of all those who have been committed to us, and to hold off from the sheepfold of our Saviour all cause of scandal, we condemn appeals of this kind by the counsel of all prelates and jurisconsults of Divine and human law adhering to the Curia and on the ground of our sure knowledge; and we denounce them as erroneous and detestable, quash and entirely annul them in the event that any such appeals, extant at present, may be discovered, and we declare and determine that they are—like something void and pestilent—of no significance. Consequently, we enjoin that nobody dares under whatever pretext to make such an appeal from any of our ordinances, sentences or commands and from those of our successors, or to adhere to such appeals, made by others, or to use them in any manner.

3. If any one, of whatever status, rank, order or condition he may be, even if adorned with Imperial, royal or Papal dignity, shall contravene this after the space of two months from the day of the publication of this Bull by the Apostolic Chancery, he shall "ipso facto" incur sentence of anathema, from which he can not be absolved except by the Roman Pontiff and at the point of death. A University or a corporation shall be subjected to an ecclesiastical interdict; nonetheless, corporations and Universities, like the aforesaid and any other persons, shall incur those penalties and censures which offenders who have committed the "crimen laesae maiestatis" and promoters of heretical depravity are known to incur. Furthermore scriveners and witnesses who shall witness acts of this kind and, in general, all those who shall knowingly furnish counsel, help or favour to such appealers, shall be punished with the same penalty.

Therefore, it is not allowed to any man to infringe or to oppose by audacious perversion this charter of our will, by which we have condemned, reproved, quashed, annulled, decreed, declared and ordered the aforesaid. If any one, however, shall so attempt, let him know that he shall incur the indignation of Almighty God and of Saint Peter and Paul, His Apostles.

Given at Mantua, in the year 1460 of the Lord's Incarnation, on the fifteenth day before the Kalends of February, in the second year of our Pontificate.

THE TEMPORAL POWER AND THE PAPAL STATES

Between the fall of the western empire and the rise of the Frankish Carolingian emperors, the popes had been given various territories in Central and South Italy. Pious feudal lords had willed some to the sovereign pontiff, others had been donated by repentant sinners; in those centuries of general insecurity and uncertainty, when life and property were tenuously and precariously held, many people disposed of their lands by deed to the only abiding authority—that of the pope.

When the pope consecrated, first Pepin in St. Denis, and then his son Charlemagne in Rome on Christmas Day, 800, he received by the Donation given by the father and confirmed by the son, a firm basis to his temporal power. The political and economic revolutions had also made the popes lords of the *Ducatus Romanus,* the duchy of Rome, which included the Holy City. The Roman citizens refused to regard any other than the pope as their lord, for only the pope kept the barbarians from plundering them, the Lombards from despoiling. When Pope Stephen II claimed the Central Provinces from Pepin, he was acknowledged as a ruling sovereign, but he placed himself under the Frankish ruler and swore he and his people would be true to the emperor. In 1077 and 1102 Countess Matilda of Tuscany added huge grants of land to the papal domain, which the pope also held in fief from the emperor.

In 1797 the temporal power was abolished by the French, who had originally granted it; and again in 1808 by Napoleon. In 1815 it was restored by the unanimous decision of the Congress of Vienna. Between 1815 and 1860 the pope "ruled" over 40,000 square kilometers and some three million people. In 1860 the King of Sardinia, of the house of Savoy, seized two thirds of the papal territory, and in 1870 the Italian State seized the whole. On May 13, 1871, the

Italian State settled the matter to its own satisfaction by a treaty never ratified by the pope, who became "the prisoner of the Vatican" in protest against the illegal seizure, and remained "incarcerated" until the "Roman Question" was finally settled by the Treaty of the Lateran in 1929.

THE CHURCH AND THE NEW WORLD

For the Church, the discoveries of the fifteenth-century explorers were interesting only as missionary journeys: the natives of the new lands had souls to be saved; now the good news of the Gospel could reach them.

In March 1493 Christopher Columbus was forced to land in Portugal. King John II maintained that the papal bull *Romanus Pontifex* of Pope Nicholas V, dated January 8, 1455, which granted the territories discovered in Africa to Portugal, also included America. The Spanish sovereigns, Ferdinand and Isabella, protested to the pope and asked him to confirm their right to the lands newly discovered by Columbus. Three bulls were issued, of which the second, Alexander VI's *Inter Caetera Divinae*[4] (1493) from which the following quotations are taken, was the most important. This bull drew a line from one pole to the other, one hundred leagues west of the Azores and Cape Verde islands. Everything west of this line was granted to Spain. The sphere east was to belong to Portugal. It was the "Line of Demarcation" so established that put what is now Brazil in Portugal's hands.

1. We have been informed, indeed, that you intended to seek and discover some remote and unknown islands and mainlands which have not been found by any one so far, and bring their habitants and natives to the worship of our Redeemer and to the confession of the Catholic faith; but being hitherto mostly occupied with the conquest and recovery of said kingdom of Granada, you were unable to fulfil this holy and praiseworthy intention as you would have desired. But then, as soon as you had recaptured the aforesaid kingdom—according to God's pleasure—you wanted to fulfil your desire and you have dispatched our beloved son Christopher Columbus, a man particularly worthy and highly recommendable, and fitted for such an undertaking, with ships and skilled men, not without great efforts, perils and expenses, in order to search carefully for such remote and unknown mainlands and islands on the sea on which no one had sailed before.

---

[4] *Ibid.*, p. 466, translation, *ibid.*, pp. 156-58.

2. They navigated on the Ocean Sea with God's help and the greatest diligence and they actually discovered some very remote islands and also mainlands which have not been found by any one else before and in which several peoples live peacefully, going unclothed—reportedly—and not eating flesh. As far as your above-said envoys could judge, these peoples inhabiting the said islands and lands believe that one God-Creator is in Heaven; they seem to be well fitted to embrace the Catholic faith and to be imbued with good morals; and there is hope that, were they instructed, the name of the Saviour, our Lord Jesus Christ, could be easily introduced into these lands and islands. The aforementioned Christopher has already caused a fort, fairly strong, to be built up and constructed in one of the principal islands and he has left it to the custody of some Christians, his companions, who are to seek for further remote and unknown islands and continents.

3. And in some islands and lands which have already been discovered gold, spices and very many precious things of various categories and qualities have been found.

4. Wherefore, all things considered maturely and, as it becomes Catholic kings and princes, considered with special regard for the exaltation and spread of the Catholic faith—as your forefathers, kings of illustrious memory, used to do—you have decided to subdue the said mainlands and islands, and their natives and inhabitants, with God's grace, and to bring them to the Catholic faith.

5. We recommend heartily in the Lord such a holy and laudable proposition and we wish it to be led to a due end, whereby the name of our Saviour would be introduced in those countries; we therefore exhort you very earnestly in the Lord and by your reception of Holy Baptism, in virtue of which you are bound to obey Apostolic orders, and by the bowels of mercy of our Lord Jesus Christ we especially enjoin that, as you intend to carry out such an expedition with a willing mind and zeal for orthodox faith, you should and must cause peoples dwelling in those islands and continents to accept the Christian religion. And no perils or hardships will ever deter you therefrom if you conceive your intention in faith and hope that Almighty God will follow with success your effort.

6. And in order that you may embark on an enterprise of such importance more readily and audaciously, endowed with the liberality of Apostolic favour, we give, concede and assign to you—out of our own initiative, not at your request or at a petition presented to us by somebody else on your behalf in this matter, but solely out of our largess, sure

knowledge and plenitude of Apostolic power, by the authority of Almighty God bestowed upon blessed Peter and by the Vicariate of Jesus Christ which we discharge on earth—all the islands and mainlands, found or to be found, discovered or to be discovered westwards or southwards by drawing and establishing a line running from the Arctic to the Antarctic Pole [i.e., from the Northern to the Southern Pole] one hundred leagues West and South from any of the islands which are commonly called the Azores and Cape Verde, irrespective of whether the mainlands and islands are situated in the direction of India or in that of any other country; with the proviso, however, that these mainlands and islands found or to be found, discovered or to be discovered as situated to the West or South of the said line, be not actually possessed by some other Christian king or prince until the day from the Nativity of our Lord Jesus Christ [i.e., of the Christian era] immediately preceding the first day of this year one thousand four hundred and ninety three, in which some of the aforesaid islands were discovered by your envoys and captains. And we concede them by the strength of the present document perpetually with all their dominions, towns, castles, localities and villages and all rights, jurisdictions and appurtenances to you and to your heirs and successors, kings of Castile and Leon; and we constitute, invest and depute you, your heirs and the said successors as lords thereof with full, free and integral power, authority and jurisdiction.

7. But we ordain that by this our donation, concession and grant no claimed right, belonging to any Christian prince who had actually possessed the said islands and mainlands until the above-mentioned day from the Nativity of our Lord Jesus Christ, can be understood as suppressed or taken away from him. Moreover, we enjoin you in virtue of holy obedience that you should dispatch—as you have already promised and as we do not doubt that you will, with your very great devotion and royal magnanimity, fulfil this promise—to the said mainlands and islands honest and God-fearing men, learned, skilled and experienced, to instruct the natives and inhabitants in Christian faith and to imbue them with good morals, and that you should apply all due diligence to this.

8. And we strictly forbid any persons of whatever dignity, even Imperial or royal, status, rank, order or condition —under the penalty of an excommunication "latae sententiae" which they will incur "ipso facto" in case of contravention—to dare, without your special licence or that of your aforesaid heirs and successors, to approach, for the

purpose of trade or for any other reason, the islands and
mainlands found or to be found, already discovered or to
be discovered towards the west and south by drawing and
establishing a line from the Arctic to the Antarctic Pole to
run at a distance of one hundred leagues from any of the
islands commonly called the Azores and Cape Verde, irrespective of whether these mainlands and islands already discovered or to be discovered are situated towards India or
towards any other country.

9. This we ordain and forbid notwithstanding any Apostolic Bulls, ordinances or other documents to the contrary,
confident in Him, from Whom empires, dominions and all
possessions proceed, that if He will direct your acts and
you will pursue this holy and praiseworthy undertaking,
within a short time your toils and efforts shall attain the
most felicitous result to the happiness and glory of all
Christendom.

10. As it would be difficult to have this present document sent to all places where it might be useful, we wish
and decree, from a similar initiative and knowledge, that to
copies of it, signed by the hand of a public notary commissioned therefor and provided with the seal of any person
endowed with an ecclesiastical dignity or an ecclesiastical
office, the same credence should be given before justice extra-
judicially, and anywhere else, as would be given to the present document, if submitted or shown.

11. Let no one, therefore, infringe or with rash daring
contravene this instrument of our recommendation, exhortation, examination.

The Church continually tried to help the wretched natives
of the lands thus distributed, and the popes issued many bulls
against their enslavement or ill treatment. For example, Pope
Paul III in the bull *Pastorale officium,* dated May 29, 1537,
condemned the enslavement of Indians, and declared that it
was heresy to say that they were irrational and incapable of
conversion. He also tried to transfer spiritual authority over
the Indians from the Spanish Inquisition, which was controlled
by the Spanish crown, to the bishop.[5]

It has come to our hearing that our very dear son in Christ,
Charles, the ever august Emperor of the Romans who is also
king of Castile and Aragon, anxious to check those who,
burning with avarice, possess an inhuman spirit, has pro-

[5] Text in C. Mirbt, *op. cit.,* 270, translation in Sidney Ehler and John B.
Morrall, *op. cit.,* p. 200.

hibited all his subjects by public edict from bringing the Western and Southern Indians into slavery, or daring to deprive them of their possessions. These Indians therefore, although they live outside the bosom of the Church, nevertheless have not been, nor are they to be, deprived of their freedom or of ownership of their own possessions, since they are human beings and, consequently, capable of faith and salvation. They are not to be destroyed by slavery, but to be invited to life by preaching and example. Furthermore, desiring to repress the shameful deeds of such wicked men and to ensure that the Indians are not alienated by injuries and punishments so that they find it more difficult to embrace the faith of Christ, we lay it as a charge and command by this present letter upon your Circumspection—in whose righteousness, foresight, zeal and experience in these matters and in others we have in the Lord special trust—that either by your own action or by that of others you provide to all the aforesaid Indians the help of an effective defence in the matters referred to previously; and we enjoin that you very strictly forbid all and sundry of whatever dignity, position, condition, rank and excellence, to bring the above-said Indians into slavery in any way or to dare to deprive them of their possessions in any manner under pain, if they do so, of incurring thereby excommunication "latae sententiae," from which they can only be absolved by ourselves or the Roman Pontiff reigning at that time, except if they are at the point of death and have previously made amends.

Chapter 6

✠

The Church and the Reformation

The Church had learned to live in a pagan world; she had faced the various, continually changing problems of living in a Christian world. With the success of the Protestant Reformation (which began in 1517), owing to the princes—German, Swedish, and later English—who defended it, the Church had to learn to live once more in a divided world, and to cope with the various non-Catholic sovereign powers. The average Christian, meanwhile, had to face a new form of free choice. Hitherto, he could be either a good Christian, a bad Christian, or a pagan; now the various forms of Protestantism offered depended very much on where the Christian lived, for the axiom *cujus regio, ejus religio* (as the ruler's faith, so the country's) was rapidly put into general practice.

The popes often had excommunicated emperors, kings and queens, but the excommunication and deposition of Queen Elizabeth of England by the pope, St. Pius V, also absolved her subjects from their allegiance, and was followed by one of the bitterest persecutions the Church has ever endured. To say Mass, to be a priest or to shelter one, was punished by death, and by the most ghastly of deaths, accompanied by torture. Catholics were not freed from some of these penalties until 1829. The bull *Regnans in excelsis,* excommunicating and deposing Queen Elizabeth I of England, was dated February 25, 1570.[1]

> Pius the Bishop, servant of the servants of God, for a perpetual memorial of the matter.
> He who reigns on high, to Whom is given all power in Heaven and on earth, has entrusted His holy Catholic and Apostolic Church, outside which there is no salvation, to one person alone on earth, namely to Peter the Prince of the Apostles, and to Peter's successor, the Roman Pontiff, to be governed (by him) with plenitude of power. Him alone He appointed Prince over all nations and kingdoms, to root up,

[1] Cherubini, *op. cit.,* II, 303, translation in Sidney Ehler and John B. Morrall, *op. cit.,* pp. 181-83.

pull down, waste, destroy, plant and build, so that he might preserve his faithful people linked together by the bond of mutual charity in the unity of the Spirit, and might present them, saved and blameless, to their Saviour.

In the fulfilment of this office, we, called by the goodness of God to the government of the aforesaid Church, spare no labour, striving with all zeal to preserve intact that unity and Catholic religion which its Author has allowed to be disturbed with such great tribulations for the proving of His people's faith and for our correction. But the number of the ungodly has grown so strong in power, that no place is left in the world which they have not tried to corrupt with their abominable doctrines; among others assisting in this work is the servant of vice, Elizabeth, pretended Queen of England, with whom, as in a place of sanctuary, the most nefarious wretches have found refuge. This same woman, having acquired the kingdom and outrageously usurped for herself the place of Supreme Head of the Church in all England and its chief authority and jurisdiction, has again plunged that same kingdom back into a wretchedly unhappy condition, after it had so recently been reclaimed for the Catholic Faith and prosperity.

For having by force prohibited the practice of the true religion (which had been formerly overthrown by Henry VIII, an apostate from it, and restored by Mary, the legitimate queen of famous memory, with the help of this See) and following and embracing the errors of heretics, she has altered the composition of the royal Council representing the nobility of England and has filled it with obscure heretical men; she has suppressed the followers of the Catholic Faith, appointed shameful preachers and ministers of impieties, and abolished the Sacrifice of the Mass, prayers, fastings, choice of meats, celibacy and Catholic ceremonies; and she has commanded that books containing manifest heresy should be distributed throughout the whole kingdom and that impious rites and institutions (accepted and observed by herself according to Calvin's precept) should be observed by her subjects also. She has dared to eject bishops, rectors of churches and other Catholic priests from their churches and benefices and to bestow these and other ecclesiastical things upon heretics and she has also presumed to decide legal cases within the Church. She has forbidden the prelates, clergy and people to acknowledge the Roman Church or to obey its orders and its canonical sanctions. She has forced most of them to assent to her wishes and laws, to abjure the authority and obedience of the Roman

Pontiff and to recognize her by oath as sole mistress in temporal and spiritual affairs; she has imposed pains and penalties on those who would not obey her commands and has exacted them from those who persevered in the unity of faith and the aforesaid obedience; she has cast Catholic bishops and rectors of churches into prison, where many of them, worn out with long weariness and sorrow, have miserably ended their span of life. All these things are clear and notorious to all nations and proved by the most weighty testimony of so many that there is no room whatever for excuse, defence or evasion.

We have seen that the impieties and crimes have been multiplied, one upon the other, and that also the persecution of the faithful and the affliction of religion through the pressure and action of the said Elizabeth grow greater every day, and since we understand her spirit to be hardened and obstinate—so that she has not only set at naught the pious prayers and warnings of Catholic princes concerning her soundness of mind and conversion, but she has not even allowed the Nuncios of this See to cross into England for this purpose—we are necessarily compelled to take up against her the weapons of justice, although we can not disguise our sorrow that we are thus forced to proceed against one whose ancestors have deserved so well of the Commonwealth of Christendom. But being strengthened by the authority of Him, Who willed to place us on the supreme throne of justice though unequal to so great a burden, out of the plenitude of our Apostolic power we declare the aforesaid Elizabeth to be heretic and an abetter of heretics, and we declare her, together with her supporters in the abovesaid matters, to have incurred the sentence of excommunication and to be cut off from the unity of the Body of Christ.

Furthermore we declare her to be deprived of her pretended claim to the aforesaid kingdom and of all lordship, dignity and privilege whatsoever.

Also we declare that the lords, subjects and peoples of the said kingdom, and all others who have sworn allegiance to her in any way, are perpetually absolved from any oath of this kind and from any type of duty in relation to lordship, fidelity and obedience; consequently we absolve them by the authority of our present statements, and we deprive the same Elizabeth of her pretended claim to the kingdom and of all other claims mentioned previously. And we command and forbid all and sundry among the lords, subjects, peoples and others aforesaid that they have not to obey her or her admonitions, orders or laws. We shall bind those who do the contrary with a similar sentence of excommunication.

Because it would be too difficult for the present words to be conveyed to those who need them, we desire that copies of them bearing the signature of a public notary and the sign of a prelate of the Church or his office, should have the same authentic strength before justice and extra-judicially and produce everywhere the same effect as this present document would produce, if submitted and shown.

Given at Rome at St. Peter's, in the year of the Incarnation of our Lord 1570, on the fifth day (before the) Kalends of March, in the fifth year of our Pontificate.

The natural sequence of Protestantism is that, having rejected the infallible authority of the pope, it develops into a system of ethical behavior that gradually discards dogmatic belief altogether. Since Luther at first had no authority other than that of the Holy See to which he could appeal, he declared that princes were not to be obeyed when they commanded submission to superstitious errors. But when he needed to secure his own church "against the application of the same dissolving principles which had served him to break off from his allegiance to Rome . . . he instantly turned from the people to the princes; he impressed on his party that character of political dependence and that habit of passive obedience to the State, which it has ever since retained."[2]

Thus the eighteenth century saw the emergence of a revolutionary deism; the sovereign enemy was no longer the Church, except in so far as the Church sided with the national ruler, and was on the side of the *status quo*. At first, extreme nationalism was everywhere the Church's chief opponent, and the famous Constitution *Unigenitus* of Clement XI was directed against Jansenism, a theological fruit of Gallicanism. The immediate reason for this Constitution was a book by one Pasquier Quesnel, a reprint of the New Testament annotated with his own moral reflections. The French Parlement took up the conflict, protesting the "papal encroachment in the internal discipline of French Catholicism."[3] The text here given of *Unigenitus* ("Only begotten") (Sept. 8, 1713) is from an early English translation.[4]

Clement XI, bishop, servant of the servants of God; to all the faithful of Christ, greeting, and the apostolical benediction.

The only begotten Son of God, made Man for our salva-

[2] Lord Acton, "The Protestant Theory of Persecution," *Essays in Freedom and Power*. New York: Noonday Press, 1955, p. 171.
[3] Father Philip Hughes, *op. cit.*, p. 208.
[4] Stephen Whatley, *A Parallel of the Doctrine of the Pagans with the Doctrine of the Jesuits*. London: J. Pemberton, 1726.

tion and that of the whole world, while he instructed his disciples in the doctrine of truth, and taught his universal Church in the Apostles, disposing of present Things and foreseeing future, has admonished us, with a singular and most salutary precept, to beware of false prophets, who come to us in sheep's clothing; by which name are chiefly pointed at, those lying teachers and mockers, well versed in the art of deceiving, who privily insinuating erroneous opinions, under the specious pretence of piety, set abroach pernicious principles, under colour of holiness: And to the end that they may more easily surprize the unwary, laying aside, in a manner, the wolf's skin, and wrapping themselves up with the expressions of the divine law, as it were with certain sheepskins, slily abuse the words of Holy Scripture, and even of the New Testament itself, which they diversely wrest to their own destruction, and that of others; imitating, without doubt, the example of the old father of lies, by whom they were begotten, and being taught by their master, that there is not a more ready way at all to beguile, than where the deceitfulness of an impious error is to be brought in, there to pretend the authority of the Divine Words.

We being instructed by these really Divine Admonitions, as soon as ever (not without the most deep bitterness of our spirit) we heard, that a certain book, in the French tongue, was some time since printed, and divided into several tomes, under the title of *The New Testament in French, with Moral Reflections upon every Verse, &c.* At Paris, 1693. And otherwise, *An Abridgment of the Morals of the Gospel, Acts of the Apostles, Epistle of St. Paul, Catholick Epistles, and Revelation:* Or, *Christian Considerations upon the Text of those Sacred Books, &c.* At Paris, 1694. Although this book was at another time condemned by us; and we perceived that falsities of corrupt doctrines were in many places thereof actually mingled together with Catholick Truths; nevertheless, as if it were free from all error, it was kept by many, every where thrust into the hands of Christ's faithful servants, and by the means of some persons, who are always for setting innovations on foot, too diligently dispersed on all sides; it was also translated into *Latin*, that the contagion of the pernicious instruction might, if it were possible, pass through from nation to nation, and from the kingdom to another people; whereupon we were mightily grieved that the Lord's flock, committed to our charge, should by degrees be led aside into the way of perdition, by such crafty delusions and fallacies: wherefore being stirred up as well by the motives of our Pastoral Care, as by the frequent complaints of the zealous assertors of the Orthodox Faith; but chiefly by the letters and entreaties of many venerable brothers, especially Bishops of *France*, We have determined to put a stop, by some stronger remedy, to the increasing disease, which may, one time or other, break out into worse effects.

And indeed, turning the view of our provident consideration upon the very cause of the spreading mischief, we clearly discern, that the utmost bane of such a book chiefly spreads itself and grows stronger, upon this account, that the fame lies hid within, and, like corrupt matter, does not break forth 'till the ulcer be lanced; since the book itself, at first sight, entices readers with a certain show of Godliness; for the words of it are as soft as oil, but are very arrows, and that too with a bent bow, so artfully prepared to hurt, that under cover they shoot at the upright in heart. Therefore We judged, that nothing could be done by Us more seasonably or profitably, than to explain, after a more clear and distinct manner, the fallacious doctrine of the book (which we have hitherto only showed in general) by particularly extracting many propositions out of the said book; and to set, as it were, before the eyes of all Christ's faithful people, the notorious seeds of tares taken out of the middle of the wheat, with which they were enveloped: So that not one or another, but many gross errors, as well those that were some while since condemned, as others lately discovered, being laid bare, and, as it were, exposed to publick view, we certainly trust, that, by the blessing of the Lord, all will be constrained to yield to the truth, which is now apparently disclosed and made manifest.

This course will most of all tend to the advantage of the Catholick cause, and be greatly profitable for composing the discords raised, especially in the most flourishing kingdom of *France*, among spirits that are of different opinions, and now proceed to more grievous dissentions; in a word, it will be very advantagious, and almost absolutely necessary, for settling the tranquillity of consciences. And indeed, not only the aforesaid bishops, but even chiefly our most dear Son in Christ, *Lewis* the most Christian King of *France* (whose singular zeal in maintaining the truth of the Catholick faith, and extirpating errors, we cannot sufficiently commend) has often made protestation to, and importunately sollicited us, to that purpose, with repeated sincerely pious offices, worthy of the most Christian King, and with earnest desires, That we would provide for the pressing necessity of souls, by forthwith issuing the censure of our Apostolical Judgment.

Whereupon, by the favour of the Lord, and relying on His Divine Assistance, we have set about the profitable work, carefully and diligently, as the importance of the affair required; and have ordered a considerable number of propositions, faithfully extracted out of the aforesaid book, respectively, according to the above mentioned editions, and expressed as well in the *French* as in the *Latin* Tongue, to be accurately discussed, by many professors of sacred theology; at first, indeed, before two of our venerable brothers, cardinals of the Holy *Roman* Church: But afterward we commanded the matter to be strictly canvassed and examined before Us (a Council of divers other cardinals being also called) by several repeated congregations, after every particular proposition, over and beside, had been most exactly compared with the very text of the book, with the greatest diligence and maturity of deliberation. The propositions are as follows, *viz.*

PROPOSITIONS CONDEMNED

I

What remains to a soul (who is deprived of God and his Infinite Goodness) but Sin, and the direful consequences thereof, a beggarly pride, a poor and indigent laziness, a total imbecility to a spiritual labour, either by prayer or good works?

II

The Grace of Jesus Christ, a principle efficacious for all manner of good, is necessary for all good-works; without it nothing is done, or can be done.

III

'Tis in vain, O Lord, that you command, unless you give yourself what you command.

IV

Yes, O Lord, all things are possible to him on whom you render all things possible in operating the same in him.

V

When God mollifies not the heart by the inward unction of his grace; then exhortations, and outward graces, serve only to make it more obdurate.

VI

The difference between the *Jewish* and Christian covenant is, that God requires in the one the relinquishing of Sin, and the fulfilling of the Law in the Sinner, though leaving him in his Corruption; and in the other, that God bestows on the Sinner whatever he desires, in purifying him by Grace.

VII

What advantage is it for the man in the old covenant, whom God leaves to his own weakness, making him subject to his law? And what happiness is it not, to be a member of that covenant in which God bestows on us that which he requires of us?

VIII

We are no longer members of the new covenant, than that we are partakers of the new Grace, which worketh in us that which we are commanded by God.

IX

The Grace of Jesus Christ is the Sovereign Grace, without which we can never confess, and with which we never deny him.

X

Grace is the operation of the hand of Almighty God, which cannot either be hindered or retarded by any thing.

XI

Grace is nothing else but the Will of Almighty God, governing and doing whatever he willeth or ordaineth.

XII

When God will save a soul, the undoubted effect, always, and every where, follows the Will of God.

XIII

When God will save a soul, and when he touches it with the inward hand of his mercy, then no human will is able to resist him.

XIV

Although the obstinate sinner be never so far off from being saved, yet must he submit himself; he must humble himself, and adore his blessed Saviour, when Jesus Christ manifests himself to him by the enlivening beams of his Grace.

XV

When God accompanies his commandment, and his Eternal Word, with the unction of his Spirit, and the inward Power of his Grace, it works in the heart an obedience, such as it requires.

XVI

There are no allurements that can resist those of Grace, because nothing is able to resist an Almighty Being.

XVII

Grace is the voice of the Father, which instructeth men inwardly, and bringeth them to Jesus Christ: whoever approaches him not, after he hath first heard the outward call of the Son, is not the father's disciple.

XVIII

The Seed of the Word, which the Hand of God waters, brings forth always its fruits.

XIX

The Grace of God is no other but his Almighty Will; it is the Idea which God gives of it in all his Writings.

XX

True Grace is the idea that God would have us be obedient to him; he worketh and all is done, he speaketh as a Lord, and all things are subject to his power.

XXI

The Grace of Jesus Christ is strong, powerful, sovereign, and invincible, because it is the operation of the will of the Almighty, the consequence and imitation of the working of God, who hath sent into the world, and raised up his Son.

XXII

The All-powerful harmony of the operation of God in the heart of man, with the free assent of his will, is immediately shown unto us in the Incarnation, as being the source and model of all the other operations of his Mercy and Grace, which are free, and have likewise their dependence on God, even as this original operation.

XXIII

God himself has given the representation of the operation of the Almighty Power of his Grace, in the figure or type of that by which he hath formed all creatures out of nothing, and restored life to the dead.

XXIV

The true conception the centurion had of the Almighty Power of God, and Jesus Christ, in healing of bodies by the motion of his will alone, is the image of the idea which we ought to have of the Almighty Power of his Grace, cleansing souls from all sinful concupiscence.

XXV

God enlightens the soul, and heals it as well as the body, by his Will alone; he commandeth, and they obey him.

XXVI

No Graces are given but through faith alone.

XXVII

Faith is the principal Grace, and the Fountain of the rest.

XXVIII

Pardon of sins is the first Grace which God granteth to sinners.

XXIX

No Grace is bestowed out of the Church.

XXX

All whom God will have to be saved through Jesus Christ, are undoubtedly saved.

XXXI

The desires of Jesus Christ are always effectual; whenever he requires, he produces peace in the heart.

XXXII

Jesus Christ yielded himself a Sacrifice, that the First-born, viz. the Elect, might be delivered by his Blood for ever, from the hand of the destroying angel.

XXXIII

Alas! to what degree must a man have carried self-denial, and his renouncing all worldly interests, before he can have the confidence truly to appropriate to himself, if I may speak so, Jesus Christ his Love, his Death, and Mysteries, as St. *Paul* does when he says, He has loved me, and has given himself for me.

XXXIV

The grace of *Adam* produceth only human merit.

XXXV

The grace of *Adam* is a sequel of the creation, which was due to nature found and entire.

XXXVI

The real Difference between the grace of *Adam,* or the state of innocency, and the Christian Grace, is, that the first was received personally by every one, and the other is not received but in the Person of Jesus Christ risen from the dead, to whom we are united.

XXXVII

The Grace of *Adam* which sanctified him in his own Person, was proportioned to him; the Christian Grace, which sanctifieth us in Jesus Christ, is Almighty, and worthy the Son of God.

XXXVIII

The sinner is not free but for the Evil, without the Grace of the Deliverer.

XXXIX

The will which Grace does not prevent, hath no light but to mistake, no heat but to precipitate, no force but to wound itself; it is capable of all wickedness, but can do no good.

XL

Without Grace we can do nothing, but what tends to our condemnation.

XLI

All the knowledge men have of God, even the natural, and that which the heathen philosophers had, proceeds from God only; and without Grace it produces nothing but presumption, vanity and opposition to God himself, instead of an inclination either of worshipping, acknowledging, or loving him.

XLII

The Grace of Jesus Christ alone renders a man fit for the sacrifice of faith; without him, there is nothing but impurity and indignity.

XLIII

The first effect of baptismal Grace, is, that we die unto sin, so that the spirit, the heart, and the senses, may have no more life for sin, than a dead man has for the things of the world.

XLIV

There are but two sorts of Love, from whence, all our affections and actions arise; the Love of God, which doth all for him and which God rewardeth; the Love, by which we love our selves and the world, and which, for not referring every thing to God as it ought, becomes thereby bad.

XLV

The Love of God not ruling in our hearts any more, carnal concupiscence must needs govern them, and every action becomes corrupted thereby.

XLVI

Concupiscence or Charity render the use of the senses either good or bad.

XLVII

The obedience of the law must necessarily arise from some source, and that source is Charity. When the Love of God is its inward principle, and God's Glory its end, then that which appears outwardly is pure, otherwise is hypocrisy or feigned righteousness.

XLVIII

What can we be without the light of faith, without Christ, and without Charity, but error and sin?

XLIX

As no sin is without the love of our selves, so no good works can be without the Love of God.

L

In vain do men call unto God, and call him Father, if they do not call upon him with the spirit of Charity.

LI

Faith justifies when it operates, but operates only by Charity.

LII

All other means of salvation are comprehended in Faith, as in their bud and seed; but this Faith is not without Love and confidence.

LIII

Charity alone performs Christian actions after a Christian manner, in respect to God and Jesus Christ.

LIV

Charity alone speaks to God and he only hears it.

LV

God crowns Charity alone; he that goes by another motive runs in vain.

LVI

God recompenses Charity alone, because Charity honors God alone.

LVII

Everything fails a sinner when hope fails him, and there can be no hope of God where there is no love of him.

LVIII

There is neither God nor religion, where there is no Charity.

LIX

The prayers of the wicked are a new sin, and that which God grants them is a new judgment against them.

LX

If the fear of punishment alone causes repentance, the more violent it is, the more it leadeth men to desperation.

LXI

Tears stop only the hand, but the heart remaineth adherent to sin as long as it is not directed by the Love of Justice.

LXII

He who abstains from evil only out of fear of punishment, commits it in his heart, and is already guilty thereof before God.

LXIII

He who is baptized, is yet under the Law, even as a *Jew*, if he doth not fulfil it; or if he fulfil only through fear.

LXIV

They that are under the curse of the law do no good, because 'tis sin either in doing evil, or in shunning of it through fear.

LXV

Moses and the prophets, the priests and doctors of the Law, are dead, without sending any children to God, since they have made but slaves through fear.

LXVI

He that approaches God should not come to him with his brutal passions, nor be led by a natural instinct, or fear, as beasts, but by Faith and Love, as children.

LXVII

Slavish fear representeth God as a severe, imperious, unjust, and unmerciful master.

LXVIII

The Goodness of God hath abridged the way of salvation, in comprehending all in Faith and prayer.

LXIX

Faith, the use, encrease, and reward of Faith, are all a gift of the mere liberality of God.

LXX

God never afflicteth the innocent; afflictions serve always either to punish the sin, or to purify the sinner.

LXXI

Man, for his preservation, can dispense with this law, for his advantage, which God hath made for its use.

LXXII

The mark of the Christian Church is, that it ought to be Catholick, or Universal, comprehending all the heavenly angels, all the elect, all the righteous of the earth, and those of all ages.

LXXIII

What is the Church but the assembly of the Children of God living in its bosom, adopted in Christ, subsisting in his Person, redeemed by his Blood, living by his Spirit, acting by his Grace, and expecting the glory of the life to come?

LXXIV

The Church hath the Word Incarnate as its Chief, and all the saints as its members.

LXXV

The Church is one Man, composed of many members, whereof Christ is the Chief, the Life, the Substance, and the Person; one Christ, composed of many saints, whereof he is the Sanctifier.

LXXVI

Nothing is more extensive than the Church of God, because it consists of all the elect and righteous of all ages.

LXXVII

He that leadeth not a life worthy of the Son of God, and a member of Christ, has God spiritually no more for his Father, and Christ for his Head.

LXXVIII

That man is separated from the elect, whose image has been the *Jewish* people, and the Head is Christ, in not living as well according to the Gospel, as in believing the Gospel.

LXXIX

It is useful and necessary, at all times, in all places, and for all sorts of persons, to study and understand the Spirit, Piety and Mysteries of the Holy Scriptures.

LXXX

The reading of the Holy Scripture is for all men.

LXXXI

The holy obscurity of the Word of God is not a sufficient reason for the laity to excuse themselves from the reading thereof.

LXXXII

Christians are to sanctify the Lord's Day with reading godly books, more particularly the Holy Scriptures; 'tis dangerous to deprive them of it.

LXXXIII

'Tis an imposition to persuade the world, that the knowledge of religious mysteries ought not to be communicated to women by reading holy books: It is not from the simplicity of women, but the haughty and proud knowledge of men, that the Scriptures have been abused, and that there are risen so many heresies.

LXXXIV

To pull the New Testament out of the hands of Christians, or in keeping it close and sealed up, by taking away from them the means of understanding it, is to shut the mouth of Christ against them.

LXXXV

To forbid Christians the reading of the Holy Scripture, and especially the Gospel, is to forbid the use of the Light to the children of Light, and to punish them with a kind of excommunication.

LXXXVI

To forbid the ignorant people the comfort of joining their voice to that of all the Church, is a custom opposite to the ancient practice of the Apostles, and even to the intention of God.

LXXXVII

'Tis a behaviour full of wisdom, of Light, and of Charity, to give to men time and opportunity of humbling themselves, and to be sensible of the nature of the sin, to ask a true contrition and humiliation from the spirit, and, at least, to begin to satisfy the justice of God, before they are admitted to a reconciliation of the Church.

LXXXVIII

We know not of what nature sin is, and true repentance, when we would be soon restored to the enjoyment of the felicity which sin has deprived us of, and that we are ashamed to bear the confusion of that separation.

LXXXIX

The 14th Degree of the conversion of a sinner from sin, is, that being already reconciled, he hath a right to assist at the offices of the Church.

XC

The Church hath power to excommunicate, which is to be executed by the chief pastors, with the consent, at least, of the whole body.

XCI

The fear of an unjust excommunication ought not to deter us from doing our duty; we never go out of the Church, no, not even when we seem to be driven out of it by the malice of men, when we adhere to God, Jesus Christ, and the Church through Charity.

XCII

To suffer excommunication, and an unjust anathema, rather than to betray the Truth, is to imitate St. *Paul*, far from opposing authority in the least, or breaking the unity.

XCIII

Jesus healeth sometime the wounds which are made without his commandment, through the too great precipitation of principal pastors; Jesus re-establisheth that which they retrench by an indiscreet zeal.

XCIV

Nothing gives a worse idea of the Church to its enemies, than to see the exercise of authority over the Faith of believers, and to foment divisions for things that are neither prejudicial to faith or manners.

XCV

Truths are now reduced under one language, which is in a manner unknown to the greatest part of Christians, and the manner of preaching them, is a kind of an unknown idiom, so different it is from the simplicity of the Apostles, and the common understanding of the Faithful; and there is no regard taken that this defect is one of the marks of the decay of the Church, and of the wrath of God against his children.

XCVI

God suffers, that all powers be contrary to the preachers of Truth, that its conquest may be attributed to the Divine Grace alone.

XCVII

It happens too often that the members which are the most holy, and the most strictly united to the Church, are regarded unworthy of being in the Church, or as if they were excluded; but the righteous liveth by Faith, and not by virtue of the opinion of men.

XCVIII

The condition of persecutions, and sufferings, that one undergoes, either as heretic, malefactor, or ungodly, is very often the last trial, and the most meritorious, because it maketh man more resembling Jesus Christ.

XCIX

The infatuation, prevention, and obstinacy, of not being willing to examine things, or to acknowledge an error or mistake, change and pervert, every day, far too many persons into an odour of death to death, which God hath placed in his Church for to be an odour of life to Life; as for example, good books, instructions, and holy performances.

C

'Tis a deplorable time, when men think of honouring God in persecuting the Truth, and its disciples: that time is now come. To be reputed and used by the ministers of religion, as impious and unworthy of all conversation with God, as a rotten member, capable to infect all things in the society of saints, is, to pious and godly men, a death more terrible than that of the body. In vain does any one flatter himself with the purity of his intentions, and with zeal of religion, in persecuting, by fire and sword, honest and godly men, if he is blinded by his own passions, or seduced by those of others, because he will not examine into the matter; we often believe to sacrifice an impious man to God, and we sacrifice a Servant of God to the devil.

CI

There is nothing more opposite to the Spirit of God, and the Doctrine of Jesus Christ, than to render oaths common in the Church, because it is to multiply the opportunities of Perjury, and lay snares for the weak and ignorant; as also occasions that the Name and Truth of God, serve sometimes for the promoting of ungodly designs.

Having, therefore, as well heard by word of mouth, as received in writing, the suffrages of the aforesaid cardinals and other divines; and having first implored the assistance of the Divine Light; by private and even publick prayers appointed to that end; we do respectively, by this our ordinance, which shall perpetually stand in force, declare, condemn, and disallow, all and singular the above-inserted Propositions, as false, captious, illsounding, offensive to pious Ears, scandalous, pernicious, rash, injurious to the Church and its practice; not only outrageous against the Church, but even against the secular powers, seditious, impious, blasphemous, suspected of heresy, and savouring of heresy itself; as also encouraging heretics and heresies, and even schism, erroneous, often condemned, and, lastly, also heretical; containing divers heresies manifestly tending to innovation, and principally those which are found in the famous propositions of *Jansenius,* nay, even as taken in that sense in which these were condemned.

We command then, all Christ's faithful people, of both sexes, that they do not presume to think, teach, or preach, touching the said propositions, otherwise than as is contained in this our Same Ordinance: So that whosoever teaches, maintains, or publishes them, or any of them, jointly or separately, or even treats of them by way of disputation, publicly or privately, unless perhaps to impugn or disprove them; shall be, *ipso facto,* without any other deliberation, liable to the ecclesiastical censures, and to other penalties appointed by law, against those that commit the like offences.

And further, by the express disallowing of the aforesaid propositions, we do not by any means, intend to approve of others contained in the said book, especially, since in the course of the examination, we have found therein, many other propositions very like and near of the same stamp with those that were condemned as above, and tainted with the same errors; and indeed, not a few, as it were under a certain imaginary colour of a persecution that is now on foot, fomenting disobedience and obstinacy, and falsely crying them up under the name of Christian patience; a particular enumeration of which, for that cause, we have judged to be both too tedious, and not at all necessary. To conclude, what is more intolerable, we have found the sacred text of the New Testament itself damnably corrupted, and, in many respects, conformable to another *French Version at Mons,* long ago disallowed; but very much disagreeing and swerving from the Vulgar edition, which is approved by the use of so many ages in the Church, and ought to be looked upon as authentic by all orthodox persons; and often, not without the greatest perverseness, wrested into strange, foreign, and even pernicious senses.

We therefore, by the apostolical authority, and the tenour of these presents, do again prohibit, and likewise condemn, the same book, inasmuch as by soft words and benedictions (as the Apostle expresses it) that is to say, under the false pretence of a pious instruction, it is exceedingly suited to seduce the minds of the innocent; whether it bears the above-mentioned titles, or any other, of whatsoever edition or version it may be, wheresoever, and in whatsoever language it is hitherto printed, or (which God forbid) may be printed for the time to come. Even as we do in like manner prohibit and strictly forbid all and singular other books or libels, composed in its defence, as well manuscript as printed copies, or such like books and libels (which God avert) as perhaps may be hereafter set forth; as also the reading, transcribing, retaining, and use of them, among all the singular the faithful People of Christ, under pain of excommunication, to be *ipso facto* incurred by those that act contrary to this Ordinance. . . .

But in the wings, while Gallicanism and Jansenism played out their acts, Liberalism was waiting to raise its bloodier, uglier head. At the end of the eighteenth century the storm broke. "The history," Christopher Dawson said in his 1955 Oriel lectures at Oxford, "of the modern revolutionary movement has been a continuous one, so that democracy, nationalism, socialism, and communism are all of them successive or simultaneous aspects of the same process." When, in the French Revolution, the Church, Voltaire's *infâme*, was, it would seem, crushed, and a harlot danced on the altar of Notre Dame, religion everywhere was threatened. Napoleon's victories swept through Italy, disrupted the Papal States, and menaced the papacy itself. But the Church survived, to face, after Waterloo, a world "where the highest consideration," as Lord Acton put it, "is the public good and the popular will, as in democracies and in constitutional monarchies." In such a world, he warned, "majority takes the place of authority; an irresistible power is substituted for an idolatrous principle, and all private rights are equally insecure."

The Church has had, in the nineteenth and twentieth centuries, to face first Liberalism, then Modernism, secularism, dialectical materialism and fascism, and has met the hydra-headed dictatorships with the same calm statement of fact with which she met the pagan empire or the Holy Roman emperor: that two loves have created two cities, love of God, to the contempt of self, the heavenly; love of self, to the contempt of God, the earthly. And every human being ever born is citizen of both and has to live in the tension caused by his dual citizenship. Meanwhile, the individual Christian painfully learned to live with civil liberty, in one world, where the industrial revolution completed the social upheaval caused by the Enlightenment, and materialism manured men's minds for Marx's sowing.

Yet the nineteenth century saw a great upswing of religion. The revolutions were met by the Vatican Council; Liberalism was answered by Pope Pius IX with one great encyclical and Syllabus cf Errors; Modernism by Pope Pius X with another. So far in the twentieth century, the Church has more and more emphasized the uniqueness, the infinite value, of the human person: to the dictatorship of the proletariat and the *mystique* of an economic interpretation of history, the Church has opposed the doctrine of the Mystical Body as the living prolongation of Jesus Christ Himself, expressing Himself in and through each and every one of His members. This twentieth century, too, is the century of the Mother of God, and from the proclamation of the dogma of the Immaculate Conception (1854) to that of the Assumption (1950), the Church has honored and proclaimed the one totally *human* being in all history who was what every human being was meant to be, and who therefore reached before the end of Time the goal of Time.

And the popes have been not only bulwarks, but builders. Thus, in the great labor encyclicals, *Rerum Novarum* and *Quadragesimo Anno,* they have set forth the dignity of the workingman and his rights; in *Mit brennender Sorge,* the Church faced the menace of Nazism; in *Non abbiamo bisogno,* that of Fascism; in *Divini Redemptoris,* that of atheistic communism. In the encyclicals on human liberty, on the function of the state in the modern world, on the Christian education of youth, and on Christian marriage, and above all in the encyclical *Mystici Corporis,* the Church has built up not only her ramparts against contemporary error but also the topless towers of her self's dear city, the city of God.

Chapter 7

✝

Benedict XIV (1740-58)

In the middle of the eighteenth century, the uninterrupted sequence of historical encyclicals begins. On the death of Clement XII on February 6, 1740, the conclave which met to elect his successor was composed of fifty-six cardinals. Various factions caused a delay of five months because the conclave could not agree on the election of a new pontiff. But on August 10 the conclave obtained the necessary majority for Cardinal Prospero Lambertini, Archbishop of Bologna, who took the name of Benedict XIV. He was sixty-five years old and had the reputation of being a man of great culture, knowledge of canon law, purity of customs, and serene and jovial character, so that he was extremely well liked in his archdiocese. His pontificate confirmed these qualities and definitely distinguished itself from those preceding it by the liberal spirit which animated his actions. Yet he was a man of culture much more than a man of politics. When he yielded the King of Portugal the right to the patronage and the control of ecclesiastical benefits, or when, in the Kingdom of the Two Sicilies, he renounced the absolute privilege ecclesiastics had had of exemption from secular jurisdiction, many thought that Benedict XIV did not defend with enough energy the rights of the Church. It may be, however, that he foresaw future times when the power and spiritual prestige of the pontiff would increase enormously just because his temporal power would have diminished. Benedict XIV dedicated himself to the intellectual mission of the papacy with the passion of the humanist and the wide outlook of a modern man. He inaugurated public works, commercial legislation, the opening of new means of communications in the Papal States, the establishment of academies, and a number of provisions leading to the modernization of Roman life. Proof of his tolerant mind is to be found in his correspondents, who included Lodovico Antonio Muratori, Frederick II of Prussia, and Voltaire. Yet his cordial exchange of letters with the last did not keep Benedict XIV from condemning his work by his decree of 1753.

He has also left his imprint as a canonist, since he established definitively the criteria for the procedure of beatification. He was the first pope to give the *name* "encyclical" to a letter sent by him to all Catholic bishops "in peace and communion." This first encyclical of modern times is called *Ubi primum* and is dated December 3, 1740.

Benedict XIV died in the eighteenth year of his pontificate, on May 3, 1758, after a long illness.

Extracts from four of his most important encyclicals follow.[1]

Inter omnigenas, February 2, 1744

14. If the wife of a Catholic runs off to the Turks and dares to contract with one of them a criminal alliance, her husband may not marry another in her stead; for marriage, indissoluble by divine right so long as the parties to it live, cannot be dissolved by this woman's crime. Therefore any man who, in such a case, marries another woman, is guilty of adultery, and must be refused access to the sacraments, unless he has completely separated himself from the woman.

Quod provinciale, August 10, 1754

In this encyclical letter we want to commend to your attention, confirm and order you to observe what the Provincial Council of Albano . . . under Pope Clement XI in 1714 said. . . .

1. With much sorrow we have heard that many of your province forget about their eternal salvation, hiding their Christian faith in a way which is almost an apostasy, and continue to use Turk or Muslim names not only in order to be free from taxes and other tributes imposed upon Christians or at least often imposed, but also in order that they and their parents be not considered apostates from Islam (*Mahumetana Secta*) and be not punished for this reason. All these things one cannot do—even if one keeps in one's heart the Faith in Christ—because it involves a faking of Muslim errors which is contrary to Christian sincerity. Such an insincerity is a serious matter and virtually is a denial of one's faith which is an offense to God, and also is a scandal to one's neighbour. It might provide the Turks with a wonderful occasion to consider all Christians as hypocrites and deceivers, who should be persecuted with good reason.

What heightens our sorrow is, that some of you, Venerable Brothers, and some of you, dear sons, Pastors and Missionaries,

[1] Text in *Tutti le Encicliche Dei Sommi Pontifici*. Milano: Edizioni Corbaccio, 1940.

connive at this nasty and detestable simulation . . . and are not ashamed of admitting almost without qualms of conscience such people to the sacraments. . . .

Thus we strictly forbid that a Christian under any circumstance or pretext or in any imaginable situation should take a Muslim or Turkish name for the purpose of being considered a Muslim. . . .

[Usury, or the receiving of interest on loans, was at first forbidden to Christians. During the Middle Ages, the moneylenders were always Jews; it was not until the fourteenth century that the Count of Flanders installed two Lombards, Christians, as head of the "Exchange" at Antwerp. Soon the Lombards were lending not only to merchants and to towns, but to the emperors, for example Charles V. About the middle of the sixteenth century, the Genoese bankers asked the Jesuit theologian, Jaime Lainez, for his opinion on the legitimacy of interest, which he gave. Leonard Leys, called Lessius, teaching theology at Louvain around 1585, also concretely discussed the problems of banking "in law and in justice," i.e., in theory and practice. Yet the situation remained far from clear, with Oratorians and Jesuits taking different sides. The pope felt it necessary to clarify the situation, and the encyclical that follows, *Vix pervenit*, of November 1, 1745, is the first on the subject.]

A short while ago we learned about the new controversy concerning several opinions now held in Italy. Immediately we thought that it pertains to our Apostolic duties to remedy efficaciously and to stop this disgraceful idea that usurious contracts should be considered valid, because we thought that were time and silence to close over this idea, it would acquire increasing respectability, and would corrupt those cities of Italy not yet infected. Therefore we have followed that method of which the Holy See always takes advantage, that is, we have explained the whole problem to some of our brethren the Cardinals of the Roman Church, who are well known for their profound knowledge of theology and for their learned experience with canon law. . . .

All these have unanimously approved what follows. Usury is that crime which has its special place in the contract of loan, and it is that guarantee, by which it is pretended that from what has been loaned more should be returned than what was originally loaned, and therefore it is pretended that above and beyond the capital a certain margin of profit may be asked because of the loan itself. In this case any profit of this type which goes beyond the capital is illicit and has the character [nature] of usury.

In order to cancel such guilt it is not possible to hope it will be mitigated by the fact that such gain is not exorbitant or excessive, but moderate; not big but small; nor from the fact that the lender is not poor but rich, and has anyway no intention of leaving the sum idle which he gives as a loan, but to invest it profitably in order to augment his fortune or to buy new properties, or to make business gains, because it is evident that he is acting against the law of loan, which necessarily consists in an equality between that which is given and that which is restored. And whoever is not ashamed to ask for more in such a case, or who fails to blush to ask for a sum which is greater than what he lent, he is obliged, if he has received such a greater sum, to give it back, because of the so-called Clause of Commutative Justice, which has the effect of maintaining equality in human contracts, and of restoring it when it has been disturbed. . . .

With this we cannot deny that sometimes it can happen that other juridical titles concur with the contract, titles which are not intrinsically connected with the loan. From such titles there might arise an absolutely just and legitimate reason to ask for more capital than has been loaned. Nor can it be denied that someone may invest and well employ his own money by means of other contracts which are completely different from the loan; either in order to procure for himself annual interest or to conclude legitimate commercial undertakings, and from this to receive honest gains. [D-1475]*

Annus qui hunc, February 19, 1749

43. This is what We recommend with all our strength and above all: that churches should be very well kept decorated, should be clean, and furnished with all the necessary sacred objects. It is easy to understand: if strangers crossing the Papal States see there, either in the towns or in the diocesan territories, buildings dedicated to worship falling into ruin, or desecrated by dirt and filth, without their sacred ornaments or with only torn, unattractive ones, it is certain that they will return home taking with them nothing but a memory of scandalous negligence and that they will, full of indignation, hold us guilty.

44. We do not intend, with these words, to insist on sumptuous or magnificent accouterments for holy buildings, nor on rich or expensive furnishings; we are aware these are not everywhere possible; what we wish is decency and cleanli-

* Section References to the Latin text in Denzinger, *Enchiridion Symbolorum*, Herder & Co., 1947, are given in brackets.

ness. These can coexist with poverty, and can be adapted to it; no one can object to our requiring these. . . .

49. The second point upon which we would rouse your zeal and your solicitude is that you take care that the canonical hours be sung or recited as is customary or is the rule in in each church, with the care and the respect due by those who are obligated to them. There is indeed nothing which is more contrary to, or bad for, church discipline, than negligently or disrespectfully to carry out liturgical worship. You are certainly aware of the obligation that canons and other metropolitan clergy have in cathedrals and college choirs, to chant the canonical hours daily in choir; and it is not sufficient, in order to meet this obligation, to execute the psalter without interior attention and simply in order to get it over with. . . .

51. Great care must be exercised lest the chant be hurried or sung faster than it should; that the pauses be made in the appropriate place; and that one part of the choir does not begin the following verse of a psalm before the other has finished the preceding verse. It is this chant which excites the souls of the faithful to devotion and to piety; and it is this chant which, if it is executed according to the rules and with the decorum which is required inside the churches of God, which the faithful prefer. . . .

53. The third thing of which we wish to warn you, is that "musical" chant which modern usage has commonly introduced into churches, and is accompanied by organs and other instruments, should be executed in such a way that it does not convey a profane, worldly or theatrical impression. The use of organs and of other instruments is not yet admitted throughout the Christian world.

Chapter 8

✠

Clement XIII (1758-69)

On July 9, 1758, after a conclave which had lasted fifty days, the Venetian Cardinal Carlo Rezzonico, who took the name of Clement XIII, was elected successor of Benedict XIV.

He was preceded by a well-deserved reputation for great competence in ecclesiastical matters, since he had spent all of his career in the most delicate and varied positions: he had first been governor of Rieti and Fano, then the adviser of various congregations, and finally bishop of Padua. He resembled his predecessor in his love of culture and his desire to put in order the administration of the Church state. He was preparing a vast plan of administrative reforms when a serious matter, which had been brewing for some time, upset the life of the Church: the battle that had broken out everywhere against the Jesuits, who for two centuries had been formidable agents of propaganda and defenders of the interest of the Church. The Catholic states, which had become powerful monarchies, did not take kindly to the Jesuits' ecclesiastical privileges in the social, cultural, educational, and economic fields. These privileges were most strongly defended by them. The campaign against the Society was such that it required the intervention of the pope, who could not always resist the pressure of the governments. First Portugal, governed by the Marquês de Pombal, voiced historically unfounded accusations against the Society of Jesus, and asked for its suppression in Portugal: Clement XIII had to give his consent. This example was followed by others: in France, the Jesuits were suppressed by royal decree in 1762; in 1767, Charles III of Spain decreed their expulsion from his kingdom, and in Catholic Austria, the empress, Maria Theresa, refused to support the protests of the Holy See in spite of Clement XIII's esteem, which had resulted in his bestowing the title of "Apostolic" on her. The struggle between the Society of Jesus and the various monarchies went on for twelve years. Clement XIII reaffirmed the position of the Society of Jesus in the Papal Bull which follows:[1]

[1] Rome, 9 January, 1765. Le Père de Ravignan, *Clement XIII et Clement XIV*, Paris: Julien Lanier, 1854, VIII, p. 524.

Our Lord Jesus Christ having charged the blessed Apostle Peter and his successor the Roman Pontiff with the obligation to feed his flock, an obligation which no circumstance of time or place, no human consideration, in a word nothing can limit, it is the duty of him who is seated upon the Chair of St. Peter to give his attention to all the different functions of the charge which Jesus Christ has confided to him, to neglect none, to extend his vigilance to all the needs of the Church. . . .

One of the principal duties of this charge is to take under his protection all the religious orders approved by the Holy See, to give new impetus to the zeal of those who having by solemn vow dedicated themselves to the religious profession work with courage sustained by piety in defense of the Catholic faith, to spread it, to cultivate the Saviour's field, to inspire and strengthen those among them who might be languishing and feeble, to console the afflicted, and above all, to remove from the Church confided to his vigilance the scandals which daily are borne in its womb and whose effect is the loss of souls.

The Institution, *The Society of Jesus,* whose author was a man to whom the Universal Church offers the cult and honor it pays to saints, this Institution, which several of our predecessors, among them Paul III, Julius III, Gregories XIII and XIV and Paul V . . . altogether a total of nineteen . . . have more than once approved and confirmed . . . recently has been traduced by men who after having defamed it with false and malignant interpretations, have not feared to call it irreligious and impious, in private conversation as well as in printed works, and have defaced it with injurious imputations, covered it with opprobrium and infamy, and have undertaken with all sorts of schemes to spread the poison from country to country . . . thus insulting in the most outrageous manner the Church of God, which they accuse both of having been mistaken, and of having judged and declared pious and pleasing of God what in itself is irreligious and impious, and to have fallen into a criminal error the more dangerous that it now has lasted more than 200 years. . . . In order to reject the atrocious injury made to the Church of God committed to us and to the Holy See which we occupy, to stop with our Apostolic Authority the circulation of such unreasonable remarks which are being spread on every side, and which are seducing souls and bringing them into proximate danger of perdition . . . using the plenitude of the Apostolic Power . . . walking in the steps of Our Predecessors by this Constitution whose effect shall be perpetual, We declare and state in the same form and manner as Our Predecessors, that the Institution *The Society of Jesus* breathes to the highest point piety and holiness, both in its final aim, which it continually has before it, which is none other than the defense and propagation of the Catholic religion, and in the means it takes to arrive at this end: this is what experience has taught us to date.

Clement XIII inaugurated the worship of the Sacred Heart of Jesus.

Good, pious and mild, Clement XIIII was obstinately attacked by almost the whole of Europe. He often repeated the noble words of Osius, Bishop of Cordova, to the Emperor Constans II: "God has confided to you the Empire; to us ecclesiastical matters. Whoever should wrest the empire from you, would disobey God; fear then to commit a great crime by usurping ecclesiastical authority."

He died in February 1769, aged seventy-five.

Chapter 9

✠

Clement XIV (1769-74)

The conclave which was to designate Clement XIII's successor was dominated by the problem of rulers who wished to obtain suppression of the Jesuit Order. After three months of effort, the conclave finally elected Cardinal Lorenzo Ganganelli of Forli on May 20, 1769. He took the name of Clement XIV and was crowned in St. John Lateran on June 2, 1769. He had belonged to the Friars Minor Conventual, and, after a long career as a preacher, he had been called to Rome to direct the Collegio di Bonaventura, and had been made a cardinal by Clement XIII.

The battle against the Jesuits had by then broken out all over Europe. The pope was unable to withstand the violence and the threat of the secular authorities and rulers. In order to avoid the imminent peril of schism and the establishment of national Churches, he suppressed the Jesuit Order in the bull *Dominus ac Redemptor noster* of July 21, 1773.

This was the final tragedy, the ultimate proof of the shackles the Catholic princes had put upon the Church. "Catholicism had reached in the West the point at which it disappeared from the East—how can it survive in absolute states that are themselves Catholic, unless its ideals dominate these states? A solution . . . a temporary release from the vicious circle, was provided by the Revolution, which broke the old absolutist monarchies, leaving the Church broken too, it is true, but, for the first time in centuries, free once more, yet so little used to freedom that, for a century or so, she halts and stumbles somewhat in the unexpected light." [1] The destruction of the Society of Jesus by the action of the Catholic monarchies, and the confirmation of their work by the papacy itself, marked "not only the defeat of Catholicism as an international force but the self-acceptance of that defeat; and the subsequent action of the Revolution in the dechristianization of France and the secularization of the European order

[1] Father Philip Hughes, *op. cit.,* p. 194.

113

was only the logical completion of this process. But from that moment the tide began to turn," wrote Christopher Dawson in his Oriel lectures.

Dominus ac Redemptor Noster[2]

We well know that the divine will has placed us above nations and kingdoms, that, cultivating the vineyard of Sabaoth, and preserving the edifice of the Christian religion, of which Christ is the corner-stone, we root up and destroy, pull down and scatter, and then build up and plant in that sacred vineyard. . . .

. . . having in view the tranquillity of the Christian republic, we have felt that we ought to neglect nothing to reconcile things in building and planting, and be ever ready and disposed, when the chain of mutual charity requires it, to tear up and destroy even what is most pleasing and dear to us, and what we can least spare, without experiencing great grief and pain. It must be explicitly admitted that, among the institutions which secure the welfare and happiness of the Catholic commonwealth, the first place belongs to the religious orders. In all ages it has been these that have furnished the most aid to the Universal Church of Christ, the most varied advantages, and who have shed most lustre on it. For this reason the Apostolic See has approved them, and has not only maintained them by its protection, but still further strengthened them by favours, exemptions, privileges and faculties. . . . But when it has occurred that in some regular order there are not found, to the advantage of the Christian people, the abundant fruits and profits that are so ardently desired, and for obtaining which the orders were instituted, but that, far from that, they appear to have become a cause of prejudice and of disturbance to the tranquillity of the nations rather than a foundation fitted to establish that tranquillity; then that same Apostolic See which had consecrated its cares to plant them . . . has not hesitated to impose new laws on them, and to recall them to their original strictness of life, or to disperse them and uproot them from the land.

It was for this cause that Pope Innocent III, our predecessor, perceiving that the excessive variety of the regular orders causes great confusion in the Church, ordered, when he presided over the fourth general Lateran Council, that no new religious orders should be founded. Whoever wished to become a regular must enter one of the approved orders. Subsequently it was decreed that who so desired to found a

[2] Tutti le Encicliche.

new order must adopt the rule of some institute already approved. Under this decree it was no longer allowable for any one to found a new order without the special authority of the Roman pontiff, which was just.

We have omitted nothing and forgotten nothing that could enable us thoroughly to understand everything that concerns the regular order that is called the Society of Jesus. We have attentively observed its progress and its present condition. It has been proven to us that that order was instituted by its holy founder for the salvation of souls, the conversion of heretics, and especially of infidels, and for the greater increase of piety and religion. . . . It was approved . . . by our predecessor Paul III. . . . On that subject he published his letters . . . on September 27 in the year of our Lord 1540.

. . . Now, we have perceived that the said Society of Jesus could no longer produce the abundant fruits and advantages for which it was instituted and was approved by so many of our predecessors, who bestowed on it so many privileges, but, on the contrary, that if it existed it was almost impossible that the Church could have true and permanent peace. Led by such considerations . . . we, after mature examination, of our own certain knowledge, and in the plenitude of the apostolic power, suppress and extinguish the said society. We take from it and abrogate each and all of its offices, ministries, administrations, houses, schools and habitations, in all provinces, kingdoms, and states whatsoever, and under whatsoever title to them belonging; we suppress all its statutes, customs, decrees and constitutions, even when fortified by oath, apostolic confirmation, or otherwise. . . . We declare, therefore, that it is perpetually broken up and dissolved, alike as to the spiritual and as to the temporal, and as to all authority whatsoever of the minister-general, and of the provincial, of the visitors and of the other superiors of the society.

The end we aim at is, in the first place, to secure the advantage of the Church and the tranquillity of the nations; then to bring aid and consolation to each of the members of the Society of Jesus, whose persons we paternally love in the Lord in order that, henceforth, being delivered from all the pains which have tormented them, and from so many discords and contentions, they may the most fruitfully cultivate the vineyard of the Lord, and more abundantly work for the salvation of souls.

Chapter 10

✠

Pius VI (1775-99)

Struggles for prestige between France, Austria and Portugal rendered the election of a successor to Clement XIV difficult. After four months and many ballots, Cardinal Giovanni Angelo Braschi of Cesena, who assumed the name of Pius VI, was elected.

His pontificate would have been memorable had it occurred during the Renaissance, since he was a man of great culture and taste. During his reign the political situation of the Church went from bad to worse, due to the approaching revolutionary tempest. The attitude of Joseph II of Austria, called the Sacristan Emperor because of his interest even in minute ecclesiastical matters, threatened the prestige of the Church more and more. Since his protests were useless, the pontiff thought that he might influence the emperor if he went personally and spoke to him. He left Rome at the end of February 1782 and, after a triumphant trip, arrived in Vienna, where he remained for a month without obtaining the least result from Joseph II. On the contrary, he had to accede to the growing demands of the emperor which contributed to diminishing the prestige of the Church in the states of the empire.

Dissensions of a doctrinal nature had also arisen in Italy, where the influence of Jansenism had led to the deviation of a bishop and his priests who had met in a synod in Pistoia and had voted propositions which the pope had to condemn. At the very time when the pontificate was in such difficulties, the Revolution broke out in France. The first concessions of Louis XVI for a civil constitution of the clergy had met with the firm resistance of the pope, who condemned the decisions of the king of France; yet Rome was still not wholly aware of the gravity of the situation in France. The papal nuncio had to leave the French capital hastily while the crowd was burning the pope in effigy. The Roman people were divided, the majority being definitely hostile to the revolutionary ideas. The tragic massacre by them in the Corso of the French ambassador Nicolas Jean Hugon de Basseville, who was flaunting a tricolor cockade, filled the pope with alarm. On March 10,

116

1791, he replied to Cardinal de la Rochefoucauld and to the French bishops who had signed the act called the Civil Constitution of the Clergy, which annihilated the Church in France. This encyclical, *Caritas quae,* is important; but since it is very long, only extracts are given.[1]

Your letter has renewed in us that immense pain that afflicted us, and that no consolation can relieve, since we learned that the Assembly of your nation, met to consider the interests of political economy, has gone so far in its decrees as to attack the Catholic religion. This Assembly, though engaged in conspiracies against itself, yet rushes on the sanctuary.

From the first we thought that, with men so inconsiderate, silence must be kept, for fear of provoking them by the word of truth to acts of greater perversity. . . . Meanwhile we have spoken to God, and ordered public prayers, to obtain for these new legislators a disposition which will recall them from the precepts of the philosophy of this age, back to the laws of our religion and their practice. . . .

. . . Venerable brethren, constantly preserve your steadfast resolution; renounce not your project for fear of danger; resist threats. . . . As for our part, we have recommended new prayers; we have urged your king to withhold his sanction; we have warned two bishops, who are consulted by the king, what to do to disarm and appease, as far as lies in us, the fury of those called the Tiers État; we have suspended the payment of the taxes for documents issued to France. . . . Moreover, we have refrained from declaring the authors of that baleful civil constitution separated and cut off from the Catholic religion. In a word, we have borne everything, in order, by mildness and patience, to avoid a deplorable schism, and to restore peace for you and your country. Nay, more, firm in the resolve of paternal charity, which you seem to share, we ask and entreat you to declare and tell us what to do to conciliate minds. Distant as we are from France, we cannot know this. You, who see things nearer, may perceive some measure not at variance with Catholic dogma and universal discipline. Propose it for our examination and deliberation. . . .

[In 1793 Pope Pius VI wrote an encyclical, condemning the French *Manifesto,* from which the following is an extract.]

Ad nostros

We happened upon a publication issued in the name of the generals of the Christian army which says among other things that the commanders of the said army, wishing to return to the

[1] This and the following encyclical are from *Tutti le Encicliche.*

Catholic religion its old splendor with all the means at their disposal, invite the curates and vicars deposed by their legitimate bishops in virtue of their general powers to approach the bishop of Agra, the apostolic vicar resident at St. Laurent-sur-Seine, in order to hear from him what to do and how to behave.

We do not know if this publication is authentic or not; he who publishes it leaves it up to the reader, in a preliminary introduction, to trust him enough to believe that these words are legitimate. Now the reinstatement of the Catholic religion, towards which the glorious and commendable efforts of the commanders of said army seem to tend, has always been the objective of our apostolic preoccupation.

The commanders of this army have chosen for this purpose a man who pretends to be the bishop of Agra and vicar apostolic. Far from reaching the goal they intend to reach they would only facilitate error and abandon the faithful to a most dangerous imposture, since we know that such a diocese does not exist and that we have never thought to confer the quality of apostolic vicar on the man who claims it. Therefore, with the intention of clearing up your minds and of eliminating any equivocacy in such an important affair, we advise you, dear children and brothers, that should anyone qualify himself as bishop of Agra and apostolic vicar you should not recognize him as such but avoid him and leave him alone since he is an impostor who usurps both titles vitiating with sacrilege and nullity all his juridical acts.

[In 1796, General Bonaparte began to threaten the Papal States. Since Pius VI could not defend them militarily, he tried to negotiate an agreement, which was reached in Bologna and by which Bonaparte gave up the invasion of the Papal States for a tribute of two million francs and a series of manuscripts, works of art, etc. For fear that the treaty would not be honored, Pius VI had secretly begun negotiations for military aid with the government of Vienna and the King of Naples. A small army was being organized in Rome as well. Napoleon, having learned of these preparations, immediately invaded Romagna and the Marches and entered Ancona. After an unsuccessful attempt at resistance by the papal troops, negotiations began and the treaty of Tolentino was signed on February 19, 1797. By it, the Papal States were to pay a new indemnity of 32,700 francs, hand over still other art treasures, give Romagna as far as Cattolica to France, and renounce their claim to Avignon and to the old county of Venaissin. As a guarantee of the fulfillment of the treaty, Ancona remained in French hands. It was the first time in the history of the Church that a pontiff had signed a treaty giving up part of the temporal patrimony.

In August 1797, when General Berthier marched upon Rome, Pius VI renounced any thought of resistance and capitulated. The French general entered the Eternal City, occupied all strategic points, took hostages, and ordered requisitions of money. Rome was proclaimed a republic. The pope had remained in the city under a guarantee by the new authorities that they would respect his spiritual function. In fact, he was, however, their prisoner, and the recent orgies of the French Revolution aroused serious fears about his fate. The French, on the other hand, feared that the pope's presence might encourage attempts at rebellion against them. He was roughly treated, even the "ring of the Fisherman" being taken from him (though later returned), and he was removed first to Siena, then to a monastery near Florence, and finally to Valence in Dauphiné, where he died at the age of eighty-one, on August 19, 1799.]

Chapter 11

✠

Pius VII (1800-23)

A Benedictine monk, and a member of the noble family of Chiaramonti, Pius VII was elected in Venice, as Rome was still occupied by French troops at the time of his election. His first encyclical, May 15, 1800, addressed to the cardinals and all the bishops of Christendom, was a letter of commiseration with the people of France. He entered Rome on June 3, and a year later, after the victory of Marengo on July 14, 1801, Italy was at Napoleon's feet. However, Napoleon had told the cardinal bishop of Vercelli that he wished to make peace with the pope, and on July 10 the pope replied: "You may tell the First Consul that we will readily enter on a negotiation, the object of which is honorable, so suitable to our apostolic ministry, so conformable to the wishes of our heart." On July 15, 1801, the Concordat was signed between the French government and Pius VII.

But Napoleon was soon annoyed by the pope's refusal to annul his brother Jerome's marriage to a Miss Patterson of Baltimore. In spite of the coronation of Napoleon and of Josephine his wife, and of the pope's journey to Paris, Napoleon chafed over his limited powers. "I find a priest more powerful than I, for he reigns over minds, while I reign over matter," said the emperor. After the Papal States had been again invaded, the pope declared the time for mildness was over, and excommunicated Napoleon. The French general Radet then took the pope prisoner, and carried him from Rome in a carriage; the pope had but one *papetto* (a dime) in his purse. He was transferred to Avignon and then Savona, while Napoleon, on February 7, 1810, annexed the Papal States to his empire. Napoleon then imprisoned the pope with much greater severity in Fontainebleau; yet, on May 24, 1814, the pope was back in Rome, and one of his first acts was the restoration of the Society of Jesus, by the bull of August 7, 1814. The following is an extract.[1]

Urgent and pressing petitions were daily laid before us from our venerable brethren the archbishops and bishops, and illustrious persons of every rank and class, calling, with the unani-

[1] This and the following encyclical are from *Tutti le Encicliche.*

120

mous consent of almost the whole Christian world, for the restoration of the said Society of Jesus. . . .

Not withstanding the apostolic constitutions and ordinances, and especially the aforesaid letters, in the form of a brief . . . of Clement XIV . . . beginning *Dominus ac Redemptor noster*, which, to give effect to these presents, we hereby intend expressly and specially to repeal. . . .

[The pope also expressed the traditional view of the Church on mixed marriages.]

Vix nova a Nobis, February 27, 1809

63. Some of you also asked from us the faculty of giving a dispensation or of permitting a contract of marriage between two parties one of whom professes the Catholic faith and another heresy; we imagine that you are perfectly aware that the true Catholic Church, the Church of Jesus Christ, has always frowned heavily on marriage with heretics; the Church holds such marriages in horror. . . . It is upon patent and forceful reasons that the Holy See has always leaned in order to remove this danger as far from itself as possible, and it is because of these reasons that it will not give, except under pressure and with great circumspection, such a permission, and only in certain grave circumstances. . . .

The restoration of the pope to the temporal power held by his predecessors was the joint work of Protestant and Catholic powers. Pius VII died on August 18, 1823, in Rome, aged eighty-one.

Chapter 12

✠

Leo XII (1823-29)

Annibale della Genga was already a sick man when, aged sixty-three, he was elected pope. The chief event of his reign was the jubilee of 1825. The following extract is from his encyclical *Caritate Christi* (December 25, 1825).[1]

129. You must love above all things the beauty of God's house; but your chief care must be that it is not violated by the indecent behaviour or clothing of those who attend, nor by any impiety which would dishonour it more than anything else. . . .

Warned by you, may the people recall the precept imposed by the Lord "Remember that thou keep holy the Sabbath day." . . . But the perversity of many is so great that they do not hesitate on that day to give themselves over to servile work; or, taking advantage of the exemption granted them from such works on that day . . . they profit by it to go to the devil. Thus, on feast days they give themselves over to banquets, to drunkenness, to debauchery, and to all the works of the devil. In so far as you can, see to it that this scandal disappears, and that it is replaced by a willingness to pray, to listen to the word of God, by the very salutary participation in the august sacrifice of the Mass, not only assisted at piously, but also by the reception of the body of Christ.

[1] *Tutti le Encicliche.*

Chapter 13

✠

Pius VIII (1829-30)

Cardinal Castiglioni, who on March 31, 1829, was elected pope, assumed the title of Pius VIII. He was a canon lawyer. Canon law is a system of ecclesiastical jurisprudence as complex and as complete as any other judicial and legislative code, and this pope was the foremost canonist of his age. He was made happy by the enactment of Catholic Emancipation in England on April 23, 1829.

On May 21, 1829, he issued an encyclical *Traditi humilitati* against the spread of religious indifferentism, and the spread of unauthorized and heretical translations of the Scriptures.[1]

... Another object of our vigilance ... is the societies which publish new translations of the Scriptures in all vernacular tongues, translations made against the most salutary rules of the Church, and in which the texts are ingeniously wrested to perverse meanings, according to a particular spirit. These translations are distributed in all places, at great expense, and gratuitously offered to the more ignorant, often mingling short explanations, that they may drink a poisonous draught where they expect to imbibe the salutary waters of wisdom. The Holy See had long since warned the Christian people of this new danger for the faith ... The rules drawn up by order of the Council of Trent, and renewed by the Congregation of the Index, were at once recalled to the minds of the faithful. ... The Council of Trent ... to arrest restless and adventurous minds, passed this decree: "That in matters of faith and matters which concern Christian doctrine, no one, relying on his own judgment, shall wrest the Holy Spirit to his particular sense, or interpret it contrary to the sense which the Church has always followed or contrary to the unanimous opinion of the Fathers."

[In Germany, the Protestant powers proclaimed a Pragmatic in 1821, in the name of the states of Württemberg, Baden, the two Hesses, Nassau and Frankfort. This Pragmatic, drawn up

[1] This and the two encyclicals following are from *Tutti le Encicliche*.

exclusively by Protestants, was to regulate Catholic faith and worship. In 1830, the free city of Frankfort produced a Pragmatic in thirty-nine articles, "intended to adapt the faith and discipline of the Universal Church, the work of the learning and sanctity of eighteen centuries, to the requirements of the Protestant burgomaster and his Council."[2] The pope, in reply to a letter from the archbishop of Cologne and various German bishops, issued a bull *Litteris alto*, dated March 25, 1830, concerning mixed marriages.]

In your letter, addressed two years since to Leo XII . . . you carefully set forth the difficult and critical position in which you were placed by an enactment of the civil law, issued in your countries a few years since, which requires that, in mixed marriages, the children of both sexes be brought up in the religion of the father, or at least according to his wish; at the same time forbidding priests to require of persons about to contract such marriages any promise in regard to the religious education of the children to spring from such union. . . . We therefore justly hope that not only you will conform entirely to our reply . . . but also that his Majesty [the king of Prussia] will not be offended if, cheerfully obeying him in temporal affairs, you nevertheless reserve the right to follow the holy rules of the Catholic religion in matters which concern not the civil effects but the very sanctity of marriage and the religious duties of the wedded.

To come more directly to the question, we need not tell you . . . that the Church has horror of these unions, which present so many deformities and spiritual dangers. . . .

It is acknowledged, in fact, that Catholics, whether men or women, who marry with non-Catholics so as rashly to expose themselves and their children to the danger of being perverted, not only violate the holy canons, but, moreover, sin directly and grievously against the paternal and divine law.

. . . According to these principles, then, whenever a Catholic, especially a woman, would marry a non-Catholic, the bishop or parish priest must carefully instruct such Catholic on the canonical provisions concerning marriage; and seriously warn such person of the grave crime of which he (or she) is about to render himself guilty before God, should he have the temerity to violate them.

It will be especially fitting to urge him to remember this firm dogma of our religion, that out of the true Catholic faith no one can be saved, and to acknowledge, consequently, that the Catholic woman would act in advance most cruelly towards the

[2] Chevalier Artaud de Montor, *The Lives and Times of the Roman Pontiffs.* New York: P. J. Kenedy and Sons, 1910.

children whom she expects from God, if she contracted a marriage where she knows that their education will depend entirely on the will of their non-Catholic father. . . . If, in some cases, the paternal care of the pastor is unavailing . . . he will refrain not only from honoring with any religious ceremony whatever the ensuing marriage, but also from any act by which he may seem to give it his approbation. All that has been tolerated in this respect in certain places is that pastors who . . . find it necessary to attend such marriages, suffer them to take place in their presence (provided there was no other canonical impediment) in order that, having heard the consent of the two parties, they might then, by virtue of their ministry, enter in the marriage register the act validly accomplished. . . . We now will and ordain that mixed marriages celebrated after this day in your dioceses without the formalities prescribed by the Council of Trent be regarded, provided that no other canonical impediment directly intervene, as valid and true marriages.

[The last encyclical before Pius VIII's death on December 1, 1830, was written to the archbishops and bishops of Germany:]

The holy Spouse of Christ, the Spotless Lamb, is free by divine institution, and is not subjected to any human power, but it is reduced by these profane novelties introduced into your country to a shameful and wretched bondage, when the lay power is permitted to confirm or reject councils, divide dioceses, select the candidates for the priesthood, and those who should be promoted to ecclesiastical functions, when the direction of instruction and religious and moral discipline is assigned to them, when the very seminaries and all that touches the spiritual government of the Church is left to the pleasure of the laity, and the faithful are prevented from communicating freely with the head of the Church, although such communion is essential to the constitution of the Catholic Church, and cannot be prevented without depriving the faithful of necessary succor and imperiling their eternal salvation.

Chapter 14

✝

Gregory XVI (1831-46)

In the whole of Italy, and even in Rome, liberal risings and conspiracies were becoming daily more frequent and threatening. It was therefore not without some uneasiness that the cardinals met on December 31, 1830, in order to nominate a successor to Pius VIII. In this conclave there was a very lively struggle between the "zealots" *(Zelanti)* and those having liberal tendencies *(Liberaleggianti)*, and the *Zelanti* got the upper hand once more with the election of Cardinal Cappellari on February 2, 1831. He took the name of Gregory XVI. He had been a monk of the Order of the Camaldolesi and was a theological scholar. Not ever having been a bishop, he had to be consecrated bishop of Rome at the time of his election to the papacy.

From the beginning of his pontificate he was faced with the necessity of fighting against revolutionary movements. This induced him, a month after his election, to request military help from Austria to maintain order in the Papal States. The resulting intervention raised a serious international problem, since France and other powers were opposed to it; they attempted to persuade the pontiff to make appropriate reforms so as to calm the restless spirit of his people. Gregory XVI, who had chosen as his secretary of state Cardinal Bernetti, who did not belong to the *Zelanti,* let himself be persuaded into some promises and concessions of reform. This calmed the people and made it possible for the pope to send the Austrian troops home. In the same year a few reforms of a legal nature were adopted, such as the right of asylum, the faculty of pardon given to certain religious congregations, and the abolition of ancient privileges. So as not to have to depend upon foreign help, a small papal army was set up for the purpose of keeping order within the territory. But these tendencies to reform were not well received in Austria, where the activities of Cardinal Bernetti were considered dangerously liberal, so that Gregory XVI, under Austrian pressure, was induced to replace him with Cardinal Lambruschini, a safe member of the *Zelanti.* This exasperated the Liberals within the Papal States and disorders and conspiracies started up again. Gregory XVI was certainly not in a position to contest the situation, the more so since he was a scholar rather than a politician. He did not like innovations and opposed the building of railroads in the Papal States and condemned severely any attempt to reconcile Catholicism with modern political ideas.

He died suddenly on June 1, 1846, at the age of eighty-one, leaving the Papal States in serious agitation and disorder.

The most important events of his reign were the two encyclicals, *Mirari vos* against Liberalism, issued in 1832, and, two years later, *Singulari nos,* which climaxed the career of the Abbé de Lamennais.

Many Frenchmen, when they saw the Revolution, terrible fruit of the Enlightenment, felt that they had to abandon human reason, whose reign had proved so disastrous. And their first and crudest reaction against rationalism (which is the conviction that human reason unaided by revelation can know everything) was the abdication of reason. No more would the way of faith go via reason, but reasonable certitude would be found by means of faith. But this faith was not to be in the word of God, but in the consensus of humanity. According to one exponent of this doctrine, the Abbé de Lamennais, a brilliant French priest, the individual, exalted as the final arbiter of knowledge by the Enlightenment, is impotent to find truth by himself. Rather "the consensus of all is for everyone the only criterion of certainty." This theory, which by rendering reason impotent makes faith unreasonable, was propounded, together with liberal political ideas, by the Abbé de Lamennais in books and especially in one newspaper personally directed by him, called *l'Avenir*. Gregory XVI, not wishing to hurt Lamennais, who had professed his readiness to rethink his position and to submit to the judgment of the Holy See, issued the encyclical *Mirari vos,* which proscribed de Lamennais's position without mentioning either him or *l'Avenir,* and which insisted on the traditional Catholic apologetic acceptance of the value of human reason.[1]

We speak to you, venerable brethren, of evils which you behold with your own eyes and which we consequently deplore in common. Perversity, science without modesty, unbridled license, are at work, full of ardor and insolence. The sanctity of the mysteries incites nothing but contempt, and the majesty of the divine worship, that power which the mind of man can neither dispense with nor resist, has become for perverse men an object of censure, profanation, and sacrilegious derision. . . .

The divine authority of the Church is attacked; its rights torn from it; it is subordinated to earthly considerations, and

[1] This and the following encyclical are from *Tutti le Encicliche*.

by force of injustice it is submitted to the contempt of nations, and reduced to a shameful servitude. The obedience due to bishops is destroyed, and their rights are trampled under foot. Academies and universities resound with new and monstrous opinions, and no longer secretly or obscurely do they attack the Catholic faith, but publicly declare against it a horrible and impious war. The lessons and examples of the masters thus pervert the youth, the disasters of religion receive an immense increase, and the most frightful immorality gains and spreads. Thus when the sacred bonds of religion are once contemptuously cast aside, bonds which alone preserve kingdoms and maintain the power and vigor of authority, public order is seen to disappear, sovereignty perish, and all legitimate power is menaced by an ever-approaching revolution-abyss of bottomless miseries, which these conspiring societies have especially dug, in which heresy and sects have so to speak vomited as into a sewer all that their bosom holds of license, sacrilege and blasphemy.

[De Lamennais immediately announced that the editors of *l'Avenir* "respectfully submit themselves to the authority of the Vicar of Christ . . . and urge all their friends to do the same."

Later, de Lamennais by his *Paroles d'un croyant* prompted Gregory to write the encyclical *Singulari nos* (June 25, 1834):]

29. The author, with captious phrases, attempts to attack and to destroy Catholic doctrine as We have defined it in Our letters: the submission due to authority; the deplorable contagion of indifferentism from which the peoples of the world must be preserved; the barrier that must be erected against the wild license of opinions and speech; finally, the condemnation of an absolute liberty of conscience, the horrid conspiration of the upholders of every erroneous doctrine against Church and state.

After this attack, de Lamennais re-examined his position, and died outside the Church.

Chapter 15

✠

Pius IX (1846-78)

Giovanni Maria Mastai-Ferretti, cardinal bishop of Imola in the Romagna, was elected pope on June 16, 1846, after the cardinal secretary of state, Lambruschini, a conservative, had led on the first count. Mastai took the name of Pius, in memory of Pius VII, who had befriended him when a seminarian, and whom he revered for his stand against Napoleon. On July 17, 1846, Pius IX* amnestied over a thousand political prisoners and many hundreds more who were in exile. This gesture made the pope tremendously popular in Rome, where the people venerated him, but it alienated the Austrians. "God," Prince Metternich observed, "never amnesties; He pardons."

The new pope appointed Gizzi, a liberal, as his secretary of state. He introduced tariff reform, admitted the Jews to share in the papal charities, reformed the criminal code, himself regularly visited the prisons, and established a free press, subject to a council of four lay and one ecclesiastical censor. He set up a *consulta* to assist him in the work of governing the Papal States, under the presidency of Cardinal Antonelli.

The Austrians moved against the pope, occupying Ferrara, and Pius IX only got rid of them by threatening excommunication. Then the Austrians gave way, but the pope found he had played into the hands of the Italian patriots, and particularly of the exile, Mazzini, who wrote him an Open Letter. As Metternich wrote: "A liberal pope is not a possibility. . . . He can destroy, but he cannot build. What the Pope has already destroyed by his liberalism is his own temporal power; what he is unable to destroy is his spiritual power." The violence of the various uprisings against the Austrians proved Metternich's prophecy true indeed and horrified the pope, and on April 29, 1848, he censured the extremists in an Allocution. Thereafter the Risorgimento (as the struggle for a united Italy was called) went on in spite of Pio Nono.

In March 1848 the pope granted a Constitution, and ap-

* Nicknamed and generally known, even during his lifetime, as "Pio Nono."

pointed as premier Count Pellegrino Rossi, who was murdered by the extremists on November 15, 1848. Then the pope, accompanied by Cardinal Antonelli, fled to Gaeta, and the Republic of Rome was proclaimed on February 9, 1849.

On April 12, 1850, escorted by French troops, Pius IX returned to Rome, and rode to the Vatican, where he remained.

On December 8, 1854, the dogma of the Immaculate Conception was solemnly proclaimed on the sole authority of the pope.

In the encyclical *Jamdudum Cernimus,* of March 18, 1861, the pope denounced Piedmontese aggression and "put an end to all idea that he would treat with Cavour."

Pius IX's first encyclical, *Qui pluribus* (November 9, 1846), pointed to the danger of communism, and is the first papal statement on the subject.[1]

32. You well know the monstrous errors and artifices which the children of this century make use of in order to wage relentless war against the Catholic faith, the divine authority of the Church, its laws, and to trample the rights of authority, ecclesiastic or civil. Such is the object of the execrable doctrine called communism: it is wholly contrary to natural law itself; nor could it establish itself without turning upside down all rights, all interests, the essence of property, and society itself.

[That the misfortunes which removed all temporal power from the Holy Father, and constituted him the "prisoner of the Vatican," did not in any way lessen his claim to legislate for the whole of Christendom is proved by his encyclical condemning a London society (September 16, 1864).[2]]

The Holy See has been informed that Catholics and even ecclesiastics have joined a society founded in London in 1857 to promote what they call Christian Unity and even that several articles in periodicals published under the auspices of this society have been written by ecclesiastics belonging to this society. The character and purpose of this society cannot easily be judged from the articles in the magazine called *The Union Review,* but rather from the pamphlet by which members are invited and registered. Founded and directed by Protestants, this society expressedly claims that the fundamental motive of its foundation is that there are three Christian communities, the Roman Catholic, the Greek Orthodox, and the Anglican, which, although separated and divided from each

[2] Text in *Acta Apostolicae Sedis, 1909.*

other, call themselves with equal right Catholic. Everywhere Catholics, Greek schismatics and Anglicans are welcome as members with the one provision, that no one be allowed to question the different doctrinal points in which they disagree and everybody be free to follow the confessions of his own religion with peace of mind. The society requests all its members to pray for its intentions and the priests to offer the sacrifice for the intention that all the three above-mentioned Christian communities, which supposedly already constitute the Catholic Church, finally be united into one body. . . .

The foundation on which the society is built is such that it turns the constitution of the Catholic Church upside down because it consists in the belief that the true church of Jesus Christ is composed of the Roman Catholics spread over the whole world, of those of the schism of Photius and of members of the Anglican heresy, who, the society declares, have, equally as the Romans, one church, one Lord, one faith, one baptism. . . .

Of course, nothing must be more important for a Catholic than that schisms and dissensions among Christians be radically abolished and that all Christians be united (Eph. 4:3). . . . But under no circumstances can it be tolerated that faithful Christians and ecclesiastics be under the leadership of heretics and, what is worse, that they should pray for Christian unity according to the intentions of the most depraved and contagious heresy.

The true church of Jesus Christ is constituted by divine authority and recognizable by the fourfold characteristic which we assert in the creed, and these four marks are so connected with each other that they cannot be separated from each other. Thence it comes that she who is really Catholic must at the same time sparkle with unity, holiness and the preogative of the Apostolic Succession. [D-1685-87]

[Clearly and forcefully he reiterated the statements made in the great bull *Unam sanctam* in his *Quanto Conficiamur* (August 10, 1863).[8]]

It is necessary, dear sons and venerable brothers, to remember again and to condemn the very serious error into which some Catholics miserably fall, who think that men who live in error and are strangers to Catholic faith and unity can reach eternal life. This of course is contrary to Catholic faith in an extreme degree [*maxime*]. It is known to me as well as to you that those who are affected by invincible ignorance about our most holy religion, and who are willing to observe

[8] Official English Version, Vatican Polyglot Press.

the natural law written into the hearts of all men by God and to obey God, and who live a righteous and worthy life can reach eternal life, helped by divine light and God's grace, since God who sees into the minds and hearts, thoughts and virtues of everybody, in His supreme goodness and pity never would allow anyone to be punished with eternal punishment who did not voluntarily commit a sin. But it is known that Catholic dogma states that nobody outside of the Catholic Church can be saved and that those who defy the authority of the Church and its definitions and are divided from the unity of the Church and the successor of Peter, the Roman pontiff, to whom the custody of the vineyard was committed by the Saviour (as the Council of Chalcedon says), cannot gain eternal life.

Far be it from us that the children of the Catholic Church ever be enemies of those who are in no way bound to us by the ties of the same faith and the same love. Even more may Catholics be always eager to offer the services of Christian charity and to help those who are poor, sick, and afflicted by other adversities, and, above all, to try to free them from the darkness of their error, in which they are miserably caught, and bring them back to Catholic Truth, and to their most loving mother the Church, who extends Her motherly arms tenderly towards them and never ceases to call them back to Her lap so that they may reach eternal life founded in faith, hope and charity "secure and growing in all good." [D-1678]

[From every part of the world, petitions had come to the Holy See requesting that the dogma of the Immaculate Conception of the Blessed Virgin Mary be solemnly defined. The Sovereign Pontiff appointed a commission of prelates and theologians to examine the matter. He begged the prayers of the faithful and requested the bishops of the universal Church to report to him on the mind of their clergy and people concerning a solemn definition.

This encyclical letter, *Ubi primum* (February 2, 1849), was written at Gaeta, Italy, where the Holy Father had taken refuge from the anticlerical revolutionists who had seized Rome.[4]]

No sooner had We been elevated to the sublime Chair of the Prince of the Apostles and undertook the government of the universal Church (not, indeed, because of Our own worthiness but by the hidden designs of Divine Providence) than We had the great consolation, Venerable Brethren, in recalling that, during the pontificate of Gregory XVI, Our Predeces-

[4] *Dogmatic Canons and Decrees.* New York: The Devin-Adair Co., 1912, pp. 1-4.

sor of happy memory, there was in the entire Catholic world a most ardent and wondrous revival of the desire that the most holy Mother of God—the beloved Mother of us all, the immaculate Virgin Mary—be finally declared by a solemn definition of the Church to have been conceived without the stain of original sin. . . .

REQUESTS FOR DEFINITION

Moreover, Venerable Brethren, many of you have sent letters to Our Predecessor and to Us begging, with repeated insistence and redoubled enthusiasm, that We define as a dogma of the Catholic Church that the most blessed Virgin Mary was conceived immaculate and free in every way of all taint of original sin.

Nor do we lack today eminent theologians—men of intellectual brilliance, of virtue, of holiness and sound doctrine—who have so effectively explained this doctrine and so impressively expounded this proposition that many persons are now wondering why this honor has not already been accorded to the Blessed Virgin by the Church and the Apostolic See—an honor which the widespread piety of the Christian people so fervently desires to have accorded to the Most Holy Virgin by a solemn decree and by the authority of the Church and the Holy See.

THE DEVOTION OF THE HOLY FATHER

Welcome indeed have such requests been to Us. They have filled Us with joy. From our earliest years nothing has ever been closer to Our heart than devotion—filial, profound, and wholehearted—to the most blessed Virgin Mary. Always have We endeavored to do everything that would redound to the greater glory of the Blessed Virgin, promote her honor, and encourage devotion to her. Accordingly, from the very beginning of Our supreme pontificate We have most fervently directed Our energies and Our thoughts to this matter of such great importance. Nor have We failed, through humble and fervent prayers, to beg almighty God to enlighten Our mind with the light of His grace in order that We might know what We should do in this matter.

Great indeed is Our trust in Mary. The resplendent glory of her merits, far exceeding all the choirs of angels, elevates her to the very steps of the throne of God. Her foot has crushed the head of Satan. Set up between Christ and His Church, Mary, ever lovable and full of grace, always has delivered the Christian people from their greatest calamities and from the snares and assaults of all their enemies, ever rescuing them from ruin. . . .

Accordingly, We have appointed certain priests of recognized piety and theological learning, as well as several cardinals of the Holy Roman Church who are renowned because of their ability, piety, wisdom, prudence, and knowledge of the things of God; and We have directed them to make, carefully and thoroughly, a most diligent examination into this most important matter and then provide Us with a complete report. Through such a procedure, We feel that We are following in the clearly marked footsteps of Our Predecessors and that We are emulating their example.

APPEAL TO THE BISHOPS

Wherefore, Venerable Brethren, We send you this communication that We may effectively encourage your admirable devotion and your pastoral zeal and thus bring it about that each of you, in such manner as you will see fit, will arrange to have public prayers offered in your diocese for this intention: that the most merciful Father of all knowledge will deign to enlighten Us with the heavenly light of His Holy Spirit, so that in a matter of such moment We may proceed to do what will redound to the greater glory of His Holy Name, to the honor of the most Blessed Virgin, and to the profit of the Church Militant. . . .

[The replies were unanimously in favor of a definition, and in the bull *Ineffabilis Deus,* of December 8, 1854, the dogma of the Immaculate Conception was proclaimed in the following words:[5]]

We declare, pronounce, and define that the doctrine which holds that the most blessed Virgin Mary, in the first instant of her conception, by a singular grace and privilege granted by almighty God, in view of the merits of Jesus Christ, the Saviour of the human race, was preserved free from all stain of original sin, is a doctrine revealed by God and therefore to be believed firmly and constantly by all the faithful. [D-1641]

[On December 8, 1864, Cardinal Antonelli, Pius IX's Secretary of State, sent out the *Syllabus of Errors,* accompanied by the encyclical *Quanta cura,* with the following note.[6]]

Our most Holy Father, Pius IX, Sovereign Pontiff, being

[5] *Ibid.*
[6] *Ibid.,* pp. 187-209.

profoundly anxious for the salvation of souls and concerned with sound doctrine, has never, since the beginning of his pontificate, ceased to proscribe and condemn the chief errors and false doctrines of our most unhappy age, by his published Encyclicals, by his Consistorial Allocutions and other Apostolic Letters. But, as it may happen that all the pontifical acts do not reach each one of the ordinaries, the same Sovereign Pontiff has willed that a Syllabus of the same errors be compiled, to be sent to all the Bishops of the Catholic world, in order that these same Bishops may have before their eyes all the errors and pernicious doctrines which he has reprobated and condemned.

He has consequently charged me with the duty of seeing to it that this Syllabus, having been printed, should be sent to your most reverend excellencies on this occasion and at this time, in which the Sovereign Pontiff, because of his great concern for the welfare and the good of the Christian Church and of the whole flock which has been divinely committed to him by the Lord, has thought it expedient to write another encyclical letter to all the Catholic Bishops. Thus fulfilling, as is my duty, with all the zeal and respect that is their due, the orders of this same Sovereign Pontiff, I hasten to send to your excellencies this syllabus with these letters.

Quanta Cura[7]

It is well known unto all men, and especially to You, Venerable Brothers, with what great care and pastoral vigilance Our Predecessors, the Roman Pontiffs, have discharged the Office entrusted by Christ Our Lord to them, in the Person of the Most Blessed Peter, Prince of the Apostles, have unremittingly discharged the duty of feeding the lambs and the sheep, and have diligently nourished the Lord's entire flock with the words of faith, imbued it with salutary doctrine, and guarded it from poisoned pastures. And those Our Predecessors, who were the assertors and Champions of the august Catholic Religion, of truth and justice, being as they were chiefly solicitous for the salvation of souls, held nothing to be of so great importance as the duty of exposing and condemning, in their most wise Letters and Constitutions, all heresies and errors which are hostile to moral honesty and to the eternal salvation of mankind, and which have frequently stirred up terrible commotions and have damaged both the Christian and civil commonwealths in a disastrous manner. Wherefore those Our Predecessors have, with Apostolic forti-

[7] Translation from version accompanying pastoral letter of Archbishop Spalding, Baltimore, 1870, pp. 4-13.

tude, continually resisted the machinations of those evil men, who, "foaming out their own confusion, like the raging waves of the sea," and "promising liberty, while they are themselves the slaves of corruption," endeavored by their fallacious opinions and most wicked writings to subvert the foundations of Religion and of civil Society, to remove from our midst all virtue and justice, to deprave the hearts and minds of all, to turn away from right discipline of morals the incautious, and especially inexperienced youth, miserably corrupting them, leading them into the nets of error, and finally withdrawing them from the bosom of the Catholic Church.

And now, Venerable Brothers, as is also very well known to you, scarcely had We (by the secret dispensation of Divine Providence, certainly by no merit of Our own) been called to this Chair of Peter, when We, to the extreme grief of Our soul, beheld a horrible tempest stirred up by so many erroneous opinions, and the dreadful and never enough to be lamented mischiefs which redound to Christian people from such errors; and We then, in discharge of Our Apostolic Ministerial Office, imitating the example of Our illustrious Predecessors, raised Our voice, and in several published Encyclical Letters, and in Allocutions delivered in Consistory, and in other Apostolical Letters, We condemned the prominent, most grievous errors of the age, and We stirred up your excellent episcopal vigilance, and again and again did We admonish and exhort all the sons of the Catholic Church, who are most dear to Us, that they should abhor and shun all the said errors, as they would the contagion of a fatal pestilence. Especially in Our first Encyclical Letter, written to You on the 9th of November, A.D. 1846, and in two Allocutions, one of which was delivered by Us in Consistory on the 9th of December, A.D. 1854, and the other on the 9th of June, A.D. 1862, We condemned the monstrous and portentous opinions, which prevail especially in the present age, to the very great loss of souls, and even to the detriment of civil society, and which are in the highest degree hostile, not only to the Catholic Church, and to her salutary doctrine and venerable laws, but also to the everlasting law of nature engraven by God upon the hearts of all men, and to right reason; and out of which almost all errors originate.

Now although hitherto We have not omitted to denounce and reprove the chief errors of this kind, yet the cause of the Catholic Church and the salvation of souls committed to Us by God, and even the interests of human society absolutely demand, that once again We should stir up Your pastoral solicitude, to drive away other erroneous opinions which flow from those errors above specified, as their source. These false and perverse opinions are so much the more detestable, by as much as they have chiefly for their object to hinder and banish that salutary influence which the Catholic Church, by the institution and command of her Divine Author, ought freely to exercise, even to the consummation of the world, not only over individual men, but nations, peoples, and sovereigns, and to abolish that mutual co-operation and agreement of counsels between the Priesthood and Governments, which has always been propitious and conducive to the welfare both of Church and State. (Gregory XVI Encyclical, 13th August, 1832.) For you know well, Venerable Brethren, that at this time there are found not a few who, applying to civil intercourse the impious and absurd principles of what they call *Naturalism,* dare teach "that the best form of Society, and the exigencies of civil progress, absolutely require human society to be constituted and governed without any regard whatsoever to Religion, as if this [Religion] did not even exist, or at least without making any distinction between true and false religions." Contrary to the teachings of the Holy Scriptures, of the Church, and of the Holy Fathers, these persons do not hesitate to assert, that "the best condition of human society is that wherein no duty is recognized by the Government of correcting, by enacted penalties, the violators of the Catholic Religion, except when the maintenance of the public peace requires it." From this totally false notion of social government, they fear not to uphold that erroneous opinion most pernicious to the Catholic Church, and to the salvation of souls, which was called by Our Predecessor, Gregory XVI (lately quoted) the insanity [*deliramentum*] (Encycl. 13 August, 1832): namely, "that the liberty of conscience and of worship is the peculiar (or inalienable) right of every man, which should be proclaimed by law, and that citizens have the right to all kinds of liberty, to be restrained by no law, whether ecclesiastical or civil, by which they may be enabled to manifest openly and publicly their ideas, by word of mouth, through the press, or by any other means." But whilst these men make these rash assertions, they do not reflect, or consider, that they preach the liberty of perdition (St. Augustine, Epistle 105, al. 166), and that, "if it is always free to human arguments to discuss, men will never be wanting who will dare to resist the truth, and to rely upon the loquacity of human wisdom, when we know from the command of Our Lord Jesus Christ, how faith and Christian wisdom ought to avoid this most mischievous vanity." (St. Leo, Epistle 164, al. 133, sec 2, Boll. ed.)

And since Religion has been excluded from civil Society, and the doctrine and authority of divine Revelation, or the true and germane notion of justice and human right have been obscured and lost, and material or brute force substituted in the place of true justice and legitimate right, it is easy to perceive why some persons, forgetting and trampling upon the most certain principles of sound reason, dare cry out together, "that the will of the people, manifested by what they call public opinion, or in any other way, constitutes the supreme law, independent of all divine and human right, and that, in the political order, accomplished facts, by the mere fact of having been accomplished, have the force of right." But who does not see and plainly understand, that the Society of man, freed from the bonds of Religion and of true justice, can certainly have no other purpose than the effort to obtain and accumulate wealth, and that in its actions it follows no other law than that of the uncurbed cupidity, which seeks to secure its own pleasures and comforts? For this reason, also, these same men persecute with such bitter hatred the Religious Orders, who have deserved so well of Religion, civil Society, and Letters; they loudly declare that these Orders have no right to exist, and, in so doing, make common cause with the falsehoods of the heretics. For, as was most wisely taught by Our Predecessor of illustrious memory, Pius VI, "the abolition of Religious Orders injures the state of public profession of the Evangelical Counsels; injures a mode of life recommended by the Church, as in conformity with Apostolical doctrine; does wrong to the illustrious founders whom we venerate upon our altars, and who constituted these societies under the inspiration of God." (Epistle to Cardinal de la Rochefoucauld, March 10, 1791.)

And these same persons also impiously pretend that citizens should be deprived of the liberty of publicly bestowing on the Church their alms for the sake of Christian charity, and that the law forbidding "servile labor on account of Divine worship" upon certain fixed days should be abolished, upon the most fallacious pretext that such liberty and such law are contrary to the principles of political economy. Not content with abolishing Religion in public Society, they desire further to banish it from families and private life. Teaching and professing these most fatal errors of Socialism and Communism, they declare "that domestic society, or the family, derives all its reason of existence solely from civil law, whence it is to be concluded that from civil law descend and depend all the rights of parents over their children, and, above all, the right of instructing and educating them." By such impious opinions and machinations, do these most false teachers endeavor to eliminate the salutary teaching and influence of the Catholic Church from the instruction and education of youth, and miserably to infect and deprave by every pernicious error and vice the tender and pliant minds of youth. All those who endeavor to throw into confusion both religious and political affairs, to destroy the good order of society, and to annihilate all Divine and human rights, have always exerted all their criminal schemes, attention, and efforts upon the manner in which they might, above all, deprave and delude unthinking youth, as We have already shown: it is upon the corruption of youth that they place all their hopes. Thus they never cease to attack by every method the Clergy, both secular and regular, from whom, as testify to us in so conspicuous a manner the most certain records of history, such considerable benefits have been bestowed in abundance upon Christian and Civil Society and upon the republic of Letters; asserting of the Clergy in general, that they are the enemies of the useful sciences, of progress, and of civilization, and that they ought to be deprived of all participation in the work of teaching and training the young.

Others, reviving the depraved fictions of innovators, errors many times condemned, presume, with extraordinary impudence, to subordinate the authority of the Church and of this Apostolic See, conferred upon it by Christ our Lord, to the judgment of civil authority, and to deny to all the rights of this same Church and this See with regard to those things which appertain to the secular order. For these persons do not blush to affirm "that the laws of the Church do not bind the conscience, if they are not promulgated by the civil power; that the acts and decrees of the Roman Pontiffs concerning religion and the Church require the sanction and approbation, or at least the assent of the civil power; and that the Apostolic Constitutions (Clement XII, Benedict XIV, Pius VII, Leo XII) condemning secret societies, whether these exact or do not exact an oath of secrecy, and branding with anathema their followers and partisans, have no force in those countries of the world where such associations are tolerated by the civil Government." It is likewise affirmed "that the excommunications launched by the Council of Trent and the Roman Pontiffs against those who invade and usurp the possessions of the Church and its rights, strive, by confounding the spiritual and temporal orders, to attain solely a mere earthly end; that the Church can decide nothing which may bind the consciences of the faithful in the temporal order of things; the right of the Church is not competent to restrain with temporal penalties the violators of her laws; and that it is in accordance with the principles of theology and of public law for the civil Government to appropriate property possessed by the churches, the Religious Orders, and other pious establishments." And they have no shame in avowing openly and publicly the heretical statement and principle, from which have emanated so many errors and perverse opinions, "that the ecclesiastical power is not, by the law of God, made distinct from and independent of the civil power, and that no distinction, no independence of this kind can be maintained without the Church invading and usurping the essential rights of the civil power." Neither can We pass over in silence the audacity of those who, not enduring sound doctrine, assert that "the judgments and decrees of the Holy See, the object of which is declared to concern the general welfare of the Church, its rights, and its discipline, do not claim acquiescence and obedience, under pain of sin and loss of the Catholic profession, if they do not treat of the dogmas of faith and of morals."

How contrary is this doctrine to the Catholic dogma, of the plenary power divinely conferred on the Sovereign Pontiff by Our Lord Jesus Christ, to guide, to supervise and to govern the Universal Church, no one can fail to see and understand, clearly and evidently.

Amid so great a perversity of depraved opinions, We, remembering Our Apostolic duty, and solicitous before all things for Our most holy Religion, for sound doctrine, for the salvation of the souls confided to Us, and for the welfare of human Society itself, have considered the moment opportune to raise anew Our Apostolic voice. Therefore do We, by our Apostolic authority, reprobate, denounce, and condemn generally and particularly all the evil opinions and doctrines specially mentioned in this Letter, and We wish that they may be held as reprobated, denounced, and condemned by all the children of the Catholic Church.

But You know further, Venerable Brothers, that in Our time the haters of all truth and justice and violent enemies of our Religion have spread abroad other impious doctrines, by means of pestilent books, pamphlets, and journals, which, distributed over the surface of the earth, deceive the people and wickedly lie. You are not ignorant that in our day men are found who, animated and excited by the spirit of Satan, have arrived at that excess of impiety as not to fear to deny Our Lord and Master Jesus Christ, and to attack His Divinity with scandalous persistence. And here We cannot abstain from awarding You well-merited praise, Venerable Brothers, for all the care and zeal, with which You have raised Your episcopal voice against so great an impiety.

And therefore in this present Letter, We speak to You with all affection; to You who, called to partake of Our cares, are Our greatest support in the midst of Our very great grief;

Our joy and consolation, by reason of the excellent piety of which You give proof in maintaining Religion, and the marvellous love, faith, and discipline with which, united by the strongest and most affectionate ties to Us and this Apostolic See. You strive valiantly and accurately to fulfil Your most weighty episcopal ministry. We do then expect, from Your excellent pastoral zeal, that, taking the sword of the Spirit, which is the Word of God, and strengthened by the grace of Our Lord Jesus Christ, You will watch with redoubled care that the faithful committed to Your charge "abstain from evil pasturage, which Jesus Christ doth not till, because His Father hath not planted it." (St. Ignatius, *M. ad. Philadelph.*, St. Leo, Epist. 156, al. 125.) Never cease, then, to inculcate on the faithful that all true happiness for mankind proceeds from our august Religion, from its doctrine and practice, and that that people is happy who have the Lord for their God (Psalm 143). Teach them "that kingdoms rest upon the foundation of the Catholic faith (St. Celest, Epist, 22 ad. Syn. Eph.), and that nothing is so deadly, nothing so certain to engender every ill, nothing so exposed to danger, as for men to believe that they stand in need of nothing else than the free will which we received at birth, if we ask nothing further from the Lord; that is to say, if, forgetting our Author, we abjure His power to show that we are free." And do not omit to teach, "that the royal power has been established, not only to exercise the government of the world, but, above all, for the protection of the Church (St. Leo, Epist. 156, al. 125); and that there is nothing more profitable and more glorious for the Sovereigns of States, and Kings, than to leave the Catholic Church to exercise her laws, and not to permit any to curtail her liberty;" as Our most wise and courageous Predecessor, St. Felix, wrote to the Emperor Zeno. "It is certain that it is advantageous for Sovereigns, when the cause of God is in question, to submit their Royal will, according to his ordinance, to the Priests of Jesus Christ, and not to prefer it before them." (Pius VII Epist., Encycl. *Diu satis,* 15th May, 1800.)

And if always, so especially at present, Venerable Brothers, in the midst of the numerous calamities of the Church and of civil Society, in view also of the terrible conspiracy of our adversaries against the Catholic Church and this Apostolic See, and the great accumulation of errors, it is before all things necessary to go with faith to the Throne of Grace, to obtain mercy and find Grace in timely aid. We have therefore judged it right to excite the piety of all the faithful, in order that, with Us and with You all, they may pray without ceasing to the Father of lights and of mercies, supplicating and beseeching Him fervently and humbly, and in the plenitude of their faith they may seek refuge in Our Lord Jesus Christ, who has redeemed us to God with his blood, that by their earnest and continual prayers, they may obtain from that most dear Heart, victim of burning charity for us, that it would draw all to Himself by the bonds of His love, that all men being inflamed by His holy love may live according to His heart, pleasing God in all things, and being fruitful in all good works.

But, as there is no doubt that the prayers most agreeable to God are those of men who approach Him with a heart pure from all stain, We have thought it good to open to Christians, with Apostolic liberality, the heavenly treasures of the Church confided to Our dispensation, so that the faithful, more strongly drawn towards true piety, and purified from the stain of their sins by the Sacrament of Penance, may more confidently offer up their prayers to God and obtain His mercy and grace.

By these Letters therefore, emanating from Our Apostolic authority, We grant to all and each of the faithful of both sexes throughout the Catholic world a Plenary Indulgence, in the manner of a Jubilee, during one month, up to the end of the coming year 1865, and not longer, to be carried into effect by You, Venerable Brethren, and the other legitimate local Ordinaries, in the form and manner laid down at the commencement of Our Sovereign Pontificate by Our Apostolical Letters in form of a Brief, dated the 20th of November, A.D. 1846, and sent to the whole Episcopate of the world, commencing with the words, *"Arcano Divinae Providentiae concilio,"* and with the faculties given by Us in those same Letters. We desire, however, that all the prescriptions of Our Letters shall be observed, saving the exceptions We have declared are to be made. And we have granted this, notwithstanding all which might make to the contrary, even those worthy of special and individual mention and derogation; and in order that every doubt and difficulty may be removed, We have ordered that copies of those Letters should again be forwarded to You.

Let us implore, Venerable Brethren, from our inmost hearts, and with all our souls, the mercy of God. He has encouraged us so to do, by saying: "I will not withdraw My mercy from them." "Let us ask and we shall receive; and if there is slowness or delay in the reception, because we have grievously offended, let us knock, because to him that knocketh it shall be opened; if our prayers, groans, and tears, in which we must persist and be obstinate, knock at the door: and if our prayers be united; let each one pray to God, not for himself alone, but for all his brethren, as the Lord hath taught us to pray." (St.

Cyprian, Epistle 11.) But, in order that God may accede more easily to Our and Your prayers, and to those of all His faithful servants, let us employ in all confidence, as our Mediatrix with Him, the Virgin Mary, Mother of God, who has destroyed all heresies throughout the world, and who, the most loving Mother of us all, is very gracious . . . and full of mercy, . . . allows herself to be entreated by all, shows herself most clement towards all, and takes under her pitying care all our necessities with a most ample affection" (St. Bernard, *Sermo de duodecim praerogativis B. V. M. in verbis Apocalyp.*), and, "sitting as queen at the right hand of her only begotten Son, our Lord Jesus Christ, in a golden vestment clothed around with various adornments," there is nothing which she cannot obtain from him. Let us implore also the intervention of the Blessed Peter, Chief of the Apostles, and his co-Apostle Paul, and of all those Saints of heaven, who, having already become the friends of God, have been admitted into the celestial kingdom, where they are crowned and bear palms in their hands; and who, henceforth certain of their own immortality, are solicitous for our salvation.

In conclusion, We ask of God from Our inmost soul the abundance of all His celestial benefits for you, and We bestow upon You, Venerable Brethren, and upon all the faithful Clergy, and Laity committed to Your care, Our Apostolic Benediction from the most loving depths of Our heart, in token of our Charity toward You.

PIUS, PP. IX.

Given at Rome, from St. Peter's this 8th day of December, 1864, the tenth anniversary of the dogmatic Definition of the Immaculate Conception of the Virgin Mary, Mother of God, in the nineteenth year of Our Pontificate. [D-1688-1780]

THE SYLLABUS OF PIUS IX[8]

Syllabus of the principal errors of our time, which are censured in the consistorial Allocutions, Encyclical and other Apostolic Letters of our Most Holy Lord, Pope Pius IX.

I. PANTHEISM, NATURALISM AND ABSOLUTE RATIONALISM

1. There exists no Supreme, all-wise, all-provident Divine Being, distinct from the universe, and God is identical with the nature of things, and is, therefore, subject to changes. In effect, God is produced in man and in the world, and all things are God and have the very substance of God, and God is one and

[8] *Dogmatic Canons and Decrees*, pp. 187-209.

the same thing with the world, and, therefore, spirit with matter, necessity with liberty, good with evil, justice with injustice.—*Allocution "Maxima quidem," June 9, 1862.*

2. All action of God upon man and the world is to be denied.—*Ibid.*

3. Human reason, without any reference whatsoever to God, is the sole arbiter of truth and falsehood, and of good and evil; it is law to itself, and suffices, by its natural force, to secure the welfare of men and of nations.—*Ibid.*

4. All the truths of religion proceed from the innate strength of human reason; hence reason is the ultimate standard by which man can and ought to arrive at the knowledge of all truths of every kind.—*Ibid. and Encyclical "Qui pluribus," Nov. 9, 1846*, etc.

5. Divine revelation is imperfect, and therefore subject to a continual and indefinite progress, corresponding with the advancement of human reason.—*Ibid.*

6. The faith of Christ is in opposition to human reason, and divine revelation not only is not useful, but is even hurtful to the perfection of man.—*Ibid.*

7. The prophecies and miracles set forth and recorded in the Sacred Scriptures are the fiction of poets, and the mysteries of the Christian faith the result of philosophical investigations. In the books of the Old and the New Testament there are contained mythical inventions, and Jesus Christ is Himself a myth.—*Ibid.*

II. MODERATE RATIONALISM

8. As human reason is placed on a level with religion itself, so theological must be treated in the same manner as philosophical sciences.—*Allocution "Singulari quadam," Dec. 9, 1854.*

9. All the dogmas of the Christian religion are indiscriminately the object of natural science or philosophy; and human reason, enlightened solely in an historical way, is able, by its own natural strength and principles, to attain to the true science of even the most abstruse dogmas; provided only that such dogmas be proposed to reason itself as its object.—*Letters to the Archbishop of Munich, "Gravissimas inter," Dec. 11, 1862, and "Tuas libenter," Dec. 21, 1863.*

10. As the philosopher is one thing, and philosophy another, so it is the right and duty of the philosopher to subject himself to the authority which he shall have proved to be true; but philosophy neither can nor ought to submit to any such authority.—*Ibid., Dec. 11, 1862.*

11. The Church not only ought never to pass judgment

on philosophy, but ought to tolerate the errors of philosophy, leaving it to correct itself.—*Ibid., Dec. 21, 1863.*

12. The decrees of the Apostolic See and of the Roman congregations impede the true progress of science.—*Ibid.*

13. The method and principles by which the old scholastic doctors cultivated theology are no longer suitable to the demands of our times and to the progress of the sciences.—*Ibid.*

14. Philosophy is to be treated without taking any account of supernatural revelation.—*Ibid.*

N.B. To the rationalistic system belong in great part the errors of Anthony Günther, condemned in the letter to the Cardinal Archbishop of Cologne, "Eximiam tuam," June 15, 1857, and in that to the Bishop of Breslau, "Dolore haud mediocri," April 30, 1860.

III. INDIFFERENTISM. LATITUDINARIANISM

15. Every man is free to embrace and profess that religion which, guided by the light of reason, he shall consider true.—*Allocution "Maxima quidem," June 9, 1862; Damnatio "Multiplices inter," June 10, 1851.*

16. Man may, in the observance of any religion whatever, find the way of eternal salvation, and arrive at eternal salvation.—*Encyclical "Qui pluribus," Nov. 9, 1846.*

17. Good hope at least is to be entertained of the eternal salvation of all those who are not at all in the true Church of Christ.—*Encyclical "Quanto conficiamur," Aug. 10, 1863,* etc.

18. Protestantism is nothing more than another form of the same true Christian religion, in which form it is given to please God equally as in the Catholic Church.—*Encyclical "Noscitis," Dec. 8, 1849.*

IV. SOCIALISM, COMMUNISM, SECRET SOCIETIES, BIBLICAL SOCIETIES, CLERICO-LIBERAL SOCIETIES

Pests of this kind are frequently reprobated in the severest terms in the Encyclical "Qui pluribus," Nov. 9, 1846, Allocution "Quibus quantisque," April 20, 1849, Encyclical "Noscitis et nobiscum," Dec. 8, 1849, Allocution "Singulari quadam," Dec. 9, 1854, Encyclical "Quanto conficiamur," Aug. 10, 1863.

V. ERRORS CONCERNING THE CHURCH AND HER RIGHTS

19. The Church is not a true and perfect society, entirely free; nor is she endowed with proper and perpetual rights of her own, conferred upon her by her Divine Founder; but it

appertains to the civil power to define what are the rights of the Church, and the limits within which she may exercise those rights.—*Allocution "Singulari quadam," Dec. 9, 1854*, etc.

20. The ecclesiastical power ought not to exercise its authority without the permission and assent of the civil government.—*Allocution "Meminit unusquisque," Sept. 30, 1861*.

21. The Church has not the power of defining dogmatically that the religion of the Catholic Church is the only true religion.—*Damnatio "Multiplices inter," June 10, 1851*.

22. The obligation by which Catholic teachers and authors are strictly bound is confined to those things only which are proposed to universal belief as dogmas of faith by the infallible judgment of the Church.—*Letter to the Archbishop of Munich, "Tuas libenter," Dec. 21, 1863*.

23. Roman pontiffs and ecumenical councils have wandered outside the limits of their powers, have usurped the rights of princes, and have even erred in defining matters of faith and morals.—*Damnatio "Multiplices inter," June 10, 1851*.

24. The Church has not the power of using force, nor has she any temporal power, direct or indirect.—*Apostolic Letter "Ad Apostolicae," Aug. 22, 1851*.

25. Besides the power inherent in the episcopate, other temporal power has been attributed to it by the civil authority, granted either explicitly or tacitly, which on that account is revocable by the civil authority whenever it thinks fit.—*Ibid*.

26. The Church has no innate and legitimate right of acquiring and possessing property.—*Allocution "Nunquam fore," Dec. 15, 1856; Encyclical "Incredibili," Sept. 7, 1863*.

27. The sacred ministers of the Church and the Roman pontiff are to be absolutely excluded from every charge and dominion over temporal affairs.—*Allocution "Maxima quidem," June 9, 1862*.

28. It is not lawful for bishops to publish even letters Apostolic without the permission of Government.—*Allocution "Nunquam fore," Dec. 15, 1856*.

29. Favours granted by the Roman pontiff ought to be considered null, unless they have been sought for through the civil government.—*Ibid*.

30. The immunity of the Church and of ecclesiastical persons derived its origin from civil law.—*Damnatio "Multiplices inter," June 10, 1851*.

31. The ecclesiastical forum or tribunal for the temporal causes, whether civil or criminal, of clerics, ought by all means to be abolished, even without consulting and against the protest of the Holy See.—*Allocution "Nunquam fore," Dec. 15, 1856; Allocution "Acerbissimum," Sept. 27, 1852*.

32. The personal immunity by which clerics are exoner-

ated from military conscription and service in the army may be abolished without violation either of natural right or equity. Its abolition is called for by civil progress, especially in a society framed on the model of a liberal government.—*Letter to the Bishop of Monreale "Singularis nobisque," Sept. 29, 1864*.

33. It does not appertain exclusively to the power of ecclesiastical jurisdiction by right, proper and innate, to direct the teaching of theological questions.—*Letter to the Archbishop of Munich, "Tuas libenter," Dec. 21, 1863*.

34. The teaching of those who compare the Sovereign Pontiff to a prince, free and acting in the universal Church, is a doctrine which prevailed in the Middle Ages.—*Apostolic Letter "Ad Apostolicae," Aug. 22, 1851*.

35. There is nothing to prevent the decree of a general council, or the act of all peoples, from transferring the supreme pontificate from the bishop and city of Rome to another bishop and another city.—*Ibid*.

36. The definition of a national council does not admit of any subsequent discussion, and the civil authority can assume this principle as the basis of its acts.—*Ibid*.

37. National churches, withdrawn from the authority of the Roman pontiff and altogether separated, can be established. —*Allocution "Multis gravibusque," Dec. 17, 1860*.

38. The Roman pontiffs have, by their too arbitrary conduct, contributed to the division of the Church into Eastern and Western.—*Apostolic Letter "Ad Apostolicae," Aug. 22, 1851*.

VI. ERRORS ABOUT CIVIL SOCIETY, CONSIDERED BOTH IN ITSELF AND IN ITS RELATION TO THE CHURCH

39. The State, as being the origin and source of all rights, is endowed with a certain right not circumscribed by any limits.—*Allocution "Maxima quidem," June 9, 1862*.

40. The teaching of the Catholic Church is hostile to the well-being and interests of society.—*Encyclical "Qui pluribus," Nov. 9, 1846; Allocution "Quibus quantisque," April 20, 1849*.

41. The civil government, even when in the hands of an infidel sovereign, has a right to an indirect negative power over religious affairs. It therefore possesses not only the right called that of *exsequatur*, but also that of appeal, called *appellatio ab abusu*.—*Apostolic Letter "Ad Apostolicae," Aug. 22, 1851*.

42. In the case of conflicting laws enacted by the two powers, the civil law prevails.—*Ibid*.

43. The secular power has authority to rescind, declare

and render null, solemn conventions, commonly called concordats, entered into with the Apostolic See, regarding the use of rights appertaining to ecclesiastical immunity, without the consent of the Apostolic See, and even in spite of its protest. —*Allocution "Multis gravibusque," Dec. 17, 1860; Allocution "In consistoriali," Nov. 1, 1850.*

44. The civil authority may interfere in matters relating to religion, morality and spiritual government: hence, it can pass judgment on the instructions issued for the guidance of consciences, conformably with their mission, by the pastors of the Church. Further, it has the right to make enactments regarding the administration of the divine sacraments, and the dispositions necessary for receiving them.—*Allocutions "In consistoriali," Nov. 1, 1850, and "Maxima quidem," June 9, 1862.*

45. The entire government of public schools in which the youth of a Christian state is educated, except (to a certain extent) in the case of episcopal seminaries, may and ought to appertain to the civil power, and belong to it so far that no other authority whatsoever shall be recognized as having any right to interfere in the discipline of the schools, the arrangement of the studies, the conferring of degrees, in the choice or approval of the teachers.—*Allocutions "Quibus luctuosissimis," Sept. 5, 1851, and "In consistoriali," Nov. 1, 1850.*

46. Moreover, even in ecclesiastical seminaries, the method of studies to be adopted is subject to the civil authority.—*Allocution "Nunquam fore," Dec. 15, 1856.*

47. The best theory of civil society requires that popular schools open to children of every class of the people, and, generally, all public institutes intended for instruction in letters and philosophical sciences and for carrying on the education of youth, should be freed from all ecclesiastical authority, control and interference, and should be fully subjected to the civil and political power at the pleasure of the rulers, and according to the standard of the prevalent opinions of the age.—*Epistle to the Archbishop of Freiburg, "Cum non sine," July 14, 1864.*

48. Catholics may approve of the system of educating youth unconnected with Catholic faith and the power of the Church, and which regards the knowledge of merely natural things, and only, or at least primarily, the ends of earthly social life.—*Ibid.*

49. The civil power may prevent the prelates of the Church and the faithful from communicating freely and mutually with the Roman pontiff.—*Allocution "Maxima quidem," June 9, 1862.*

50. Lay authority possesses of itself the right of present-

ing bishops, and may require of them to undertake the administration of the diocese before they receive canonical institution, and the Letters Apostolic from the Holy See.—*Allocution "Nunquam fore," Dec. 15, 1856.*

51. And, further, the lay government has the right of deposing bishops from their pastoral functions, and is not bound to obey the Roman pontiff in those things which relate to the institution of bishoprics and the appointment of bishops.—*Allocution "Acerbissimum," Sept. 27, 1852; Damnatio "Multiplices inter," June 10, 1851.*

52. Government can, by its own right, alter the age prescribed by the Church for the religious profession of women and men; and may require of all religious orders to admit no person to take solemn vows without its permission.—*Allocution "Nunquam fore," Dec. 15, 1856.*

53. The laws enacted for the protection of religious orders and regarding their rights and duties ought to be abolished; nay, more, civil Government may lend its assistance to all who desire to renounce the obligation which they have undertaken of a religious life, and to break their vows. Government may also suppress the said religious orders, as likewise collegiate churches and simple benefices, even those of advowson, and subject their property and revenues to the administration and pleasure of the civil power.—*Allocutions "Acerbissimum," Sept. 27, 1852; "Probe memineritis," Jan. 22, 1855; "Cum saepe," July 26, 1855.*

54. Kings and princes are not only exempt from the jurisdiction of the Church, but are superior to the Church in deciding questions of jurisdiction.—*Damnatio "Multiplices inter," June 10, 1851.*

55. The Church ought to be separated from the State, and the State from the Church.—*Allocution "Acerbissimum," Sept. 27, 1852.*

VII. ERRORS CONCERNING NATURAL AND CHRISTIAN ETHICS

56. Moral laws do not stand in need of the divine sanction, and it is not at all necessary that human laws should be made conformable to the laws of nature, and receive their power of binding from God.—*Allocution "Maxima quidem," June 9, 1862.*

57. The science of philosophical things and morals and also civil laws may and ought to keep aloof from divine and ecclesiastical authority.—*Ibid.*

58. No other forces are to be recognized except those which reside in matter, and all the rectitude and excellence of morality ought to be placed in the accumulation and in-

crease of riches by every possible means, and the gratification of pleasure.—*Ibid.; Encyclical "Quanto conficiamur," Aug. 10, 1863.*

59.   Right consists in the material fact. All human duties are an empty word, and all human facts have the force of right.—*Allocution "Maxima quidem," June 9, 1862.*

60.   Authority is nothing else but numbers and the sum total of material forces.—*Ibid.*

61.   The injustice of an act when successful inflicts no injury on the sanctity of right.—*Allocution "Jamdudum cernimus," March 18, 1861.*

62.   The principle of non-intervention, as it is called, ought to be proclaimed and observed.—*Allocution "Novos et ante," Sept. 28, 1860.*

63.   It is lawful to refuse obedience to legitimate princes, and even to rebel against them.—*Encyclical "Qui pluribus," Nov. 9, 1864; Allocution "Quibusque vestrum," Oct. 4, 1847; "Noscitis et Nobiscum," Dec. 8, 1849; Letter Apostolic "Cum Catholica."*

64.   The violation of any solemn oath, as well as any wicked and flagitious action repugnant to the eternal law, is not only not blamable but is altogether lawful and worthy of the highest praise when done through love of country.—*Allocution "Quibus quantisque," April 20, 1849.*

VIII.   ERRORS CONCERNING CHRISTIAN MARRIAGE

65.   The doctrine that Christ has raised marriage to the dignity of a sacrament cannot be at all tolerated.—*Apostolic Letter "Ad Apostolicae," Aug. 22, 1851.*

66.   The Sacrament of Marriage is only a something accessory to the contract and separate from it, and the sacrament itself consists in the nuptial benediction alone.—*Ibid.*

67.   By the law of nature, the marriage tie is not indissoluble, and in many cases divorce properly so called may be decreed by the civil authority.—*Ibid.; Allocution "Acerbissimum," Sept. 27, 1852.*

68.   The Church has not the power of establishing diriment impediments of marriage, but such a power belongs to the civil authority by which existing impediments are to be removed.—*Damnatio "Multiplices inter," June 10, 1851.*

69.   In the dark ages the Church began to establish diriment impediments, not by her own right, but by using a power borrowed from the State.—*Apostolic Letter "Ad Apostolicae," Aug. 22, 1851.*

70.   The canons of the Council of Trent, which anathe-

matize those who dare to deny to the Church the right of establishing diriment impediments, either are not dogmatic, or must be understood as referring to such borrowed power. —*Ibid.*

71. The form of solemnizing marriage prescribed by the Council of Trent, under pain of nullity, does not bind in cases where the civil law lays down another form, and declares that when this new form is used the marriage shall be valid. —*Ibid.*

72. Boniface VIII was the first who declared that the vow of chastity taken at ordination renders marriage void.— *Ibid.*

73. In force of a merely civil contract there may exist between Christians a real marriage, and it is false to say either that the marriage contract between Christians is always a sacrament, or that there is no contract if the sacrament be excluded.—*Ibid.; Letter to the King of Sardinia, Sept. 9, 1852; Allocutions "Acerbissimum," Sept. 27, 1852; "Multis gravibusque," Dec. 17, 1860.*

74. Matrimonial causes and espousals belong by their nature to civil tribunals.—*Encyclical "Qui pluribus," Nov. 9, 1846; Damnatio "Multiplices inter," June 10, 1851; "Ad Apostolicae," Aug. 22, 1851; Allocution "Acerbissimum," Sept. 27, 1852.*

N.B.—To the preceding questions may be referred two other errors regarding the celibacy of priests and the preference due to the state of marriage over that of virginity. These have been stigmatized: the first in the Encyclical "Qui pluribus," Nov. 9, 1846; the second, in the Letter Apostolic "Multiplices inter," June 10, 1851.

IX. ERRORS REGARDING THE CIVIL POWER OF THE SOVEREIGN PONTIFF

75. The children of the Christian and Catholic Church are divided amongst themselves about the compatibility of the temporal with the spiritual power.—*"Ad Apostolicae," Aug. 22, 1851.*

76. The abolition of the temporal power of which the Apostolic See is possessed would contribute in the greatest degree to the liberty and prosperity of the Church.—*Allocutions "Quibus quantisque," April 20, 1849; "Si semper antea," May 20, 1850.*

N.B.—Besides these errors, explicitly censured, very many others are implicitly condemned by the doctrine propounded and established, which all Catholics are bound most firmly to hold touching the temporal sovereignty of the Roman pontiff. This doctrine is clearly stated in the Allocutions "Quibus quantisque," April 20, 1849, and "Si semper antea," May 20, 1850; Letter Apostolic "Cum Catholica ecclesia," March 26, 1860; Allocutions, "Noves et antea," Sept. 28, 1860; "Jamdudum cernimus," March 18, 1861; "Maxima quidem," June 9, 1862.

X. ERRORS HAVING REFERENCE TO MODERN LIBERALISM

77. In the present day it is no longer expedient that the Catholic religion should be held as the only religion of the State, to the exclusion of all other forms of worship.—*Allocution "Nemo vestrum," July 26, 1855.*

78. Hence it has been wisely decided by law, in some Catholic countries, that persons coming to reside therein shall enjoy the public exercise of their own peculiar worship. —*Allocution "Acerbissimum," Sept. 27, 1852.*

79. Moreover, it is false that the civil liberty of every form of worship, and the full power, given to all, of overtly and publicly manifesting any opinions whatsoever and thoughts, conduce more easily to corrupt the morals and minds of the people, and to propagate the pest of indifferentism. —*Allocution "Nunquam fore," Dec. 15, 1856.*

80. The Roman Pontiff can, and ought to, reconcile himself, and come to terms with progress, liberalism and modern civilization.—*Allocution "Jamdudum cernimus," March 18, 1861.*

[On December 8, 1869, the Vatican Council met in Rome. All Christian bishops had been invited, the schismatic Greeks and Russians not less than those "in peace and communion." The Canons have been quoted in Chapter 1. Suffice it to say that at the last of the votes in the General Congregation, on July 13, 1870, the Constitution *Pastor aeternus* in which the pope's primacy and infallibility were defined, 451 voted *placet,* or yea, 88 voted *non placet,* or nay, and 62 voted *placet juxta modum,* "yea subject to certain amendments." The Franco-Prussian War and Infallibility were declared the same week. In spite of the horrors, in spite of the gathering darkness, Pius IX had only one concern, the welfare of the Church Universal, as his sad encyclical *Etsi multa luctuosa* shows (November 21, 1873)."]

The faith teaches us and human reason demonstrates that

a double order of things exists, and that we must therefore distinguish between the two earthly powers, the one of natural origin which provides for secular affairs and the tranquillity of human society, the other of supernatural origin, which presides over the City of God, that is to say the Church of Christ, which has been divinely instituted for the sake of souls and of eternal salvation. . . . The duties of this twofold power are most wisely ordered in such a way that to God is given what is God's (Matt. 22:21), and because of God to Caesar what is Caesar's, who is great because he is smaller than heaven. Certainly the Church has never disobeyed this divine command, the Church which always and everywhere instructs the faithful to show the respect which they should inviolably have for the supreme authority and its secular rights. . . .

. . . Venerable Brethren, you see clearly enough how sad and full of perils is the condition of Catholics in the regions of Europe which We have mentioned. Nor are things any better or circumstances calmer in America, where some regions are so hostile to Catholics that their governments seem to deny by their actions the Catholic faith they claim to profess. In fact, there, for the last few years, a ferocious war on the Church, its institutions and the rights of the Apostolic See has been raging. . . . Venerable Brothers, it is surprising that in our time such a great war is being waged against the Catholic Church. But anyone who knows the nature, desires and intentions of the sects, whether they be called masonic, or bear another name, and compares them with the nature, the systems and the vastness of the obstacles by which the Church has been assailed almost everywhere, cannot doubt that the present misfortune must mainly be imputed to the frauds and machinations of these sects. It is from them that the synagogue of Satan, which gathers its troops against the Church of Christ, takes its strength. In the past Our predecessors, vigilant even from the beginning in Israel, had already denounced them to the kings and the nations, and had condemned them time and time again, and even We have not failed in this duty. If those who would have been able to avert such a deadly scourge had only had more faith in the supreme Pastors of the Church! But this scourge, winding through sinuous caverns, . . . deceiving many with astute frauds, finally has arrived at the point where it comes forth impetuously from its hiding places and triumphs as a powerful master. Since the throng of its propagandists has grown enormously, these wicked groups think that they have already become masters of the world and that they have almost reached their pre-established goal. Having sometimes obtained what they desired, and that is power, in several countries, they boldly turn the help of powers and authorities which they have secured to trying to submit the Church of God to the most cruel servitude, to undermine the foundations on which it rests, to contaminate its splendid qualities; and, moreover, to strike it with frequent blows, to shake it, to overthrow it, and, if possible, to make it disappear completely from the earth. Things being thus, Venerable Brothers, make every effort to defend the faithful which are entrusted to you against the insidious contagion of these sects and to save from perdition those who unfortunately have inscribed themselves in such sects. Make known and attack those who, whether suffering from, or planning, deception, are not afraid to affirm that these shady congregations aim only at the profit of society, at progress and mutual benefit. Explain to them often and impress deeply on their souls the Papal constitutions on this subject and teach them that the masonic associations are anathematized by them not only in Europe but also in America and wherever they may be in the whole world.

[The closing years of Pius IX's episcopate were darkened by the shadow of Prussia. The *Kulturkampf*, which was Bismarck's pet project, began with the expulsion of the Jesuits and ended "by subjecting the training of priests to the will of the State." [10] What Bismarck began, Hitler completed: for seventy years the attack of German paganism on Christendom was to be continual. In his very last encyclical, *Quod nunquam*, of February 5, 1875, Pius IX faced and foresaw the future.[11]]

To the Archbishops and Bishops of Prussia concerning the situation of the Catholic Church faced with persecution by that Government. . . .
But although they (the bishops resisting persecution) should be praised rather than pitied, the scorn of episcopal dignity, the violation of the liberty and the rights of the Church, the ill treatment which does not only oppress those dioceses, but also the others of the Kingdom of Prussia, demand that We, owing to the Apostolic office with which God has entrusted us in spite of Our insufficient merit, protest against laws which have produced such great evils and make one fear even greater ones; and as far as we are able to do so with the sacred authority of divine law, We vindicate for the Church the freedom which has been trodden underfoot with

10 E. E. Y. Hales, *Pio Nono*. New York: P. J. Kenedy & Sons, 1954, P. 324.
11 *Tutti le Encicliche*.

sacrilegious violence. That is why by this letter we intend to do Our duty by announcing openly to all those whom this matter concerns and to the whole Catholic world, that these laws are null and void because they are absolutely contrary to the divine constitution of the Church. In fact, with respect to matters which concern the holy ministry, Our Lord did not put the mighty of this century in charge, but Saint Peter, whom he entrusted not only with feeding his sheep, but also the goats; therefore no power in the world, however great it may be, can deprive of the pastoral office those whom the Holy Ghost has made Bishops in order to feed the Church of God.

Chapter 16

✝

Leo XIII (1878-1903)

Gioacchino Vincenzo Pecci, born on March 2, 1810, in the Papal States, studied first with the Jesuits, then at the Collegio Romano, and finally at the Sapienza, where he took his doctorate in canon law. Ordained at twenty-seven, he served as head of the police in Benevento, and then as Governor of Perugia. Later papal nuncio to Brussels, he became bishop of Perugia in 1846. Thirteen days after the death of Pius IX, Cardinal Pecci was elected pope, taking the name of Leo XIII. He is one of the greatest of all the popes, and his eighty-six encyclicals constitute a collection of statements on various modern problems that is the most important single contribution to Catholic doctrine since the Middle Ages. All good everywhere belongs absolutely to the Church, but hers is the job of distinguishing it from error, and also of assimilating it, so that she can nourish the weakest of her children with it without fear of their taking harm.

"Never was science so arrogant as when Leo XIII began to recommend to Catholics the study of sound philosophy. . . . Scientists everywhere were proclaiming the victory of science over religion, when Leo declared that there could be no question of victory where there was no conflict," wrote Father John Wynne, S.J.[1] The real value to the Church of the new awareness of labor problems is distilled in the greatest of all Leo's encyclicals, *Rerum novarum;* the true nature and the real limits of human liberty are set forth in *Libertae praestantissimum;* Christian citizenship is discussed in *Sapientiae Christiane,* and the Christian constitution of states in *Immortate Dei.*

"Liberalism having come to stay, Catholics must be shown how to live in a Liberal world, and yet live by their Catholic principles; they must learn, not only how they could survive in such a world, but how to be active loyal citizens of the liberal states." [2] Leo XIII had to cope with a violently anti-

[1] *The Great Encyclical Letters of Leo XIII.* New York: Benziger, 1903, p. 4.
[2] Father Philip Hughes, *op. cit.,* p. 257.

clerical France; with the *Kulturkampf* of Bismarck in Germany; with a hostile Italy digesting the temporal lands and powers it had taken from the Church. The Italian revolutionaries almost succeeded in throwing Pius IX's body into the Tiber, when it was being removed to the cemetery of San Lorenzo, and the Italian government actually tried to confiscate Catholic alms, but the pope was undeterred, working twelve hours a day seven days a week in the Vatican. His death in 1903 ended a notably productive twenty-five years as pope.

His encyclical *Divinum Illud,* on the Holy Spirit, and that of the Holy Eucharist, *Mirae caritatis,* are among his major purely theological utterances.

Divinum Illud, May 4, 1897[8]

Now We have earnestly striven, by the help of His grace, to follow the example of Christ Our Saviour, the Prince of pastors, and the Bishop of our souls, by diligently carrying on His office, entrusted by Him to the apostles and chiefly to Peter, "whose dignity faileth not, even in his unworthy successor." * In pursuance of this object We have endeavored to direct all that we have attempted and persistently carried out during a long pontificate towards two chief ends: in the first place, towards the restoration, both in rulers and peoples, of the principles of the Christian life in civil and domestic society, since there is no true life for men except from Christ; and, secondly, to promote the reunion of those who have fallen away from the Catholic Church either by heresy or by schism, since it is most undoubtedly the will of Christ that all should be united in one flock under one Shepherd. But now that We are looking forward to the approach of the closing days of Our life, Our soul is deeply moved to dedicate to the Holy Ghost, who is the life-giving Love, all the work We have done during Our pontificate, that He may bring it to maturity and fruitfulness. In order better and more fully to carry out this Our intention, We have resolved to address you at the approaching sacred season of Pentecost concerning the indwelling and miraculous power of the Holy Ghost; and the extent and efficiency of His action, both in the whole body of the Church and in the individual souls of its members, through the glorious abundance of His divine graces. We earnestly desire that, as a result, faith may be aroused in your minds concerning the mystery of the adorable Trinity, and especially that piety may increase and be inflamed towards the Holy Ghost, to whom especially all of us owe the grace of following the paths of truth and virtue. . . .

[8] Father John Wynne, S.J., *op. cit.,* pp. 424-29.
* St. Leo the Great, Sermon ii., on the Anniversary of his Election.

Before We enter upon this subject, it will be both desirable and useful to say a few words about the mystery of the Blessed Trinity. This dogma is called by the Doctors of the Church "the substance of the New Testament," that is to say, the greatest of all mysteries, since it is the fountain and origin of them all. In order to know and contemplate this mystery, the angels were created in heaven and men upon earth. In order to teach more fully this mystery, which was but foreshadowed in the Old Testament, God Himself came down from the angels unto men: *No man hath seen God at any time; the only begotten Son, who is in the bosom of the Father, He hath declared Him.** . . . The danger that arises is lest the divine persons be confounded one with the other in faith or worship, or lest the one nature in them be separated: for "This is the Catholic faith, that we should adore one God in Trinity and Trinity in Unity." Therefore Our predecessor Innocent XII absolutely refused the petition of those who desired a special festival in honor of God the Father. For, although the separate mysteries connected with the Incarnate Word are celebrated on certain fixed days, yet there is no special feast on which the Word is honored according to His divine nature alone. And even the Feast of Pentecost was instituted in the earliest times, not simply to honor the Holy Ghost in Himself, but to commemorate His coming, or His external mission. And all this has been wisely ordained, lest from distinguishing the persons men should be led to distinguish the divine essence . . . The Church is accustomed most fittingly to attribute to the Father those works of the divinity in which power excels, to the Son those in which wisdom excels, and those in which love excels to the Holy Ghost. Not that all perfections and external operations are not common to the divine persons; for "the operations of the Trinity are indivisible, even as the essence of the Trinity is indivisible"** because as the three divine persons "are inseparable, so do they act inseparably."† But by a certain comparison, and a kind of affinity between the operations and the properties of the persons, these operations are attributed or, as it is said, "appropriated" to one person rather than to the others. "Just as we make use of the traces of similarity or likeness which we find in creatures for the manifestation of the divine persons, so do we use their essential attributes; and this manifestation of the persons by their essential attributes is called *appropriation*."†† In this manner

---

* Summ. Th. 1a., q. xxxi. De Trin. 1. i., c. 3.
** St. Aug. *De Trin.*, 1. i., cc. 4, 5.
† *Ibid.*
†† St. Th. 1a., q. xxxix., 7.

the Father, who is "the principal of the whole Godhead,"* is also the efficient cause of all things, of the Incarnation of the Word, and the sanctification of souls; "of Him are all things," *of Him* referring to the Father. But the Son, the Word, the Image of God, is also the exemplary cause, whence all creatures borrow their form and beauty, their order and harmony. He is for us the way, the truth, and the life: the reconciler of man with God. "By Him are all things," *by Him* referring to the Son. The Holy Ghost is the ultimate cause of all things, since, as the will and all other things finally rest in their end, so He, who is the divine goodness and the mutual love of the Father and Son, completes and perfects, by His strong yet gentle power, the secret work of man's eternal salvation. "In Him are all things," *in Him* referring to the Holy Ghost.

THE HOLY GHOST AND THE INCARNATION

Having thus paid the due tribute of faith and worship owing to the Blessed Trinity, and which ought to be more and more inculcated upon the Christian people, We now turn to the exposition of the power of the Holy Ghost. And, first of all, we must look to Christ, the Founder of the Church and Redeemer of our race. Among the external operations of God, the highest of all is the mystery of the Incarnation of the Word, in which the splendor of the divine perfections shines forth so brightly that nothing more sublime can even be imagined, nothing else could have been more salutary to the human race. Now this work, although belonging to the whole Trinity, is still appropriated especially to the Holy Ghost, so that the gospels thus speak of the Blessed Virgin: *She was found with child of the Holy Ghost,* and *that which is conceived in her is of the Holy Ghost.*** And this is rightly attributed to Him who is the Love of the Father and the Son, since this *great mystery of piety*† proceeds from the infinite love of God towards man, as St. John tells us: *God so loved the world as to give His only begotten son.*†† Moreover, human nature was thereby elevated to a *personal* union with the Word; and this dignity is given, not on account of any merits, but entirely and absolutely through grace, and therefore, as it were, through the special gift of the Holy Ghost. . . .

---

* St. Aug. *De Trin.* 1. iv., c. 20.
** Matt. i. 18, 20.
† 1 Tim. iii. 16.
†† John iii. 16.

THE HOLY GHOST AND THE CHURCH

The Church which, already conceived, came forth from the side of the second Adam in His sleep on the cross, first showed herself before the eyes of men on the great day of Pentecost. On that day the Holy Ghost began to manifest His gifts in the mystic body of Christ, by that miraculous outpouring already foreseen by the prophet Joel,* for the Paraclete "sat upon the apostles as though new spiritual crowns were placed upon their heads in tongues of fire."** . . . Thus was fully accomplished that last promise of Christ to His apostles of sending the Holy Ghost, who was to complete and, as it were, to seal the deposit of doctrine committed to them under His inspiration. *I have yet many things to say to you, but you cannot bear them now; but when He, the Spirit of Truth, shall come, He will teach you all truth.*† For He who is the Spirit of Truth, inasmuch as He proceedeth both from the Father, who is the eternally True, and from the Son, who is the substantial Truth, receiveth from each both His essence and the fulness of all truth. This truth He communicates to His Church, guarding her by His all-powerful help from ever falling into error, and aiding her to foster daily more and more the germs of divine doctrine and to make them fruitful for the welfare of the peoples. And since the welfare of the peoples, for which the Church was established, absolutely requires that this office should be continued for all time, the Holy Ghost perpetually supplies life and strength to preserve and increase the Church. *I will ask the Father, and He will give you another Paraclete, that He may abide with you forever, the Spirit of Truth.*††

By Him the bishops are constituted, and by their ministry are multiplied not only the children, but also the fathers— that is to say, the priests—to rule and feed the Church by that blood wherewith Christ has redeemed her. *The Holy Ghost hath placed you bishops to rule the Church of God, which He hath purchased with His own blood.*§ And both bishops and priests, by the miraculous gift of the Spirit, have the power of absolving sins, according to those words of Christ to the apostles: *Receive ye the Holy Ghost; whose sins you shall forgive they are forgiven them, and whose you shall retain they are retained.* That the Church is a divine insti-

* Joel ii. 28, 29.
** S. Cyril Hier. Catech. 17.
† John xvi. 12, 13.
†† John xiv. 16, 17.
§ Acts xx. 28.

tution is most clearly proved by the splendor and glory of those gifts and graces with which she is adorned, and whose author and giver is the Holy Ghost. Let it suffice to state that, as Christ is the Head of the Church, so is the Holy Ghost her soul. "What the soul is in our body, that is the Holy Ghost in Christ's body, the Church." This being so, no further and fuller "manifestation and revelation of the divine Spirit" may be imagined or expected; for that which now takes place in the Church is the most perfect possible, and will last until that day when the Church herself, having passed through her militant career, shall be taken up into the joy of the saints triumphing in heaven.

Mirae caritatis, May 28, 1902[4]

. . . To examine into the nature and to promote the effects of those manifestations of His wondrous love which, like rays of light, stream forth from Jesus Christ, this, as befits Our sacred office, has ever been and this, with His help to the last breath of Our life, will ever be Our earnest aim and endeavor. And now . . . ever watchful over the vicissitudes of the Church, apostolic charity in a manner compels Us to add one thing more, in order to fill up the measure of what We have already conceived and carried out. This is, to commend to all Christians, more earnestly than heretofore, the all-holy Eucharist, forasmuch as it is a divine gift proceeding from the very Heart of the Redeemer, who "with desire desireth" this singular mode of union with men, a gift most admirably adapted to be the means whereby the salutary fruits of His redemption may be distributed. . . .

Accordingly, Venerable Brethren, it has seemed good to Us to address you on certain points connected with this same mystery, for the defence and honor of which the solicitude of the Church has been so constantly engaged, for which martyrs have given their lives, which has afforded to men of the highest genius a theme to be illustrated by their learning, their eloquence, their skill in all the arts; and this We will do in order to render more clearly evident and more widely known those special characteristics by virtue of which it is so singularly adapted to the needs of these our times. It was towards the close of His mortal life that Christ our Lord left this memorial of His measureless love for men, this powerful means of support *for the life of the world*.[*] And precisely for this reason, We, being so soon to depart from this life, can wish for nothing better than that it may be granted to Us to

[4] Father John Wynne, S. J., *op. cit.*, pp. 518-29.
[*] John vi. 52.

stir up and foster in the hearts of all men the dispositions of mindful gratitude and due devotion towards this wonderful Sacrament, wherein most especially lie, as We hold, the hope and the efficient cause of salvation and of that peace which all men so anxiously seek.

Some there are, no doubt, who will express their surprise that for the manifold troubles and grievous afflictions by which our age is harassed We should have determined to seek for remedies and redress in this quarter rather than elsewhere, and in some, perchance, Our words will excite a certain peevish disgust. But this is only the natural result of pride; for when this vice has taken possession of the heart, it is inevitable that Christian faith, which demands a most willing docility, should languish, and that a murky darkness in regard of divine truths should close in upon the mind; so that in the case of many these words should be made good: *whatever things they know not, they blaspheme.** . . .

To know with an entire faith what is the excellence of the Most Holy Eucharist is in truth to know what that work is which, in the might of His mercy, God, made man, carried out on behalf of the human race. For as a right faith teaches us to acknowledge and to worship Christ as the sovereign cause of our salvation, since He by His wisdom, His laws, His ordinances, His example, and by the shedding of His blood, made all things new; so the same faith likewise teaches us to acknowledge Him and to worship Him as really present in the Eucharist, as verily abiding through all time in the midst of men, in order that their Master, their Good Shepherd, their most acceptable Advocate with the Father, He may impart to them of His own inexhaustible abundance the benefits of that redemption which He has accomplished. Now if any one will seriously consider the benefits which flow from the Eucharist he will understand that conspicuous and chief among them all is that in which the rest, without exception, are included; in a word, it is for men the source of life, of that life which best deserves the name. *The bread which I will give is My flesh, for the life of the world.*** In more than one way, as We have elsewhere declared, is Christ *the life.* He Himself declared that the reason of His advent among men was this, that He might bring them the assured fulness of a more than merely human life. *I am come that they may have life, and may have it more abundantly.*† Every one is aware that no sooner had *the goodness and kindness of God our Saviour appeared*†† than there at once burst forth a certain

* Jude 10.   † John x. 10.
** John vi. 52.   †† Tit. iii. 4.

creative force which issued in a new order of things and pulsed through all the veins of society, civil and domestic. Hence arose new relations between man and man; new rights and new duties, public and private; henceforth a new direction was given to government, to education, to the arts; and most important of all, man's thoughts and energies were turned towards religious truth and the pursuit of holiness. Thus was life communicated to man, a life truly heavenly and divine. . . .

. . . And here it will be opportune to recall to mind on what occasion and in what manner Christ moved and prepared the hearts of men for the worthy and due reception of the living bread which He was about to give them. No sooner had the rumor spread of the miracle which He had wrought on the shores of the lake of Tiberias, when with the multiplied loaves He fed the multitude, than many forthwith flocked to Him in the hope that they, too, perchance, might be the recipients of a like favor. And, just as He had taken occasion from the water which she had drawn from the well to stir up in the Samaritan woman a thirst for that *water which springeth up unto life everlasting,** so now Jesus availed Himself of this opportunity to excite in the minds of the multitude a keen hunger for the bread *which endureth unto life everlasting.*** Nor, as He was careful to explain to them, was the bread which He promised the same as that heavenly manna which had been given to their fathers during their wanderings in the desert, or again the same as that which, to their amazement, they had recently received from Him; but He was Himself that bread: *I*, said He, *am the bread of life.*† And He urges this still further upon them all both by invitation and by precept: *If any man shall eat of this bread, he shall live forever; and the bread which I will give is My flesh, for the life of the world.*†† And in these other words He brings home to them the gravity of the precept: *Amen, amen, I say to you, unless you shall eat the flesh of the Son of man and drink His blood, you shall not have life in you.*§ Away then with the widespread but most mischievous error of those who give it as their opinion that the reception of the Eucharist is in a manner reserved for those narrow-minded persons (as they are deemed) who rid themselves of the cares of the world in order to find rest in some kind of professedly religious life. For this gift, than which nothing can be more excellent or more conductive to salvation, is offered to all

---

* John iv. 14.   † John vi. 48.   § John vi. 54.
** John vi. 27.   †† John vi. 52.

those, whatever their office or dignity may be, who wish—as every one ought to wish—to foster in themselves that life of divine grace whose goal is the attainment of the life of blessedness with God. . . .

. . . For as men and states alike necessarily have their being from God, so they can do nothing good except in God through Jesus Christ, through whom every best and choicest gift has ever proceeded and proceeds. But the source and chief of all these gifts is the venerable Eucharist, which not only nourishes and sustains that life the desire whereof demands our most strenuous efforts, but also enhances beyond measure that dignity of man of which in these days we hear so much. For what can be more honorable or a more worthy object of desire than to be made, as far as possible, sharers and partakers in the divine nature? Now this is precisely what Christ does for us in the Eucharist, wherein, after having raised man by the operation of His grace to a supernatural state, He yet more closely associates and unites him with Himself. For there is this difference between the food of the body and that of the soul, that whereas the former is changed into our substance, the latter changes us into its own; so that St. Augustine makes Christ Himself say: "You shall not change Me into yourself as you do the food of your body, but you shall be changed into me."*

. . . The Eucharist, according to the testimony of the holy Fathers, should be regarded as in a manner a continuation and extension of the Incarnation. For in and by it the substance of the Incarnate Word is united with individual men, and the supreme Sacrifice offered on Calvary is in a wondrous manner renewed, as was signified beforehand by Malachy in the words: *In every place there is sacrifice, and there is offered to My name a pure oblation.*** And this miracle, itself the very greatest of its kind, is accompanied by innumerable other miracles; for here all the laws of nature are suspended; the whole substance of the bread and wine are changed into the body and the blood; the species of bread and wine are sustained by the divine power without the support of any underlying substance; the body of Christ is present in many places at the same time, that is to say, wherever the Sacrament is consecrated. . . .

To this it must be added that by this same Sacrament our hope of everlasting blessedness, based on our trust in the divine assistance, is wonderfully strengthened. For the edge of that longing for happiness which is so deeply rooted in the hearts of all men from their birth is whetted even more and

* Confessions 1. vii., c. x.
** Mal. i. 11.

more by the experience of the deceitfulness of earthly goods, by the unjust violence of wicked men, and by all those other afflictions to which mind and body are subject. Now the venerable Sacrament of the Eucharist is both the source and the pledge of blessedness and of glory, and this, not for the soul alone, but for the body also. For it enriches the soul with an abundance of heavenly blessings, and fills it with a sweet joy which far surpasses man's hope and expectations; it sustains him in adversity, strengthens him in the spiritual combat, preserves him for life everlasting, and as a special provision for the journey accompanies him thither. And in the frail and perishable body that divine Host, which is the immortal body of Christ, implants a principle of resurrection, a seed of immortality, which one day must germinate. That to this source man's soul and body will be indebted for both these boons has been the constant teaching of the Church, which has dutifully reaffirmed the affirmation of Christ: *He that eateth My flesh and drinketh My blood hath everlasting life; and I will raise him up at the last day.**

In connection with this matter it is of importance to consider that in the Eucharist, seeing that it is instituted by Christ as "a perpetual memorial of His passion,"** is proclaimed to the Christian the necessity of a salutary self-chastisement. For Jesus said to those first priests of His: *Do this in memory of Me;*† that is to say, do this for the commemoration of My pains, My sorrows, My grievous afflictions, My death upon the cross. Wherefore this Sacrament is at the same time a sacrifice, seasonable throughout the entire period of our penance; and it is likewise a standing exhortation to all manner of toil, and a solemn and severe rebuke to those carnal pleasures which some are not ashamed so highly to praise and extol: *As often as ye shall eat this bread, and drink this chalice, ye shall announce the death of the Lord, until He come.*††

. . . Nor is it possible that there should be any lack of charity among men, or rather it must needs be enkindled and flourish, if man would but ponder well the charity which Christ has shown in this Sacrament. For in it He has not only given a splendid manifestation of His power and wisdom, but "has in a manner poured out the riches of His divine love towards men."§ Having before our eyes this noble example set us by Christ, who bestows on us all that He has, assuredly

* John vi. 55.
** Opusc. lvii. Offic. de festo Corporis Christi.
† Luke xxii. 18.
†† 1 Cor. xi. 26.
§ Conc. Trid., Sess. XIII. De Euch. c. ii.

we ought to love and help one another to the utmost, being daily more closely united by the strong bond of brotherhood. . . .

Besides all this, the grace of mutual charity among the living, which derives from the Sacrament of the Eucharist so great an increase of strength, is further extended by virtue of the sacrifice to all those who are numbered in the communion of saints. For the communion of saints, as every one knows, is nothing but the mutual communication of help, expiation, prayers, blessings, among all the faithful, who, whether they have already attained to the heavenly country, or are detained in the purgatorial fire, or are yet exiles here on earth, all enjoy the common franchise of that city whereof Christ is the head, and the constitution.

[The twelve great social encyclicals of Pope Leo XIII, which form the so-called "Leonine Corpus," are readily available in many editions, and have recently been quite admirably edited, with a splendid introduction and copious notes, by Professor Étienne Gilson, one of the most distinguished Catholic scholars of our times.[5]

Rerum Novarum (of new things), generally called "Of the Condition of the Working Classes," is the most famous of the Leonine Corpus. It is the Church's complete answer to *Das Kapital* of Marx, and, indeed, to Communism and Socialism in whatever forms. It has been quoted, commented on, and printed many times, and is required reading for any student of economic history. It is given here in its entirety.]

Rerum Novarum, May 15, 1891[6]

The Condition of the Working Classes

That the spirit of revolutionary change, which has long been disturbing the nations of the world, should have passed beyond the sphere of politics and made its influence felt in the cognate sphere of practical economics is not surprising. The elements of the conflict now raging are unmistakable in the vast expansion of industrial pursuits and the marvellous discoveries of science; in the changed relations between masters and workmen; in the enormous fortunes of some few individuals, and the utter poverty of the masses; in the increased self-reliance and closer mutual combination of the working classes; as also, finally, in the prevailing moral degeneracy. The momentous gravity of the state of things now obtaining fills every mind

---

[5] *The Church Speaks to the Modern World:* The Social Teachings of Leo XIII. New York: Doubleday & Co., (Image Books), 1954.
[6] Father John Wynne, S.J., *op. cit.*, pp. 208-48.

with painful apprehension; wise men are discussing it; practical men are proposing schemes; popular meetings, legislatures, and rulers of nations are all busied with it—and actually there is no question which has taken a deeper hold on the public mind.

Therefore, Venerable Brethren, as on former occasions when it seemed opportune to refute false teaching, We have addressed you in the interests of the Church and of the commonweal, and have issued Letters bearing on "Political Power," "Human Liberty," "The Christian Constitution of the State," and like matters, so have We thought it expedient now to speak on THE CONDITION OF THE WORKING CLASSES. It is a subject on which We have already touched more than once, incidentally. But in the present Letter, the responsibility of the Apostolic office urges us to treat the question of set purpose and in detail, in order that no misapprehension may exist as to the principles which truth and justice dictate for its settlement. The discussion is not easy, nor is it void of danger. It is no easy matter to define the relative rights and mutual duties of the rich and of the poor, of capital and of labor. And the danger lies in this, that crafty agitators are intent on making use of these differences of opinion to pervert men's judgments and to stir up the people to revolt.

But all agree, and there can be no question whatever, that some remedy must be found, and found quickly, for the misery and wretchedness pressing so heavily and unjustly at this moment on the vast majority of the working classes.

For the ancient workingmen's guilds were abolished in the last century, and no other organization took their place. Public institutions and the very laws have set aside the ancient religion. Hence by degrees it has come to pass that workingmen have been surrendered, all isolated and helpless, to the hardheartedness of employers and the greed of unchecked competition. The mischief has been increased by rapacious usury, which, although more than once condemned by the Church, is nevertheless, under a different guise, but with the like injustice, still practised by covetous and grasping men. To this must be added the custom of working by contract, and the concentration of so many branches of trade in the hands of a few individuals; so that a small number of very rich men have been able to lay upon the teeming masses of the laboring poor a yoke little better than that of slavery itself.

To remedy these wrongs the Socialists, working on the poor man's envy of the rich, are striving to do away with private property, and contend that individual possessions should become the common property of all, to be administered by the State or by municipal bodies. They hold that by thus transferring property from private individuals to the community, the present mischievous state of things will be set to rights, inasmuch as each citizen will then get his fair share of whatever there is to enjoy. But their contentions are so clearly powerless to end the controversy that were they carried into effect the workingman himself would be among the first to suffer. They are, moreover, emphatically unjust, because they would rob the lawful possessor, bring State action into a sphere not within its competence, and create utter confusion in the community.

It is surely undeniable that, when a man engages in remunerative labor, the impelling reason and motive of his work is to obtain property, and thereafter to hold it as his very own. If one man hires out to another his strength or skill, he does so for the purpose of receiving in return what is necessary for sustenance and education; he therefore expressly intends to acquire a right full and real, not only to the remuneration, but also to the disposal of such remuneration, just as he pleases. Thus, if he lives sparingly, saves money, and, for greater security, invests his savings in land, the land, in such case, is only his wages under another form; and, consequently, a workingman's little estate thus purchased should be as completely at his full disposal as are the wages he received for his labor. But it is precisely in such power of disposal that ownership obtains, whether the property consist of land or chattels. Socialists, therefore, by endeavoring to transfer the possessions of individuals to the community at large, strike at the interests of every wage-earner, since they would deprive him of the liberty of disposing of his wages, and thereby of all hope and possibility of increasing his stock and of bettering his condition in life.

What is of far greater moment, however, is the fact that the remedy they propose is manifestly against justice. For every man has by nature the right to possess property as his own. This is one of the chief points of distinction between man and the animal creation, for the brute has no power of self-direction, but is governed by two main instincts, which keep his powers on the alert, impel him to develop them in a fitting manner, and stimulate and determine him to action without any power of choice. One of these instincts is self-preservation, the other the propagation of the species. But both can attain their purpose by means of things which lie within range; beyond their verge the brute creation cannot go, for they are moved to action by their senses only, and in the special direction which these suggest. But with man it is wholly different. He possesses, on the one hand, the full perfection of the animal being, and hence enjoys, at least as much as the rest of the animal kind, the fruition of things material. But animal nature, however perfect, is far from representing the human being in its completeness, and is in truth but humanity's humble hand-maid, made to serve and to obey. It is the mind, or reason, which is the predominant element in us who are human creatures; it is this which renders a human being human, and distinguishes him essentially and generically from the brute. And on this very account—that man alone among the animal creation is endowed with reason—it must be within his right to possess things not merely for temporary and momentary use, as other living things do, but to have and to hold them in stable and permanent possession; he must have not only things that perish in the use of them, but those also which, though they have been reduced into use, remain his own for further use.

This becomes still more clearly evident if man's nature be considered a little more deeply. For man, fathoming by his faculty of reason matters without number, and linking the future with the present, becoming, furthermore, by taking enlightened forethought, master of his own acts, guides his ways under the eternal law and the power of God, whose providence governs all things. Wherefore it is in his power to exercise his choice not only as to matters that regard his present welfare, but also about those which he deems may be for his advantage in time yet to come. Hence man not only can possess the fruits of the earth, but also the very soil, in-asmuch as from the produce of the earth he has to lay by provision for the future. Man's needs do not die out, but recur; although satisfied today they demand fresh supplies for tomorrow. Nature accordingly owes to man a storehouse that shall never fail, affording the daily supply for his daily wants. And this he finds solely in the inexhaustible fertility of the earth.

Neither do we, at this stage, need to bring into action the in-terference of the State. Man precedes the State, and possesses, prior to the formation of any State, the right of providing for the sustenance of his body. Now to affirm that God has given the earth for the use and enjoyment of the whole human race is not to deny that private property is lawful. For God has granted the earth to mankind in general, not in the sense that all without distinction can deal with it as they like, but rather that no part of it has been assigned to any one in particular, and that the limits of private possession have been left to be fixed by man's own industry, and by the laws of individual races. Moreover, the earth, even though apportioned among private owners, ceases not thereby to minister to the needs of all, inasmuch as there is no one who does not sustain life from what the land produces. Those who do not possess the soil, contribute their labor; hence it may truly be said that all human subsistence is derived either from labor on one's own land, or from some toil, some calling which is paid for either in the produce of the land itself, or in that which is exchanged for what the land brings forth.

Here, again, we have further proof that private ownership is in accordance with the law of nature. Truly, that which is required for the preservation of life, and for life's well-being, is produced in great abundance from the soil, but not until man has brought it into cultivation and expended upon it his solicitude and skill. Now, when man thus turns the activity of his mind and the strength of his body towards procuring the fruits of nature, by such act he makes his own that portion of nature's field which he cultivates—that portion on which he leaves, as it were, the impress of his individuality; and it cannot but be just that he should possess that portion as his very own, and have a right to hold it without any one being justified in violating that right. [D-1938 *et seq.*]

So strong and convincing are these arguments, that it seems amazing that some should now be setting up anew certain obsolete opinions in opposition to what is here laid down. They assert that it is right for private persons to have the use of the soil and its various fruits, but that it is unjust for any one to possess outright either the land on which he has built, or the estate which he has brought under cultivation. But those who deny these rights do not perceive that they are defrauding man of what his own labor has produced. For the soil which is tilled and cultivated with toil and skill utterly changes its conditions: it was wild before, now it is fruitful; was barren, but now brings forth in abundance. That which has thus altered and improved the land becomes so truly part of itself as to be in great measure indistinguishable and inseparable from it. Is it just that the fruit of a man's own sweat and labor should be possessed and enjoyed by any one else? As effects follow their cause, so is it just and right that the results of labor should belong to those who have bestowed their labor.

With reason, then, the common opinion of mankind, little affected by the few dissentients who have contended for the opposite view, has found in the careful study of nature, and in the laws of nature, the foundations of the division of property, and the practice of all ages has consecrated the principle of private ownership, as being pre-eminently in conformity with human nature, and as conducing in the most unmistakable manner to the peace and tranquillity of human existence. The same principle is confirmed and enforced by the civil laws—laws which, so long as they are just, derive from the law of nature their binding force. The authority of the divine law adds its sanction, forbidding us in severest terms even to covet that which is another's:—*Thou shalt not covet thy neighbor's wife; nor his house, nor his field, nor his man-servant, nor his maid-servant, nor his ox, nor his ass, nor any-thing which is his.*[1]

The rights here spoken of, belonging to each individual man, are seen in much stronger light when considered in relation to man's social and domestic obligations. In choosing a state of life, it is indisputable that all are at full liberty to follow the counsel of Jesus Christ as to observing virginity, or to bind themselves by the marriage tie. No human law can abolish the natural and original right of marriage, nor in any way limit the chief and principal purpose of marriage, ordained by God's authority from the beginning. *Increase and multiply.*[2] Hence we have the family; the "society" of a man's house—a society limited indeed in numbers, but no less a true "society," anterior to every kind of State or nation, invested with rights and duties of its own, totally independent of the civil community.

The right of property, therefore, which has been proved to belong naturally to individual persons, must in like wise belong to a man in his capacity of head of a family; nay, such person must possess this right so much the more clearly in proportion as his position multiplies his duties. For it is a most sacred law of nature that a father should provide food and all necessaries for those whom he has begotten; and, similarly, nature dictates that a man's children, who carry on, so to speak, and continue his own personality, should be by him provided with all that is needful to enable them to keep themselves honorably from want and misery amid the uncertainties of this mortal life. Now in no other way can a father effect this except by the ownership of lucrative property, which he can transmit to his children by inheritance. A family, no less than a State, is, as we have said, a true society, governed by a power within its sphere, that is to say, by the father. Provided, therefore, the limits which are prescribed by the very purposes for which it exists be not transgressed, the family has at least equal rights with the State in the choice and pursuit of the things needful to its preservation and its just liberty.

We say, at least equal rights; for inasmuch as the domestic household is antecedent, as well in idea as in fact, to the gathering of men into a community, the family must neces-sarily have rights and duties which are prior to those of the Community, and founded more immediately in nature. If the citizens of a State—in other words the families—on entering into association and fellowship, were to experience at the hands of the State hindrance instead of help, and were to find their

[1] Deuteronomy v. 21.　　　　[2] Genesis i. 28.

rights attacked instead of being upheld, such association should be held in detestation, rather than be an object of desire.

The contention, then, that the civil government should at its option intrude into and exercise intimate control over the family and the household, is a great and pernicious error. True, if a family finds itself in exceeding distress, utterly deprived of the counsel of friends, and without any prospect of extricating itself, it is right that extreme necessity be met by public aid, since each family is a part of the commonwealth. In like manner, if within the precincts of the household there occur grave disturbance of mutual rights, public authority should intervene to force each party to yield to the other its proper due; for this is not to deprive citizens of their rights, but justly and properly to safeguard and strengthen them. But the rulers of the State must go no further: here nature bids them stop. Paternal authority can be neither abolished nor absorbed by the State; for it has the same source as human life itself. "The child belongs to the father," and is, as it were, the continuation of the father's personality; and, speaking strictly, the child takes its place in civil society, not of its own right, but in its quality as member of the family in which it is born. And for the very reason that "the child belongs to the father," it is, as St. Thomas of Aquin says, "before it attains the use of free-will, under power and charge of its parents."[3] The Socialists, therefore, in setting aside the parent and setting up a State supervision, act *against natural justice,* and break into pieces the stability of all family life.

And not only is such interference unjust, but it is quite certain to harass and worry all classes of citizens, and subject them to odious and intolerable bondage. It would throw open the door to envy, to mutual invective, and to discord; the sources of wealth themselves would run dry, for no one would have any interest in exerting his talents or his industry; and that ideal equality about which they entertain pleasant dreams would be in reality the levelling down of all to a like condition of misery and degradation.

Hence it is clear that the main tenet of Socialism, community of goods, must be utterly rejected, since it only injures those whom it would seem meant to benefit, is directly contrary to the natural rights of mankind, and would introduce confusion and disorder into the commonweal. The first and most fundamental principle, therefore, if one would undertake to alleviate the condition of the masses, must be the inviolability of private property. This being established, we proceed to show where the remedy sought for must be found.

We approach the subject with confidence, and in the exercise

[3] St. Thomas, Summa Theologica, 2a 2æ, Q. x. Art. 12.

of the rights which manifestly appertain to us, for no practical solution of this question will be found apart from the intervention of Religion and of the Church. It is We who are the chief guardian of Religion and the chief dispenser of what pertains to the Church, and We must not by silence neglect the duty incumbent on Us. Doubtless this most serious question demands the attention and the efforts of others besides ourselves —to wit, of the rulers of States, of employers of labor, of the wealthy, aye, of the working classes themselves, for whom We are pleading. But We affirm without hesitation that all the striving of men will be vain if they leave out the Church. It is the Church that insists, on the authority of the Gospel, upon those teachings whereby the conflict can be brought to an end, or rendered, at least, far less bitter; the Church uses her efforts not only to enlighten the mind but to direct by her precepts the life and conduct of each and all; the Church improves and betters the condition of the workingman by means of numerous useful organizations; does her best to enlist the services of all ranks in discussing and endeavoring to meet, in the most practical way, the claims of the working classes; and acts from the positive view that for these purposes recourse should be had, in due measure and degree, to the intervention of the law and of State authority.

Let it, then, be taken as granted, in the first place, that the condition of things human must be endured, for it is impossible to reduce civil society to one dead level. Socialists may in that intent do their utmost, but all striving against nature is in vain. There naturally exist among mankind manifold differences of the most important kind; people differ in capacity, skill, health, strength; and unequal fortune is a necessary result of unequal condition. Such inequality is far from being disadvantageous either to individuals or to the community. Social and public life can only be maintained by means of various kinds of capacity for business and the playing of many parts; and each man, as a rule, chooses the part which suits his own peculiar domestic condition. As regards bodily labor, even had man never fallen from *the state of innocence,* he would not have remained wholly unoccupied; but that which would then have been his free choice and his delight became afterwards compulsory, and the painful expiation for his disobedience. *Cursed be the earth in thy work; in thy labor thou shalt eat of it all the days of thy life.*[4] In like manner, the other pains and hardships of life will have no end or cessation on earth; for the consequences of sin are bitter and hard to bear, and they must accompany man so long as life lasts. To suffer and to endure, therefore, is the lot of

[4] Genesis iii. 17.

humanity; let them strive as they may, no strength and no artifice will ever succeed in banishing from human life the ills and troubles which beset it. If any there are who pretend differently—who hold out to a hard-pressed people the boon of freedom from pain and trouble, and undisturbed repose, and constant enjoyment—they delude the people and impose upon them, and their lying promises will only one day bring forth evils worse than the present. Nothing is more useful than to look upon the world as it really is—and at the same time to seek elsewhere, as we have said, for the solace to its troubles.

The great mistake made in regard to the matter now under consideration is to take up with the notion that class is naturally hostile to class, and that the wealthy and the working-men are intended by nature to live in mutual conflict. So irrational and so false is this view, that the direct contrary is the truth. Just as the symmetry of the human frame is the resultant of the disposition of the bodily members, so in a State is it ordained by nature that these two classes should dwell in harmony and agreement, and should, as it were, groove into one another, so as to maintain the balance of the body politic. Each needs the other: Capital cannot do without Labor, nor Labor without Capital. Mutual agreement results in pleasantness of life and the beauty of good order; while perpetual conflict necessarily produces confusion and savage barbarity. Now, in preventing such strife as this, and in uprooting it, the efficacy of Christian institutions is marvellous and manifold. First of all, there is no intermediary more powerful than Religion (whereof the Church is the interpreter and guardian) in drawing the rich, and the poor bread-winners, together, by reminding each class of its duties to the other, and especially of the obligations of justice. Thus Religion teaches the laboring man and the artisan to carry out honestly and fairly all equitable agreements freely entered into; never to injure the property, nor to outrage the person, of an employer; never to resort to violence in defending their own cause, nor to engage in riot or disorder; and to have nothing to do with men of evil principles, who work upon the people with artful promises, and excite foolish hopes which usually end in useless regrets, followed by insolvency. Religion teaches the wealthy owner and the employer that their work-people are not to be accounted their bondsmen; that in every man they must respect his dignity and worth as a man and as a Christian; that labor is not a thing to be ashamed of, if we lend ear to right reason and to Christian philosophy, but is an honorable calling, enabling a man to sustain his life in a way upright and creditable; and that it is shameful and inhuman to treat men like chattels to make money by, or to look upon them merely as so much muscle or physical power. Again, therefore, the Church teaches that, as Religion and things spiritual and mental are among the workingman's main concerns, the employer is bound to see that the worker has time for his religious duties; that he be not exposed to corrupting influences and dangerous occasions; and that he be not led away to neglect his home and family, or to squander his earnings. Furthermore, the employer must never tax his workpeople beyond their strength, or employ them in work unsuited to their sex or age. His great and principal duty is to give every one a fair wage. Doubtless, before deciding whether wages are adequate, many things have to be considered; but wealthy owners and all masters of labor should be mindful of this—that to exercise pressure upon the indigent and the destitute for the sake of gain, and to gather one's profit out of the need of another, is condemned by all laws, human and divine. To defraud any one of wages that are his due is a crime which cries to the avenging anger of Heaven. *Behold, the hire of the laborers . . . which by fraud hath been kept back by you, crieth aloud; and the cry of them hath entered into the ears of the Lord of Sabaoth.*[5] Lastly, the rich must religiously refrain from cutting down the workmen's earnings, whether by force, by fraud, or by usurious dealing; and with all the greater reason because the laboring man is, as a rule, weak and unprotected, and because his slender means should in proportion to their scantiness be accounted sacred.

Were these precepts carefully obeyed and followed out, would they not be sufficient of themselves to keep under all strife and all its causes?

But the Church, with Jesus Christ as her Master and Guide, aims higher still. She lays down precepts yet more perfect, and tries to bind class to class in friendliness and good feeling. The things of earth cannot be understood or valued aright without taking into consideration the life to come, the life that will know no death. Exclude the idea of futurity, and forthwith the very notion of what is good and right would perish; nay, the whole scheme of the universe would become a dark and unfathomable mystery. The great truth which we learn from Nature herself is also the grand Christian dogma on which Religion rests as on its foundation—that when we have given up this present life, then shall we really begin to live. God has not created us for the perishable and transitory things of earth, but for things heavenly and everlasting; He has given us this world as a place of exile, and not as our abiding-place. As for riches and the other things which men call good

---

[5] St. James v. 4.

and desirable, whether we have them in abundance, or lack them altogether—so far as eternal happiness is concerned—it matters little; the only important thing is to use them aright. Jesus Christ, when He redeemed us with *plentiful redemption,* took not away the pains and sorrows which in such large proportion are woven together in the web of our mortal life. He transformed them into motives of virtue and occasions of merit: and no man can hope for eternal reward unless he follow in the blood-stained footprints of his Saviour. *If we suffer with Him, we shall also reign with Him.*[6] Christ's labors and sufferings, accepted of His own free-will, have marvellously sweetened all suffering and all labor. And not only by His example, but by His grace and by the hope held forth of everlasting recompense, has He made pain and grief more easy to endure; *for that which is at present momentary and light of our tribulation, worketh for us above measure exceedingly an eternal weight of glory.*[7]

Therefore those whom fortune favors are warned that freedom from sorrow and abundance of earthly riches are no warrant for the bliss that shall never end, but rather are obstacles;[8] that the rich should tremble at the threatenings of Jesus Christ—threatenings so unwonted in the mouth of Our Lord[9]—and that a most strict account must be given to the Supreme Judge for all we possess. The chief and most excellent rule for the right use of money is one which the heathen philosophers hinted at, but which the Church has traced out clearly, and has not only made known to men's minds, but has impressed upon their lives. It rests on the principle that it is one thing to have a right to the possession of money, and another to have a right to use money as one wills. Private ownership, as we have seen, is the natural right of man; and to exercise that right, especially as members of society, is not only lawful, but absolutely necessary. "It is lawful," says St. Thomas of Aquin, "for a man to hold private property; and it is also necessary for the carrying on of human existence."[10] But if the question be asked, How must one's possessions be used? the Church replies without hesitation in the words of the same holy Doctor: "Man should not consider his outward possessions as his own, but as common to all, so as to share them without hesitation when others are in need. Whence the Apostle saith, Command the rich of this world . . . to offer with no stint, to apportion largely."[11] True, no one is commanded to distribute to others that which is required for his own needs and those of his household; nor even to give away what is reasonably required to keep up

[6] 2 Tim. ii. 12.
[7] 2 Cor. iv. 17.
[8] St. Matt. xix. 23, 24.
[9] St. Luke vi. 24, 25.
[10] 2a 2æ Q. lxvi. Art. 2.
[11] Ibid. Q. lxv. Art. 2.

becomingly his condition in life; "for no one ought to live other than becomingly."[12] But when what necessity demands has been supplied, and one's standing fairly taken thought for, it becomes a duty to give to the indigent out of what remains over. *Of that which remaineth, give alms.*[13] It is a duty, not of justice (save in extreme cases), but of Christian charity —a duty not enforced by human law. But the laws and judgments of men must yield place to the laws and judgments of Christ the true God, who in many ways urges on His followers the practice of almsgiving—*It is more blessed to give than to receive;*[14] and who will count a kindness done or refused to the poor as done or refused to Himself—*As long as you did it to one of My least brethren, you did it to Me.*[15] To sum up, then, what has been said: Whoever has received from the divine bounty a large share of temporal blessings, whether they be external and corporeal, or gifts of the mind, has received them for the purpose of using them for the perfecting of his own nature, and, at the same time, that he may employ them, as the steward of God's providence, for the benefit of others. "He that hath a talent," says St. Gregory the Great, "let him see that he hide it not; he that hath abundance, let him quicken himself to mercy and generosity; he that hath art and skill, let him do his best to share the use and the utility thereof with his neighbor."[16]

As for those who possess not the gifts of fortune, they are taught by the Church that in God's sight poverty is no disgrace, and that there is nothing to be ashamed of in seeking one's bread by labor. This is enforced by what we see in Christ Himself, who *whereas He was rich, for our sakes became poor;*[17] and who, being the Son of God, and God Himself, chose to seem and to be considered the son of a carpenter— nay, did not disdain to spend a great part of His life as a carpenter Himself. *Is not this the carpenter, the son of Mary?*[18] From contemplation of this divine exemplar, it is more easy to understand that the true worth and nobility of man lies in his moral qualities, that is, in virtue; that virtue is moreover the common inheritance of men, equally within the reach of high and low, rich and poor; and that virtue, and virtue alone, wherever found, will be followed by the rewards of everlasting happiness. Nay, God Himself seems to incline rather to those who suffer misfortune; for Jesus Christ calls the poor

[12] Ibid. Q. xxxii. Art. 6.
[13] St. Luke xi. 41.
[14] Acts xx. 35.
[15] St. Matt. xxv. 40.
[16] St. Gregory the Great, Hom. ix. in Evangel. n. 7.
[17] 2 Cor. viii. 9.
[18] St. Mark vi. 3.

"blessed";[19] He lovingly invites those in labor and grief to come to Him for solace;[20] and He displays the tenderest charity towards the lowly and the oppressed. These reflections cannot fail to keep down the pride of those who are well to do, and to embolden the spirit of the afflicted; to incline the former to generosity and the latter to meek resignation. Thus the separation which pride would set up tends to disappear, nor will it be difficult to make rich and poor join hands in friendly concord.

But, if Christian precepts prevail, the respective classes will not only be united in the bonds of friendship, but also in those of brotherly love. For they will understand and feel that all men are children of the same common Father, who is God; that all have alike the same last end, which is God Himself, who alone can make either men or angels absolutely and perfectly happy; that each and all are redeemed and made sons of God, by Jesus Christ, *the first-born among many brethren;* that the blessings of nature and the gifts of grace belong to the whole human race in common, and that from none except the unworthy is withheld the inheritance of the kingdom of heaven. *If sons, heirs also; heirs indeed of God, and co-heirs of Christ.*[21]

Such is the scheme of duties and of rights which is shown forth to the world by the Gospel. Would it not seem that, were society penetrated with ideas like these, strife must quickly cease?

But the Church, not content with pointing out the remedy, also applies it. For the Church does her utmost to teach and to train men, and to educate them; and by the intermediary of her bishops and clergy diffuses her salutary teachings far and wide. She strives to influence the mind and the heart so that all may willingly yield themselves to be formed and guided by the commandments of God. It is precisely in this fundamental and momentous matter, on which everything depends, that the Church possesses a power peculiarly her own. The agencies which she employs are given to her by Jesus Christ Himself for the very purpose of reaching the hearts of men, and derive their efficiency from God. They alone can reach the innermost heart and conscience, and bring men to act from a motive of duty, to resist their passions and appetites, to love God and their fellow-men with a love that is singular and supreme, and to break down courageously every barrier which impedes the way of a life of virtue.

On this subject we need but recall for one moment the examples recorded in history. Of these facts there cannot be

[19] St. Matt. v. 3: Blessed are the poor in spirit.
[20] St. Matt. xi. 28: Come to Me all you that labor and are burdened, and I will refresh you.
[21] Rom. viii. 17.

any shadow of doubt: for instance, that civil society was renovated in every part by the teachings of Christianity; that in the strength of that renewal the human race was lifted up to better things—nay, that it was brought back from death to life, and to so excellent a life that nothing more perfect had been known before, or will come to be known in the ages that have yet to be. Of this beneficent transformation Jesus Christ was at once the First Cause and the final end; as from Him all came, so to Him was all to be brought back. For when the human race, by the light of the Gospel message, came to know the grand mystery of the Incarnation of the Word and the redemption of man, at once the life of Jesus Christ, God and Man, pervaded every race and nation, and interpenetrated them with His faith, His precepts and His laws. And if society is to be healed now, in no other way can it be healed save by a return to Christian life and Christian institutions. When a society is perishing, the wholesome advice to give to those who would restore it is to recall it to the principles from which it sprang; for the purpose and perfection of an association is to aim at and to attain that for which it was formed; and its efforts should be put in motion and inspired by the end and object which originally gave it being. Hence to fall away from its primal constitution implies disease; to go back to it, recovery. And this may be asserted with utmost truth both of the State in general and of that body of its citizens—by far the great majority—who sustain life by their labor.

Neither must it be supposed that the solicitude of the Church is so preoccupied with the spiritual concerns of her children as to neglect their temporal and earthly interests. Her desire is that the poor, for example, should rise above poverty and wretchedness, and better their condition in life; and for this she makes a strong endeavor. By the very fact that she calls men to virtue and forms them to its practice, she promotes this in no slight degree. Christian morality, when adequately and completely practised, leads of itself to temporal prosperity, for it merits the blessing of that God who is the source of all blessings; it powerfully restrains the greed of possession and the thirst for pleasure—twin plagues, which too often make a man who is void of self-restraint miserable in the midst of abundance;[22] it makes men supply for the lack of means through economy, teaching them to be content with frugal living, and further, keeping them out of the reach of those vices which devour not small incomes merely, but large fortunes, and dissipate many a goodly inheritance.

The Church, moreover, intervenes directly in behalf of the poor by setting on foot and maintaining many associations

---

[22] The desire of money is the root of all evils.—1 Tim. vi. 10.

which she knows to be efficient for the relief of poverty. Herein again she has always succeeded so well as to have even extorted the praise of her enemies. Such was the ardor of brotherly love among the earliest Christians that numbers of those who were in better circumstances despoiled themselves of their possessions in order to relieve their brethren; whence *neither was there any one needy among them.*[23] To the order of Deacons, instituted in that very intent, was committed by the apostles the charge of the daily doles; and the Apostle Paul, though burdened with the solicitude of all the churches, hesitated not to undertake laborious journeys in order to carry the alms of the faithful to the poorer Christians. Tertullian calls these contributions, given voluntarily by Christians in their assemblies, deposits of piety; because, to cite his own words, they were employed "in feeding the needy, in burying them, in the support of youths and maidens destitute of means and deprived of their parents, in the care of the aged, and the relief of the shipwrecked."[24]

Thus by degrees came into existence the patrimony which the Church has guarded with religious care as the inheritance of the poor. Nay, to spare them the shame of begging, the common mother of rich and poor has exerted herself to gather together funds for the support of the needy. The Church has aroused everywhere the heroism of charity, and has established congregations of religious and many other useful institutions for help and mercy, so that hardly any kind of suffering could exist which was not afforded relief. At the present day many there are who, like the heathen of old, seek to blame and condemn the Church for such eminent charity. They would substitute in its stead a system of relief organized by the State. But no human expedients will ever make up for the devotedness and self-sacrifice of Christian charity. Charity, as a virtue, pertains to the Church; for virtue it is not, unless it be drawn from the Sacred Heart of Jesus Christ; and whosoever turns his back on the Church cannot be near to Christ.

It cannot, however, be doubted that to attain the purpose we are treating of, not only the Church but all human agencies must concur. All who are concerned in the matter should be of one mind and according to their ability act together. It is with this, as with the Providence that governs the world: the results of causes do not usually take place save where all the causes co-operate.

It is sufficient, therefore, to inquire what part the State should play in the work of remedy and relief.

By the State we here understand, not the particular form

[23] Acts iv. 34.
[24] Apologia Secunda, xxxix.

of government prevailing in this or that nation, but the State as rightly apprehended; that is to say, any government conformable in its institutions to right reason and natural law, and to those dictates of the divine wisdom which we have expounded in the Encyclica on "The Christian Constitution of the State." The foremost duty, therefore, of the rulers of the State should be to make sure that the laws and institutions, the general character and administration of the commonwealth, shall be such as of themselves to realize public wellbeing and private prosperity. This is the proper scope of wise statesmanship and is the work of the heads of the State. Now, a State chiefly prospers and thrives through moral rule, wellregulated family life, respect for religion and justice, the moderation and equal allocation of public taxes, the progress of the arts and of trade, the abundant yield of the land— through everything, in fact, which makes the citizens better and happier. Hereby, then, it lies in the power of a ruler to benefit every class in the State, and amongst the rest to promote to the utmost the interests of the poor; and this in virtue of his office, and without being open to any suspicion of undue interference—since it is the province of the State to consult the common good. And the more that is done for the benefit of the working classes by the general laws of the country, the less need will there be to seek for special means to relieve them.

There is another and deeper consideration which must not be lost sight of. As regards the State, the interests of all, whether high or low, are equal. The poor are members of the national community equally with the rich; they are real component living members which constitute, through the family, the living body; and it need hardly be said that they are in every State very largely in the majority. It would be irrational to neglect one portion of the citizens and favor another; and, therefore, the public administration must duly and solicitously provide for the welfare and the comfort of the working classes; otherwise that law of justice will be violated which ordains that each man shall have his due. To cite the wise words of St. Thomas of Aquin: "As the part and the whole are in a certain sense identical, the part may in some sense claim what belongs to the whole."[25] Among the many and grave duties of rulers who would do their best for the people, the first and chief is to act with strict justice—with that justice which is called by the schoolmen *distributive*—towards each and every class alive.

But although all citizens, without exception, can and ought to contribute to that common good in which individuals share so advantageously to themselves, yet it should not be supposed

[25] 2a 2æ Q. lxi. Art. 1 ad 2.

that all can contribute in the like way and to the same extent. No matter what changes may occur in forms of government, there will ever be differences and inequalities of condition in the State. Society cannot exist or be conceived of without them. Some there must be who devote themselves to the work of the commonwealth, who make the laws or administer justice, or whose advice and authority govern the nation in times of peace and defend it in war. Such men clearly occupy the foremost place in the State, and should be held in highest estimation, for their work concerns most nearly and effectively the general interests of the community. Those who labor at a trade or calling do not promote the general welfare in such measure as this; but they benefit the nation, if less directly, in a most important manner. Still we have insisted that, since the end of society is to make men better, the chief good that society can possess is virtue. Nevertheless, in all well-constituted States it is in no wise a matter of small moment to provide those bodily and external commodities *the use of which is necessary to virtuous action.*[26] And in order to provide such material well-being, the labor of the poor—the exercise of their skill, and the employment of their strength, in the culture of the land and in the workshops of trade—is of great account and quite indispensable. Indeed, their cooperation is in this respect so important that it may be truly said that it is only by the labor of workingmen that States grow rich. Justice, therefore, demands that the interests of the poorer classes should be carefully watched over by the administration, so that they who contribute so largely to the advantage of the community may themselves share in the benefits which they create—that being housed, clothed, and enabled to sustain life, they may find their existence less hard and more endurable. It follows that whatever shall appear to prove conducive to the well-being of those who work should obtain favorable consideration. Let it not be feared that solicitude of this kind will be harmful to any interest; on the contrary, it will be to the advantage of all; for it cannot but be good for the commonwealth to shield from misery those on whom it so largely depends.

We have said that the State must not absorb the individual or the family; both should be allowed free and untrammelled action so far as is consistent with the common good and the interests of others. Rulers should, nevertheless, anxiously safeguard the community and all its members: the community, because the conservation thereof is so emphatically the business of the supreme power that the safety of the commonwealth is not only the first law, but it is a government's whole

---

[26] St. Thomas of Aquin, De Regimine Principum, i. 15.

reason of existence; and the members, because both philosophy and the Gospel concur in laying down that the object of the government of the State should be, not the advantage of the ruler, but the benefit of those over whom he is placed. The gift of authority derives from God, and is, as it were, a participation in the highest of all sovereignties; and should be exercised as the power of God is exercised—with a fatherly solicitude which not only guides the whole but reaches also to details.

Whenever the general interest or any particular class suffers, or is threatened with mischief which can in no other way be met or prevented, the public authority must step in to deal with it. Now, it interests the public, as well as the individual, that peace and good order should be maintained; that family life should be carried on in accordance with God's laws and those of nature; that religion should be reverenced and obeyed; that a high standard of morality should prevail, both in public and private life; that the sanctity of justice should be respected, and that no one should injure another with impunity; that the members of the commonwealth should grow up to man's estate strong and robust, and capable, if need be, of guarding and defending their country. If by a strike, or other combination of workmen, there should be imminent danger of disturbance to the public peace; or if circumstances were such as that among the laboring population the ties of family life were relaxed; if religion were found to suffer through the operatives not having time and opportunity afforded them to practise its duties; if in workshops and factories there were danger to morals through the mixing of the sexes or from other harmful occasions of evil; or if employers laid burdens upon their workmen which were unjust, or degraded them with conditions repugnant to their dignity as human beings; finally, if health were endangered by excessive labor, or by work unsuited to sex or age—in such cases, there can be no question but that, within certain limits, it would be right to invoke the aid and authority of the law. The limits must be determined by the nature of the occasion which calls for the law's interference—the principle being that the law must not undertake more, nor proceed further, than is required for the remedy of the evil or the removal of the mischief.

Rights must be religiously respected wherever they exist; and it is the duty of the public authority to prevent and to punish injury, and to protect every one in the possession of his own. Still, when there is a question of defending the rights of individuals, the poor and helpless have a claim to especial consideration. The richer class have many ways of shielding themselves, and stand less in need of help from the State;

whereas those who are badly off have no resources of their own to fall back upon, and must chiefly depend upon the assistance of the State. And it is for this reason that wage-earners, who are undoubtedly among the weak and necessitous, should be specially cared for and protected by the Government.

Here, however, it is expedient to bring under special notice certain matters of moment. It should ever be borne in mind that the chief thing to be realized is the safeguarding of private property by legal enactment and public policy. Most of all it is essential, amid such a fever of excitement, to keep the multitude within the line of duty; for if all may justly strive to better their condition, neither justice nor the common good allows any individual to seize upon that which belongs to another, or, under the futile and shallow pretext of equality, to lay violent hands on other people's possessions. Most true it is that by far the larger part of the workers prefer to better themselves by honest labor rather than by doing any wrong to others. But there are not a few who are imbued with evil principles and eager for revolutionary change, whose main purpose is to stir up tumult and bring about measures of violence. The authority of the State should intervene to put restraint upon such firebrands, to save the working classes from their seditious arts, and protect lawful owners from spoliation.

When working men have recourse to a strike, it is frequently because the hours of labor are too long, or the work too hard, or because they consider their wages insufficient. The grave inconvenience of this not uncommon occurrence should be obviated by public remedial measures; for such paralyzing of labor not only affects the masters and their work-people alike, but is extremely injurious to trade and to the general interests of the public; moreover, on such occasions, violence and disorder are generally not far distant, and thus it frequently happens that the public peace is imperilled. The laws should forestall and prevent such troubles from arising; they should lend their influence and authority to the removal in good time of the causes which lead to conflicts between employers and employed.

But if owners of property should be made secure, the workingman, in like manner, has property and belongings in respect to which he should be protected; and foremost of all, his soul and mind. Life on earth, however good and desirable in itself, is not the final purpose for which man is created; it is only the way and the means to that attainment of truth and that practice of goodness in which the full life of the soul consists. It is the soul which is made after the image and likeness of God; it is in the soul that the sovereignty resides in virtue whereof man is commanded to rule the creatures below him and to use all the earth and the ocean for his profit and advantage. *Fill the earth and subdue it; and rule over the fishes of the sea, and the fowls of the air, and all living creatures which move upon the earth.*[27] In this respect all men are equal; there is no difference between rich and poor, master and servant, ruler and ruled, *for the same is Lord over all.*[28] No man may with impunity outrage that human dignity which God Himself treats *with reverence,* nor stand in the way of that higher life which is the preparation for the eternal life of heaven. Nay, more: no man has in this matter power over himself. To consent to any treatment which is calculated to defeat the end and purpose of his being is beyond his right; he cannot give up his soul to servitude; for it is not man's own rights which are here in question, but the rights of God, the most sacred and inviolable of rights.

From this follows the obligation of the cessation from work and labor on Sundays and certain holy days. The rest from labor is not to be understood as mere giving way to idleness; much less must it be an occasion for spending money and for vicious indulgence, as many would have it to be; but it should be rest from labor, hallowed by religion. Rest (combined with religious observances), disposes man to forget for a while the business of his every-day life, to turn his thoughts to things heavenly, and to the worship which he so strictly owes to the Eternal Godhead. It is this, above all, which is the reason and motive of Sunday rest; a rest sanctioned by God's great law of the ancient covenant—*Remember thou keep holy the Sabbath day,*[29] and taught to the world by His own mysterious "rest" after the creation of man: *He rested on the seventh day from all His work which He had done.*[30]

If we turn now to things external and corporeal, the first concern of all is to save the poor workers from the cruelty of greedy speculators, who use human beings as mere instruments of money-making. It is neither just nor human so to grind men down with excessive labor as to stupefy their minds and wear out their bodies. Man's powers, like his general nature, are limited, and beyond these limits he cannot go. His strength is developed and increased by use and exercise, but only on condition of due intermission and proper rest. Daily labor, therefore, should be so regulated as not to be protracted over longer hours than strength admits. How many and how long the intervals of rest should be must depend on the nature of the work, on circumstances of time and place, and on the health and strength of the workmen. Those who work in mines and quarries, and extract coal, stone, and metals

[27] Genesis i. 28.   [29] Exod. xx. 8.
[28] Rom. x. 12.   [30] Genesis ii. 2.

from the bowels of the earth, should have shorter hours in proportion as their labor is more severe and trying to health. Then, again, the season of the year should be taken into account; for not infrequently a kind of labor is easy at one time which at another is intolerable or exceedingly difficult. Finally, work which is quite suitable for a strong man cannot reasonably be required from a woman or a child. And, in regard to children, great care should be taken not to place them in workshops and factories until their bodies and minds are sufficiently developed. For just as very rough weather destroys the buds of spring, so does too early an experience of life's hard toil blight the young promise of a child's faculties, and render any true education impossible. Women, again, are not suited for certain occupations; a woman is by nature fitted for home work, and it is that which is best adapted at once to preserve her modesty and to promote the good bringing up of children and the well-being of the family. As a general principle it may be laid down that a workman ought to have leisure and rest proportionate to the wear and tear of his strength; for waste of strength must be repaired by cessation from hard work.

In all agreements between masters and work-people there is always the condition, expressed or understood, that there should be allowed proper rest for soul and body. To agree in any other sense would be against what is right and just; for it can never be just or right to require on the one side, or to promise on the other, the giving up of those duties which a man owes to his God and to himself.

We now approach a subject of great and urgent importance, and one in respect of which, if extremes are to be avoided, right notions are absolutely necessary. Wages, as we are told, are regulated by free consent, and therefore the employer, when he pays what was agreed upon, has done his part and seemingly is not called upon to do anything beyond. The only way, it is said, in which injustice might occur would be if the master refused to pay the whole of the wages, or if the workman should not complete the work undertaken; in such cases the State should intervene, to see that each obtains his due—but not under any other circumstances.

This mode of reasoning is, to a fair-minded man, by no means convincing, for there are important considerations which it leaves out of account altogether. To labor is to exert one's self for the sake of procuring what is necessary for the purposes of life, and chief of all for self-preservation. *In the sweat of thy brow thou shalt eat thy bread.*[31] Hence a man's labor bears two notes or characters. First of all, it is *personal,*

[31] Genesis iii. 19.

inasmuch as the exertion of individual strength belongs to the individual who puts it forth, employing such strength to procure that personal advantage on account of which it was bestowed. Secondly, man's labor is *necessary;* for without the result of labor a man cannot live; and self-preservation is a law of nature, which it is wrong to disobey. Now, were we to consider labor so far as it is *personal* merely, doubtless it would be within the workman's right to accept any rate of wages whatsoever; for in the same way as he is free to work or not, so is he free to accept a small remuneration or even none at all. But this is a mere abstract supposition; the labor of the workingman is not only his personal attribute, but it is *necessary;* and this makes all the difference. The preservation of life is the bounden duty of one and all, and to be wanting therein is a crime. It follows that each one has a right to procure what is required in order to live; and the poor can procure it in no other way than through work and wages.

Let it be then taken for granted that workman and employer should, as a rule, make free agreements, and in particular should agree freely as to the wages; nevertheless, there underlies a dictate of natural justice more imperious and ancient than any bargain between man and man, namely, that remuneration ought to be sufficient to support a frugal and well-behaved wage-earner. If through necessity or fear of a worse evil the workman accept harder conditions because an employer or contractor will afford him no better, he is made the victim of force and injustice. In these and similar questions, however—such as, for example, the hours of labor in different trades, the sanitary precautions to be observed in factories and workshops, etc.—in order to supersede undue interference on the part of the State, especially as circumstances, times, and localities differ so widely, it is advisable that recourse be had to societies or boards such as We shall mention presently, or to some other mode of safeguarding the interests of the wage-earners; the State being appealed to, should circumstances require, for its sanction and protection.

If a workman's wages be sufficient to enable him to maintain himself, his wife, and his children in reasonable comfort, he will not find it difficult, if he be a sensible man, to study economy; and he will not fail, by cutting down expenses, to put by some little savings and thus secure a small income. Nature and reason alike would urge him to this. We have seen that this great labor question cannot be solved save by assuming as a principle that private ownership must be held sacred and inviolable. The law, therefore, should favor ownership, and its policy should be to induce as many as possible of the humbler class to become owners.

Many excellent results will follow from this; and first of all, property will certainly become more equitably divided. For the result of civil change and revolution has been to divide society into two widely differing castes. On the one side there is the party which holds power because it holds wealth; which has in its grasp the whole of labor and trade; which manipulates for its own benefit and its own purposes all the sources of supply, and which is even represented in the councils of the State itself. On the other side there is the needy and powerless multitude, broken down and suffering, and ever ready for disturbance. If working-people can be encouraged to look forward to obtaining a share in the land, the consequence will be that the gulf between vast wealth and sheer poverty will be bridged over, and the respective classes will be brought nearer to one another. A further consequence will result in the greater abundance of the fruits of the earth. Men always work harder and more readily when they work on that which belongs to them; nay, they learn to love the very soil that yields, in response to the labor of their hands, not only food to eat but an abundance of good things for themselves and those that are dear to them. That such a spirit of willing labor would add to the produce of the earth and to the wealth of the community is self-evident. And a third advantage would spring from this: men would cling to the country in which they were born; for no one would exchange his country for a foreign land if his own afforded him the means of living a decent and happy life. These three important benefits, however, can be reckoned on only provided that a man's means be not drained and exhausted by excessive taxation. The right to possess private property is derived from nature, not from man; and the State has the right to control its use in the interests of the public good alone, but by no means to absorb it altogether. The State would therefore be unjust and cruel if under the name of taxation it were to deprive the private owner of more than is fitting.

In the last place—employers and workmen may of themselves effect much in the matter we are treating, by means of such associations and organizations as afford opportune aid to those who are in distress, and which draw the two classes more closely together. Among these may be enumerated societies for mutual help; various benevolent foundations established by private persons to provide for the workman, and for his widow or his orphans, in case of sudden calamity, in sickness, and in the event of death; and what are called "patronages," or institutions for the care of boys and girls, for young people, as well as homes for the aged.

The most important of all are workingmen's unions; for

these virtually include all the rest. History attests what excellent results were brought about by the artificers' guilds of olden times. They were the means of affording not only many advantages to the workmen, but in no small degree of promoting the advancement of art, as numerous monuments remain to bear witness. Such unions should be suited to the requirements of this our age—an age of wider education, of different habits, and of far more numerous requirements in daily life. It is gratifying to know that there are actually in existence not a few associations of this nature, consisting either of workmen alone, or of workmen and employers together; but it were greatly to be desired that they should become more numerous and more efficient. We have spoken of them more than once; yet it will be well to explain here how notably they are needed, to show that they exist of their own right, and what should be their organization and their mode of action.

The consciousness of his own weakness urges man to call in aid from without. We read in the pages of holy writ: *It is better that two should be together than one; for they have the advantage of their society. If one fall he shall be supported by the other. Woe to him that is alone, for when he falleth he hath none to lift him up.*[32] And further: *A brother that is helped by his brother is like a strong city.*[33] It is this natural impulse which binds men together in civil society; and it is likewise this which leads them to join together in associations of citizen with citizen; associations which, it is true, cannot be called societies in the full sense of the word, but which, notwithstanding, *are* societies.

These lesser societies and the society which constitutes the State differ in many respects, because their immediate purpose and aim is different. Civil society exists for the common good, and hence is concerned with the interests of all in general, albeit with individual interests also in their due place and degree. It is therefore called *public* society, because by its agency, as St. Thomas of Aquin says, "Men establish relations in common with one another in the setting up of a commonwealth."[34] But societies which are formed in the bosom of the State are styled *private,* and rightly so, since their immediate purpose is the private advantage of the associates. "Now a private society," says St. Thomas again, "is one which is formed for the purpose of carrying out private objects; as when two or three enter into partnership with the view of trading in common."[35] Private societies, then, although they exist within the

---

[32] Ecclesiastes iv. 9, 10.
[33] Prov. xviii. 19.
[34] Contra impugnantes Dei cultum et religionem, ii.
[35] Ibid.

State, and are severally part of the State, cannot nevertheless be absolutely, and as such, prohibited by the State. For to enter into a "society" of this kind is the natural right of man; and the State is bound to protect natural rights, not to destroy them; and if it forbid its citizens to form associations, it contradicts the very principle of its own existence; for both they and it exist in virtue of the like principle, namely, the natural tendency of man to dwell in society.

There are occasions, doubtless, when it is fitting that the law should intervene to prevent associations; as when men join together for purposes which are evidently bad, unlawful, or dangerous to the State. In such cases public authority may justly forbid the formation of associations, and may dissolve them if they already exist. But every precaution should be taken not to violate the rights of individuals and not to impose unreasonable regulations under pretence of public benefit. For laws only bind when they are in accordance with right reason, and hence with the eternal law of God.[36]

And here we are reminded of the confraternities, societies, and religious orders which have arisen by the Church's authority and the piety of Christian men. The annals of every nation down to our own days bear witness to what they have accomplished for the human race. It is indisputable that on grounds of reason alone such associations, being perfectly blameless in their objects, possess the sanction of the law of nature. In their religious aspect, they claim rightly to be responsible to the Church alone. The rulers of the State accordingly have no rights over them, nor can they claim any share in their control; on the contrary, it is the duty of the State to respect and cherish them, and, if need be, to defend them from attack. It is notorious that a very different course has been followed, more especially in our own times. In many places the State authorities have laid violent hands on these communities, and committed manifold injustice against them; it has placed them under control of the civil law, taken away their rights as corporate bodies, and despoiled them of their property. In such property the Church had her rights, each member of the body had his or her rights, and there were also the rights of those who had founded or endowed these communities for a definite purpose, and furthermore, of those for whose benefit and assistance they had their being. Therefore We cannot refrain from complaining of such spoliation as unjust and fraught with evil results; and with all the more rea-

---

[36] "Human law is law only by virtue of its accordance with right reason; and thus it is manifest that it flows from the eternal law. And in so far as it deviates from right reason it is called an unjust law; in such case it is no law at all, but rather a species of violence."—St. Thomas of Aquin, Summa Theologica, 1a 2æ Q. xciii. art. 3.

son do We complain because, at the very time when the law proclaims that association is free to all, We see that Catholic societies, however peaceful and useful, are hampered in every way, whereas the utmost liberty is conceded to individuals whose purposes are at once hurtful to religion and dangerous to the State.

Associations of every kind, and especially those of working-men, are now far more common than heretofore. As regards many of these there is no need at present to inquire whence they spring, what are their objects, or what the means they employ. There is a good deal of evidence, however, which goes to prove that many of these societies are in the hands of secret leaders, and are managed on principles ill-according with Christianity and the public well-being; and that they do their utmost to get within their grasp the whole field of labor, and force workingmen either to join them or to starve. Under these circumstances Christian workingmen must do one of two things: either join associations in which their religion will be exposed to peril, or form associations among themselves— unite their forces and shake off courageously the yoke of so unrighteous and intolerable an oppression. No one who does not wish to expose man's chief good to extreme risk will for a moment hesitate to say that the second alternative should by all means be adopted.

Those Catholics are worthy of all praise—and they are not a few—who, understanding what the times require, have striven, by various undertakings and endeavors, to better the condition of the working class without any sacrifice of principle being involved. They have taken up the cause of the working-man, and have spared no efforts to better the condition both of families and individuals; to infuse a spirit of equity into the mutual relations of employers and employed; to keep before the eyes of both classes the precepts of duty and the laws of the Gospel—that Gospel which by inculcating self-restraint, keeps men within the bounds of moderation, and tends to establish harmony among the divergent interests, and the various classes which compose the State. It is with such ends in view that we see men of eminence meeting together for discussion, for the promotion of concerted action, and for practical work. Others, again, strive to unite working-men of various grades into associations, help them with their advice and means, and enable them to obtain fitting and profitable employment. The bishops, on their part, bestow their ready good-will and support; and with their approval and guidance many members of the clergy, both secular and regular, labor assiduously in behalf of the spiritual and mental interests of the members of such associations. And there are not wanting Catholics blessed with affluence, who have, as it were, cast in their lot with the wage-earners, and who have spent large sums in founding and widely spreading benefit and insurance societies, by means of which the workingman may without difficulty acquire, through his labor, not only many present advantages but also the certainty of honorable support in days to come. How greatly such manifold and earnest activity has benefited the community at large is too well known to require Us to dwell upon it. We find therein grounds for most cheering hope in the future, provided always that the associations We have described continue to grow and spread, and are well and wisely administered. Let the State watch over these societies of citizens banded together for the exercise of their rights; but let it not thrust itself into their peculiar concerns and their organization; for things move and live by the spirit inspiring them, and may be killed by the rough grasp of a hand from without.

In order, then, that an association may be carried on with unity of purpose and harmony of action, its organization and government should be firm and wise. All such societies, being free to exist, have the further right to adopt such rules and organizations as may best conduce to the attainment of their respective objects. We do not judge it expedient to enter into minute particulars touching the subject of organization: this must depend on national character, on practice and experience, on the nature and aim of the work to be done, on the scope of the various trades and employments, and on other circumstances of fact and of time:—all of which should be carefully considered.

To sum up, then, We may lay it down as a general and lasting law, that workingmen's associations should be so organized and governed as to furnish the best and most suitable means for attaining what is aimed at; that is to say, for helping each individual member to better his condition to the utmost in body, mind, and property. It is clear that they must pay special and chief attention to the duties of religion and morality, and that their internal discipline must be guided very strictly by these weighty considerations; otherwise they would lose wholly their special character, and end by becoming little better than those societies which take no account whatever of religion. What advantage can it be to a workingman to obtain by means of a society all that he requires, and to endanger his soul for lack of spiritual food? *What doth it profit a man if he gain the whole world and suffer the loss of his own soul?*[37] This, as Our Lord teaches, is the mark or character that distinguishes the Christian from the

[37] Matt. xvi. 26.

heathen. *After all these things do the heathens seek. . . . Seek
ye first the kingdom of God and His justice, and all these
things shall be added unto you.*[38] Let our associations, then,
look first and before all things to God; let religious instruction
have therein the foremost place, each one being carefully
taught what is his duty to God, what he has to believe, what
to hope for, and how he is to work out his salvation; and let
all be warned and strengthened with special care against
wrong principles and false teaching. Let the workingman be
urged and led to the worship of God, to the earnest practice
of religion, and, among other things, to the keeping holy of
Sundays and holydays. Let him learn to reverence and love
Holy Church, the common Mother of us all; and hence to
obey the precepts of the Church, and to frequent the sacraments, since they are the means ordained by God for obtaining forgiveness of sin and for leading a holy life.

The foundations of the organization being thus laid in religion, We next proceed to make clear the relations of the
members one to another, in order that they may live together
in concord and go forward prosperously and with good results.
The offices and charges of the society should be apportioned
for the good of the society itself, and in such mode that difference in degree or standing should not interfere with
unanimity and good-will. Office-bearers should be appointed
with due prudence and discretion, and each one's charge
should be carefully mapped out. Hereby no member will
suffer injury. Let the common funds be administered with
strict honesty, in such a way that a member may receive assistance in proportion to his necessities. The rights and duties
of the employers, as compared with the rights and duties of
the employed, ought to be the subject of careful consideration.
Should it happen that either a master or a workman believe
himself injured, nothing would be more desirable than that a
committee should be appointed composed of reliable and
capable members of the association, whose duty would be,
conformably with the rules of the association, to settle the
dispute. Among the several purposes of a society one should
be to try to arrange for a continuous supply of work at all
times and seasons, as well as to create a fund out of which the
members may be effectually helped in their needs, not only
in cases of accident but also in sickness, old age, and distress.

Such rules and regulations, if willingly obeyed by all, will
sufficiently ensure the well-being of the poor; whilst such
mutual associations among Catholics are certain to be productive in no small degree of prosperity to the State. It is
not rash to conjecture the future from the past. Age gives

[38] Matt. vi. 32, 33.

way to age, but the events of one century are wonderfully like those of another; for they are directed by the providence of God, who overrules the course of history in accordance with His purposes in creating the race of man. We are told that it was cast as a reproach on the Christians in the early ages of the Church that the greater number among them had to live by begging or by labor. Yet, destitute though they were of wealth and influence, they ended by winning over to their side the favor of the rich and the good-will of the powerful. They showed themselves industrious, hard-working, assiduous, and peaceful, ruled by justice, and, above all, bound together in brotherly love. In presence of such mode of life and such example, prejudice gave way, the tongue of malevolence was silenced, and the lying legends of ancient superstition little by little yielded to Christian truth.

At the time being, the condition of the working classes is the pressing question of the hour; and nothing can be of higher interest to all classes of the State than that it should be rightly and reasonably adjusted. But it will be easy for Christian workingmen to decide it aright if they will form associations, choose wise guides, and follow on the path which with so much advantage to themselves and the commonweal was trodden by their fathers before them. Prejudice, it is true, is mighty, and so is the greed of money; but if the sense of what is just and rightful be not debased through depravity of heart, their fellow-citizens are sure to be won over to a kindly feeling towards men whom they see to be in earnest as regards their work and who prefer so unmistakably right dealing to mere lucre, and the sacredness of duty to every other consideration.

And further great advantage would result from the state of things We are describing; there would exist so much more ground for hope, and likelihood even, of recalling to a sense of their duty those workingmen who have either given up their faith altogether, or whose lives are at variance with its precepts. Such men feel in most cases that they have been fooled by empty promises and deceived by false pretexts. They cannot but perceive that their grasping employers too often treat them with great inhumanity and hardly care for them outside the profit their labor brings; and if they belong to any union, it is probably one in which there exists, instead of charity and love, that intestine strife which ever accompanies poverty when unresigned and unsustained by religion. Broken in spirit and worn down in body, how many of them would gladly free themselves from such galling bondage! But human respect, or the dread of starvation, makes them tremble to take the step. To such as these Catholic associations are of incalculable service, by helping them out of their difficulties, inviting them to companionship, and receiving the returning wanderers to a haven where they may securely find repose.

We have now laid before you, Venerable Brethren, both who are the persons and what are the means whereby this most arduous question must be solved. Every one should put his hand to the work which falls to his share, and that at once and straightway, lest the evil which is already so great become through delay absolutely beyond remedy. Those who rule the State should avail them of the laws and institutions of the country; masters and wealthy owners must be mindful of their duty; the poor, whose interests are at stake, should make every lawful and proper effort; and since religion alone, as We said at the beginning, can avail to destroy the evil at its root, all men should rest persuaded that the main thing needful is to return to real Christianity, apart from which all the plans and devices of the wisest will prove of little avail.

In regard to the Church, her co-operation will never be found lacking, be the time or the occasion what it may; and she will intervene with all the greater effect in proportion as her liberty of action is the more unfettered. Let this be carefully taken to heart by those whose office it is to safe-guard the public welfare. Every minister of holy religion must bring to the struggle the full energy of his mind and all his power of endurance. Moved by your authority, Venerable Brethren, and quickened by your example, they should never cease to urge upon men of every class, upon the high-placed as well as the lowly, the Gospel doctrines of Christian life; by every means in their power they must strive to secure the good of the people; and above all must earnestly cherish in themselves, and try to arouse in others, charity, the mistress and the queen of virtues. For the happy results we all long for must be chiefly brought about by the plenteous outpouring of charity; of that true Christian charity which is the fulfilling of the whole Gospel law, which is always ready to sacrifice itself for others' sake, and is man's surest antidote against worldly pride and immoderate love of self; that charity whose office is described and whose Godlike features are outlined by the Apostle St. Paul in these words: *Charity is patient, is kind, . . . seeketh not her own, . . . suffereth all things, . . . endureth all things.*[39]

On each one of you, Venerable Brothers, and on your clergy and people, as an earnest of God's mercy and a mark of Our affection, We, lovingly in the Lord, bestow the Apostolic Benediction.

[39] 1 Cor. xiii. 4-7.

Chapter 17

✠

St. Pius X (1903-14)

Cardinal Joseph Sarto, who was elected on August 4, 1903, to succeed Leo XIII, was born near Venice on June 2, 1835, and was the son of a postman. He had been curate, parish priest, seminary professor, vicar general and bishop of Mantua before becoming cardinal patriarch of Venice and then pope. In 1904 he was insulted, very deliberately, by the French president. When the new pope, who had taken the title of Pius X, protested, the French withdrew their ambassador from the Vatican, and seized all ecclesiastical property in France, separating church and state, and removing from the French clergy all means of subsistence. This crisis was followed by the one which occurred among the clergy themselves, some of whom had been infected by the Modernist heresy. The pope dealt with this crisis by issuing against the Modernist heresy the decree *Lamentabili* in July 1907, and the encyclical *Pascendi* on September 8, 1907.

Pope Pius X's motto was the "Restoration of all things in Christ," and his first action was to encourage frequent Communion, and to allow children to make their first Communion as soon as they knew the truths necessary for salvation, and the difference between the Eucharist and ordinary bread. He also restored Gregorian plain chant to its place in the liturgy, and founded a Pontifical Institute of Sacred Music in Rome; he reformed the Roman Curia and recodified the canon law. He died on August 20, 1914, and was canonized on May 31, 1954. He is the first pope of modern times to have been canonized.

The movement then called Modernism was philosophical and theological, and its adherents were almost all priests; it was exclusively within the Church. The characteristics of the Modernists were their rejection of the traditional scholastic metaphysics, substituting for it hegelian immanentism and nineteenth-century historicism. The Catholic answer was given in *Pascendi,* longest of encyclicals. Its doctrine, in the form

of an oath, is professed publicly each year by all professors
of philosophy and theology at Catholic seminaries.

Pascendi Dominici Gregis, September 8, 1907[1]

One of the primary obligations assigned by Christ to the
office divinely committed to Us of feeding the Lord's flock
is that of guarding with the greatest vigilance the deposit of
the faith delivered to the saints, rejecting the profane novelties
of words and the gainsaying of knowledge falsely so called.
There has never been a time when this watchfulness of the
supreme pastor was not necessary to the Catholic body, for,
owing to the efforts of the enemy of the human race, there
have never been lacking "men speaking perverse things" (Acts
xx. 30), "vain talkers and seducers" (Tit. i. 10), "erring and
driving into error" (2 Tim. iii. 13). It must, however, be confessed that these latter days have witnessed a notable increase
in the number of the enemies of the Cross of Christ, who, by
arts entirely new and full of deceit, are striving to destroy the
vital energy of the Church, and, as far as in them lies, utterly
to subvert the very Kingdom of Christ. Wherefore We may
no longer keep silence, lest We should seem to fail in Our
most sacred duty, and lest the kindness that, in the hope of
wiser counsels, We have hitherto shown them, should be set
down to lack of diligence in the discharge of Our office.

That We should act without delay in this matter is made
imperative especially by the fact that the partisans of error
are to be sought not only among the Church's open enemies;
but, what is to be most dreaded and deplored, in her very
bosom, and are the more mischievous the less they keep in
the open. We allude, Venerable Brethren, to many who belong
to the Catholic laity, and, what is much more sad, to the
ranks of the priesthood itself, who, animated by a false zeal
for the Church, lacking the solid safeguards of philosophy and
theology, nay more, thoroughly imbued with the poisonous
doctrines taught by the enemies of the Church, and lost to all
sense of modesty, put themselves forward as reformers of the
Church; and, forming more boldly into line of attack, assail all
that is most sacred in the work of Christ, not sparing even the
Person of the Divine Redeemer, Whom, with sacrilegious
audacity, they degrade to the condition of a simple and
ordinary man. . . .

It is one of the cleverest devices of the Modernists (as they
are commonly and rightly called) to present their doctrines
without order and systematic arrangement, in a scattered and

[1] Translation in A. Leslie Lilley, *The Programme of Modernism*. London:
T. Fisher Unwin, 1908.

disjointed manner, so as to make it appear as if their minds were in doubt or hesitation, whereas in reality they are quite fixed and steadfast. . . .

To proceed in an orderly manner in this somewhat abstruse subject, it must first of all be noted that the Modernist sustains and includes within himself a manifold personality; he is a philosopher, a believer, a theologian, an historian, a critic, an apologist, a reformer. These roles must be clearly distinguished one from another by all who would accurately understand their system and thoroughly grasp the principles and the outcome of their doctrines.

We begin, then, with the philosopher. Modernists place the foundation of religious philosophy in that doctrine which is commonly called *Agnosticism*. According to this teaching human reason is confined entirely within the field of *phenomena*, that is to say, to things that appear, and in the manner in which they appear: it has neither the right nor the power to overstep these limits. Hence it is incapable of lifting itself up to God, and of recognising His existence, even by means of visible things. From this it is inferred that God can never be the direct object of science, and that, as regards history, He must not be considered as an historical subject. Given these premises, every one will at once perceive what becomes of *Natural Theology*, of the *motives of credibility*, of *external revelation*. The Modernists simply sweep them entirely aside; they include them in *Intellectualism* which they denounce as a system which is ridiculous and long since defunct. Nor does the fact that the Church has formally condemned these portentous errors exercise the slightest restraint upon them. . . . Yet it is a fixed and established principle among them that both science and history must be atheistic: and within their boundaries there is room for nothing but *phenomena;* God and all that is divine are utterly excluded. . . .

However, this *Agnosticism* is only the negative part of the system of the Modernists: the positive part consists in what they call *vital immanence*. Thus they advance from one to the other. Religion, whether natural or supernatural, must, like every other fact, admit of some explanation. But when natural theology has been destroyed, and the road to revelation closed by the rejection of the arguments of credibility, and all external revelation absolutely denied, it is clear that this explanation will be sought in vain outside of man himself. It must, therefore, be looked for in man; and since religion is a form of life, the explanation must certainly be found in the life of man. In this way is formulated the principle of *religious immanence*. Moreover, the first actuation, so to speak, of every vital phenomenon—and religion, as noted above, belongs to this category—is due to a certain need or impulsion; but speaking more particularly of life, it has its origin in a movement of the heart, which movement is called a *sense*. Therefore, as God is the object of religion, we must conclude that faith, which is the basis and foundation of all religion, must consist in a certain interior sense, originating in a need of the divine. This need of the divine, which is experienced only in special and favourable circumstances, cannot, of itself, appertain to the domain of consciousness,* but is first latent beneath consciousness, or, to borrow a term from modern philosophy, in the *subconsciousness,* where also its root lies hidden and undetected.

It may perhaps be asked how it is that this need of the divine which man experiences within himself resolves itself into religion? To this question the Modernist reply would be as follows: Science and history are confined within two boundaries, the one external, namely, the visible world, the other internal, which is consciousness. When one or other of these limits has been reached, there can be no further progress, for beyond is the *unknowable.* In presence of this *unknowable,* whether it is outside man and beyond the visible world of nature, or lies hidden within the *subconsciousness,* the need of the divine in a soul which is prone to religion, excites—according to the principles of *Fideism,* without any previous advertence of the mind—a certain special *sense,* and this sense possesses, implied within itself both as its own object and as its intrinsic cause, the divine *reality* itself, and in a way unites man with God. It is this *sense* to which Modernists give the name of faith, and this is what they hold to be the beginning of religion.

But we have not yet reached the end of their philosophising, or, to speak more accurately, of their folly. Modernists find in this *sense,* not only faith, but in and with faith, as they understand it, they affirm that there is also to be found *revelation.* For, indeed, what more is needed to constitute a revelation? Is not that religious *sense* which is perceptible in the conscience, revelation, or at least the beginning of revelation? Nay, is it not God Himself manifesting Himself, indistinctly, it is true, in this same religious *sense,* to the soul? And they add: Since God is both the object and the cause of faith, this revelation is at the same time *of* God and *from* God, that is to say, God is both the Revealer and the Revealed.

From this, Venerable Brethren, springs that most absurd

---

* In the Latin text the word is *conscientia,* which may be rendered in English as "conscience" or "consciousness," and in the present translation it is so used as the context seems to require.—*Translator's note.*

tenet of the Modernists, that every religion, according to the different aspect under which it is viewed, must be considered as both natural and supernatural. It is thus that they make consciousness and revelation synonymous. From this they derive the law laid down as the universal standard, according to which *religious consciousness* is to be put on an equal footing with revelation, and that to it all must submit, even the supreme authority of the Church, whether in the capacity of teacher, or in that of legislator in the province of sacred liturgy or discipline. . . .

It is thus that the *religious sense,* which through the agency of *vital immanence* emerges from the lurking-places of the *subconsciousness,* is the germ of all religion, and the explanation of everything that has been or ever will be in any religion. This *sense,* which was at first only rudimentary and almost formless, under the influence of that mysterious principle from which it originated, gradually matured with the progress of human life, of which, as has been said, it is a certain form. This, then, is the origin of all, even of supernatural religion. For religions are mere developments of this *religious sense.* Nor is the Catholic religion an exception; it is quite on a level with the rest; for it was engendered, by the process of *vital immanence,* and by no other way, in the consciousness of Christ, who was a man of the choicest nature, whose like has never been, nor will be. In hearing these things we shudder indeed at so great an audacity of assertion and so great a sacrilege. And yet, Venerable Brethren, these are not merely the foolish babblings of unbelievers. There are Catholics, yea, and priests too, who say these things openly; and they boast that they are going to reform the Church by these ravings!

. . . In their writings and addresses they seem not unfrequently to advocate doctrines which are contrary one to the other, so that one would be disposed to regard their attitude as double and doubtful. But this is done deliberately and advisedly, and the reason of it is to be found in their opinion as to the mutual separation of science and faith. Thus in their books one finds some things which might well be approved by a Catholic, but on turning over the page one is confronted by other things which might well have been dictated by a rationalist. When they write history they make no mention of the divinity of Christ, but when they are in the pulpit they profess it clearly; again, when they are dealing with history they take no account of the Fathers and the Councils, but when they catechise the people, they cite them respectfully. In the same way they draw their distinctions

between exegesis which is theological and pastoral and exegesis which is scientific and historical. So, too, when they
treat of philosophy, history, and criticism, acting on the
principle that science in no way depends upon faith, they feel
no especial horror in treading in the footsteps of Luther and
are wont to display a manifold contempt for Catholic doctrines,
for the Holy Fathers, for the Oecumenical Councils, for the
ecclesiastical Magisterium; and should they be taken to task
for this, they complain that they are being deprived of their
liberty. Lastly, maintaining the theory that faith must be
subject to science, they continuously and openly rebuke the
Church on the ground that she resolutely refuses to submit
and accommodate her dogmas to the opinions of philosophy;
while they, on their side, having for this purpose blotted out
the old theology, endeavour to introduce a new theology
which shall support the aberrations of philosophers. . . .

But it is not only within her own household that the Church
must come to terms. Besides her relations with those within,
she has others with those who are outside. The Church does
not occupy the world all by herself; there are other societies
in the world, with which she must necessarily have dealings
and contact. The rights and duties of the Church towards
civil societies must, therefore, be determined, and determined,
of course, by her own nature, that to wit, which the Modernists
have already described to us. The rules to be applied in this
matter are clearly those which have been laid down for
science and faith, though in the latter case the question turned
upon the *object*, while in the present case we have one of *ends*.
In the same way, then, as faith and science are alien to each
other by reason of the diversity of their *objects,* Church and
State are strangers by reason of the diversity of their ends,
that of the Church being spiritual while that of the State is
temporal. . . .

. . . The State must, therefore, be separated from the
Church, and the Catholic from the citizen. Every Catholic,
from the fact that he is also a citizen, has the right and the
duty to work for the common good in the way he thinks best,
without troubling himself about the authority of the Church,
without paying any heed to its wishes, its counsels, its orders
—nay, even in spite of its rebukes. For the Church to trace
out and prescribe for the citizen any line of action, on any
pretext whatsoever, is to be guilty of an abuse of authority,
against which one is bound to protest with all one's might.
Venerable Brethren, the principles from which these doctrines
spring have been solemnly condemned by Our Predecessor,
Pius VI, in his Apostolic Constitution *Auctorem fidei*. [D-
2071 *et seq.*]

Lamentabili Sane, July 3, 1907
Syllabus Condemning the Errors of the Modernists[2]

With truly lamentable results, our age, casting aside all restraint in its search for the ultimate causes of things, frequently pursues novelties so ardently that it rejects the legacy of the human race. Thus it falls into very serious errors, which are even more serious when they concern sacred authority, the interpretation of Sacred Scripture, and the principal mysteries of Faith. The fact that many Catholic writers also go beyond the limits determined by the Fathers and the Church herself is extremely regrettable. In the name of higher knowledge and historical research (they say), they are looking for that progress of dogmas which is, in reality, nothing but the corruption of dogmas.

These errors are being daily spread among the faithful. Lest they captivate the faithfuls' minds and corrupt the purity of their faith, His Holiness, Pius X, by Divine Providence, Pope, has decided that the chief errors should be noted and condemned by the Office of this Holy Roman and Universal Inquisition.

Therefore, after a very diligent investigation and consultation with the Reverend Consultors, the Most Eminent and Reverend Lord Cardinal, the General Inquisitors in matters of faith and morals have judged the following propositions to be condemned and proscribed. In fact, by this general decree, they are condemned and proscribed.

*   *   *   *   *

1. The ecclesiastical law which prescribes that books concerning the Divine Scriptures are subject to previous examination does not apply to critical scholars and students of scientific exegesis of the Old and New Testament.

2. The Church's interpretation of the Sacred Books is by no means to be rejected; nevertheless, it is subject to the more accurate judgment and correction of the exegetes.

3. From the ecclesiastical judgments and censures passed against free and more scientific exegesis, one can conclude that the Faith the Church proposes contradicts history and that Catholic teaching cannot really be reconciled with the true origins of the Christian religion.

4. Even by dogmatic definitions the Church's magisterium cannot determine the genuine sense of the Sacred Scriptures.

5. Since the deposit of Faith contains only revealed truths,

[2] Translation in *All Things in Christ*, Vincent A. Yzermans. Westminster, Maryland: The Newman Press, 1954, pp. 223 ff.

the Church has no right to pass judgment on the assertions of the human sciences.

6. The "Church learning" and the "Church teaching" collaborate in such a way in defining truths that it only remains for the "Church teaching" to sanction the opinions of the "Church learning."

7. In proscribing errors, the Church cannot demand any internal assent from the faithful by which the judgments she issues are to be embraced.

8. They are free from all blame who treat lightly the condemnations passed by the Sacred Congregation of the Index or by the Roman Congregations.

9. They display excessive simplicity or ignorance who believe that God is really the author of the Sacred Scriptures.

10. The inspiration of the books of the Old Testament consists in this: The Israelite writers handed down religious doctrines under a peculiar aspect which was either little or not at all known to the Gentiles.

11. Divine inspiration does not extend to all of Sacred Scriptures so that it renders its parts, each and every one, free from every error.

12. If he wishes to apply himself usefully to Biblical studies, the exegete must first put aside all preconceived opinions about the supernatural origin of Sacred Scripture and interpret it the same as any other merely human document.

13. The Evangelists themselves, as well as the Christians of the second and third generation, artificially arranged the evangelical parables. In such a way they explained the scanty fruit of the preaching of Christ among the Jews.

14. In many narrations the Evangelists recorded, not so much things that are true, as things which, even though false, they judged to be more profitable for their readers.

15. Until the time the canon was defined and constituted, the Gospels were increased by additions and corrections. Therefore there remained in them only a faint and uncertain trace of the doctrine of Christ.

16. The narrations of John are not properly history, but a mystical contemplation of the Gospel. The discourses contained in his Gospel are theological meditations, lacking historical truth concerning the mystery of salvation.

17. The fourth Gospel exaggerated miracles not only in order that the extraordinary might stand out but also in order that it might become more suitable for showing forth the work and glory of the Word Incarnate.

18. John claims for himself the quality of witness concerning Christ. In reality, however, he is only a distinguished witness of the Christian life, or of the life of Christ in the Church at the close of the first century.

19. Heterodox exegetes have expressed the true sense of the Scriptures more faithfully than Catholic exegetes.

20. Revelation could be nothing else than the consciousness man acquired of his relation to God.

21. Revelation, constituting the object of the Catholic faith, was not completed with the Apostles.

22. The dogmas the Church holds out as revealed are not truths which have fallen from heaven. They are an interpretation of religious facts which the human mind has acquired by laborious effort.

23. Opposition may, and actually does, exist between the facts narrated in Sacred Scripture and the Church's dogmas which rest on them. Thus the critic may reject as false facts the Church holds as most certain.

24. The exegete who constructs premises from which it follows that dogmas are historically false or doubtful is not to be reproved as long as he does not directly deny the dogmas themselves.

25. The assent of faith ultimately rests on a mass of probabilities.

26. The dogmas of the Faith are to be held only according to their practical sense; that is to say, as preceptive norms of conduct and not as norms of believing.

27. The divinity of Jesus Christ is not proved from the Gospels. It is a dogma which the Christian conscience has derived from the notion of the Messias.

28. While He was exercising His ministry, Jesus did not speak with the object of teaching He was Messias, nor did His miracles tend to prove it.

29. It is permissible to grant that the Christ of history is far inferior to the Christ Who is the object of faith.

30. In all the evangelical texts the name "Son of God" is equivalent only to that of "Messias." It does not in the least way signify that Christ is the true and natural Son of God.

31. The doctrine concerning Christ taught by Paul, John, and the Councils of Nicaea, Ephesus and Chalcedon is not that which Jesus taught but that which the Christian conscience conceived concerning Jesus.

32. It is impossible to reconcile the natural sense of the Gospel texts with the sense taught by our theologians concerning the conscience and the infallible knowledge of Jesus Christ.

33. Everyone who is not led by preconceived opinions can readily see that either Jesus professed an error concerning the immediate Messianic coming or the greater part of His doctrine as contained in the Gospels is destitute of authenticity.

34. The critics can ascribe to Christ a knowledge without

limits only on a hypothesis which cannot be historically conceived and which is repugnant to the moral sense. That hypothesis is that Christ as man possessed the knowledge of God and yet was unwilling to communicate the knowledge of a great many things to His disciples and posterity.

35. Christ did not always possess the consciousness of His Messianic dignity.

36. The Resurrection of the Saviour is not properly a fact of the historical order. It is a fact of merely the supernatural order (neither demonstrated nor demonstrable) which the Christian conscience gradually derived from other facts.

37. In the beginning, faith in the Resurrection of Christ was not so much in the fact itself of the Resurrection as in the immortal life of Christ with God.

38. The doctrine of the expiatory death of Christ is Pauline and not evangelical.

39. The opinions concerning the origin of the Sacraments which the Fathers of Trent held and which certainly influenced their dogmatic canons are very different from those which now rightly exist among historians who examine Christianity.

40. The Sacraments had their origin in the fact that the Apostles and their successors, swayed and moved by circumstances and events, interpreted some idea and intention of Christ.

41. The Sacraments are intended merely to recall to man's mind the ever-beneficent presence of the Creator.

42. The Christian community imposed the necessity of Baptism, adopted it as a necessary rite, and added to it the obligation of the Christian profession.

43. The practice of administering Baptism to infants was a disciplinary evolution, which became one of the causes why the Sacrament was divided into two, namely, Baptism and Penance.

44. There is nothing to prove that the rite of the Sacrament of Confirmation was employed by the Apostles. The formal distinction of the two Sacraments of Baptism and Confirmation does not pertain to the history of primitive Christianity.

45. Not everything which Paul narrates concerning the institution of the Eucharist (I Cor. 11: 23-25) is to be taken historically.

46. In the primitive Church the concept of the Christian sinner reconciled by the authority of the Church did not exist. Only very slowly did the Church accustom herself to this concept. As a matter of fact, even after Penance was recognized as an institution of the Church, it was not called

a Sacrament since it would be held as a disgraceful Sacrament.

47. The words of the Lord, "Receive the Holy Spirit; whose sins you shall forgive, they are forgiven them; and whose sins you shall retain, they are retained" (John 20: 22-23), in no way refer to the Sacrament of Penance, in spite of what it pleased the Fathers of Trent to say.

48. In his Epistle (Ch. 5:14-15) James did not intend to promulgate a Sacrament of Christ but only commend a pious custom. If in this custom he happens to distinguish a means of grace, it is not in that rigorous manner in which it was taken by the theologians who laid down the notion and number of the Sacraments.

49. When the Christian supper gradually assumed the nature of a liturgical action those who customarily presided over the supper acquired the sacerdotal character.

50. The elders who fulfilled the office of watching over the gatherings of the faithful were instituted by the Apostles as priests or bishops to provide for the necessary ordering of the increasing communities and not properly for the perpetuation of the Apostolic mission and power.

51. It is impossible that Matrimony could have become a Sacrament of the new law until later in the Church since it was necessary that a full theological explication of the doctrine of grace and the Sacraments should first take place before Matrimony should be held as a Sacrament.

52. It was far from the mind of Christ to found a Church as a society which would continue on earth for a long course of centuries. On the contrary, in the mind of Christ the kingdom of heaven together with the end of the world was about to come immediately.

53. The organic constitution of the Church is not immutable. Like human society, Christian society is subject to a perpetual evolution.

54. Dogmas, Sacraments and hierarchy, both their notion and reality, are only interpretations and evolutions of the Christian intelligence which have increased and perfected by an external series of additions the little germ latent in the Gospel.

55. Simon Peter never even suspected that Christ entrusted the primacy in the Church to him.

56. The Roman Church became the head of all the churches, not through the ordinance of Divine Providence, but merely through political conditions.

57. The Church has shown that she is hostile to the progress of the natural and theological sciences.

58. Truth is no more immutable than man himself, since it evolved with him, in him, and through him.

59. Christ did not teach a determined body of doctrine applicable to all times and all men, but rather inaugurated a religious movement adapted or to be adapted to different times and places.

60. Christian Doctrine was originally Judaic. Through successive evolutions it became first Pauline, then Joannine, finally Hellenic and universal.

61. It may be said without paradox that there is no chapter of Scripture, from the first of Genesis to the last of the Apocalypse, which contains a doctrine absolutely identical with that which the Church teaches on the same matter. For the same reason, therefore, no chapter of Scripture has the same sense for the critic and the theologian.

62. The chief articles of the Apostles' Creed did not have the same sense for the Christians of the first ages as they have for the Christians of our time.

63. The Church shows that she is incapable of effectively maintaining evangelical ethics since she obstinately clings to immutable doctrines which cannot be reconciled with modern progress.

64. Scientific progress demands that the concepts of Christian doctrine concerning God, creation, revelation, the Person of the Incarnate Word, and Redemption be readjusted.

65. Modern Catholicism can be reconciled with true science only if it is transformed into a non-dogmatic Christianity; that is to say, into a broad and liberal Protestantism. [D-2001 *et seq.*]

*   *   *   *   *

The following Thursday, the fourth day of the same month and year, all these matters were accurately reported to our Most Holy Lord, Pope Pius X. His Holiness approved and confirmed the decree of the Most Eminent Fathers and ordered that each and every one of the above-listed propositions be held by all as condemned and proscribed.

Peter Palombelli,
Notary of the Holy Roman and Universal Inquisition

Acerbo nimis, April 15, 1905
On the Catechism[3]

. . . It is a common complaint, unfortunately too well founded, that there are large numbers of Christians in our own time who are entirely ignorant of those truths necessary

[3] Translation by Joseph Collins, *Catechetical Documents of Pius X.* Vatican Polyglot Press.

for salvation. . . . It is hard to find words to describe how profound is the darkness in which they are engulfed and, what is most deplorable of all, how tranquilly they repose there. They rarely give thought to God, the Supreme Author and Ruler of all things, or to the teachings of the faith of Christ. They know nothing of the Incarnation of the Word of God, nothing of the perfect restoration of the human race which He accomplished. Grace, the greatest of the helps for attaining eternal things, the Holy Sacrifice and the Sacraments by which we obtain grace, are entirely unknown to them. They have no conception of the malice and baseness of sin; hence they show no anxiety to avoid sin or to renounce it. And so they arrive at life's end in such a condition that, lest all hope of salvation be lost, the priest is obliged to give in the last few moments of life a summary teaching of religion, a time which should be devoted to stimulating the soul to greater love for God. And even this as too often happens only when the dying man is not so sinfully ignorant as to look upon the ministration of the priest as useless, and then calmly faces the fearful passage to eternity without making his peace with God. . . .

Intellect is the guide to holiness. 3. There is then, Venerable Brethren, no reason for wonder that the corruption of morals and depravity of life is already so great, and ever increasingly greater, not only among uncivilized peoples but even in those very nations that are called Christian. . . . For the will of man retains but little of that divinely implanted love of virtue and righteousness by which it was, as it were, attracted strongly toward the real and not merely apparent good. Disordered by the stain of the first sin, and almost forgetful of God, its Author, it improperly turns every affection to a love of vanity and deceit. This erring will, blinded by its own evil desires, has need therefore of a guide to lead it back to the paths of justice whence it has so unfortunately strayed. The intellect itself is this guide, which need not be sought elsewhere, but is provided by nature itself. It is a guide, though, that, if it lack its companion light, the knowledge of divine things, will be only an instance of the blind leading the blind so that both will fall into the pit. . . .

Intellect moves the will to action. 5. We by no means wish to conclude that a perverse will and unbridled conduct may not be joined with a knowledge or religion. Would to God that facts did not too abundantly prove the contrary! But We do maintain that the will cannot be upright nor the conduct good when the mind is shrouded in the darkness of crass ignorance. A man who walks with open eyes may, indeed, turn aside from the right path, but a blind man is in much more imminent danger of wandering away. Furthermore, there is always some hope for a reform of perverse conduct so long as the light of faith is not entirely extinguished; but if lack of faith is added to depraved morality because of ignorance, the evil hardly admits of remedy, and the road to ruin lies open. . . .

Duty of Pastors. 7. We must now consider upon whom rests the obligation to dissipate this most pernicious ignorance and to impart in its stead the knowledge that is wholly indispensable. There can be no doubt, Venerable Brethren, that this most important duty rests upon all w o are pastors of souls. On them, by command of Christ, rest the obligations of knowing and of feeding the flocks committed to their care; and to feed implies, first of all, to teach. . . .

Priestly holiness and learning. 9. Here then it is well to emphasize and insist that for a priest there is no duty more grave or obligation more binding than this. Who, indeed, will deny that knowledge should be joined to holiness of life in the priest? "For the lips of the priest shall keep knowledge." The Church demands this knowledge of those who are to be ordained to the priesthood. Why? Because the Christian people expect from them knowledge of the divine law, and it was for that end that they were sent by God. . . .

Parish priests must teach. 10. If what We have just said is applicable to all priests, does it not apply with much greater force to those who possess the title and the authority of parish priests, and who, by virtue of their rank and in a sense by virtue of a contract, hold the office of pastors of souls?

Teaching is their primary duty. 11. For this reason the Council of Trent, treating of the duties of pastors of souls, decreed that their first and most important work is the instruction of the faithful. It therefore prescribes that they shall teach the truths of religion on Sundays and on the more solemn feast days; moreover during the holy seasons of Advent and Lent they are to give such instruction every day or at least three times a week. This, however, was not considered enough. The Council provided for the instruction of youth by adding that the pastors, either personally or through others, must explain the truths of religion at least on Sundays and feast days to the children of the parish, and inculcate obedience to God and to their parents. When the Sacraments are to be administered, it enjoins upon pastors the duty to explain their efficacy in plain and simple language. . . .

Primacy of catechetical instruction. 14. We are indeed aware that the work of teaching the Catechism is unpopular with many because as a rule it is deemed of little account and for the reason that it does not lend itself easily to the winning of public praise. But this in Our opinion is a judgment based on vanity and devoid of truth. We do not disapprove of those pulpit orators who, out of genuine zeal for the glory of God, devote themselves to defense of the faith and to its spread, or who eulogize the saints of God. But their labor presupposes labor of another kind, that of the catechist. And so if this be lacking, then the foundation is wanting; and they labor in vain who build the house. Too often it happens that ornate sermons which receive the applause of crowded congregations serve but to tickle the ears and fail utterly to touch the hearts of the hearers. Catechetical instruction, on the other hand, plain and simple though it be, is the word of which God Himself speaks through the lips of the prophet Isaias: "And as the rain and the snow come down from heaven, and return no more thither, but soak the earth and water it, and make it to spring and give seed to the sower and bread to the eater: so shall my word be, which shall go forth from my mouth. It shall not return to me void, but it shall do whatsoever I please and shall prosper in the things for which I sent it." We believe the same may be said of those priests who work hard to produce books which explain the truths of religion. They are surely to be commended for their zeal, but how many are there who read these works and take from them a fruit commensurate with the labor and intention of the writers? The teaching of the Catechism, on the other hand, when rightly done, never fails to profit those who listen to it.

Supernatural motives for the catechist. 15. In order to enkindle the zeal of the ministers of God, We again insist on the need to reach the ever-increasing numbers of those who know nothing at all of religion, or who possess at most only such knowledge of God and Christian truths as befits idolaters. How many there are, alas, not only among the young, but among adults and those advanced in years, who know nothing of the chief mysteries of faith; who on hearing the name of Christ can only ask, "Who is he . . . that I may believe in him?" In consequence of this ignorance, they do not consider it a crime to excite and nourish hatred against their neighbor, to enter into most unjust contracts, to do business in dishonest fashion, to hold the funds of others at an exorbitant interest rate, and to commit other iniquities no less reprehensible. They are, moreover, ignorant of the law of Christ which not only condemns immoral actions but also forbids deliberate immoral thoughts and desires. Even when for some reason or other they avoid sensual pleasures, they nevertheless entertain evil thoughts without the least scruple, thereby multiplying their sins above the number of the hairs of the head. These persons are found, we deem it necessary to repeat, not merely among the poorer classes of the people or in sparsely settled districts, but also among those in the higher walks of life, even, indeed, among those puffed up with learning, who, relying upon a vain erudition, feel free to ridicule religion and to "deride whatever they do not know. . . ."

Regulations to be universally observed. 18. We, therefore, Venerable Brethren, desirous of fulfilling this most important obligation of Our Teaching Office, and likewise wishing to introduce uniformity everywhere in so weighty a matter, do by Our Supreme Authority enact the following regulations and strictly command that they be observed and carried out in all dioceses of the world.

One hour weekly instruction for youth. 19. I. On every Sunday and holy day, with no exception, throughout the year, all parish priests and in general all those having the care of souls, shall instruct the boys and girls, for the space of an hour, from the text of the Catechism on those things they must believe and do in order to attain salvation.

Preparation for the Sacraments. 20 II. At certain times throughout the year, they shall prepare boys and girls to receive properly the Sacraments of Penance and Confirmation, by a continued instruction over a period of days.

Lenten Eucharistic instruction. 21. III. With a very special zeal, on every day in Lent and, if necessary, on the days following Easter, they shall instruct with the use of apt illustrations and exhortations the youth of both sexes to receive their First Communion in a holy manner. . . .

Il Fermo Proposito, June 11, 1905
On the Catholic Action in Italy[4]

. . . *To restore all things in Christ* has ever been the Church's motto, and it is specially Ours, in the perilous times in which we live. To restore all things, not in any fashion, but in Christ; *that are in heaven, and on earth, in Him,* adds the Apostle; to restore in Christ not only what directly depends on the divine mission of the Church to conduct souls to God, but also, as We have explained, that which flows spontaneously

[4] Translation in *The Pope and The People*. London: The Catholic Truth Society, 1932, pp. 190-198.

from this divine mission, viz., Christian civilization in each and every one of the elements which compose it.

To dwell only on this last part of the desired restoration, you see well what support is given to the Church by those chosen bands of Catholics whose aim is to unite all their forces in order to combat anti-Christian civilization by every just and lawful means, and to repair in every way the grievous disorders which flow from it; to reinstate Jesus Christ in the family, the school and society; to re-establish the principle that human authority represents that of God; to take intimately to heart the interests of the people, especially those of the working and agricultural classes, not only by the inculcation of religion, the only true source of comfort in the sorrows of life, but also by striving to dry their tears, to soothe their sufferings, and by wise measures to improve their economic condition; to endeavor, consequently, to make public laws conformable to justice, to amend or suppress those which are not so; finally, with a true Catholic spirit, to defend and support the rights of God in everything, and the no less sacred rights of the Church.

All these works, of which Catholic laymen are the principal supporters and promoters, and whose form varies according to the special needs of each nation, and the particular circumstances of each country, constitute what is generally known by a distinctive, and surely a very noble name: *Catholic Action* or *Action of Catholics*. This has always come to the aid of the Church, and the Church has always welcomed and blessed it, although it has acted in various ways in accordance with the age. . . .

Further, in order that Catholic Action may be effectual on all points, it is not enough that it be adapted to actual social needs only; it ought also to be invigorated by all the practical methods furnished at the present day by progress in social and economic studies, by experience already gained elsewhere, by the condition of civil society, and even by the public life of States. Otherwise there will be a risk of groping for a long time for new and hazardous things, while good and safe ones are ready to hand, and have been already well tried; or again, there will be the danger of proposing institutions and methods suitable, perhaps, in former times, but not understood by people of the present day; or finally, there will be the danger of stopping half-way by not using, in the measure in which they are granted, those rights of citizenship which modern constitutions offer to all, and, therefore, also to Catholics.

We dwell on this last point, for it is certain that the present constitution of States offers to all without distinction the power of influencing public opinion, and Catholics, while recognizing the obligations imposed by the law of God and the precepts of the Church, may with safe conscience enjoy this liberty, and prove themselves capable, as much as, and even more than others, of co-operating in the material and civil well-being of the people, thus acquiring that authority and respect which may make it even possible for them to defend and promote a higher good, namely, that of the soul.

These civil rights are many and various, going as far as a direct share in the political life of the country by representing the people in the legislature. . . . This makes it incumbent on all Catholics to prepare themselves prudently and seriously for political life in case they should be called to it. . . .

Chapter 18

✠

Benedict XV (1914-22)

Born in Genoa on November 21, 1854, Giacomo della Chiesa was a nobleman who trained first as a lawyer before studying for the priesthood. He was then trained as a diplomat, serving under Leo XIII and Cardinal Rampolla before becoming pope on September 2, 1914. His whole reign was given over to the problems of World War I, which involved millions of Catholics on both sides. Two principles guided him, that of maintaining strict neutrality toward all the belligerents, and of exploring all possibilities that might lead to peace. Through his secretary of state, Cardinal Gasparri, and his legate to Germany, Monsignor Pacelli (later Pope Pius XII) he offered both sides a basis for opening peace negotiations in 1917; but both rejected it. He was able to persuade both sides to a truce on Christmas Day during each of the war years; and through the co-operation of the neutral Swiss he was able to effect the exchange of countless war prisoners, and to work for better care for the wounded. He also helped establish an international organization for providing the families of dead soldiers with definite information. The three great documents of his reign are his encyclical *Ad Beatissimi* (November 1, 1914), his concrete proposals for peace, *Dès le début,* of August 1, 1917, addressed to the belligerent peoples and to their leaders, and the encyclical *Pacem Dei munus* of May 20, 1920. He protested against the deportation of French and Belgian workmen to Germany; against German reprisals on prisoners of war; against the bombardment of open towns, and against the violations of international law by both Germany and Austria.

After the war, the pope was excluded from participating in the peace settlement, by a clause in the secret Treaty of London, made between the Allies and Italy in 1915, prior to Italy's entering the war.

Pope Benedict XV died of influenza on January 22, 1922.

Ad Beatissimi[1]

. . . It is not only the murderous struggle now going on that is ruining the nations, and filling Us with anxious alarm. There is another dreadful evil, which goes deep down in modern society, an evil that inspires fear in the minds of thoughtful men, because while it has already caused, and is threatening still to cause immense mischief to nations, it must also be recognized as the true source of the present deplorable conflict. Truly, as soon as the rules and dictates of Christian wisdom, which are the assured basis of stability and peace, came to be disregarded in the ordering of public life, the very structure of the State began to be shaken to its fall; and there has also ensued so great a change of thought and conduct, that, unless God comes to the rescue, the dissolution of human society itself would seem to be at hand. The more prominent disorders are these: the lack of mutual love among men; disregard for authority; unjust quarrels between the various classes; material prosperity become the absorbing object of human endeavor, as though there were nothing higher and better to be gained. These We regard as the four chief causes why the world is so terribly shaken. We must labor earnestly therefore, by putting in practice Christian principles, to remove such disorders from our midst, if indeed we have at heart the common peace and welfare. . . .

. . . Never perhaps was human brotherhood more preached than now; nay, it is pretended that, without any help from the teaching of the Gospel, or from the work of Christ and the Church, the spirit of brotherhood has been one of the highest creations of modern civilization. Yet the truth is that men never acted towards each other in less brotherly fashion than now. Race hatreds are becoming almost a frenzy; nation is divided from nation more by enmity and jealousy than by geographical position; in the same city, within the same walls, the different ranks are on fire with mutual envy; all take as their supreme law their own self-interest. . . .

Allorchè Focili, July 28, 1915
To the Belligerent Peoples and to Their Leaders[2]

. . . When We, though all unworthy, were called to succeed on the Apostolic Throne the meek Pius X, whose life of holiness and well-doing was cut short by grief at the fratricidal struggle that had just burst forth in Europe, We, too, on turn-

[1] Official English Version, *Acta Apostolicae Sedis.*
[2] Official English Version, *Acta Apostolicae Sedis*, Vol. 7, pp. 375-77.

ing a fearful glance on the blood-stained battlefields, felt the anguish of a father who sees his homestead devastated and in ruins before the fury of the hurricane. And thinking with unspeakable regret of Our young sons, who were being mown down by death in thousands, We opened Our heart, enlarged by the charity of Christ, to all the crushing sorrow of the mothers, and of the wives made widows before their time, and to all the inconsolable laments of the little ones, too early bereft of a father's care. Sharing in the anxious fears of innumerable families, and fully conscious of the imperative duties imposed upon Us by the sublime mission of peace and of love, entrusted to Our care in days of so much sadness, We conceived at once the firm purpose of consecrating all Our energy and all Our power to the reconciling of the peoples at war: indeed, We made it a solemn promise to Our Divine Saviour, Who willed to make all men brothers at the cost of His Blood. . . .

In the holy name of God, and in the name of our heavenly Father and Lord, by the Blessed Blood of Jesus, Price of man's redemption, We conjure you, whom Divine Providence has placed over the nations at war, to put an end at last to this horrible slaughter, which for a whole year has dishonored Europe. It is the blood of brothers that is being poured out on land and sea. The most beautiful regions of Europe, this garden of the world, are sown with corpses and with ruin: there, where but a short time ago flourished the industry of manufactures and the fruitful labor of the fields, now thunders fearfully the cannon, and in its destructive fury it spares neither village nor city, but spreads everywhere havoc and death. You bear before God and man the tremendous responsibility of peace and war; give ear to Our prayer, to the fatherly voice of the Vicar of the Eternal and Supreme Judge, to Whom you must render an account as well of your public undertakings, as of your own individual deeds.

The abounding wealth, with which God, the Creator, has enriched the lands that are subject to you, allow you to go on with the struggle; but at what cost? Let the thousands of young lives quenched every day on the fields of battle make answer: answer, the ruins of so many towns and villages, of so many monuments raised by the piety and genius of your ancestors. And the bitter tears shed in the secrecy of home, or at the foot of altars where suppliants beseech—do not these also repeat that the price of the long-drawn-out struggle is great —too great?

Nor let it be said that the immense conflict cannot be settled without the violence of war. Lay aside your mutual purpose of destruction; remember that nations do not die; humbled and oppressed, they chafe under the yoke imposed upon them, preparing a renewal of the combat, and passing down from generation to generation a mournful heritage of hatred and revenge.

Why not from this moment weigh with serene mind the rights and lawful aspirations of the peoples? Why not initiate with a good will an exchange of views, directly or indirectly, with the object of holding in due account, within the limits of possibility, those rights and aspirations, and thus succeed in putting an end to the monstrous struggle, as has been done under other similar circumstances? Blessed be he who will first raise the olive-branch, and hold out his right hand to the enemy with an offer of reasonable terms of peace. The equilibrium of the world, and the prosperity and assured tranquillity of nations, rest upon mutual benevolence and respect for the rights and the dignity of others, much more than upon hosts of armed men and the ring of formidable fortresses. . . .

Dès le Début, August 1, 1917.
To the Belligerent Peoples and to Their Leaders[3]

. . . Since the beginning of Our Pontificate, in the midst of the horrors of the terrible war which has burst upon Europe, We have considered three things among others:

To maintain an absolute impartiality towards all belligerents, as becomes him who is the Common Father, and who loves all his children with an equal affection;

To endeavor continually to do the utmost good to all without distinction of persons, nationality or religion, in accordance not only with the universal law of charity, but also with the supreme spiritual duty laid upon Us by Christ; and

Finally, as is demanded by Our pacific mission to omit nothing, as far as in Our power lies, to contribute to hasten the end of this calamity by trying to bring the peoples and their leaders to more moderate resolutions in the discussion of means that will secure a "just and lasting peace."

Whoever has followed Our work during these three sorrowful years that have just ended has been able easily to recognize that, as We remained ever faithful to Our resolution of absolute impartiality and Our work of well-doing, so We have not ceased to exhort the belligerent peoples and Governments to become once again brothers, even though publicity was not given to all that We have done in order to attain this noble end.

Toward the end of the first year of war We addressed to

[3] Translation in John Eppstein, *The Catholic Tradition of the Law of Nations.* Washington, D.C.: The Catholic Association for International Peace, 1936, pp. 215-18.

the nations who are at grips the most earnest exhortations, and, further, We indicated the road to be followed in order to reach a peace which would be stable and honorable for all. Unhappily, Our appeal was not heard and the war continued desperately for another two years with all its horrors.

It became even more cruel, and spread upon the face of the earth, upon the sea, and even into the sky; and on defenseless cities, on tranquil villages, on their innocent populations, were seen to descend desolation and death.

And now anyone can imagine how the sufferings of all would be multiplied and aggravated if yet more months, or worse still, more years, were to be added to this bloodstained time. Must the civilized world be nothing more than a field of death, and shall Europe, so glorious and flourishing, rush to the abyss, as if dragged by some universal madness, and lend a hand in her own destruction? . . .

But that We may no longer limit Ourselves to general terms, as circumstances counseled Us in the past, We desire now to put forward some more concrete and practical propositions, and invite the Governments of the belligerents to come to some agreement on the following points, which seem to offer the bases of a just and lasting peace, though leaving to them the duty of adjusting and completing them: First of all, the fundamental point must be that the moral force of right shall be substituted for the material force of arms; thence must follow a just agreement of all for the simultaneous and reciprocal diminution of armaments, in accordance with rules and guarantees to be established hereafter, in a measure sufficient and necessary for the maintenance of public order in each State; next, as a substitute for armies, the institution of arbitration, with its high peace-making function, subject to regulations to be agreed on and sanctions to be determined against the State which should refuse either to submit international questions to arbitration or to accept its decision.

Once the supremacy of right is thus established, let all obstacles to the free intercourse of people be swept aside, in assuring, by means of rules, to be fixed in the same way, the true liberty of and common rights over the sea, which on the one hand would eliminate numerous causes of conflict, and, on the other, would open to all new sources of prosperity and progress.

As to the damage to be made good and the cost of the war, We see no other way of solving the question but to lay down, as a general principle, an entire and reciprocal condonation, justified moreover by the immense benefits which will accrue from disarmament—the more so as the continuation of such carnage solely for economic reasons would be inconceivable.

If in certain cases there are, on the other hand, particular reasons, let them be weighed justly and equitably.

But these peaceful agreements, with the immense advantages which flow from them, are not possible without the reciprocal restitution of territories at the moment occupied—consequently, on the part of Germany, a total evacuation of Belgium, with a guarantee of her complete political, military and economic independence, as against any other Power whatever; similar evacuation of French territory; on the part of other belligerent Powers a similar restitution of the German Colonies.

As regards territorial questions—as, for instance, those pending between Italy and Austria, and between Germany and France—there is ground for hope that in view of the immense advantages of a permanent peace with disarmament, the disputants would feel disposed to examine them in a conciliatory spirit, giving due weight, within the limits of justice and feasibility, as We have said previously, to the aspirations of the populations, and, on occasion, bringing their particular interests into harmony with the general welfare of the great community of mankind.

The same spirit of equity and justice must direct the examination of the remaining territorial and political questions, and particularly those which concern Armenia, the Balkan States, and the territories which form part of the former kingdom of Poland, which in particular, by reason of her noble historical traditions and the sufferings endured, specially during the present war, has a just claim on the sympathies of all nations.

Such are the principal foundations on which We believe that the future reorganization of the peoples must be built. They are of a nature to make impossible the return of similar conflicts, and to prepare the solution of the economic question, which is so important for the material well-being of all the belligerent States. . . .

Chapter 19

✠

Pius XI (1922-39)

Achille Cardinal Ratti, who, as Pius XI, succeeded Benedict XV in 1922, was born in Lombardy, the fourth son of a silk weaver. Ordained in 1879, he took his doctorates in theology and canon law and then became a curate in a country parish near Milan. Later librarian of the Ambrosian Library in Milan for thirty-eight years, he was an enthusiastic mountain climber, and was the first Italian to make the ascent of Monte Rosa from the Italian side. Prefect of the Vatican Library from 1914 to 1918, when he became nuncio to Poland, he became cardinal of Milan in 1921 and a year later was elected pope on February 6. He chose as his motto "The peace of Christ in the reign of Christ," and he kept on Cardinal Gasparri as his secretary of state, the first time a pope had retained the secretary of state of his predecessor. In 1929 he ended the *impasse* between Italy and the Vatican by concluding the Treaty of the Lateran. He concluded concordats with Latvia, Poland, Bavaria, Rumania, Lithuania, Prussia, Baden, Germany, Austria, and Yugoslavia, and agreements with Portugal and Czechoslavakia. Diplomatic relations with France were improved by a settlement about ecclesiastical property pending since 1904, and new Catholic universities were founded at Milan, in Poland and Holland. He established pontifical institutes for Oriental studies and celebrated the fortieth anniversary of Leo XIII's *Rerum Novarum* with a new encyclical on labor questions, *Quadragesimo Anno*.

This pope early faced the danger offered to the individual soul and the human community by extreme nationalism, and condemned the Action Française, the organ of the French extreme right, in 1925. In *Non abbiamo bisogno* he made it clear that "no Catholic could be a genuine convinced Fascist," and on March 14, 1937, his encyclical *Mit brennender Sorge* denounced "the whole Nazi conception of life as utterly, and, necessarily, anti-Christian."[1]

Against the Soviet cruelties he was not less vehement, and in his great encyclical *Divini Redemptoris* of March 1, 1937, he made it abundantly clear that for the Catholic Church totalitarian regimes, whether of the right or of the left, are equally against that liberty which is man's first and greatest attribute,

[1] Father Philip Hughes, *op. cit.*, p. 276.

since it mirrors the divine liberty and is necessary to man for his pursuit of his true end. As Lord Acton put it, "When Christ said 'Render unto Caesar the things that are Caesar's, and unto God the things that are God's' He gave to the civil power, under the protection of conscience, a sacredness it had never enjoyed, and bounds it had never acknowledged." These words were "the repudiation of absolutism and the inauguration of freedom. For our Lord not only delivered the precept, but created the force to execute it. To limit the power of the State became the perpetual charge of the universal Church," and of that supreme charge no pope has been more conscious than was Pius XI.

He died on February 10, 1939.

Ubi Arcano Dei, December 23, 1922
On the Peace of Christ in the Kingdom of Christ[2]

. . . Public life is so enveloped, even at the present hour, by the dense fog of mutual hatreds and grievances that it is almost impossible for the common people so much as freely to breathe therein. If the defeated nations continue to suffer most terribly, no less serious are the evils which afflict their conquerors. Small nations complain that they are being oppressed and exploited by great nations. The great powers, on their side, contend that they are being judged wrongly and circumvented by the smaller. All nations, great and small, suffer acutely from the sad effects of the late War. Neither can those nations which were neutral contend that they have escaped altogether the tremendous sufferings of the War or failed to experience its evil results almost equally with the actual belligerents. These evil results grow in volume from day to day because of the utter impossibility of finding anything like a safe remedy to cure the ills of society, and this in spite of all the efforts of politicians and statesmen whose work has come to naught if it has not unfortunately tended to aggravate the very evils they tried to overcome. Conditions have become increasingly worse because the fears of the people are being constantly played upon by the ever-present menace of new wars, likely to be more frightful and destructive than any which have preceded them. Whence it is that the nations of today live in a state of armed peace which is scarcely better than war itself, a condition which tends to exhaust national finances, to waste the flower of youth, to muddy and poison the very fountainheads of life, physical, intellectual, religious, and moral.

[2] Official English Version, *Acta Apostolicae Sedis*.

A much more serious and lamentable evil than these threats of external aggression is the internal discord which menaces the welfare not only of nations but of human society itself. In the first place, we must take cognizance of the war between the classes, a chronic and mortal disease of present-day society, which like a cancer is eating away the vital forces of the social fabric, labor, industry, the arts, commerce, agriculture—everything in fact which contributes to public and private welfare and to national prosperity. This conflict seems to resist every solution and grows worse because those who are never satisfied with the amount of their wealth contend with those who hold on most tenaciously to the riches which they have already acquired, while to both classes there is common the desire to rule the other and to assume control of the other's possessions. From this class war there result frequent interruptions of work, the causes for which most often can be laid to mutual provocations. There result, too, revolutions, riots, and forcible repression of one side or other by the government, all of which cannot but end in general discontent and in grave damage to the common welfare. . . .

Peace indeed was signed in solemn conclave between the belligerents of the late war. This peace, however, was only written into treaties. It was not received into the hearts of men, who still cherish the desire to fight one another and to continue to menace in a most serious manner the quiet and stability of civil society. Unfortunately, the law of violence held sway so long that it has weakened and almost obliterated all traces of those natural feelings of love and mercy which the law of Christian charity has done so much to encourage. Nor has this illusory peace, written only on paper, served as yet to reawaken similar noble sentiments in the souls of men. On the contrary, there has been born a spirit of violence and of hatred which, because it has been indulged in for so long, has become almost second nature in many men. There has followed the blind rule of the inferior parts of the soul over the superior, that rule of the lower elements *fighting against the law of the mind,* which St. Paul grieved over.

Men today do not act as Christians, as brothers, but as strangers, and even enemies. The sense of man's personal dignity and of the value of human life has been lost in the brutal domination begotten of might and mere superiority in numbers. . . .

It is in the very nature of material objects that an inordinate desire for them becomes the root of every evil, of every discord, and, in particular, of a lowering of the moral sense. On the one hand, things which are naturally base and vile can never give rise to noble aspirations in the human heart, which was created by and for God alone and is restless until it finds repose in Him. On the other hand, material goods (and in this they differ greatly from those of the spirit which the more of them we possess the more remain to be acquired) the more they are divided among men the less each one has and, by consequence, what one man has another cannot possibly possess unless it be forcibly taken away from the first. Such being the case, worldly possessions can never satisfy all in equal manner nor give rise to a spirit of universal contentment, but must become perforce a source of division among men. . . .

The inordinate desire for pleasure, *concupiscence of the flesh,* sows the fatal seeds of division not only among families but likewise among states; the inordinate desire for possessions, *concupiscence of the eyes,* inevitably turns into class warfare and into social egotism; the inordinate desire to rule or to domineer over others, *pride of life,* soon becomes mere party or factional rivalries, manifesting itself in constant displays of conflicting ambitions and ending in open rebellion, in the crime of *lèse majesté,* and even in national parricide.

These unsuppressed desires, this inordinate love of the things of the world, are precisely the source of all international misunderstandings and rivalries, despite the fact that oftentimes men dare to maintain that acts prompted by such motives are excusable and even justifiable because, forsooth, they were performed for reasons of state or of the public good, or out of love for country. Patriotism—the stimulus of so many virtues and of so many noble acts of heroism when kept within the bounds of the law of Christ—becomes merely an occasion, an added incentive to grave injustice when true love of country is debased to the condition of an extreme nationalism, when we forget that all men are our brothers and members of the same great human family, that other nations have an equal right with us both to life and to prosperity, that it is never lawful nor even wise, to dissociate morality from the affairs of practical life, that, in the last analysis, it is "justice which exalteth a nation: but sin maketh nations miserable." (Proverbs xiv, 34)

There exists an institution able to safeguard the sanctity of the law of nations. This institution is a part of every nation; at the same time it is above all nations. She enjoys, too, the highest authority, the fullness of the teaching power of the Apostles. Such an institution is the Church of Christ. She alone is adapted to do this great work, for she is not only divinely commissioned to lead mankind, but moreover, because of her very make-up and the constitution which she possesses, by reason of her age-old traditions and her great prestige, which has not been lessened but has been greatly increased since the close of the war, cannot but succeed in such a venture where others assuredly will fail. . . .

The Church does not desire, neither ought she to desire, to mix up without a just cause in the direction of purely civil affairs. On the other hand, she cannot permit or tolerate that the State use the pretext of certain laws or unjust regulations to do injury to the rights of an order superior to that of the State, to interfere with the constitution given the Church by Christ, or to violate the rights of God Himself over civil society. . . . [D-2190]

[The following is the pope's comment on the foundation of the League of Nations. He points out how its theological basis rests on St. Thomas Aquinas.]

Studiorum Ducem,[3] June 29, 1923

. . . Hence, in the second part of the *Summa Theologica,* those teachings are famous which regard the paternal or domestic rule, the legal rule of State or nation, the law of peoples, peace, war, justice and dominion, laws and their observance, the duty of providing for private necessity as for public prosperity, and all this as well in the natural as in the supernatural order. Because, if privately and publicly and in the mutual relations of nation with nation, these precepts are preserved holily and inviolately, nothing else is required for that conciliating "Peace of Christ in the Reign of Christ" which the whole world so much desires.

It is, therefore, to be hoped that the doctrines of Aquinas, concerning the ruling of peoples and the laws which establish their relations with one another, may be better known, since they contain the true foundations of that which is termed the "League of Nations. . . ." [D-2192]

Rappresentanti in terra, December 31, 1929
Christian Education of Youth[4]

. . . Since education consists essentially in preparing man for what he must be and for what he must do here below, in order to attain the sublime end for which he was created, it is clear that there can be no true education which is not wholly directed to man's last end, and that in the present order of Providence, since God has revealed Himself to us in the Person of His Only Begotten Son, who alone is "the way,

[3] Translation from *The Catholic Mind,* Vol. 21, pp. 311-12 (August 22, 1923).
[4] Official English Version, Vatican Polyglot Press.

the truth and the life," there can be no ideally perfect education which is not Christian education.

From this we see the supreme importance of Christian education, not merely for each individual, but for families and for the whole of human society, whose perfection comes from the perfection of the elements that compose it. From these same principles, the excellence, we may well call it the unsurpassed excellence, of the work of Christian education becomes manifest and clear; for after all it aims at securing the Supreme Good, that is, God, for the souls of those who are being educated, and the maximum of well-being possible here below for human society. And this it does as efficaciously as man is capable of doing it, namely by co-operating with God in the perfecting of individuals and of society. . . .

Education is essentially a social and not a mere individual activity. Now there are three necessary societies, distinct from one another and yet harmoniously combined by God, into which man is born: two, namely the family and civil society, belong to the natural order; the third, the Church, to the supernatural order.

In the first place comes the family, instituted directly by God for its peculiar purpose, the generation and formation of offspring; for this reason it has priority of nature and therefore of rights over civil society. Nevertheless, the family is an imperfect society, since it has not in itself all the means for its own complete development; whereas civil society is a perfect society, having in itself all the means for its peculiar end, which is the temporal well-being of the community; and so, in this respect, that is, in view of the common good, it has pre-eminence over the family, which finds its own suitable temporal perfection precisely in civil society.

The third society, into which man is born when through Baptism he reaches the divine life of grace, is the Church; a society of the supernatural order and of universal extent; a perfect society, because it has in itself all the means required for its own end, which is the eternal salvation of mankind; hence it is supreme in its own domain.

Consequently, education which is concerned with man as a whole, individually and socially, in the order of nature and in the order of grace, necessarily belongs to all these three societies, in due proportion, corresponding, according to the disposition of Divine Providence, to the co-ordination of their respective ends.

And first of all education belongs pre-eminently to the Church, by reason of a double title in the supernatural order, conferred exclusively upon her by God Himself; absolutely superior therefore to any other title in the natural order. . . .

Again it is the inalienable right as well as the indispensable duty of the Church to watch over the entire education of her children, in all institutions, public or private, not merely in regard to the religious instruction there given, but in regard to every other branch of learning and every regulation in so far as religion and morality are concerned. . . .

However, it is clear that in all these ways of promoting education and instruction, both public and private, the State should respect the inherent rights of the Church and of the family concerning Christian education, and moreover have regard for distributive justice. Accordingly, unjust and unlawful is any monopoly, educational or scholastic, which, physically or morally, forces families to make use of government schools, contrary to the dictates of their Christian conscience, or contrary even to their legitimate preferences.

This does not prevent the State from making due provision for the right administration of public affairs and for the protection of its peace, within or without the realm. These are things which directly concern the public good and call for special aptitudes and special preparation. The State may therefore reserve to itself the establishment and direction of schools intended to prepare for certain civic duties and especially for military service, provided it be careful not to injure the rights of the Church or of the family in what pertains to them. It is well to repeat this warning here; for in these days there is spreading a spirit of nationalism which is false and exaggerated, as well as dangerous to true peace and prosperity. Under its influence various excesses are committed in giving a military turn to the so-called physical training of boys (sometimes even for girls, contrary to the very instincts of human nature); or again in usurping unreasonably on Sunday, the time which should be devoted to religious duties and to family life at home. It is not our intention, however, to condemn what is good in the spirit of discipline and legitimate bravery promoted by these methods; We condemn only what is excessive, as for example violence, which must not be confounded with courage nor with the noble sentiment of military valour in defense of country and public order; or again exaltation of athleticism, which even in classic pagan times marked the decline and downfall of genuine physical training.

In general also it belongs to civil society and the State to provide what may be called civic education, not only for its youth, but for all ages and classes. This consists in the practice of presenting publicly to groups of individuals information having an intellectual, imaginative and emotional appeal, calculated to draw their wills to what is upright and honest, and to urge its practice by a sort of moral compulsion, positively by disseminating such knowledge, and negatively by suppressing what is opposed to it. . . .

Accordingly in the matter of education, it is the right, or to speak more correctly, it is the duty, of the State to protect in its legislation the prior rights, already described, of the family as regards the Christian education of its offspring, and consequently also to respect the supernatural rights of the Church in this same realm of Christian education.

It also belongs to the State to protect the rights of the child itself when the parents are found wanting either physically or morally in this respect, whether by default, incapacity or misconduct, since, as has been shown, their right to educate is not an absolute and despotic one, but dependent on the natural and divine law, and therefore subject alike to the authority and jurisdiction of the Church, and to the vigilance and administrative care of the State in view of the common good. Besides, the family is not a perfect society, that is, it has not in itself all the means necessary for its full development. In such cases, exceptional no doubt, the State does not put itself in the place of the family, but merely supplies deficiencies, and provides suitable means, always in conformity with the natural rights of the child and the supernatural rights of the Church.

In general, then, it is the right and duty of the State to protect, according to the rules of right reason and faith, the moral and religious education of youth, by removing public impediments that stand in the way.

In the first place it pertains to the State, in view of the common good, to promote in various ways the education and instruction of youth. It should begin by encouraging and assisting, of its own accord, the initiative and activity of the Church and the family, whose successes in this field have been clearly demonstrated by history and experience. It should, moreover, supplement their work whenever this falls short of what is necessary, even by means of its own schools and institutions. For the State more than any other society is provided with the means put at its disposal for the needs of all, and it is only right that it use these means to the advantage of those who have contributed them.

Over and above this, the State can exact, and take measures to secure that all its citizens have the necessary knowledge of their civic and political duties, and a certain degree of physical, intellectual and moral culture, which, considering the conditions of our times, is really necessary for the common good. . . .

Quadragesimo Anno, May 15, 1931
On Reconstructing the Social Order[5]

[This is the pope's restatement, on its fortieth anniversary, of his predecessor Leo XIII's greatest encyclical on labor, *Rerum Novarum*. *See also* D-2253-70]

Forty years have passed since Leo XIII's peerless Encyclical, *On the Condition of Workers*, first saw the light, and the whole Catholic world, filled with grateful recollection, is undertaking to commemorate it with befitting solemnity. Other Encyclicals of Our Predecessor had in a way prepared the path for that outstanding document and proof of pastoral care: namely, those on the family and the holy Sacrament of matrimony as the source of human society, on the origin of civil authority and its proper relations with the Church, on the chief duties of Christian citizens, against the tenets of Socialism, against false teachings on human liberty, and others of the same nature fully expressing the mind of Leo XIII. Yet the Encyclical *On the Condition of Workers*, compared with the rest, had this special distinction that at a time when it was most opportune and actually necessary to do so, it laid down for all mankind the surest rules to solve aright that difficult problem of human relations, called "the social question."

For, toward the close of the nineteenth century, the new kind of economic life that had arisen and the new developments of industry had gone to the point in most countries that human society was clearly becoming divided more and more into two classes. One class, very small in number, was enjoying almost all the advantages which modern inventions so abundantly provided; the other, embracing the huge multitude of working people, oppressed by wretched poverty, was vainly seeking escape from the straits wherein it stood.

Quite agreeable, of course, was this state of things to those who thought it, in their abundant riches, the result of inevitable economic laws and, accordingly, as if it were for charity to veil the violation of justice which lawmakers not only tolerated but at times sanctioned, wanted the whole care of supporting the poor committed to charity alone. The workers, on the other hand, crushed by their hard lot, were barely enduring it and were refusing longer to bend their necks beneath so galling a yoke; and some of them, carried away by the heat

[5] Translation in *Two Basic Social Encyclicals*. Washington, D.C.: Catholic University of America Press, 1943. Distributed by Benziger Brothers, New York.

of evil counsel, were seeking the overturn of everything, while others, whom Christian training restrained from such evil designs, stood firm in the judgment that much in this had to be wholly and speedily changed. . . .

. . . The Supreme Pastor, . . . grieving that so large a portion of mankind should "live undeservedly in miserable and wretched conditions," took it upon himself with great courage to defend "the cause of the workers whom the present age had handed over, each alone and defenseless, to the inhumanity of employers and the unbridled greed of competitors." He sought no help from either Liberalism or Socialism, for the one had proved that it was utterly unable to solve the social problem aright, and the other, proposing a remedy far worse than the evil itself, would have plunged human society into greater dangers.

Since a problem was being treated "for which no satisfactory solution" is found "unless religion and the Church have been called upon to aid," the Pope, clearly exercising his right and correctly holding that the guardianship of religion and the stewardship over those things that are closely bound up with it had been entrusted especially to him and relying solely upon the unchangeable principles drawn from the treasury of right reason and Divine Revelation, confidently and *as one having authority,* declared and proclaimed "the rights and duties within which the rich and the proletariat—those who furnish material things and those who furnish work—ought to be restricted in relation to each other," and what the Church, heads of States and the people themselves directly concerned ought to do.

The Apostolic voice did not thunder forth in vain. On the contrary, not only did the obedient children of the Church hearken to it with marveling admiration and hail it with the greatest applause, but many also who were wandering far from the truth, from the unity of the Faith, and nearly all who since then, either in private study or in enacting legislation, have concerned themselves with the social and economic question. Feeling themselves vindicated and defended by the Supreme Authority on earth, Christian workers received this Encyclical with special joy. . . .

And so, with Leo's Encyclical pointing the way and furnishing the light, a true Catholic social science has arisen, which is daily fostered and enriched by the tireless efforts of those chosen men whom We have termed auxiliaries of the Church. . . .

Nor is the benefit that has poured forth from Leo's Encyclical confined within these bounds; for the teaching which *On the Condition of Workers* contains has gradually and imperceptibly worked its way into the minds of those outside Catholic unity who do not recognize the authority of the Church. Catholic principles on the social question have, as a result, passed little by little into the patrimony of all human society. . . .

Meanwhile, as Leo's teachings were being widely diffused in the minds of men, with learned investigations leading the way, they have come to be put into practice. In the first place, zealous efforts have been made, with active good-will, to lift up that class which, on account of the modern expansion of industry, had increased to enormous numbers but not yet had obtained its rightful place or rank in human society and was, for that reason, all but neglected and despised—the workers. . . .

With regard to civil authority, Leo XIII, boldly breaking through the confines imposed by Liberalism, fearlessly taught that government must not be thought a mere guardian of law and of good order, but rather must put forth every effort so that "through the entire scheme of laws and institutions . . . both public and individual well-being may develop spontaneously out of the very structure and administration of the State." Just freedom of action must, of course, be left both to individual citizens and to families, yet only on condition that the common good be preserved and wrong to any individual be abolished. The function of the rulers of the State, moreover, is to watch over the community and its parts; but in protecting private individuals in their rights, chief consideration ought to be given to the weak and the poor. . . .

However, in spite of such great agreement, there were some who were no little disturbed; and so it happened that the teaching of Leo XIII, so noble and lofty and so utterly new to worldly ears, was held suspect by some, even among Catholics, and to certain ones it even gave offense. For it boldly attacked and over-turned the idols of Liberalism, ignored long-standing prejudices, and was in advance of its time beyond all expectation, so that the slow of heart disdained to study this new social philosophy and the timid feared to scale so lofty a height. There were some also who stood, indeed, in awe at its splendor, but regarded it as a kind of imaginary ideal of perfection more desirable than attainable.

Our Predecessor of happy memory strongly defended the right of property against the tenets of the Socialists of his time by showing that its abolition would result, not to the advantage of the working class, but to their extreme harm. Yet since there are some who calumniate the Supreme Pontiff and the Church herself, as if she had taken and were still taking the part of the rich against the non-owning workers —certainly no accusation is more unjust than that—and since Catholics are at variance with one another concerning the true and exact mind of Leo, it has seemed best to vindicate this, that is, the Catholic teaching on this matter, from calumnies and safeguard it from false interpretations.

First, then, let it be considered as certain and established that neither Leo nor those theologians who have taught under the guidance and authority of the Church have ever denied or questioned the twofold character of ownership, called usually individual or social according as it regards either separate persons or the common good. For they have always unanimously maintained that nature, rather the Creator Himself, has given man the right of private ownership not only that individuals may be able to provide for themselves and their families but also that the goods which the Creator destined for the entire family of mankind, may, through this institution, truly serve this purpose. All this can be achieved in no wise except through the maintenance of a certain and definite order.

Accordingly, twin rocks of shipwreck must be carefully avoided. For, as one is wrecked upon, or comes close to, what is known as "individualism" by denying or minimizing the social and public character of the right of property, so by rejecting or minimizing the private and individual character of this same right, one inevitably runs into "collectivism" or at least closely approaches its tenets. Unless this is kept in mind, one is swept from his course upon the shoals of moral, juridical and social modernism. . . .

In order to place definite limits on the controversies that have arisen over ownership and its inherent duties, there must be first laid down as a foundation a principle established by Leo XIII: the right of property is distinct from its use. That justice called commutative commands sacred respect for the division of possessions and forbids invasion of others' rights through the exceeding of the limits of one's own property; but the duty of owners to use their property only in a right way does not come under this type of justice, but under other virtues, obligations of which "cannot be enforced by legal action." Therefore, they are in error who assert that ownership and its right use are limited by the same boundaries; and it is much farther still from the truth to hold that a right to property is destroyed or lost by reason of abuse or non-use. . . .

It follows from what We have termed the individual and at the same time social character of ownership, that men must consider in this matter not only their own advantage but also the common good. To define these duties in detail, when necessity requires and the natural law has not done so, is the function of those in charge of the State. Therefore, public authority, under the guiding light always of the natural and divine law, can determine more accurately upon consideration of the true requirements of the common good, what is permitted and what is not permitted to owners in the use of their property. . . .

Labor, as Our Predecessor explained well in his Encyclical, is not a mere commodity. On the contrary, the worker's human dignity in it must be recognized. It, therefore, cannot be bought and sold like a commodity. Nevertheless, as the situation now stands, hiring and offering for hire in the so-called labor market separate men into two divisions, as into battle lines, and the contest between these divisions turns the labor market itself almost into a battlefield where face to face the opposing lines struggle bitterly. Everyone understands that this grave evil which is plunging all human society to destruction must be remedied as soon as possible. But complete cure will not come until this opposition has been abolished and well-ordered members of the social body—industries and professions—are constituted in which men may have their place, not according to the position each has in the labor market but according to the respective social functions which each performs. For under nature's guidance it comes to pass that just as those who are joined together by nearness of habitation establish towns, so those who follow the same industry or profession—whether in the economic or other field—form guilds or associations, so that many are wont to consider these self-governing organizations, if not essential, at least natural to civil society.

The teaching of Leo XIII on the form of political government, namely, that men are free to choose whatever form they please, provided that proper regard is had for the requirements of justice and of the common good, is equally applicable in due proportion, it is hardly necessary to say, to the guilds of the various industries and professions. Moreover, just as inhabitants of a town are wont to found associations with the widest diversity of purposes, which each is quite free to join or not, so those engaged in the same industry or profession will combine with one another into associations equally free for purposes connected in some manner with the pursuit of the calling itself. Since these free associations are clearly and lucidly explained by Our Predecessor of illustrious memory, We consider it enough to emphasize this one point: People are quite free not only to found such associations, which are a matter of private order and private right, but also in respect to them "freely to adopt the organization and the rules which they judge most appropriate to achieve their purpose." The same freedom must be asserted for founding associations that go beyond the boundaries of individual callings. . . .

Attention must be given also to another matter that is closely connected with the foregoing. Just as the unity of human society cannot be founded on an opposition of classes, so also the right ordering of economic life cannot be left to a free competition of forces. For from this source, as from a poisoned spring, have originated and spread all the errors of individualist economic teaching. Destroying through forgetfulness or ignorance the social and moral character of economic life, it is held that economic life must be considered and treated as altogether free from and independent of public authority, because in the market, that is, in the free struggle of competitors, it would have a principle of self-direction which governs it much more perfectly than through the intervention of any created intellect. But free competition, while justified and certainly useful, provided it is kept within certain limits, clearly cannot direct economic life—a truth which the outcome of the application in practice of the tenets of this evil individualistic spirit has more than sufficiently demonstrated. Therefore, it is most necessary that economic life be again subjected to and governed by a true and effective directing principle. This function is one that the economic dictatorship which has recently displaced free competition can still less perform, since it is a headstrong power and a violent energy that, to benefit people, needs to be strongly curbed and wisely ruled. But it cannot curb and rule itself. Loftier and nobler principles—social justice and social charity—must, therefore, be sought whereby this dictatorship may be governed firmly and fully. Hence, the institutions themselves of peoples, and particularly those of all social life, ought to be penetrated with this justice, and it is most necessary that it be truly effective, that is, establish a juridical and social order which will, as it were, give form and shape to all economic life. . . .

The civil authority itself constitutes the syndicate as a juridical personality in such a manner as to confer on it simultaneously a certain monopoly-privilege, since only such a syndicate, when thus approved, can maintain the rights (according to the type of syndicate) of workers or employers, and since it alone can arrange for the placement of labor and conclude the so-termed labor agreements. Anyone is free to join a syndicate or not, and only within these limits can this kind of syndicate be called free; for syndical dues and special assessments are exacted of absolutely all members of every specified calling or profession, whether they are workers or employers; likewise all are bound by the labor agreements made by the legally recognized syndicate. Nevertheless, it has been officially stated that this legally recognized syndicate does not prevent the existence, without legal status, however, of other associations made up of persons following the same calling. . . .

With the diffusion of modern industry throughout the whole world, the "capitalist" economic regime has spread everywhere to such a degree, particularly since the publication of Leo XIII's Encyclical, that it has invaded and pervaded the economic and social life of even those outside its orbit and is unquestionably impressing on it its advantages, disadvantages and vices, and, in a sense, is giving its own shape and form.

Accordingly, when directing Our special attention to the changes which the capitalist economic system has undergone since Leo's time, We have in mind the good not only of those who dwell in regions given over to "capital" and industry, but of all mankind. In the first place, it is obvious that not only is wealth concentrated in our times but an immense power and despotic economic dictatorship is consolidated in the hands of a few, who often are not owners but only the trustees and managing directors of invested funds which they administer according to their own arbitrary will and pleasure.

This dictatorship is being most forcibly exercised by those who, since they hold the money and completely control it, control credit also and rule the lending of money. Hence, they regulate the flow, so to speak, of the lifeblood whereby the entire economic system lives, and have so firmly in their grasp the soul, as it were, of economic life, that no one can breathe against their will.

This concentration of power and might, the characteristic mark, as it were, of contemporary economic life, is the fruit that the unlimited freedom of struggle among competitors has of its own nature produced, and which lets only the strongest survive, which is often the same as saying, those who fight the most violently, those who give least heed to their conscience.

This accumulation of might and of power generates in turn three kinds of conflict. First, there is the struggle for economic supremacy itself; then there is the bitter fight to gain supremacy over the State in order to use in economic struggles its resources and authority; finally, there is conflict between States themselves, not only because countries employ their power and shape their policies to promote every economic advantage of their citizens, but also because they seek to decide political controversies that arise among nations through the use of their economic supremacy and strength.

The ultimate consequences of the individualist spirit in economic life are these: free competition has destroyed itself; economic dictatorship has supplanted the free market; unbridled ambition for power has likewise succeeded greed for gain; all economic life has become tragically hard, inexorable and cruel. To these are to be added the grave evils that have resulted from an intermingling and shameful confusion of the functions and duties of public authority with those of the economic sphere. . . . And as to international relations, two different streams have issued from the one fountain-head: On the one hand, economic nationalism or even economic imperialism; on the other, a no less deadly and accursed internationalism of finance or international imperialism whose country is where profit is. . . .

Since the present system of economy is founded chiefly upon ownership and labor, the principles of right reason, that is, of Christian social philosophy, must be kept in mind in theory regarding ownership and labor and their association together, and must be put into actual practice. . . .

The many deviations from the Christian ideal of marriage provoked the pope's strong statement: [*See also,* D-2225-50]

Casti Connubi, December 31, 1930
On Christian Marriage[6]

How great is the dignity of chaste wedlock, Venerable Brethren, may be judged best from this that Christ Our Lord, Son of the Eternal Father, having assumed the nature of fallen man, not only, with His loving desire of compassing the redemption of our race, ordained it in an especial manner as the principle and foundation of domestic society and therefore of all human intercourse, but also raised it to the rank of a truly and great sacrament of the New Law, restored it to the original purity of its divine institution, and accordingly entrusted all its discipline and care to His spouse the Church. . . .

. . . And to begin with let it be repeated as an immutable and inviolable fundamental doctrine that matrimony was not instituted or restored by man but by God; not by man were the laws made to strengthen and confirm and elevate it but by God, the Author of nature, and by Christ Our Lord by Whom nature was redeemed, and hence these laws cannot be

---

[6] Official English Version, Vatican Polyglot Press.

subject to any human decrees or to any contrary pact even of the spouses themselves. This is the doctrine of Holy Scripture; this is the constant tradition of the Universal Church; this is the solemn definition of the sacred Council of Trent, which declares and establishes from the words of Holy Writ itself that God is the Author of the perpetual stability of the marriage bond, its unity and its firmness.

Yet although matrimony is of its very nature of divine institution, the human will, too, enters into it and performs a most noble part. For each individual marriage, inasmuch as it is a conjugal union of a particular man and woman, arises only from the free consent of each of the spouses; and this free act of the will, by which each party hands over and accepts those rights proper to the state of marriage, is so necessary to constitute true marriage that it cannot be supplied by any human power. This freedom, however, regards only the question whether the contracting parties really wish to enter upon matrimony or to marry this particular person; but the nature of matrimony is entirely independent of the free will of man, so that if one has once contracted matrimony he is thereby subject to its divinely made laws and its essential properties. For the Angelic Doctor, writing on conjugal honour and on the offspring which is the fruit of marriage, says: "These things are so contained in matrimony by the marriage pact itself that, if anything to the contrary were expressed in the consent which makes the marriage, it would not be a true marriage. . . ."

. . . [According to the teaching of Leo XIII,] "To take away from man the natural and primeval right of marriage, to circumscribe in any way the principal ends of marriage laid down in the beginning by God Himself in the words 'Increase and multiply,' is beyond the power of any human law."

Therefore the sacred partnership of true marriage is constituted both by the will of God and the will of man. From God comes the very institution of marriage, the ends for which it was instituted, the laws that govern it, the blessings that flow from it; while man, through generous surrender of his own person made to another for the whole span of life, becomes, with the help and co-operation of God, the author of each particular marriage, with the duties and blessings annexed thereto from divine institution. . . .

. . . That mutual familiar intercourse between the spouses themselves, if the blessing of conjugal faith is to shine with becoming splendour, must be distinguished by chastity so that husband and wife bear themselves in all things with the law of God and of nature, and endeavour always to follow the will of their most wise and holy Creator with the greatest reverence towards the work of God.

This conjugal faith, however, which is most aptly called by St. Augustine the "faith of chastity," blooms more freely, more beautifully and more nobly, when it is rooted in that more excellent soil, the love of husband and wife which pervades all the duties of married life and holds pride of place in Christian marriage. For matrimonial faith demands that husband and wife be joined in an especially holy and pure love, not as adulterers love each other, but as Christ loved the Church. This precept the Apostle laid down when he said: "Husbands, love your wives as Christ also loved the Church," that Church which of a truth He embraced with a boundless love not for the sake of His own advantage, but seeking only the good of His Spouse. The love, then, of which We are speaking is not that based on the passing lust of the moment nor does it consist in pleasing words only, but in the deep attachment of the heart which is expressed in action, since love is proved by deeds. This outward expression of love in the home demands not only mutual help but must go further; must have as its primary purpose that man and wife help each other day by day in forming and perfecting themselves in the interior life, so that through their partnership in life they may advance ever more and more in virtue, and above all that they may grow in true love towards God and their neighbour, on which indeed "dependeth the whole Law and the Prophets." For all men of every condition, in whatever honourable walk of life they may be, can and ought to imitate that most perfect example of holiness placed before man by God, namely Christ Our Lord, and by God's grace to arrive at the summit of perfection, as is proved by the example set us of many saints.

By this same love it is necessary that all the other rights and duties of the marriage state be regulated as the words of the Apostle: "Let the husband render the debt to the wife, and the wife also in like manner to the husband," express not only a law of justice but of charity.

Domestic society being confirmed, therefore, by this bond of love, there should flourish in it that "order of love," as St. Augustine calls it. This order includes both the primacy of the husband with regard to the wife and children, the ready subjection of the wife and her willing obedience, which the Apostle commends in these words: "Let women be subject to their husbands as to the Lord, because the husband is the head of the wife, as Christ is the head of the Church."

This subjection, however, does not deny or take away the liberty which fully belongs to the woman both in view of her dignity as a human person, and in view of her most noble office as wife and mother and companion; nor does it bid her obey her husband's every request if not in harmony with right reason or with the dignity due to wife; nor, in fine, does it imply that the wife should be put on a level with those persons who in law are called minors, to whom it is not customary to allow free exercise of their rights on account of their lack of mature judgment, or of their ignorance of human affairs. But it forbids that exaggerated liberty which cares not for the good of the family; it forbids that in this body which is the family, the heart be separated from the head to the great detriment of the whole body and the proximate danger of ruin. For if the man is the head, the woman is the heart, and as he occupies the chief place in ruling, so she may and ought to claim for herself the chief place in love.

Again, this subjection of wife to husband in its degree and manner may vary according to the different conditions of persons, place and time. In fact, if the husband neglect his duty, it falls to the wife to take his place in directing the family. But the structure of the family and its fundamental law, established and confirmed by God, must always and everywhere be maintained intact. . . .

These, then, are the elements which compose the blessing of conjugal faith: unity, chastity, charity, honourable noble obedience, which are at the same time an enumeration of the benefits which are bestowed on husband and wife in their married state, benefits by which the peace, the dignity and the happiness of matrimony are securely preserved and fostered. Wherefore it is not surprising that this conjugal faith has always been counted amongst the most priceless and special blessings of matrimony.

But this accumulation of benefits is completed and, as it were, crowned by that blessing of Christian marriage which in the words of St. Augustine we have called the sacrament, by which is denoted both the indissolubility of the bond and the raising and hallowing of the contract by Christ Himself, whereby He made it an efficacious sign of grace. . . .

. . . Considering the benefits of the Sacrament, besides the firmness and indissolubility, there are also much higher emoluments, as the word "sacrament" itself very aptly indicates; for to Christians this is not a meaningless and empty name. Christ the Lord, the Institutor and "Perfecter" of the holy sacraments, by raising the matrimony of His faithful to the dignity of a true sacrament of the New Law, made it a sign and source of that peculiar internal grace by which "it perfects natural love, it confirms an indissoluble union, and sanctifies both man and wife."

And since the valid matrimonial consent among the faithful was constituted by Christ as a sign of grace, the sacramental nature is so intimately bound up with Christian wedlock that there can be no true marriage between baptized persons "without it being by that very fact a sacrament. . . ."

And now, Venerable Brethren, we shall explain in detail the evils opposed to each of the benefits of matrimony. First consideration is due to the offspring, which many have the boldness to call the disagreeable burden of matrimony and which they say is to be carefully avoided by married people not through virtuous continence (which Christian law permits in matrimony when both parties consent) but by frustrating the marriage act. Some justify this criminal abuse on the ground that they are weary of children and wish to gratify their desires without their consequent burden. Others say that they cannot on the one hand remain continent nor on the other can they have children because of the difficulties whether on the part of the mother or on the part of family circumstances.

But no reason, however grave, may be put forward by which anything intrinsically against nature may become conformable to nature and morally good. Since, therefore, the conjugal act is destined primarily by nature for the begetting of children, those who in exercising it deliberately frustrate its natural power and purpose sin against nature and commit a deed which is shameful and intrinsically vicious. . . .

Since, therefore, openly departing from the uninterrupted Christian tradition, some recently have judged it possible solemnly to declare another doctrine regarding this question, the Catholic Church, to whom God has entrusted the defence of the integrity and purity of morals, standing erect in the midst of the moral ruin which surrounds her, in order that she may preserve the chastity of the nuptial union from being defiled by this foul stain, raises her voice in token of her divine ambassadorship and through Our mouth proclaims anew: any use whatsoever of matrimony exercised in such a way that the act is deliberately frustrated in its natural power to generate life is an offence against the law of God and of nature, and those who indulge in such are branded with the guilt of a grave sin. . . .

As regards the evil use of matrimony, to pass over the arguments which are shameful, not infrequently others that are false and exaggerated are put forward. Holy Mother Church very well understands and clearly appreciates all that is said regarding the health of the mother and the danger to her life. And who would not grieve to think of these things? Who is not filled with the greatest admiration when he sees a mother risking her life with heroic fortitude, that she may preserve the life of the offspring which she has conceived? God alone, all bountiful and all merciful as He is, can reward her for the fulfilment of the office allotted to her by nature, and will assuredly repay her in a measure full to overflowing.

Holy Church knows well that not infrequently one of the parties is sinned against rather than sinning, when for a grave cause he or she reluctantly allows the perversion of the right order. In such a case, there is no sin, provided that, mindful of the law of charity, he or she does not neglect to seek to dissuade and to deter the partner from sin. Nor are those considered as acting against nature who in the married state use their right in the proper manner although on account of natural reasons either of time or of certain defects, new life cannot be brought forth. For in matrimony as well as in the use of the matrimonial rights there are also secondary ends, such as mutual aid, the cultivating of mutual love, and the quieting of concupiscence which husband and wife are not forbidden to consider so long as they are subordinated to the primary end and so long as the intrinsic nature of the act is preserved. . . .

But another very grave crime is to be noted, Venerable Brethren, which regards the taking of the life of the offspring hidden in the mother's womb. Some wish it to be allowed and left to the will of the father or the mother; others say it is unlawful unless there are weighty reasons which they call by the name of medical, social, or eugenic "indication." Because this matter falls under the penal laws of the state by which the destruction of the offspring begotten but unborn is forbidden, these people demand that the "indication," which in one form or another they defend, be recognized as such by the public law and in no way penalized. There are those, moreover, who ask that the public authorities provide aid for these death-dealing operations, a thing, which, sad to say, everyone knows is of very frequent occurrence in some places.

As to the "medical and therapeutic indication" to which, using their own words, we have made reference, Venerable Brethren, however much we may pity the mother whose health and even life is gravely imperiled in the performance of the duty allotted to her by nature, nevertheless what could ever be a sufficient reason for excusing in any way the direct murder of the innocent? This is precisely what we are dealing with here. Whether inflicted upon the mother or upon the child, it is against the precept of God and the law of nature: "Thou shalt not kill." The life of each is equally sacred, and no one has the power, not even the public authority, to destroy it. It is of no use to appeal to the right of taking away life for here it is a question of the innocent, whereas that right has regard only to the guilty; nor is there here question of defense by bloodshed against an unjust aggressor (for who would call an innocent child an unjust aggressor?); again there is no question here of what is called the "law of extreme necessity" which could even extend to the direct killing of the innocent. Upright and skilful doctors strive most praiseworthily to guard and preserve the lives of both mother and child; on the contrary, those show themselves most unworthy of the noble medical profession who encompass the death of one or the other, through a pretence at practicing medicine or through motives of misguided pity. . . .

Those who hold the reins of government should not forget that it is the duty of public authority by appropriate laws and sanctions to defend the lives of the innocent, and this all the more so since those whose lives are endangered and assailed cannot defend themselves. Among whom we must mention in the first place infants hidden in the mother's womb. And if the public magistrates not only do not defend them, but by their laws and ordinances betray them to death at the hands of doctors and others, let them remember that God is the Judge and Avenger of innocent blood which cries from earth to Heaven.

Finally, that pernicious practice must be condemned which closely touches upon the natural right of man to enter matrimony but affects also in a real way the welfare of the offspring. For there are some who, oversolicitous for the cause of eugenics, not only give salutary counsel for more certainly procuring the strength and health of the future child—which, indeed, is not contrary to right reason—but put eugenics before aims of a higher order, and by public authority wish to prevent from marrying all those who, even though naturally fit for marriage, they consider, according to the norms and conjectures of their investigations, would, through hereditary transmission, bring forth defective offspring. And more, they wish to legislate to deprive these of that natural faculty by medical action despite their unwillingness; and this they do not propose as an infliction of grave punishment under the authority of the state for a crime committed, nor to prevent future crimes by guilty persons, but against every right and good they wish the civil authority to arrogate to itself a power over a faculty which it never had and can never legitimately possess. . . .

Public magistrates have no direct power over the bodies of their subjects; therefore, where no crime has taken place and there is no cause present for grave punishment, they can never directly harm, or tamper with the integrity of the body, either for the reasons of eugenics or for any other reason. . . .

Furthermore, Christian doctrine establishes, and the light of human reason makes it most clear, that private individuals have no other power over the members of their bodies than that which pertains to their natural ends; and they are not free to destroy or mutilate their members, or in any other way render themselves unfit for their natural functions, except when no other provision can be made for the good of the whole body. . . .

The advocates of the neo-paganism of to-day have learned nothing from the sad state of affairs, but instead, day by day, more and more vehemently, they continue by legislation to attack the indissolubility of the marriage bond, proclaiming that the lawfulness of divorce must be recognised, and that the antiquated laws should give place to a new and more humane legislation. Many and varied are the grounds put forward for divorce, some arising from the wickedness and the guilt of the persons concerned, others arising from the circumstances of the case; the former they describe as subjective, the latter as objective; in a word, whatever might make married life hard or unpleasant. . . .

Opposed to all these reckless opinions, Venerable Brethren, stands the unalterable law of God, fully confirmed by Christ, a law that can never be deprived of its force by the decrees of men, the ideas of a people or the will of any legislator: "What God hath joined together, let no man put asunder." And if any man, acting contrary to this law, shall have put asunder, his action is null and void, and the consequence remains, as Christ Himself has explicitly confirmed: "Everyone that putteth away his wife and marrieth another, committeth adultery: and he that marrieth her that is put away from her husband committeth adultery." Moreover, these words refer to every kind of marriage, even that which is natural and legitimate only; for, as has already been observed, that indissolubility by which the loosening of the bond is once and for all removed from the whim of the parties and from every secular power, is a property of every true marriage. . . .

. . . Those who have the care of the State and of the public good cannot neglect the needs of married people and their families, without bringing great harm upon the State and on the common welfare. Hence, in making the laws and in disposing of public funds they must do their utmost to relieve the needs of the poor, considering such a task as one of the most important of their administrative duties.

We are sorry to note that not infrequently nowadays it happens that through a certain inversion of the true order of things, ready and bountiful assistance is provided for the unmarried mother and her illegitimate offspring (who, of course, must be helped in order to avoid a greater evil) which is denied to legitimate mothers or given sparingly or almost grudgingly.

But not only in regard to temporal goods, Venerable Brethren, is it the concern of the public authority to make proper provision for matrimony and the family, but also in other things which concern the good of souls. Just laws must be made for the protection of chastity, for reciprocal conjugal aid, and for similar purposes, and these must be faithfully enforced, because, as history testifies, the prosperity of the State and the temporal happiness of its citizens cannot remain safe and sound where the foundation on which they are established, which is the moral order, is weakened and where the very fountainhead from which the State draws its life, namely, wedlock and the family, is obstructed by the vices of its citizens. . . .

[Although the following encyclical seems to concern itself only with Catholic Action, it was, in reality, a strong condemnation of the Fascist claim to dominate all citizens' associations, youth groups, and public and private meetings. It carried more weight, being written in the vernacular and specifically directed to Italy.]

Non abbiamo bisogno, June 29, 1931
Concerning Catholic Action[7]

We must needs speak to you, Venerable Brethren, about events which have recently occurred in this, Our Episcopal City of Rome, and throughout Italy, that is to say, in the very territory of which We are Primate—events which have had such a vast and such a strong repercussion everywhere, conspicuously so in all of the dioceses of Italy and throughout the Catholic World.

These occurrences are summarized in a very few and very sad words. There has been an attempt made to strike unto death that which was and that which always will be dearest to Our heart as Father and as Shepherd of Souls; and We can, We even must, subjoin "and the way in which it was done offends Us still more. . . ."

It has been for Us an exquisite satisfaction to see the Catholic Action organizations of all countries, both near and distant, united about the Common Father, inspired by an unique spirit of faith, of filial sorrow and of generous impulses, expressing all their astonishment and grief in seeing Catholic Action societies persecuted and assailed here in the very centre of the Apostolic Hierarchy, in Italy, where, as in all parts of the world, Catholic Action was existing, and did not wish to exist otherwise, nor could have existed otherwise, than in accordance with its authentic and essential definition—as the par-

[7] Official English Version, Vatican Polyglot Press.

ticipation and the collaboration of the laity with the Apostolic Hierarchy.

This was what Catholic Action societies were actually doing in strict accordance with its definition and under Our painstaking and vigilant direction and with the helpful cooperation of yourselves, Venerable Brethren. . . .

. . . Particularly appreciative are We of the unanimous and most satisfactory and convincing proofs which you have brought to Us concerning Italian Catholic Action societies, and particularly regarding Catholic Youth associations, affording demonstrations that these organizations have remained docile and faithful to your and to Our instructions in refraining absolutely from any and every kind of political party activity. . . .

Already on several occasions, Venerable Brethren, in the most solemn and explicit manner and assuming entire responsibility for what We were saying, we have protested against the campaign of false and unjust accusations which preceded the disbanding of the associations of the young people and of the university students affiliated with Catholic Action. It was a disbanding which was carried out in a way and with the use of tactics which would give the impression that action was being taken against a vast and dangerous organization of criminals. And the proceedings were directed against young men and young women who are certainly some of the best among the good and concerning whom We are happy and paternally proud to pay them tribute still once more. It is noteworthy that even among the officers of the law charged to carry out these orders of suppression, there were many who were ill at ease and showed by their expressions and courtesies that they were almost asking pardon for doing that which they had been commanded. We have appreciated the delicate feelings of these officers, and We have reserved for them a special blessing.

However, in sad contrast to the manner of acting of these officials, there were how many acts of mistreatment and of violence, extending even to the striking of blows and the drawing of blood! How many insults in the press, how many injurious words and acts against things and persons, not excluding Ourself, preceded, accompanied and followed the carrying into effect of this lightning-like police order which very frequently, either through ignorance or malicious zeal, was extended to include associations and organizations not contemplated in the orders of the superiors, such as the oratories of the little ones and the sodalities of the Children of Mary. And all of this sad accompaniment of irreverences and of violences took place in the presence of and with the participation of members of a political party some of whom were in uniform, and was carried into effect with such a unison of action throughout all Italy and with such a passive acquiescence on the part of the civil authorities and the police as to make one necessarily think of some uniform directions received from some high authority. It is very easy to admit, and it was also equally easy to have foreseen, that the limits of these directions could and would have almost necessarily been exceeded. We have been obliged to refer to these sorrowful and painful occurrences because there has been an attempt made to have the public and the world at large believe that the disbanding of these associations so dear to Us took place without any troubles and almost as if it were quite a normal occurrence.

But there have been other attacks on truth and justice on a larger scale. Of all the inventions, falsehoods and real calumnies diffused by the hostile press of the party, which is the only press which is free to say and to dare to say anything and is often ordered, or almost ordered, what it must say, there was certainly a large portion of these fabrications, if not all of them, summarized in a message which was cautiously characterized as unofficial and yet which was administered to the general public with the most powerful means of diffusion existing at present. The history of documents prepared not in the service of Truth but in offense of Truth and Justice is a long and sad story. But We must say, with a certain deep dismay, that in Our many years of active life as a librarian, rarely have We seen an article so tendentious and so contrary to Truth and Justice in its references to this Holy See, to Italian Catholic Action, and particularly to the associations so harshly treated. . . .

Among other things the above-mentioned message stated was that the revelations of the hostile press of the party had been almost completely confirmed, at least in substance, and confirmed no less than by the *Osservatore Romano*. The truth is that the *Osservatore Romano* has, time and time again, demonstrated that the so-called revelations were either actual fabrications or at least false in the interpretation given to facts. It is sufficient to read without bad faith and with a modest capacity to understand.

The message further stated that it was ridiculous to try to make the Holy See appear as a victim in a country where thousands of travelers could give testimony of the respect shown toward priests, prelates, the Church and religious functions. Yes, Venerable Brethren, the attempt unfortunately would be ridiculous, just as it would be ridiculous to break through an open door; because, unfortunately, thousands of visitors who are always present in Italy and in Rome have observed the irreverences, oftentimes of an impious and blasphemous character, and the acts of violence and vandalism committed against places, things and persons throughout the country and in Our very Episcopal City, and which have been repeatedly deplored by Us after We had had sure and precise information about them.

The message denounces the "black ingratitude" of the priests who are against the party which has been (so the message says) the guarantee of religious liberty throughout all Italy. The clergy, and the bishops and this Holy See have never failed to acknowledge everything that has been done during all these years for the benefit and advantage of religion, and they have on many occasions expressed their genuine and sincere appreciation. But We and the bishops and the clergy and all the faithful—in fact, all citizens desirous of peace and order— have worried and suffered and are worrying and suffering in the presence of a systematic campaign all too quickly begun against the most reasonable and precious liberties of religion and of consciences, such as were the attacks on Catholic Action and its different associations, especially those of the young —attacks which had their culmination in the police measures taken against these organizations and in the manner to which We have already alluded, attacks and measures such as to lead one seriously to doubt that the former benevolences and favors were actuated by a sincere love and zeal for religion, and rather incline to the opinion that they were due to pure calculation and with the intention of solidifying power. . . .

The police measures having been put into effect with their accompaniment and consequence of acts of violence and of irreverence—acts which were unfortunately acquiesced in and connived at by the authorities of public order—We suspended the mission of our Cardinal Legate to the centenary celebration in Padua, and the festive processions in Rome and in Italy. . . .

. . . We know of impious parodies of sacred processions, all of which were permitted to take place to the profound sorrow of the faithful and the great amazement of all citizens who desire peace and order, who were obliged to witness peace and order undefended, and even worse than undefended, by those very persons who have both the solemn duty and vital interest to defend them. . . .

And it was with a grief inexpressible that We saw a real and a true persecution break out in this Our Italy and in this very city of Rome against that which the Church and its head have characterized as most precious and dear to them from the standpoint of liberty and of right, liberty and right that are the heritage of souls and especially of the souls of the young entrusted to the Church in a particular way by the Divine Creator and Redeemer.

As is well known, We have repeatedly and solemnly affirmed and protested that Catholic Action, both from its very nature and essence (the participation and the collaboration of the laity with the Apostolic Hierarchy) and by Our precise and categorical directions and dispositions, is outside and above every political party. We have also affirmed and protested that We are sure that in Italy Our directions and dispositions have been faithfully obeyed and followed. The message makes the pronouncement that the assertion that Catholic Action did not have a true political character is absolutely false. We wish to call attention to the discourtesy of such a statement; also, because of the motives which the message gives to justify the statement, demonstrate completely the untruth and the lightness of the remark so that We would term it ridiculous if the case were not so sad. For the reason given, that Catholic Action is a political party, is because Catholic Action has banners, badges, identification cards and all the other external forms of a political party, just as if banners, badges and identification cards and other similar external appurtenances were not today the most common thing in every country of the world for the most varied kind of associations and activities which have nothing, and wish to have nothing, in common with politics, such as, for example, sports and professional organizations, civil and military clubs, commercial and industrial groups, school children even organized exclusively in a religious way, as little ones who belong to the Crusaders of the Blessed Sacrament. The message itself reveals all the weakness and the futility of this alleged motive, and, almost as if hastening to make reparations, it adds three other reasons. The first reason is that the heads of Catholic Action were almost to a man members or heads of the Popular Party, which was one of the strongest opponents of Fascism. This accusation has been launched many times against Catholic Action, but always in a generic manner and without specifying any names. Many times We have asked for precise data and for names, but without result. . . .

"However," continues the message, "the strongest argument that can be used as justification for the destruction of the Catholic circles of youth is the defense of the state, which is no more than the simple duty of every government." There is no doubt of the solemnity and the vital importance of such a duty and of such a right, We add, since We hold, and We wish at all costs to practice with all honest and reasonable individuals, that the first right is to do one's own duty.

But all the receivers and readers of the message would

have smiled with incredulity or wondered greatly if the message has added what is true, namely that of the Catholic circles of the young which were objects of the measure, 10,000 were—rather, actually are—composed of girls and young women with a total membership of about 500,000. Who can see a serious danger and a real threat against the security of the state in this question? And it must be considered that only 220,000 are inscribed as "effective members." More than 100,000 are little "aspirants"; more than 150,000, still smaller children, are called "benjamins."

There still remain the circles of the Catholic young men, that same Catholic youth which, in the publications of the youth of the party and in the circular letters of the so-called leaders of the party, are represented and held up to ridicule and to scorn (with what sense of pedagogical responsibility, to say only this, anyone may see) as an assembly of "rabbits" and able only to carry candles and to recite rosaries in sacred processions. And this is perhaps the reason that they have been in these recent days so many times, and with such cowardice, assailed and maltreated even to the shedding of blood, and left undefended by those who could and should protect and defend them, if for no other reason than, being harmless and peaceful, they have been assailed by individuals who frequently bore arms. . . .

We dare to say that even Catholic Action itself is only a pretext. That which was desired and that which was attempted was to tear away from the Catholic Action society, and through this process to tear away from the Church, the young, and all the young. . . .

We state, Venerable Brethren, the sacred and inviolable rights of the soul and of the Church, and this is the reflection and conclusion that more than any other concerns Us, as it is, than any other, more grave. . . . We said sacred and inviolable rights of souls and of the Church because the matter concerns the right of souls to procure for themselves the greatest spiritual good according to the teaching and under the formation work of the Church, of such a teaching and of such an unique work that it is constituted by Divine mandate in this supernatural order, established in the Blood of God the Redeemer, necessary and obligatory to all in order to participate in the Divine Redemption. It concerns the right of souls so formed to bring the treasures of the Redemption to other souls, thus participating in the activities of the Apostolic Hierarchy.

And in consideration of this double right of souls, We are, as We stated above, happy and proud to wage the good fight for the liberty of conscience which is an equivocal expression too often distorted to mean the absolute independence of conscience, which is absurd in a soul created and redeemed by God. . . .

And here We find Ourselves in the presence of a contrast between authentic affirmations on the one hand and not less authentic facts on the other hand, which reveal, without the slightest possibility of doubt, the proposal, already in great part actually put into effect, to monopolize completely the young, from the tenderest years up to manhood and womanhood, and all for the exclusive advantage of a party, of a regime based on ideology which clearly resolves itself into a true and real pagan worship of the state, which is no less in contrast with the natural rights of the family than it is in contradiction to the supernatural rights of the Church. To propose and promote such a monopoly, to persecute for this reason Catholic Action, as has been done for some time more or less openly or under cover, to reach this end by striking Catholic Action in the way that has recently occurred, is truly and actually to prevent children from going to Jesus Christ, since it impedes them from going to His Church and even arrives at the point of snatching them with violence from the bosom of both, because where the Church is, there is Jesus Christ.

The Church of Jesus Christ has never contested the rights and the duties of the state concerning the education of its citizens and We Ourselves have recalled and proclaimed them in Our recent Encyclical Letter on the Christian Education of Youth; rights and duties which are unchallengeable as long as they remain within the limits of the state's proper competency, a competency which in its turn is clearly indicated and determined by the missions of the state, missions certainly not only bodily and material, but missions that by the very necessity of their character are contained within the limits of the natural, the earthly and the temporary. . . .

A conception of the state which makes the young generations belong entirely to it without any exception from the tenderest years up to adult life cannot be reconciled by a Catholic with the Catholic doctrine nor can it be reconciled with the natural right of the family. It is not possible for a Catholic to reconcile with Catholic doctrine the pretense that the Church and the Pope must limit themselves to the external practices of religion, such as Mass and the Sacraments, and then to say that the rest of education belongs to the state. . . .

[The following was read, at the peril of their lives, by the Catholic clergy in Germany from their pulpits. It was the basis upon which Catholic resistance to Hitler was built, and its words sustained the many martyred priests and nuns who were murdered by the Nazis.]

Mit brennender Sorge, March 14, 1937
On the Present Position of the Catholic Church in the German Empire[8]

It is with deep anxiety and growing surprise that We have long been following the painful trials of the Church and the increasing vexations which afflict those who have remained loyal in heart and action in the midst of a people that once received from St. Boniface the bright message and the Gospel of Christ and God's Kingdom. . . .

When, in 1933, We consented, Venerable Brethren, to open negotiations for a concordat, which the Reich Government proposed on the basis of a scheme of several years' standing; and when, to your unanimous satisfaction, We concluded the negotiations by a solemn treaty, We were prompted by the desire, as it behooved Us, to secure for Germany the freedom of the Church's beneficent mission and the salvation of the souls in her care, as well as by the sincere wish to render the German people a service essential for its peaceful development and prosperity. Hence, despite many and grave misgivings, We then decided not to withhold Our consent, for We wished to spare the Faithful of Germany, as far as it was humanly possible, the trials and difficulties they would have had to face, given the circumstances, had the negotiations fallen through. . . .

. . . Whoever has left in his soul an atom of love for truth, and in his heart a shadow of a sense of justice, must admit that, in the course of these anxious and trying years following upon the conclusion of the concordat, every one of Our words, every one of Our acts, has been inspired by the binding law of treaties. At the same time, anyone must acknowledge, not without surprise and reprobation, how the other contracting party emasculated the terms of the treaty, distorted their meaning, and eventually considered its more or less official violation as a normal policy. The moderation We showed in spite of all this was not inspired by motives of worldly interest, still less by unwarranted weakness, but merely by Our anxiety not to draw out the wheat with the cockle; not to pronounce open judgment, before the public was ready to see its force; not to impeach other people's honesty, before the evidence of events should have torn the mask off the systematic hostility leveled at the Church.

[8] Official English Text as issued by *The London Tablet*, 1937.

Even now that a campaign against the confessional schools, which are guaranteed by the concordat, and the destruction of free election, where Catholics have a right to their children's Catholic education, afford evidence, in a matter so essential to the life of the Church, of the extreme gravity of the situation and the anxiety of every Christian conscience; even now Our responsibility for Christian souls induces Us not to overlook the last possibilities, however slight, of a return to fidelity to treaties, and to any arrangement that may be acceptable to the episcopate. We shall continue without failing, to stand before the rulers of your people as the defender of violated rights, and in obedience to Our Conscience and Our pastoral mission, whether We be successful or not, to oppose the policy which seeks, by open or secret means, to strangle rights guaranteed by a treaty. . . .

TRUE FAITH IN GOD

Take care, Venerable Brethren, that above all, faith in God, the first and irreplaceable foundation of all religion, be preserved in Germany pure and unstained. The believer in God is not he who utters the name in his speech, but he for whom this sacred word stands for a true and worthy concept of the Divinity. Whoever identifies, by pantheistic confusion, God and the universe, by either lowering God to the dimensions of the world, or raising the world to the dimensions of God, is not a believer in God. Whoever follows that so-called pre-Christian Germanic conception of substituting a dark and impersonal destiny for the personal God, denies thereby the Wisdom and Providence of God. . . .

Whoever exalts race, or the people, or the State, or a particular form of State, or the depositories of power, or any other fundamental value of the human community—however necessary and honorable be their function in worldly things—whoever raises these notions above their standard value and divinizes them to an idolatrous level, distorts and perverts an order of the world planned and created by God: he is far from the true faith in God and from the concept of life which that faith upholds.

Beware, Venerable Brethren, of that growing abuse, in speech as in writing, of the name of God as though it were a meaningless label, to be affixed to any creation, more or less arbitrary, of human speculation. Use your influence on the Faithful, that they refuse to yield to this aberration. Our God is the Personal God, supernatural, omnipotent, infinitely perfect, one in the Trinity of Persons, tri-personal in the unity of divine essence, the Creator of all existence, Lord,

King and ultimate Consummator of the history of the world, who will not, and cannot, tolerate a rival god by His side.

This God, this Sovereign Master, has issued commandments whose value is independent of time and space, of country and race. As God's sun shines on every human face, so His law knows neither privilege nor exception. Rulers and subjects, crowned and uncrowned, rich and poor, are equally subject to His word. From the fulness of the Creator's right there naturally arises the fulness of His right to be obeyed by individuals and communities, whoever they are. This obedience permeates all branches of activity in which moral values claim harmony with the law of God, and pervades all integration of the ever-changing laws of man into the immutable laws of God.

None but superficial minds could stumble into concepts of a national God, of a national religion; or attempt to lock within the frontiers of a single people, within the narrow limits of a single race, God, the Creator of the universe, King and Legislator of all nations, before whose immensity they are "as a drop of a bucket" (Isaiah xl, 15). . . .

RECOGNITION OF NATURAL RIGHTS

Such is the rush of present-day life that it severs from the divine foundation of Revelation, not only morality, but also theoretical and practical rights. We are especially referring to what is called the natural law, written by the Creator's hand on the tablet of the heart (Rom. ii. 14) and which reason, not blinded by sin or passion, can easily read. It is in the light of the commands of this natural law, that all positive law, whoever be the lawgiver, can be gauged in its moral content, and hence, in the authority it wields over conscience. Human laws in flagrant contradiction with the natural law are vitiated with a taint which no force, no power can mend. In the light of this principle one must judge the axiom, that "right is common utility," a proposition which may be given a correct significance: it means that what is morally indefensible, can never contribute to the good of the people. But ancient paganism acknowledged that the axiom, to be entirely true, must be reversed and be made to say: "Nothing can be useful, if it is not at the same time morally good" (Cicero, De Off. ii. 30). Emancipated from this moral rule, the principle would in international law carry a perpetual state of war between nations; for it ignores in national life, by confusing right and utility, the basic fact that man as a person possesses rights he holds from God, and which any collectivity must protect against denial, suppression or neglect. To overlook this truth is to forget that the real common good ultimately takes its measure from man's nature, which balances personal rights and social obligations, and from the purpose of society, established for the benefit of human nature. Society was intended by the Creator for the full development of individual possibilities, and for the social benefits, which by a give and take process, every one can claim for his own sake and that of others. Higher and more general values, which collectivity alone can provide, also derive from the Creator for the good of man, and for the full development, natural and supernatural, and the realization of his perfection. To neglect this order is to shake the pillars on which society rests, and to compromise social tranquillity, security and existence.

The believer has an absolute right to profess his Faith and live according to its dictates. Laws which impede this profession and practice of Faith are against natural law.

Parents who are earnest and conscious of their educative duties, have a primary right to the education of the children God has given them in the spirit of their Faith, and according to its prescriptions. Laws and measures which in school questions fail to respect this freedom of the parents go against natural law, and are immoral. The Church, whose mission it is to preserve and explain the natural law, as it is divine in its origin, cannot but declare that the recent enrolment into schools organized without a semblance of freedom, is the result of unjust pressure, and is a violation of every common right.

TO THE YOUTH

. . . If the State organizes a national youth, and makes this organization obligatory to all, then, without prejudice to rights of religious associations, it is the absolute right of youths as well as of parents to see to it that this organization is purged of all manifestations hostile to the Church and Christianity. These manifestations are even today placing Christian parents in a painful alternative, as they cannot give to the State what they owe to God alone.

No one would think of preventing young Germans establishing a true ethnical community in a noble love of freedom and loyalty to their country. What We object to is the voluntary and systematic antagonism raised between national education and religious duty. That is why We tell the young: Sing your hymns to freedom, but do not forget the freedom of the children of God. Do not drag the nobility of that freedom in the mud of sin and sensuality. He who sings hymns of loyalty to his terrestrial country should not, for that reason, become unfaithful to God and His Church, or a deserter and traitor to His heavenly country. You are often told about heroic greatness, in lying opposition to evangelical humility and patience. Why conceal the fact that there are heroisms in moral life? That the preservation of baptismal innocence is an act of heroism which deserves credit? . . .

TO THE FAITHFUL OF THE LAITY

We visualize the immense multitudes of Our faithful children, Our sons and daughters, for whom the sufferings of the Church in Germany and their own have left intact their devotion to the cause of God, their tender love for the Father of Christendom, their obedience to their pastors, their joyous resolution to remain ever faithful, happen what may, to the sacred inheritance of their ancestors. To all of them We send Our paternal greetings. And first to the members of those religious associations which, bravely and at the cost of untold sacrifices, have remained faithful to Christ and have stood by the rights which a solemn treaty had guaranteed to the Church and to themselves according to the rules of loyalty and good faith.

We address Our special greetings to the Catholic parents. Their rights and duties as educators, conferred on them by God, are at present the stake of a campaign pregnant with consequences. The Church cannot wait to deplore the devastation of its altars, the destruction of its temples, if an education, hostile to Christ, is to profane the temple of the child's soul consecrated by baptism, and extinguish the eternal light of the faith in Christ for the sake of counterfeit light alien to the Cross. Then the violation of temples is nigh, and it will be every one's duty to sever his responsibility from the opposite camp, and free his conscience from guilty cooperation with such corruption. The more the enemies attempt to disguise their designs, the more a distrustful vigilance will be needed, in the light of bitter experience. Religious lessons maintained for the sake of appearances, controlled by unauthorized men, within the frame of an educational system which systematically works against religion, do not justify a vote in favor of non-confessional schools. We know, dear Catholic parents, that your vote was not free, for a free and secret vote would have meant the triumph of the Catholic schools. Therefore, We shall never cease frankly to represent to the responsible authorities the iniquity of the pressure brought to bear on you and the duty of respecting the freedom of education. Yet do not forget this: none can free you from the responsibility God has placed on you over your children. None of your oppressors, who pretend to relieve you of your duties, can answer for you to the eternal Judge, when He will ask: "Where are those I confided to you?" May every one of you be able to answer: "Of them whom thou hast given me, I have not lost any one" (John xviii. 9). . . .

[The pope never ceased to insist that all human dictatorships, of right and of left, are contrary to the Divine Will and Plan whenever and wherever they violate that essential freedom of the individual will which is the necessary attribute of man's reason.]

Divini Redemptoris, March 28, 1937
On Atheistic Communism[9]

1. The promise of a Redeemer brightens the first page of the history of mankind, and the confident hope aroused by this promise softened the keen regret for a paradise which had been lost. It was this hope that accompanied the human race on its weary journey, until in the fullness of time the expected Saviour came to begin a new universal civilization, the Christian civilization, far superior even to that which up to this time had been laboriously achieved by certain more privileged nations.

2. Nevertheless, the struggle between good and evil remained in the world as a sad legacy of the original fall. Nor has the ancient tempter ever ceased to deceive mankind with false promises. It is on this account that one convulsion following upon another has marked the passage of the centuries, down to the revolution of our own days. This modern revolution, it may be said, has actually broken out or threatens everywhere, and it exceeds in amplitude and violence anything yet experienced in the preceding persecutions launched against the Church. Entire peoples find themselves in danger of falling back into a barbarism worse than that which oppressed the greater part of the world at the coming of the Redeemer.

3. This all too imminent danger, Venerable Brethren, as you have already surmised, is bolshevistic and atheistic communism, which aims at upsetting the social order and at undermining the very foundations of Christian civilization. . . .

8. The communism of today, more emphatically than similar movements in the past, conceals in itself a false messianic idea. A pseudo-ideal of justice, of equality and fraternity in labor impregnates all its doctrine and activity with a deceptive mysticism, which communicates a zealous

[9] Official English Version, Vatican Polyglot Press.

and contagious enthusiasm to the multitudes entrapped by
delusive promises. This is especially true in an age like ours,
when unusual misery has resulted from the unequal distribution of the goods of this world. This pseudo-ideal is even
boastfully advanced as if it were responsible for a certain
economic progress. As a matter of fact, when such progress
is at all real, its true causes are quite different, as for instance
the intensification of industrialism in countries which were
formerly almost without it, the exploitation of immense natural resources, and the use of the most brutal methods to
insure the achievement of gigantic projects with a minimum
of expense.

9. The doctrine of modern communism, which is often
concealed under the most seductive trappings, is in substance
based on the principles of dialectical and historical materialism previously advocated by Marx, of which the theoreticians
of bolshevism claim to possess the only genuine interpretation. According to this doctrine there is in the world only
one reality, matter, the blind forces of which evolve into
plant, animal and man. Even human society is nothing but
a phenomenon and form of matter, evolving in the same way.
By a law of inexorable necessity and through a perpetual
conflict of forces, matter moves towards the final synthesis
of a classless society. In such a doctrine, as is evident, there
is no room for the idea of God; there is no difference between
matter and spirit, between soul and body; there is neither
survival of the soul after death nor any hope in a future
life. Insisting on the dialectical aspect of their materialism,
the communists claim that the conflict which carries the
world towards its final synthesis can be accelerated by man.
Hence they endeavor to sharpen the antagonisms which
arise between the various classes of society. Thus the class
struggle with its consequent violent hate and destruction takes
on the aspect of a crusade for the progress of humanity. On
the other hand, all other forces whatever, as long as they resist such systematic violence, must be annihilated as hostile
to the human race.

10. Communism, moreover, strips man of his liberty, robs
human personality of all its dignity, and removes all the
moral restraints that check the eruptions of blind impulse.
There is no recognition of any right of the individual in his
relations to the collectivity; no natural right is accorded to
human personality, which is a mere cog-wheel in the com-
munist system. In man's relations with other individuals,
besides, communists hold the principle of absolute equality,
rejecting all hierarchy and divinely constituted authority, including the authority of parents. What men call authority and

subordination is derived from the community as its first and only font. Nor is the individual granted any property rights over material goods or the means of production, for inasmuch as these are the source of further wealth, their possession would give one man power over another. Precisely on this score, all forms of private property must be eradicated, for they are at the origin of all economic enslavement.

11. Refusing to human life any sacred or spiritual character, such a doctrine logically makes of marriage and the family a purely artificial and civil institution, the outcome of a specific economic system. There exists no matrimonial bond of a juridico-moral nature that is not subject to the whim of the individual or of the collectivity. Naturally, therefore, the notion of an indissoluble marriage tie is scouted. Communism is particularly characterized by the rejection of any link that binds woman to the family and the home, and her emancipation is proclaimed as a basic principle. She is withdrawn from the family and the care of her children, to be thrust instead into public life and collective production under the same conditions as man. The care of home and children then devolves upon the collectivity.

Finally, the right of education is denied to parents, for it is conceived as the exclusive prerogative of the community, in whose name and by whose mandate alone parents may exercise this right.

12. What would be the condition of a human society based on such materialistic tenets? It would be a collectivity with no other hierarchy than that of the economic system. It would have only one mission: the production of material things by means of collective labor, so that the goods of this world might be enjoyed in a paradise where each would "give according to his powers" and would "receive according to his needs." Communism recognizes in the collectivity the right, or rather, unlimited discretion, to draft individuals for the labor of the collectivity with no regard for their personal welfare; so that even violence could be legitimately exercised to dragoon the recalcitrant against their wills. In the communistic commonwealth morality and law would be nothing but a derivation of the existing economic order, purely earthly in origin and unstable in character. In a word, the communists claim to inaugurate a new era and a new civilization which is the result of blind evolutionary forces culminating in a "humanity without God."

13. When all men have finally acquired the collectivist mentality in this Utopia of a really classless society, the political State, which is now conceived by communists merely as the instrument by which the proletariat is oppressed by

the capitalists, will have lost all reason for its existence and will "wither away." However, until that happy consummation is realized, the State and the powers of the State furnish communism with the most efficacious and most extensive means for the achievement of its goal.

14. Such, Venerable Brethren, is the new gospel which bolshevistic and atheistic communism offers the world as the glad tidings of deliverance and salvation! It is a system full of errors and sophisms. It is in opposition both to reason and to divine Revelation. It subverts the social order, because it means the destruction of its foundations; because it ignores the true origin and purpose of the State; because it denies the rights, dignity and liberty of human personality. . . .

19. . . . Where communism has been able to assert its power—and here We are thinking with special affection of the people of Russia and Mexico—it has striven by every possible means, as its champions openly boast, to destroy Christian civilization and the Christian religion by banishing every remembrance of them from the hearts of men, especially of the young. Bishops and priests were exiled, condemned to forced labor, shot and done to death in inhuman fashion: laymen suspected of defending their religion were vexed, persecuted, dragged off to trial and thrown into prison. . . .

22. . . . For the first time in history we are witnessing a struggle, cold-blooded in purpose and mapped out to the least detail, between man and "all that is called God." Communism is by its nature antireligious. It considers religion as "the opiate of the people" because the principles of religion which speak of a life beyond the grave dissuade the proletariat from the dream of a soviet paradise which is of this world.

23. But the law of nature and its Author cannot be flouted with impunity. Communism has not been able, and will not be able, to achieve its objectives even in the merely economic sphere. It is true that in Russia it has been a contributing factor in rousing men and materials from the inertia of centuries, and in obtaining by all manner of means, often without scruple, some measure of material success. Nevertheless We know from reliable and even very recent testimony that not even there, in spite of slavery imposed on millions of men, has communism reached its promised goal. After all, even the sphere of economics needs some morality, some moral sense of responsibility, which can find no place in a system so thoroughly materialistic as communism. Terrorism is the only possible substitute, and it is terrorism that reigns today in Russia, where former comrades in revolution are exterminating each other. Terrorism, having failed despite all

to stem the tide of moral corruption, cannot even prevent the dissolution of society itself.

24. In making these observations it is no part of Our intention to condemn *en masse* the peoples of the Soviet Union. For them We cherish the warmest paternal affection. We are well aware that not a few of them groan beneath the yoke imposed on them by men who in very large part are strangers to the real interests of the country. We recognize that many others were deceived by fallacious hopes. We blame only the system, with its authors and abettors who considered Russia the best-prepared field for experimenting with a plan elaborated decades ago, and who from there continue to spread it from one end of the world to the other.

29. . . . In the plan of the Creator, society is a natural means which man can and must use to reach his destined end. Society is for man and not vice versa. This must not be understood in the sense of liberalistic individualism, which subordinates society to the selfish use of the individual; but only in the sense that by means of an organic union with society and by mutual collaboration the attainment of earthly happiness is placed within the reach of all. In a further sense, it is society which affords the opportunities for the development of all the individual and social gifts bestowed on human nature. These natural gifts have a value surpassing the immediate interests of the moment, for in society they reflect the divine perfection, which would not be true were man to live alone. But on final analysis, even in this latter function society is made for man, that he may recognize the reflection of God's perfection, and refer it in praise and adoration to the Creator. Only man, the human person, and not society in any form is endowed with reason and a morally free will.

30. Man cannot be exempted from his divinely imposed obligations toward civil society, and the representatives of authority have the right to coerce him when he refuses without reason to do his duty. Society, on the other hand, cannot defraud man of his God-granted rights, the most important of which We have indicated above. Nor can society systematically void these rights by making their use impossible. It is therefore according to the dictates of reason that ultimately all material things should be ordained to man as a person, that through his mediation they may find their way to the Creator. . . .

33. In view of this organized common effort towards peaceful living, Catholic doctrine vindicates to the State the dignity and authority of a vigilant and provident defender of those divine and human rights on which the Sacred Scriptures and

the Fathers of the Church insist so often. It is not true that all have equal rights in civil society. It is not true that there exists no lawful social hierarchy. . . . The enslavement of man despoiled of his rights, the denial of the transcendental origin of the State and its authority, the horrible abuse of public power in the service of a collectivistic terrorism, are the very contrary of all that corresponds with natural ethics and the will of the Creator. Both man and civil society derive their origin from the Creator, Who has mutually ordained them one to the other. Hence neither can be exempted from their correlative obligations, nor deny or diminish each other's rights. The Creator Himself has regulated this mutual relationship in its fundamental lines, and it is by an unjust usurpation that communism arrogates to itself the right to enforce, in place of the divine law based on the immutable principles of truth and charity, a partisan political program which derives from the arbitrary human will and is replete with hate. . . .

36. . . . It was Christianity that first affirmed the real and universal brotherhood of all men of whatever race and condition. This doctrine she proclaimed by a method, and with an amplitude and conviction, unknown to preceding centuries; and with it she potently contributed to the abolition of slavery. Not bloody revolution, but the inner force of her teaching made the proud Roman matron see in her slave a sister in Christ. It is Christianity that adores the son of God, made Man for love of man, and become not only the "Son of a Carpenter" but Himself a "Carpenter." It was Christianity that raised manual labor to its true dignity. . . .

38. It may be said in all truth that the Church, like Christ, goes through the centuries doing good to all. There would be today neither socialism nor communism if the rulers of the nations had not scorned the teachings and maternal warnings of the Church. On the bases of liberalism and laicism they wished to build other social edifices which, powerful and imposing as they seemed at first, all too soon revealed the weakness of their foundations, and today are crumbling one after another before our eyes, as everything must crumble that is not grounded on the one corner stone which is Christ Jesus. . . .

39. . . . The most urgent need of the present day is therefore the energetic and timely application of remedies which will effectively ward off the catastrophe that daily grows more threatening. . . .

41. As in all the stormy periods of the history of the Church, the fundamental remedy today lies in a sincere renewal of private and public life according to the principles of the Gospel by all those who belong to the Fold of Christ, that

they may be in truth the salt of the earth to preserve human society from total corruption.

43. . . . There is still much to be done in the way of spiritual renovation. Even in Catholic countries there are still too many who are Catholics hardly more than in name. . . . The Catholic who does not live really and sincerely according to the Faith he professes will not long be master of himself in these days when the winds of strife and persecution blow so fiercely, but will be swept away defenceless in this new deluge which threatens the world. And thus, while he is preparing his own ruin, he is exposing to ridicule the very name of Christian. . . .

51. . . . Now it is of the very essence of social justice to demand from each individual all that is necessary for the common good. But just as in the living organism it is impossible to provide for the good of the whole unless each single part and each individual member is given what it needs for the exercise of its proper functions, so it is impossible to care for the social organism and the good of society as a unit unless each single part and each individual member—that is to say, each individual man in the dignity of his human personality—is supplied with all that is necessary for the exercise of his social functions. If social justice be satisfied, the result will be an intense activity in economic life as a whole, pursued in tranquillity and order. This activity will be proof of the health of the social body, just as the health of the human body is recognized in the undisturbed regularity and perfect efficiency of the whole organism. [D-2277]

52. But social justice cannot be said to have been satisfied as long as workingmen are denied a salary that will enable them to secure proper sustenance for themselves and for their families; as long as they are denied the opportunity of acquiring a modest fortune and forestalling the plague of universal pauperism; as long as they cannot make suitable provision through public or private insurance for old age, for periods of illness and unemployment. . . .

54. If, therefore, We consider the whole structure of economic life, as We have already pointed out in Our Encyclical *Quadragesimo anno,* the reign of mutual collaboration between justice and charity in social-economic relations can only be achieved by a body of professional and interprofessional organizations, built on solidly Christian foundatio s. . . .

58. . . . Communism is intrinsically wrong, and no one who would save Christian civilization may collaborate with it in any undertaking whatsoever. Those who permit themselves to be deceived into lending their aid towards the triumph of com-

munism in their own country, will be the first to fall victims of their error. . . .

75. It must likewise be the special care of the State to create those material conditions of life without which an orderly society cannot exist. The State must take every measure necessary to supply employment, particularly for the heads of families and for the young. To achieve this end demanded by the pressing needs of the common welfare, the wealthy classes must be induced to assume those burdens without which human society cannot be saved nor they themselves remain secure. However, measures taken by the State with this end in view ought to be of such a nature that they will really affect those who actually possess more than their share of capital resources, and who continue to accumulate them to the grievous detriment of others.

76. The State itself, mindful of its responsibility before God and society, should be a model of prudence and sobriety in the administration of the commonwealth. Today more than ever the acute world crisis demands that those who dispose of immense funds, built up on the sweat and toil of millions, keep constantly and singly in mind the common good. State functionaries and all employees are obliged in conscience to perform their duties faithfully and unselfishly, imitating the brilliant example of distinguished men of the past and of our own day, who with unremitting labor sacrificed their all for the good of their country. In international trade relations let all means be sedulously employed for the removal of those artificial barriers to economic life which are the effects of distrust and hatred. All must remember that the peoples of the earth form but one family in God.

77. At the same time the State must allow the Church full liberty to fulfil her divine and spiritual mission, and this in itself will be an effectual contribution to the rescue of nations from the dread torment of the present hour. Everywhere today there is an anxious appeal to moral and spiritual forces; and rightly so, for the evil we must combat is at its origin primarily an evil of the spiritual order. From this polluted source the monstrous emanations of the communistic system flow with satanic logic. Now, the Catholic Church is undoubtedly preeminent among the moral and religious forces of today. Therefore the very good of humanity demands that her work be allowed to proceed unhindered. . . .

Chapter 20

✠

Pius XII (1939–1958)

Eugenio Cardinal Pacelli was born March 2, 1876, the son of the dean of the Vatican lawyers. An aristocrat, he studied at the Capranica, and was ordained in 1899. Appointed professor of law at the Roman Seminary, he left to enter the papal secretariat of state at Cardinal Gasparri's invitation. Throughout World War I he supervised the work of exchanging prisoners, moving the wounded to hospitals, etc. In May, 1917, he was sent as papal nuncio to Bavaria, and stayed in Munich during revolutionary outbreaks in which his life was threatened. In 1925, after concluding a Concordat with Bavaria, Archibishop Pacelli was sent to Berlin. Recalled to Rome in 1929, he succeeded his teacher and friend, Cardinal Gasparri, as secretary of state. He traveled to South America as legate to the Eucharistic Congress in Buenos Aires in 1934, and was in the United States in 1936. The conclave of 1939 which elected him pope on the first ballot was the shortest since 1623. Cardinal Pacelli was the first secretary of state to be elected pope since 1775.

Pius XII spoke seven languages fluently, and during World War II he made no fewer than thirty appeals in the first sixteen months of the war. He was above all the Pope of the Mystical Body; yet his great encyclical *Mystici Corporis* is but one of the many he addressed to all kinds and conditions of men. Through his radio addresses and television appearances, no less than his encyclicals, this pope strove to bring the Church's message to every human creature.

He died on October 8, 1958.

In his first encyclical he made it plain that he realized that one of the chief problems for the Church in the world of today was its relation to civil society.

Summi Pontificatus, October 20, 1939
On the Function of the State in the Modern World[1]

. . . What age has been, for all its technical and purely civic progress, more tormented than ours by spiritual emptiness and deep-felt interior poverty?

[1] Official English Version, Vatican Polyglot Press.

16. As Vicar of Him Who in a decisive hour pronounced before the highest earthly authority of that day, the great words: "For this was I born, and for this came I into the world; that I should give testimony to the truth. Every one that is of the truth, heareth my voice." (*St. John* xviii:37), We feel We owe no greater debt to Our office and to Our time than to testify to the truth with Apostolic firmness: "to give testimony to the truth." This duty necessarily entails the exposition and confutation of errors and human faults; for these must be made known before it is possible to tend and to heal them, "you shall know the truth, and the truth shall make you free" (*St. John* viii: 32). . . .

23. . . . Before all else, it is certain that the radical and ultimate cause of the evils which We deplore in modern society is the denial and rejection of a universal norm of morality as well for individual and social life as for international relations; We mean the disregard, so common nowadays, and the forgetfulness of the natural law itself, which has its foundation in God, Almighty Creator and Father of all, supreme and absolute Lawgiver, all-wise and just Judge of human actions. When God is hated, every basis of morality is undermined; the voice of conscience is stilled or at any rate grows very faint, that voice which teaches even to the illiterate and to uncivilized tribes what is good and what is bad, what lawful, what forbidden, and makes men feel themselves responsible for their actions to a Supreme Judge.

24. The denial of the fundamentals of morality had its origin, in Europe, in the abandonment of that Christian teaching of which the Chair of Peter is the depository and exponent. That teaching had once given spiritual cohesion to a Europe which, educated, ennobled and civilized by the Cross, had reached such a degree of civil progress as to become the teacher of other peoples, of other continents. But, cut off from the infallible teaching authority of the Church, not a few separated brethren have gone so far as to overthrow the central dogma of Christianity, the Divinity of the Saviour, and have hastened thereby the progress of spiritual decay. . . .

29. Among the many errors which derive from the poisoned source of religious and moral agnosticism, We would draw your attention, Venerable Brethren, to two in particular, as being those which more than others render almost impossible or at least precarious and uncertain, the peaceful intercourse of peoples.

30. The first of these pernicious errors, widespread today, is the forgetfulness of that law of human solidarity and charity which is dictated and imposed by our common origin and by the equality of rational nature in all men, to what-

ever people they belong, and by the redeeming Sacrifice offered by Jesus Christ on the Altar of the Cross to His Heavenly Father on behalf of sinful mankind. . . .

37. In the light of this unity of all mankind, which exists in law and in fact, individuals do not feel themselves isolated units, like grains of sand, but united by the very force of their nature and by their internal destiny, into an organic, harmonious mutual relationship which varies with the changing of times.

38. And the nations, despite a difference of development due to diverse conditions of life and of culture, are not destined to break the unity of the human race, but rather to enrich and embellish it by the sharing of their own peculiar gifts and by that reciprocal interchange of goods which can be possible and efficacious only when a mutual love and a lively sense of charity unite all the sons of the same Father and all those redeemed by the same Divine Blood.

39. The Church of Christ, the faithful depository of the teaching of Divine Wisdom, cannot and does not think of deprecating or disdaining the particular characteristics which each people, with jealous and intelligible pride, cherishes and retains as a precious heritage. Her aim is a supernatural union in all-embracing love, deeply felt and practiced, and not the unity which is exclusively external and superficial and by that very fact weak. . . .

43. In accordance with these principles of equality, the Church devotes her care to forming cultured native clergy and gradually increasing the number of native Bishops. And in order to give external expression to these, Our intentions, We have chosen the forthcoming Feast of Christ the King to raise to the Episcopal dignity at the Tomb of the Apostles twelve representatives of widely different peoples and races. In the midst of the disruptive contrasts which divide the human family, may this solemn act proclaim to all Our sons, scattered over the world, that the spirit, the teaching and the word of the Church can never be other than that which the Apostle of the Gentiles preached: "putting on the new [man], him who is renewed unto knowledge, according to the image of him that created him. Where there is neither Gentile nor Jew, circumcision nor uncircumcision, Barbarian nor Scythian, bond nor free. But Christ is all, and in all" (*Colossians* iii:10,11).

44. Nor is there any fear lest the consciousness of universal brotherhood aroused by the teaching of Christianity, and the spirit which it inspires, be in contrast with love of traditions or the glories of one's fatherland, or impede the progress of prosperity or legitimate interests. For that same Christianity

teaches that in the exercise of charity we must follow a God-given order, yielding the place of honor in our affections and good works to those who are bound to us by special ties. Nay, the Divine Master Himself gave an example of this preference for His Own country and fatherland, as He wept over the coming destruction of the Holy City. But legitimate and well-ordered love of our native country should not make us close our eyes to the all-embracing nature of Christian charity, which calls for consideration of others and of their interests in the pacifying light of love. . . .

47. But there is yet another error no less pernicious to the well-being of the nations and to the prosperity of that great human society which gathers together and embraces within its confines all races. It is the error contained in those ideas which do not hesitate to divorce civil authority from every kind of dependence upon the Supreme Being—First Source and absolute Master of man and of society—and from every restraint of a Higher Law derived from God as from its First Source. Thus they accord the civil authority an unrestricted field of action that is at the mercy of the changeful tide of human will, or of the dictates of casual historical claims, and of the interests of a few.

48. Once the authority of God and the sway of His law are denied in this way, the civil authority as an inevitable result tends to attribute to itself that absolute autonomy which belongs exclusively to the Supreme Maker. It puts itself in the place of the Almighty and elevates the State or group into the last end of life, the supreme criterion of the moral and juridical order, and therefore forbids every appeal to the principles of natural reason and of the Christian conscience. . . .

54. . . . It is the noble prerogative and function of the State to control, aid and direct the private and individual activities of national life that they converge harmoniously towards the common good. That good can neither be defined according to arbitrary ideas nor can it accept for its standard primarily the material prosperity of society, but rather it should be defined according to the harmonious development and the natural perfection of man. It is for this perfection that society is designed by the Creator as a means.

55. To consider the State as something ultimate to which everything else should be subordinated and directed, cannot fail to harm the true and lasting prosperity of nations. This can happen either when unrestricted dominion comes to be conferred on the State as having a mandate from the nation, people, or even a social order, or when the State arrogates such dominion to itself as absolute master, despotically, without any mandate whatsoever. If, in fact, the State lays claim

to and directs private enterprises, these, ruled as they are by
delicate and complicated internal principles which guarantee
and assure the realization of their special aims, may be damaged to the detriment of the public good, by being wrenched
from their natural surroundings, that is, from responsible
private action. . . .

59. True courage and a heroism worthy in its degree of
admiration and respect, are often necessary to support the
hardships of life, the daily weight of misery, growing want
and restrictions on a scale never before experienced, whose
reason and necessity are not always apparent. Whoever has
the care of souls and can search hearts knows the hidden
tears of mothers, the resigned sorrow of so many fathers, the
countless bitternesses of which no statistics tell or can tell.
He sees with sad eyes the mass of sufferings ever on the increase; he knows how the powers of disorder and destruction
stand on the alert ready to make use of all these things for
their dark designs. No one of good-will and vision will think
of refusing the State, in the exceptional conditions of the
world of today, correspondingly wider and exceptional rights
to meet the popular needs. But even in such emergencies, the
moral law, established by God, demands that the lawfulness
of each such measure and its real necessity be scrutinized
with the greatest rigor according to the standards of the common good.

60. In any case, the more burdensome the material sacrifices demanded of the individual and the family by the State,
the more must the rights of conscience be to it sacred and
inviolable. Goods, blood it can demand; but the soul redeemed by God, never. The charge laid by God on parents
to provide for the material and spiritual good of their offspring and to procure for them a suitable training saturated
with the true spirit of religion, cannot be wrested from them
without grave violation of their rights. . . .

64. The idea which credits the State with unlimited authority is not simply an error harmful to the internal life of
nations, to their prosperity, and to the larger and well-ordered
increase in their well-being, but likewise it injures the relations
between peoples, for it breaks the unity of supranational
society, robs the law of nations of its foundation and vigor,
leads to violation of others' rights and impedes agreement
and peaceful intercourse.

65. A disposition, in fact, of the divinely sanctioned
natural order divides the human race into social groups,
nations or States, which are mutually independent in organization and in the direction of their internal life. But for all
that, the human race is bound together by reciprocal ties,

moral and juridical, into a great commonwealth directed to the good of all nations and ruled by special laws which protect its unity and promote its prosperity.

66. Now no one can fail to see how the claim to absolute autonomy for the State stands in open opposition to this natural way that is inherent in man—nay, denies it utterly—and therefore leaves the stability of international relations at the mercy of the will of rulers, while it destroys the possibility of true union and fruitful collaboration directed to the general good.

67. So, Venerable Brethren, it is indispensable for the existence of harmonious and lasting contacts and of fruitful relations, that the peoples recognize and observe these principles of international natural law which regulate their normal development and activity. Such principles demand respect for corresponding rights to independence, to life and to the possibility of continuous development in the paths of civilization; they demand, further, fidelity to compacts agreed upon and sanctioned in conformity with the principles of the law of nations.

68. The indispensable presupposition, without doubt, of all peaceful intercourse between nations, and the very soul of the juridical relations in force among them, is mutual trust: the expectation and conviction that each party will respect its plighted word; the certainty that both sides are convinced that "Better is wisdom, than weapons of war" (*Ecclesiastes* ix: 18), and are ready to enter into discussion and to avoid recourse to force or to threats of force in case of delays, hindrances, changes or disputes, because all these things can be the result not of bad-will, but of changed circumstances and of genuine interests in conflict.

69. But on the other hand, to tear the law of nations from its anchor in Divine law, to base it on the autonomous will of States, is to dethrone that very law and deprive it of its noblest and strongest qualities. Thus it would stand abandoned to the fatal drive of private interest and collective selfishness exclusively intent on the assertion of its own rights and ignoring those of others.

70. Now, it is true that with the passage of time and the substantial change of circumstances, which were not and perhaps could not have been foreseen in the making of a treaty, such a treaty or some of its clauses can in fact become, or at least seem to become, unjust, impracticable or too burdensome for one of the parties. It is obvious that should such be the case, recourse should be had in good time to a frank discussion with a view to modifying the treaty or making another in its stead. But to consider treaties on principle

as ephemeral and tacitly to assume the authority of rescinding them unilaterally when they are no longer to one's advantage, would be to abolish all mutual trust among States. In this way, natural order would be destroyed and there would be seen dug between different peoples and nations trenches of division impossible to refill.

71. Today, Venerable Brethren, all men are looking with terror into the abyss to which they have been brought by the errors and principles which We have mentioned, and by their practical consequences. Gone are the proud illusions of limitless progress. . . . [D-2279-82]

[The great and increasing role played by the Catholic Church in the United States is emphasized in the following encyclical, which was written after World War II had broken out in Europe.]

Sertum Laetitiae, November 1, 1939
Encyclical Letter to the Church in the United States[2]

1. In our desire to enrich the crown of your holy joy We cross in spirit the vast spaces of the seas and find Ourselves in your midst as you celebrate, in company with all your faithful people, the one hundred and fiftieth anniversary of the establishment of the Ecclesiastical Hierarchy in the United States of America. And this We do with great gladness, because an occasion is thus afforded Us, as gratifying as it is solemn, of giving public testimony of Our esteem and Our affection for the youthfully vigorous and illustrious American people. . . .

7. At the present time there are in the United States 19 ecclesiastical provinces, 115 dioceses, almost 200 seminaries and innumerable houses of worship, elementary and high schools, colleges, hospitals, asylums for the poor and monasteries. It is with good reason then that visitors from other lands admire the organization and system under which your schools of various grades are conducted, the generosity of the faithful upon whom they depend, the vigilant care with which they are watched over by the directors. . . .

9. We confess that We feel a special paternal affection, which is certainly inspired of Heaven, for the Negro people dwelling among you; for in the field of religion and education We know that they need special care and comfort and are very deserving of it. . . .

39. Because sociability is one of man's natural requirements and since it is legitimate to promote by common effort

[2] Official English Version, Vatican Polyglot Press.

decent livelihood, it is not possible without injustice to deny or to limit either to the producers or to the laboring and farming classes the free faculty of uniting in associations by means of which they may defend their proper rights and secure the betterment of the goods of soul and of body, as well as the honest comforts of life. But to unions of this kind, which in past centuries have procured immortal glory for Christianity and for the professions an untarnishable splendor, one cannot everywhere impose an identical discipline and structure which therefore can be varied to meet the different temperament of the people and the diverse circumstances of time. . . .

[The most complete of contemporary statements on the nature and function of the Church is contained in perhaps the greatest of Pope Pius XII's encyclicals. *See also* D-2286-91]

Mystici Corporis, June 29, 1943
On the Mystical Body of Christ[8]

The doctrine of the mystical Body of Christ, which is the Church, was first taught us by the Redeemer Himself. Illustrating as it does the great and inestimable privilege of our intimate union with so exalted a Head, this doctrine by its sublime dignity invites all those who are drawn by the Holy Spirit to study it, and gives them, in the truths which it proposes to the mind, a strong incentive to the performance of such good works as are conformable to its teaching. . . .

The chief reason for Our present exposition of this sublime doctrine is Our solicitude for the souls entrusted to Us. Much indeed has been written on this subject; and We know that many today are turning with greater zest to a study which delights and nourishes Christian piety. This, it would seem, is chiefly because a revived interest in the sacred liturgy, the more widely spread custom of frequent Communion, and the more fervent devotion to the Sacred Heart of Jesus practised today, have brought many souls to a deeper consideration of the unsearchable riches of Christ which are preserved in the Church. Moreover, recent pronouncements on Catholic Action, by drawing closer the bonds of union between Christians and between them and the ecclesiastical hierarchy and especially the Roman Pontiff, have undoubtedly helped not a little to place this truth in its proper light. Nevertheless, while We can derive legitimate joy from these considerations, We must confess that grave errors with regard to this doctrine are being spread among those outside the true Church, and that among

[8] Official English Version, Vatican Polyglot Press.

the faithful, also, inaccurate or thoroughly false ideas are being disseminated which turn minds aside from the straight path of truth.

For while there still survives a false *rationalism*, which ridicules anything that transcends and defies the power of human genius, and which is accompanied by a cognate error, the so-called *popular naturalism*, which sees and wills to see in the Church nothing but a juridical and social union, there is on the other hand a false *mysticism* creeping in, which, in its attempt to eliminate the immovable frontier that separates creatures from their Creator, falsifies the Sacred Scriptures.

As a result of these conflicting and mutually antagonistic schools of thought, some, through vain fear, look upon so profound a doctrine as something dangerous, and so they shrink from it as from the beautiful but forbidden fruit of paradise. But this is not so. Mysteries revealed by God cannot be harmful to men, nor should they remain as treasures hidden in a field, useless. They have been given from on high precisely to help the spiritual progress of those who study them in a spirit of piety. . . .

As the word of God willed to make use of our nature, when in excruciating agony He would redeem mankind, so in the same way throughout the centuries He makes use of the Church that the work begun might endure.

If we would define and describe this true Church of Jesus Christ—which is the One, Holy, Catholic, Apostolic Roman Church—we shall find nothing more noble, more sublime, or more divine than the expression "the mystical Body of Jesus Christ"—an expression which springs from and is, as it were, the fair flowering of the repeated teaching of the Sacred Scriptures and the holy Fathers.

That the Church is a body is frequently asserted in the Sacred Scriptures. . . . But it is not enough that the Body of the Church should be an unbroken unity; it must also be something definite and perceptible to the senses as Our predecessor of happy memory, Leo XIII, in his Encyclical *Satis Cognitum* asserts: "The Church is visible because she is a body." Hence they err in a matter of divine truth, who imagine the Church to be invisible, intangible, a something "pneumatological" as they say, by which many Christian communities, though they differ from each other in their profession of faith, are united by an invisible bond.

But a body calls also for a multiplicity of members, which are linked together in such a way as to help one another. And as in the body when one member suffers, all the other members share its pain, and the healthy members come to the assistance of the ailing, so in the Church the individual members do not live for themselves alone, but also help their fellows, and all work in mutual collaboration for the common comfort and for the more perfect building up of the whole Body. . . .

Nor must one imagine that the Body of the Church, just because it bears the name of Christ, is made up during the days of its earthly pilgrimage only of members conspicuous for their holiness, or that it consists only of those whom God has predestined to eternal happiness. It is owing to the Saviour's infinite mercy that place is allowed in His mystical Body here below for those whom, of old, He did not exclude from the banquet. For not every sin, however grave it may be, is such as of its own nature to sever a man from the Body of the Church, as does schism or heresy or apostasy. Men may lose charity and divine grace through sin, thus becoming incapable of supernatural merit, and yet not be deprived of all life if they hold fast to faith and Christian hope, and if, illumined from above, they are spurred on by interior promptings of the Holy Spirit to salutary fear and are moved to prayer and penance for their sins. . . .

But if our Saviour, by His death, became, in the full and complete sense of the word, the Head of the Church, it was likewise through His blood that the Church was enriched with the fullest communication of the Holy Spirit, through which, from the time when the Son of man was lifted up and glorified on the Cross by His sufferings, she is divinely illumined. For then, as Augustine notes, with the rending of the veil of the temple it happened that the dew of the Paraclete's gifts, which heretofore had descended only on the fleece, that is on the people of Israel, fell copiously and abundantly (while the fleece remained dry and deserted) on the whole earth, that is on the Catholic Church, which is confined by no boundaries of race or territory. Just as at the first moment of the Incarnation the Son of the Eternal Father adorned with the fullness of the Holy Spirit the human nature which was substantially united to Him, that it might be a fitting instrument of the Divinity in the sanguinary work of the Redemption, so at the hour of His precious death He willed that His Church should be enriched with the abundant gifts of the Paraclete in order that in dispensing the divine fruits of the Redemption she might be, for the Incarnate Word, a powerful instrument that would never fail. For both the juridical mission of the Church, and the power to teach, govern and administer the Sacraments, derive their supernatural efficacy and force for the building up of the Body of Christ from the fact that Jesus Christ, hanging on the Cross, opened up to His Church the fountain of those divine gifts, which prevent her from ever teaching false doctrine and enable her to rule them for the salvation of their souls through divinely enlightened pastors and to bestow on them an abundance of heavenly graces. . . .

It is the will of Jesus Christ that the whole body of the Church, no less than the individual members, should resemble Him. And we see this realized when, following in the footsteps of her Founder, the Church teaches, governs, and offers the divine Sacrifice. When she embraces the evangelical counsels she reflects the Redeemer's poverty, obedience, and virginal purity. Adorned with institutes of many different kinds as with so many precious jewels, she represents Christ deep in prayer on the mountain, or preaching to the people, or healing the sick and wounded and bringing sinners back to the path of virtue—in a word, doing good to all. What wonder then, if, while on this earth she, like Christ, suffer persecutions, insults and sorrows. . . .

And now, Venerable Brethren, We come to that part of Our explanation in which We desire to make clear why the Body of Christ, which is the Church, should be called mystical. This name, which is used by many early writers, has the sanction of numerous Pontifical documents. There are several reasons why it should be used; for by it we may distinguish the Body of the Church, which is a Society whose Head and Ruler is Christ, from His physical Body, which, born of the Virgin Mother of God, now sits at the right hand of the Father and is hidden under the Eucharistic veils; and, that which is of greater importance in view of modern errors, this name enables us to distinguish it from any other body, whether in the physical or the moral order.

In a natural body the principle of unity unites the parts in such a manner that each lacks its own individual subsistence; on the contrary, in the mystical Body the mutual union, though intrinsic, links the members by a bond which leaves to each the complete enjoyment of his own personality. Moreover, if we examine the relations existing betwen the several members and the whole body, in every physical, living body, all the different members are ultimately destined to the good of the whole alone; while if we look to its ultimate usefulness, every moral association of men is in the end directed to the advancement of all in general and of each single member in particular; for they are persons. And thus—to return to Our theme—as the Son of the Eternal Father came down from heaven for the salvation of us all, He likewise established the body of the Church and enriched it with the divine Spirit to ensure that immortal souls should attain eternal happiness according to the words of the Apostle: "All things are yours; and you are Christ's; and Christ is God's." For the Church exists both for the good of the faithful and for the glory of God and of Jesus Christ whom He sent.

But if we compare a mystical body with a moral body, it is to be noted that the difference between them is not slight; rather it is very considerable and very important. In the moral body the principle of union is nothing else than the common end, and the common co-operation of all under the authority of Society for the attainment of that end; whereas in the mystical Body of which We are speaking, this collaboration is supplemented by another internal principle, which exists effectively in the whole and in each of its parts, and whose excellence is such that of itself it is vastly superior to whatever bonds of union may be found in a physical or moral body. As We said above, this is something not of the natural but of the supernatural order; rather it is something in itself infinite, uncreated: the Spirit of God, who, as the Angelic Doctor says, "numerically one and the same, fills and unifies the whole Church."

Hence, this word in its correct signification gives us to understand that the Church, a perfect society of its kind, is not made up of merely moral and juridical elements and principles. It is far superior to all other human societies; it surpasses them as grace surpasses nature, as things immortal are above all those that perish. Such human societies, and in the first place civil Society, are by no means to be despised or belittled; but the Church in its entirety is not found within this natural order, any more than the whole of man is encompassed within the organism of our mortal body. Although the juridical principles, on which the Church rests and is established, derive from the divine constitution given to it by Christ and contribute to the attaining of its supernatural end, nevertheless that which lifts the Society of Christians far above the whole natural order is the Spirit of our Redeemer who penetrates and fills every part of the Church's being and is active within it until the end of time as the source of every grace and every gift and every miraculous power. Just as our composite mortal body, although it is a marvellous work of the Creator, falls far short of the eminent dignity of our soul, so the social structure of the Christian community, though it proclaims the wisdom of the divine Architect, still remains something inferior when compared to the spiritual gifts which give it beauty and life, and to the divine source whence they flow. . . .

From all that We have hitherto said, you will readily understand, Venerable Brethren, why Paul the Apostle so often writes that Christ is in us and we in Christ. In proof of which, there is this other more subtle reason. Christ is in us through His Spirit, whom He gives to us and through whom He acts within us in such a way that all divine activity of the Holy Spirit within our souls must also be attributed to Christ. "If a man hath not the Spirit of Christ, he is none of his," says the Apostle, "but if Christ be in you . . . the spirit liveth because of justification."

This communication of the Spirit of Christ is the channel through which all the gifts, powers, and extraordinary graces found superabundantly in the Head as in their source flow into all the members of the Church, and are perfected daily in them according to the place they hold in the mystical Body of Jesus Christ. Thus the Church becomes, as it were, the filling out and the complement of the Redeemer, while Christ in a sense attains through the Church a fullness in all things. Herein we find the reason why, according to the opinion of Augustine already referred to, the mystical Head, which is Christ, and the Church, which here below as another Christ shows forth His person, constitute one new man, in whom heaven and earth are joined together in perpetuating the saving work of the Cross: Christ We mean, the Head and the Body, the whole Christ. . . .

Divino Afflante Spiritu, Sept. 30, 1945
On Promotion of Biblical Studies[4]

* * * * *

I
Historical Part
Work of Leo XIII and of His Successors in Favor of Biblical Studies

3. The first and greatest care of Leo XIII was to set forth the teaching on the truth of the Sacred Books and to defend it from attack. Hence with grave words did he proclaim that there is no error whatsoever if the sacred writer, speaking of things of the physical order "went by what sensibly appeared" as the Angelic Doctor says,[5] speaking either in "figurative language, or in terms which were commonly used at the time, and which in many instances are in daily use at this day, even among the most eminent men of science." For "the sacred writers, or to speak more accurately—the words are St. Augustine's—[6] the Holy Ghost, Who spoke by them, did not intend to teach men these things—that is the essential nature of the things of the universe—things in no way profitable to salva-

---

[4] Official English Version, *Acta* Apostolicae Sedis.
[5] Cf. I[a]-, q. 70, art. I ad 3.
[6] *De Gen. ad litt.* 2, 9, 20; *PL.* XXXIV, col. 270 s.; *CSEL.* XXVIII (Sectio III pars. 2), p. 46.

tion:"[7] which principle "will apply to cognate sciences, and especially to history," that is, by refuting "in a somewhat similar way the fallacies of the adversaries and defending the historical truth of Sacred Scripture from their attacks."[8] Nor is the sacred writer to be taxed with error, if "copyists have made mistakes in the text of the Bible," or, "if the real meaning of a passage remains ambiguous." Finally it is absolutely wrong and forbidden "either to narrow inspiration to certain passages of Holy Scripture, or to admit that the sacred writer has erred," since divine inspiration "not only is essentially incompatible with error but excludes and rejects it as absolutely and necessarily as it is impossible that God Himself, the supreme Truth, can utter that which is not true. That is the ancient and constant faith of the Church."[9]

4. This teaching, which Our Predecessor Leo XIII set forth with such solemnity, We also proclaim with Our authority and We urge all to adhere to it religiously. No less earnestly do We inculcate obedience at the present day to the counsels and exhortations which he, in his day, so wisely enjoined. For whereas there arose new and serious difficulties and questions, from the wide-spread prejudices of rationalism and more especially from the discovery and investigation of the antiquities of the East, this same Our Predecessor, moved by zeal of the apostolic office, not only that such an excellent source of Catholic revelation might be more securely and abundantly available to the advantage of the Christian flock, but also that he might not suffer it to be in any way tainted, wished and most earnestly desired "to see an increase in the number of the approved and persevering laborers in the cause of Holy Scripture; and more especially that those whom Divine Grace has called to Holy Orders, should day-by-day, as their state demands, display greater diligence and industry in reading, meditating and explaining it."[10]

5. Wherefore the same Pontiff, as he had already praised and approved the school for biblical studies, founded at St. Shephen's, Jerusalem, by the Master General of the Sacred Order of Preachers—from which, to use his own words, "biblical science itself had received no small advantage, while giving promise of more"[11]—so in the last year of his life he provided yet another way, by which these same studies, so warmly commended in the Encyclical Letter *Providentissimus*

[7] LEONIS XIII *Acta* XIII, p. 355; *Ench. Bibl*, n. 106.
[8] Cf. BENEDICTUS XV, Enc. *Spiritus Paraclitus, Acta Ap. Sedis* XII (1920), p. 396; *Ench. Bibl.* n. 471.
[9] LEONIS XIII *Acta* XIII p. 357 sq.; *Ench. Bibl.* n. 109 sq.
[10] LEONIS XIII *Acta* XIII, p. 328; *Ench. Bibl.* n. 67 sq.
[11] Apostolic Letter *Hierosolymae in coenobio*, Sept. 17, 1892; LEONIS XIII *Acta* XII, pp. 239-241; v. p. 240.

Deus, might daily make greater progress and be pursued with the greatest possible security. By the Apostolic Letter *Vigilantiae,* published on October 30 in the year 1902, he founded a Council or Commission, as it is called, of eminent men, "whose duty it would be to procure by every means that the sacred texts may receive everywhere among us that more thorough exposition which the times demand, and be kept safe not only from every breath of error, but also from all inconsiderate opinions."[12] Following the example of Our Predecessors, We also have effectively confirmed and amplified this Council using its good offices, as often before, to remind commentators of the Sacred Books of those safe rules of Catholic exegesis, which have been handed down by the Holy Fathers and Doctors of the Church, as well as by the Sovereign Pontiffs themselves.[13] . . .

II

Doctrinal Part

Biblical Studies at the Present Day

11. There is no one who cannot easily perceive that the conditions of biblical studies and their subsidiary sciences have greatly changed within the last fifty years. For, apart from anything else, when Our Predecessor published the Encyclical Letter *Providentissimus Deus,* hardly a single place in Palestine had begun to be explored by means of relevant excavations. Now, however, this kind of investigation is much more frequent and, since more precise methods and technical skill have been developed in the course of actual experience, it gives us information at once more abundant and more accurate. How much light has been derived from these explorations for the more correct and fuller understanding of the Sacred Books all experts know, as well as all those who devote themselves to these studies. The value of these excavations is enhanced by the discovery from time to time of written documents, which help much towards the knowledge of the languages, letters, events, customs, and forms of worship of most ancient times. And of no less importance is the discovery and investigation, so frequent in our times, of papyri which have contributed so much to the knowledge of letters and institutions, both public and private, especially of the time of Our Saviour.

[12] Cf. LEONIS XIII *Acta XXII,* p. 232 ss.; *Ench. Bibl.* n. 130–141; v. nn. 130, 132.
[13] Letter of the Pontifical Biblical Commission to their Excellencies the Archbishops and Bishops of Italy, Aug. 20, 1941; *Acta Ap. Sedis XXXIII* (1941), pp. 465-472.

12. Moreover ancient codices of the Sacred Books have been found and edited with discerning thoroughness; the exegesis of the Fathers of the Church has been more widely and thoroughly examined; in fine the manner of speaking, relating and writing in use among the ancients is made clear by innumerable examples. All these advantages which, not without a special design of Divine Providence, our age has acquired, are as it were an invitation and inducement to interpreters of the Sacred Literature to make diligent use of this light, so abundantly given, to penetrate more deeply, explain more clearly and expound more lucidly the Divine Oracles. If, with the greatest satisfaction of mind, We perceive that these same interpreters have resolutely answered and still continue to answer this call, this is certainly not the last or least of the fruits of the Encyclical Letter *Providentissimus Deus,* by which Our Predecessor Leo XIII, foreseeing as it were this new development of biblical studies, summoned Catholic exegetes to labor and wisely defined the direction and the method to be followed in that labor. . . .

Recourse to Original Texts. 14. The Fathers of the Church in their time, especially Augustine, warmly recommended to the Catholic scholar, who undertook the investigation and explanation of the Sacred Scriptures, the study of the ancient languages and recourse to the original texts.[14] However, such was the state of letters in those times, that not many,—and these few but imperfectly—knew the Hebrew language. In the middle ages, when Scholastic Theology was at the height of its vigor, the knowledge of even the Greek language had long since become so rare in the West, that even the greatest Doctors of that time, in their exposition of the Sacred Text, had recourse only to the Latin version, known as the Vulgate.

15. On the contrary in this our time, not only the Greek language, which since the humanistic renaissance has been, as it were, restored to new life, is familiar to almost all students of antiquity and letters, but the knowledge of Hebrew also and of other oriental languages has spread far and wide among literary men. Moreover there are now such abundant aids to the study of these languages that the biblical scholar, who by neglecting them would deprive himself of access to the original texts, could in no wise escape the stigma of levity and sloth. For it is the duty of the exegete to lay hold, so to speak, with the greatest care and reverence of the very least expressions which, under the inspiration of the Divine Spirit,

[14] Cf. ex. gr. St. Jerome *Praef. in IV Evang. ad Damasum; PL. XXIX,* col. 526-527; St. Augustine, *De Doctr. christ.* II, 16; *PL. XXXIV,* col. 42-43.

have flowed from the pen of the sacred writer, so as to arrive at a deeper and fuller knowledge of his meaning.

16. Wherefore let him diligently apply himself so as to acquire daily a greater facility in biblical as well as in other oriental languages and to support his interpretation by the aids which all branches of philology supply. This indeed St. Jerome strove earnestly to achieve, as far as the science of his time permitted; to this also aspired with untiring zeal and no small fruit not a few of the great exegetes of the sixteenth and seventeenth centuries, although the knowledge of languages then was much less than at the present day. In like manner therefore ought we to explain the original text which, having been written by the inspired author himself, has more authority and greater weight than any even the very best translation, whether ancient or modern; this can be done all the more easily and fruitfully, if to the knowledge of languages be joined a real skill in literary criticism of the same text.

Importance of textual criticism. 17. The great importance which should be attached to this kind of criticism was aptly pointed out by Augustine, when, among the precepts to be recommended to the student of the Sacred Books, he put in the first place the care to possess a corrected text. "The correction of the codices"—so says this most distinguished Doctor of the Church—"should first of all engage the attention of those who wish to know the Divine Scripture so that the uncorrected may give place to the corrected." [15] In the present day indeed this art, which is called textual criticism and which is used with great and praiseworthy results in the editions of profane writings, is also quite rightly employed in the case of the Sacred Books, because of that very reverence which is due to the Divine Oracles. For its very purpose is to insure that the sacred text be restored, as perfectly as possible, be purified from the corruptions due to the carelessness of the copyists and be freed, as far as may be done, from glosses and omissions, from the interchange and repetition of words and from all other kinds of mistakes, which are wont to make their way gradually into writings handed down through many centuries.

18. It is scarcely necessary to observe that this criticism, which some fifty years ago not a few made use of quite arbitrarily and often in such wise that one would say they did so to introduce into the sacred text their own preconceived ideas, today has rules so firmly established and secure, that it has become a most valuable aid to the purer and more accurate editing of the sacred text and that any abuse can easily be discovered. Nor is it necessary here to call to mind

[15] *De doctr. christ.* II, 21; *PL.* XXXIV, col. 40.

—since it is doubtless familiar and evident to all students of
Sacred Scripture—to what extent namely the Church has
held in honor these studies in textual criticism from the
earliest centuries down even to the present day.

19. Today therefore, since this branch of science has
attained to such high perfection, it is the honorable, though
not always easy, task of students of the Bible to procure by
every means that as soon as possible may be duly published
by Catholics editions of the Sacred Books and of ancient versions, brought out in accordance with these standards, which,
that is to say, unite the greatest reverence for the sacred text
with an exact observance of all the rules of criticism. And let
all know that this prolonged labor is not only necessary for the
right understanding of the divinely-given writings, but also
is urgently demanded by that piety by which it behooves us
to be grateful to the God of all providence, Who from the
throne of His majesty has sent these books as so many paternal
letters to His own children. . . .

Interpretation of Sacred Books.   23.   Being thoroughly prepared by the knowledge of the ancient languages and
by the aids afforded by the art of criticism, let the Catholic
exegete undertake the task, of all those imposed on him the
greatest, that namely of discovering and expounding the genuine meaning of the Sacred Books. In the performance of this
task let the interpreters bear in mind that their foremost and
greatest endeavor should be to discern and define clearly that
sense of the biblical words which is called literal. Aided by
the context and by comparison with similar passages, let them
therefore by means of their knowledge of languages search
out with all diligence the literal meaning of the words; all
these helps indeed are wont to be pressed into service in the
explanation also of profane writers, so that the mind of the
author may be made abundantly clear.

24. The commentators of the Sacred Letters, mindful of
the fact that here there is question of a divinely inspired text,
the care and interpretation of which have been confided to
the Church by God Himself, should no less diligently take
into account the explanations and declarations of the teaching
authority of the Church, as likewise the interpretation given
by the Holy Fathers, and even "the analogy of faith" as Leo
XIII most wisely observed in the Encyclical Letter *Providentissimus Deus.*[16] With special zeal should they apply themselves
not only to expounding exclusively these matters which belong
to the historical, archaeological, philological and other auxiliary

[16] LEONIS XIII *Acta* XIII, pp. 345-346; *Ench. Bibl.* n. 94-96.

sciences—as, to Our regret, is done in certain commentaries, —but, having duly referred to these, in so far as they may aid the exegesis, they should set forth in particular the theological doctrine in faith and morals of the individual books or texts so that their exposition may not only aid the professors of theology in their explanations and proofs of the dogmas of faith, but may also be of assistance to priests in their presentation of Christian doctrine to the people, and in fine may help all the faithful to lead a life that is holy and worthy of a Christian.

Right use of spiritual sense. 25. By making such an exposition, which is above all, as We have said, theological, they will efficaciously reduce to silence those who, affirming that they scarcely ever find anything in biblical commentaries to raise their hearts to God, to nourish their souls or promote their interior life, repeatedly urge that we should have recourse to a certain spiritual and, as they say, mystical interpretation. With what little reason they thus speak is shown by the experience of many, who, assiduously considering and meditating the word of God, advanced in perfection and were moved to an intense love for God; and this same truth is clearly proved by the constant tradition of the Church and the precepts of the greatest Doctors. Doubtless all spiritual sense is not excluded from the Sacred Scripture.

26. For what was said and done in the Old Testament was ordained and disposed by God with such consummate wisdom, that things past prefigured in a spiritual way those that were to come under the new dispensation of grace. Wherefore the exegete, just as he must search out and expound the literal meaning of the words, intended and expressed by the sacred writer, so also must he do likewise for the spiritual sense, provided it is clearly intended by God. For God alone could have known this spiritual meaning and have revealed it to us. Now Our Divine Saviour Himself points out to us and teaches us this same sense in the Holy Gospel; the Apostles also, following the example of the Master, profess it in their spoken and written words; the unchanging tradition of the Church approves it; finally the most ancient usage of the liturgy proclaims it, wherever may be rightly applied the well-known principle: "The rule of prayer is the rule of faith."

27. Let Catholic exegetes then disclose and expound this spiritual significance, intended and ordained by God, with that care which the dignity of the divine word demands; but let them scrupulously refrain from proposing as the genuine meaning of Sacred Scripture other figurative senses. It may indeed be useful, especially in preaching, to illustrate and

present the matters of faith and morals by a broader use of
the Sacred Text in the figurative sense, provided this be done
with moderation and restraint; it should, however, never be
forgotten that this use of the Sacred Scripture is, as it were,
extrinsic to it and accidental, and that, especially in these
days, it is not free from danger, since the faithful, in particular
those who are well-informed in the sciences sacred and profane, wish to know what God has told us in the Sacred Letters
rather than what an ingenious orator or writer may suggest
by a clever use of the words of Scripture. Nor does "the word
of God, living and effectual and more piercing than any two-
edged sword and reaching unto the division of the soul and
the spirit, of the joints also and the marrow, and a discerner
of the thoughts and intents of the heart" [17] need artificial devices and human adaptation to move and impress souls; for
the Sacred Pages, written under the inspiration of the Spirit
of God, are of themselves rich in original meaning; endowed
with a divine power, they have their own value; adorned
with heavenly beauty, they radiate of themselves light and
splendor, provided they are so fully and accurately explained
by the interpreter, that all the treasures of wisdom and prudence, therein contained, are brought to light. . . .

Importance of mode of writing. 35. What is the literal sense
of a passage is not always as obvious in the speeches and
writings of the ancient authors of the East, as it is in the
works of the writers of our own time. For what they wished
to express is not to be determined by the rules of grammar
and philology alone, nor solely by the context; the interpreter
must, as it were, go back wholly in spirit to those remote
centuries of the East and with the aid of history, archaeology,
ethnology and other sciences, accurately determine what
modes of writing, so to speak, the authors of that ancient
period would be likely to use, and in fact did use.

36. For the ancient peoples of the East, in order to express
their ideas, did not always employ those forms or kinds of
speech, which we use today; but rather those used by the
men of their times and countries. What those exactly were
the commentator cannot determine as it were in advance, but
only after a careful examination of the ancient literature of
the East. The investigation, carried out, on this point, during
the past forty or fifty years with greater care and diligence
than ever before, has more clearly shown what forms of expression were used in those far off times, whether in poetic
description or in the formulation of laws and rules of life or
in recording the facts and events of history. The same inquiry

[17] Hebr. iv, 12.

has also clearly shown the special preeminence of the people of Israel among all the other ancient nations of the East in their mode of compiling history, both by reason of its antiquity and by reason of the faithful record of the events; qualities which may well be attributed to the gift of divine inspiration and to the peculiar religious purpose of biblical history.

37.   Nevertheless no one, who has a correct idea of biblical inspiration, will be surprised to find, even in the Sacred Writers, as in other ancient authors, certain fixed ways of expounding and narrating, certain definite idioms, especially of a kind peculiar to the Semitic tongues, so-called approximations, and certain hyperbolical modes of expression, nay, at times, even paradoxical, which help to impress the ideas more deeply on the mind. For of the modes of expression which, among ancient peoples, and especially those of the East, human language used to express its thought, none is excluded from the Sacred Books, provided the way of speaking adopted in no wise contradicts the holiness and truth of God, as, with his customary wisdom, the Angelic Doctor already observed in these words: "In Scripture divine things are presented to us in the manner which is in common use amongst men."[18] For as the substantial Word of God became like to men in all things, "except sin," [19] so the words of God, expressed in human language, are made like to human speech in every respect, except error. In this consists that "condescension" of the God of providence, which St. John Chrysostom extolled with the highest praise and repeatedly declared to be found in the Sacred Books.[20] . . .

Studies of biblical antiquities.   40.   Let those who cultivate biblical studies turn their attention with all due diligence towards this point and let them neglect none of those discoveries, whether in the domain of archaeology or in ancient history or literature, which serve to make better known the mentality of the ancient writers, as well as their manner and art of reasoning, narrating and writing. In this connection Catholic laymen also should consider that they will not only further profane science, but moreover will render a conspicuous service to the Christian cause if they devote themselves with all due diligence and application to the exploration and investigation of the monuments of antiquity and contribute, according to their abilities, to the solution of questions hitherto obscure.

[18] *Comment ad Hebr.* cap. I, lectio 4.
[19] Hebr. iv, 15.
[20] Cf. v. gr. *In Gen.* I, 4 (*PG LIII*, col. 34-35); *In Gen.* II, 21 (*ib.* col. 121); *In Gen.* iii, 8 (*ib.* col. 135); *Hom.* 15 *in Joan.*, ad. I, 18 (*PG.* LIX, col. 97 sq.).

41. For all human knowledge, even the non-sacred, has indeed its own proper dignity and excellence, being a finite participation of the infinite knowledge of God, but it acquires a new and higher dignity and, as it were, a consecration, when it is employed to cast a brighter light upon the things of God.

Way of Treating More Difficult Questions. 42. The progressive exploration of the antiquities of the East, mentioned above, the more accurate examination of the original text itself, the more extensive and exact knowledge of languages both biblical and oriental, have with the help of God, happily provided the solution of not a few of those questions, which, in the time of Our Predecessor Leo XIII of immortal memory, were raised by critics outside or hostile to the Church against the authenticity, antiquity, integrity and historical value of the Sacred Books. For Catholic exegetes, by a right use of those same scientific arms, not infrequently abused by the adversaries, proposed such interpretations, which are in harmony with Catholic doctrine and the genuine current of tradition, and at the same time are seen to have proved equal to the difficulties, either raised by new explorations and discoveries, or bequeathed by antiquity for solution in our time.

43. Thus has it come about that confidence in the authority and historical value of the Bible, somewhat shaken in the case of some by so many attacks, today among Catholics is completely restored; moreover there are not wanting even non-Catholic writers, who by serious and calm inquiry have been led to abandon modern opinion and to return, at least in some points, to the more ancient ideas. This change is due in great part to the untiring labor, by which Catholic commentators of the Sacred Letters, in no way deterred by difficulties and obstacles of all kinds, strove with all their strength to make suitable use of what learned men of the present day, by their investigations in the domain of archaeology or history or philology, have made available for the solution of new questions.

Difficulties not yet solved. 44. Nevertheless no one will be surprised, if all difficulties are not yet solved and overcome; but that even today serious problems greatly exercise the minds of Catholic exegetes. We should not lose courage on this account; nor should we forget that in the human sciences the same happens as in the natural world; that is to say, new beginnings grow little by little and fruits are gathered only after many labors. Thus it has happened that certain disputed points, which in the past remained unsolved and in suspense, in our days, with the progress of studies, have found a satisfactory solution. Hence there are grounds for hope that those also will by constant effort be at last made clear, which now seem most complicated and difficult. . . .

Use of Scripture in Instruction of Faithful. 49. Whosoever considers the immense labors undertaken by Catholic exegetes during well nigh two thousand years, so that the word of God, imparted to men through the Sacred Letters, might daily be more deeply and fully understood and more intensely loved, will easily be convinced that it is the serious duty of the faithful, and especially of priests, to make free and holy use of this treasure, accumulated throughout so many centuries by the greatest intellects. For the Sacred Books were not given by God to men to satisfy their curiosity or to provide them with material for study and research, but, as the Apostle observes, in order that these Divine Oracles might "instruct us to salvation, by the faith which is in Christ Jesus" and "that the man of God may be perfect, furnished to every good work." [21]

50. Let priests therefore, who are bound by their office to procure the eternal salvation of the faithful, after they have themselves by diligent study perused the sacred pages and made them their own by prayer and meditations assiduously distribute the heavenly treasures of the divine word by sermons, homilies and exhortations; let them confirm the Christian doctrine by sentences from the Sacred Books and illustrate it by outstanding examples from sacred history and in particular from the Gospel of Christ Our Lord; and— avoiding with the greatest care those purely arbitrary and far-fetched adaptations, which are not a use, but rather an abuse of the divine word—let them set forth all this with such eloquence, lucidity and clearness that the faithful may not only be moved and inflamed to reform their lives, but may also conceive in their hearts the greatest veneration for the Sacred Scripture.

51. The same veneration the Bishops should endeavor daily to increase and perfect among the faithful committed to their care, encouraging all those initiatives by which men, filled with apostolic zeal, laudably strive to excite and foster among Catholics a greater knowledge of and love for the Sacred Books. Let them favor therefore and lend help to those pious associations whose aim it is to spread copies of the Sacred Letters, especially of the Gospels, among the faithful, and to procure by every means that in Christian families the same be read daily with piety and devotion; let them efficaciously recommend by word and example, whenever the liturgical laws permit, the Sacred Scriptures translated, with the approval of

[21] Cf. II Tim. iii, 15, 17.

the Ecclesiastical authority, into modern languages; let them themselves give public conferences or dissertations on biblical subjects, or see that they are given by other public orators well versed in the matter. . . .

[The pope's concern for the Church's worship is admirably illustrated by the following encyclical, which insists on the participation of the laity in the ceremonies. *See also* D-2297-2300.]

Mediator Dei, November 20, 1947
On the Sacred Liturgy[22]

3. In obedience, therefore, to her Founder's behest, the Church prolongs the priestly mission of Jesus Christ mainly by means of the sacred Liturgy. She does this in the first place at the altar, where constantly the Sacrifice of the Cross is re-presented and, with a single difference in the manner of its offering, renewed. She does it next by means of the Sacraments, those special channels through which men are made partakers in the supernatural life. She does it finally by offering to God, all Good and Great, the daily tribute of her prayer of praise. . . .

4. You are of course familiar with the fact, Venerable Brethren, that a remarkably widespread revival of scholarly interest in the sacred Liturgy took place towards the end of the last century and has continued through the early years of this one. The movement owed its rise to commendable private initiative and more particularly to the zealous and persistent labor of several monasteries within the distinguished Order of Saint Benedict. Thus there developed in this field among many European nations and in lands beyond the seas as well, a rivalry as welcome as it was productive of results. Indeed, the salutary fruits of this rivalry among the scholars were plain for all to see, both in the sphere of the Sacred Sciences, where the liturgical rites of the Western and Eastern Church were made the object of extensive research and profound study, and in the spiritual life of considerable numbers of individual Christians.

5. The majestic ceremonies of the Sacrifice of the altar became better known, understood and appreciated. With more widespread and more frequent reception of the Sacraments, with the beauty of liturgical prayers more fully savored, the

[22] Official English Version, Vatican Polyglot Press.

worship of the Eucharist came to be regarded for what it really is: the fountain-head of genuine Christian devotion. Bolder relief was given likewise to the fact that all the faithful make up a single and very compact body with Christ for its Head, and that the Christian community is in duty bound to participate in the liturgical rites according to their station. . . .

8. Indeed, though We are sorely grieved to note, on the one hand, that there are places where the spirit, understanding or practice of the sacred Liturgy is defective, or all but inexistent, We observe with considerable anxiety and some misgiving, that elsewhere certain enthusiasts, over-eager in their search for novelty, are straying beyond the path of sound doctrine and prudence. Not seldom, in fact, they interlard their plans and hopes for a revival of the sacred Liturgy with principles which compromise this holiest of causes in theory or practice, and sometimes even taint it with errors touching Catholic faith and ascetical doctrine.

9. Yet the integrity of faith and morals ought to be the special criterion of this sacred science, which must conform exactly to what the Church out of the abundance of her wisdom teaches and prescribes. It is consequently Our prerogative to commend and approve whatever is done properly, and to check or censure any aberration from the path of truth and rectitude.

10. Let not the apathetic or half-hearted imagine, however, that We agree with them when We reprove the erring and restrain the overbold. No more must the imprudent think that We are commending them when We correct the faults of those who are negligent and sluggish.

11. If in this Encyclical Letter We treat chiefly of the Latin Liturgy, is is not because We esteem less highly the venerable Liturgies of the Eastern Church, whose ancient and honorable ritual traditions are just as dear to Us. The reason lies rather in a special situation prevailing in the Western Church, of sufficient importance, it would seem, to require this exercise of Our Authority. . . .

20. . . . Along with the Church . . . her divine Founder is present at every liturgical function: Christ is present at the august Sacrifice of the altar both in the person of His minister and above all under the Eucharistic species. He is present in the Sacraments, infusing into them the power which makes them ready instruments of sanctification. He is present finally in the prayer of praise and petition we direct to God, as it is written: "Where there are two or three gathered together in My Name, there am I in the midst of them." The sacred Liturgy is consequently the public worship which our Re-

deemer as Head of the Church renders to the Father as well as the worship which the community of the faithful renders to its Founder, and through Him to the Heavenly Father. It is, in short, the worship rendered by the Mystical Body of Christ in the entirety of its Head and members. . . .

23. The worship rendered by the Church to God must be, in its entirety, interior as well as exterior. It is exterior because the nature of man as a composite body and soul requires it to be so. Likewise, because divine Providence has disposed that "while we recognize God visibly, we may be drawn by Him to love of things unseen." Every impulse of the human heart, besides, expresses itself naturally through the senses; and the worship of God, being the concern not merely of individuals but of the whole community of mankind, must therefore be social as well. This obviously it cannot be unless religious activity is also organized and manifested outwardly. Exterior worship, finally, reveals and emphasizes the unity of the Mystical Body, feeds new fuel to its holy zeal, fortifies its energy, intensifies its action day by day. . . .

24. But the chief element of divine worship must be interior. For we must always live in Christ and give ourselves to Him completely, so that in Him, with Him and through Him the heavenly Father may be duly glorified. The sacred Liturgy requires, however, that both of these elements be intimately linked with each other. This recommendation the Liturgy itself is careful to repeat, as often as it prescribes an exterior act of worship. Thus we are urged, when there is question of fasting, for example, "to give interior effect to our outward observance." Otherwise religion clearly amounts to mere formalism, without meaning and without content. . . . It is, therefore, the keen desire of the Church that all of the faithful kneel at the feet of the Redeemer to tell Him how much they venerate and love Him. She wants them present in crowds—like the children whose joyous cries accompanied His entry into Jerusalem. . . . She would have them move their lips in prayer, sometimes in petition, sometimes in joy and gratitude, and in this way experience His merciful aid and power like the Apostles at the lakeside of Tiberias, or abandon themselves totally, like Peter on Mount Thabor, to mystic union with the Eternal God in contemplation.

25. It is an error consequently and a mistake to think of the sacred Liturgy as merely the outward or visible part of divine worship or as an ornamental ceremonial. No less erroneous is the notion that it consists solely in a list of laws and prescriptions according to which the ecclesiastical Hierarchy orders the sacred rites to be performed.

26. It should be clear to all, then, that God cannot be honored worthily unless the mind and heart turn to Him in quest of the perfect life, and that the worship rendered to God by the Church in union with her divine Head is the most efficacious means of achieving sanctity. . . .

31. Very truly, the Sacraments and the Sacrifice of the altar, being Christ's own actions, must be held to be capable in themselves of conveying and dispensing grace from the divine Head to the members of the Mystical Body. But if they are to produce their proper effect, is is absolutely necessary that our hearts be rightly disposed to receive them. Hence the warning of Paul the Apostle with reference to Holy Communion: "But let a man first prove himself; and then let him eat of this bread and drink of the chalice." This explains why the Church in a brief and significant phrase calls the various acts of mortification, especially those practiced during the season of Lent, "the Christian army's defenses." They represent, in fact, the personal effort and activity of members who desire, as grace urges and aids them, to join forces with their Captain—"that we may discover . . . in our Captain," to borrow Saint Augustine's words, "the fountain of grace itself." But observe that these members are alive, endowed and equipped with an intelligence and will of their own. It follows that they are strictly required to put their own lips to the fountain, imbibe and absorb for themselves the life-giving water, and rid themselves personally of anything that might hinder its nutritive effect in their souls. Emphatically, therefore, the work of Redemption, which in itself is independent of our will, requires a serious interior effort on our part if we are to achieve eternal salvation. . . .

36. In the spiritual life, consequently, there can be no opposition between the action of God, Who pours forth His grace into men's hearts so that the work of the Redemption may always abide, and the tireless collaboration of man, who must not render vain the gift of God. No more can the efficacy of the external administration of the Sacraments, which comes from the rite itself [*ex opere operato*], be opposed to the meritorious action of their ministers or recipients, which we call the agent's action [*opus operantis*]. Similarly, no conflict exists between public prayer and prayers in private, between morality and contemplation, between the ascetical life and devotion to the Liturgy. Finally there is no opposition between the jurisdiction and teaching office of the ecclesiastical Hierarchy, and the specifically priestly power exercised in the sacred ministry. . . .

44. Since therefore it is the priest chiefly who performs

the sacred Liturgy in the name of the Church, its organization, regulation and details cannot but be subject to Church authority. This conclusion, based on the nature of Christian worship itself, is further confirmed by the testimony of history. . . .

51. Several causes, really, have been instrumental in the progress and development of the sacred Liturgy during the long and glorious life of the Church.

52. Thus, for example, as Catholic doctrine on the Incarnate Word of God, the Eucharistic Sacrament and Sacrifice, and Mary the Virgin Mother of God came to be determined with greater certitude and clarity, new ritual forms were introduced through which the acts of the Liturgy proceeded to reproduce this brighter light issuing from the decrees of the teaching Authority of the Church, and to reflect it, in a sense, so that it might reach the minds and hearts of Christ's people more readily.

53. The subsequent advances in ecclesiastical discipline for the administering of the Sacrament, that of Penance for example; the institution and later suppression of the Catechumenate; and again, the practice of Eucharistic Communion under a single species, adopted in the Latin Church; these developments were assuredly responsible in no little measure for the modification of the ancient ritual in the course of time, and for the gradual introduction of new rites considered more in accord with prevailing discipline in these matters. . . .

59. . . . It has pained Us grievously to note, Venerable Brethren, that such innovations are actually being introduced, not merely in minor details but in matters of major importance as well. We instance, in point of fact, those who make use of the vernacular in the celebration of the august Eucharistic Sacrifice; those who transfer certain feast-days—which have been appointed and established after mature deliberation—to other dates; those finally who delete from the prayerbooks approved for public use the sacred texts of the Old Testament, deeming them little suited and inopportune for modern times.

60. The use of the Latin language, customary in a considerable portion of the Church, is a manifest and beautiful sign of unity, as well as an effective antidote for any corruption of doctrinal truth. In spite of this, the use of the mother tongue in connection with several of the rites may be of much advantage to the people. But the Apostolic See alone is empowered to grant this permission. It is forbidden, therefore, to take any action whatever of this nature without having requested and obtained such consent, since the sacred

Liturgy, as We have said, is entirely subject to the discretion and approval of the Holy See.

61. The same reasoning holds in the case of some persons who are bent on the restoration of all the ancient rites and ceremonies indiscriminately. The Liturgy of the early ages is most certainly worthy of all veneration. But ancient usage must not be esteemed more suitable and proper, either in its own right or in its significance for later times and new situations, on the simple ground that it carries the savor and aroma of antiquity. The more recent liturgical rites likewise deserve reverence and respect. They too owe their inspiration to the Holy Spirit, Who assists the Church in every age even to the consummation of the world. . . .

62. . . . Thus . . . one would be straying from the straight path were he to wish the altar restored to its primitive table-form; were he to want black excluded as a colour for the liturgical vestments; were he to forbid the use of sacred images and statues in Churches; were he to order the crucifix so designed that the Divine Redeemer's Body shows no trace of His cruel sufferings; and lastly were he to disdain and reject polyphonic music or singing in parts, even where it conforms to regulations issued by the Holy See. . . .

82. The fact, however, that the faithful participate in the Eucharistic Sacrifice, does not mean that they also are endowed with priestly power. It is very necessary that you make this quite clear to your flocks.

83. For there are today, Venerable Brethren, those who, approximating to errors long since condemned, teach that in the New Testament by the word "priesthood" is meant only that priesthood which applies to all who have been baptized, and hold that the command by which Christ gave power to His Apostles at the Last Supper to do what He Himself had done, applies directly to the entire Christian Church, and that thence, and thence only, arises the hierarchical priesthood. Hence they assert that the people are possessed of a true priestly power, while the priest only acts in virtue of an office committed to him by the community. Wherefore they look on the Eucharistic Sacrifice as a "concelebration," in the literal meaning of that term, and consider it more fitting that priests should "concelebrate" with the people present than that they should offer the Sacrifice privately when the people are absent. . . .

84. . . . We deem it necessary to recall that the priest acts for the people only because he represents Jesus Christ, Who is Head of all His members and offers Himself in their stead. Hence he goes to the altar as the minister of Christ, inferior

to Christ but superior to the people. The people, on the other hand, since they in no sense represent the Divine Redeemer and are not a mediator between themselves and God, can in no way possess the sacerdotal power.

85. All this has the certitude of faith. However, it must also be said that the faithful do offer the Divine Victim, though in a different sense. . . .

92. . . . The faithful participate in the oblation, understood in this limited sense, after their own fashion and in a two-fold manner, namely because they not only offer the Sacrifice by the hands of the priest, but also, to a certain extent, in union with him. It is by reason of this participation, that the offering made by the people is also included in liturgical worship. . . .

98. In order that the oblation by which the faithful offer the Divine Victim in this Sacrifice to the Heavenly Father may have its full effect, it is necessary that the people add something else, namely the offering of themselves as a victim. . . .

99. . . . At that time especially when the faithful take part in the liturgical service with such piety and recollection that it can truly be said of them: "whose faith and devotion is known to Thee," it is then, when with the High Priest and through Him they offer themselves as a spiritual sacrifice, that each one's faith ought to become more ready to work through charity. . . .

130. The Sacred Councils teach that it is the Church's tradition right from the beginning to worship with the same adoration, "the Word Incarnate as well as His own flesh," and St. Augustine asserts that: "No one eats that flesh, without first adoring it," while he adds that "not only do we not commit a sin by adoring it, but that we do sin by not adoring it. . . ."

136. Strive then, Venerable Brethren, with your customary devoted care so that the Churches, which the faith and piety of Christian peoples have built in the course of centuries for the purpose of singing a perpetual hymn of glory to God Almighty and of providing a worthy abode for our Redeemer concealed beneath the Eucharistic species, may be entirely at the disposal of greater numbers of the faithful who, called to the feet of their Saviour, hearken to His most consoling invitation: "Come to Me all you who labor and are heavily burdened, and I will refresh you. . . ."

138. The ideal of Christian life is that each one be united to God in the closest and most intimate manner. For this reason, the worship that the Church renders to God, and which is based especially on the Eucharistic Sacrifice and the use of the Sacraments, is directed and arranged in such a way

that it embraces, by means of the Divine Office, the hours of the day, the weeks and the whole cycle of the year, and reaches all the aspects and phases of human life. . . .

165. Hence the Liturgical Year devotedly fostered and accompanied by the Church, is not a cold and lifeless representation of the events of the past, or a simple and bare record of a former age. It is rather Christ Himself Who is ever living in His Church. Here He continues that journey of immense mercy which He lovingly began in His mortal life, going about doing good with the design of bringing men to know His mysteries and in a way live by them. These mysteries are ever present and active not in a vague and uncertain way as some modern writers hold, but in the way that Catholic doctrine teaches us. According to the Doctors of the Church, they are shining examples of Christian perfection, as well as sources of divine grace, due to the merit and prayers of Christ; they still influence us because each mystery brings its own special grace for our salvation. . . .

192. Besides, "so that the faithful take a more active part in divine worship, let Gregorian chant be restored to popular use in the parts proper to the people. Indeed it is very necessary that the faithful attend the sacred ceremonies not as if they were outsiders or mute onlookers, but let them fully appreciate the beauty of the Liturgy and take part in the sacred ceremonies, alternating their voices with the priest and the choir, according to the prescribed norms. If, please God, this is done, it will not happen that the congregation hardly ever or only in a low murmur answer the prayers in Latin or in the vernacular. . . ."

195. . . . Modern art should be given free scope in the due and reverent service of the Church and the sacred rites, provided that they preserve a correct balance between styles tending neither to extreme realism nor to excessive "symbolism," and that the needs of the Christian community are taken into consideration rather than the particular taste or talent of the individual artist. Thus modern art will be able to join its voice to that wonderful choir of praise to which have contributed, in honor of the Catholic faith, the greatest artists throughout the centuries. Nevertheless, in keeping with the duty of Our office, We cannot help deploring and condemning those works of art, recently introduced by some, which seem to be a distortion and perversion of true art and which at times openly shock Christian taste, modesty and devotion, and shamefully offend the true religious sense: these must be entirely excluded and banished from our Churches, like "anything else that is not in keeping with the sanctity of the place. . . ."

[The First World War palpably refuted much of the optimistic naturalism current in the thought centers of Europe. In consequence, a new feeling of awareness for Catholicism emerged. Instead of a rationalistic empiricism, the philosophic mood was "existentialist." Many European Catholic intellectuals noted the change and were anxious to take advantage of it. They soon found that the Catholic philosophic language and approach were quite unintelligible to their contemporaries, and in consequence there was an earnest effort to enter into the non-Catholic intellectual's abode by his own door. As early as 1935 attempts at new formulations of the Catholic message were being made. This became stronger as the result of the Second World War, especially in France where many Catholic intellectuals entered into the underground resistance movement, where they were intimately connected with non-Catholics. After the war the need for contemporary expression of the age-old doctrine was keenly felt, and the need was being met. There were dangers involved in it. To meet these dangers Pius XII published *Humani generis*. The encyclical is very moderate, giving the new approach its full due. No one was condemned and the zeal of the men interested in the new work was praised. The encyclical merely pointed out with clarity how contemporary moods could be accepted and where they were unacceptable. The encyclical was directed primarily to Catholic intellectuals, and it was well received by all, even by those engaged in the new enterprise. *See also* D-2305-30.]

Humani generis, August 12, 1950
Concerning Certain False Opinions[23]

. . . The truths we have to learn about God and about the relations between God and man are truths which wholly transcend this visible order of things, and truths of that kind, if they are to be translated into human action and influence human action, call for self-surrender and self-sacrifice. Meanwhile, the human mind is hampered in the attaining of such truths, not only by the impact of the senses and the imagination, but by disordered appetites which are the consequences of the Fall. What wonder if men who are faced by such problems persuade themselves, all too readily, that any conclusion which is unwelcome to them personally is groundless, or at best uncertain?

We have to admit, then, the moral necessity of a revelation from God. Without that, religious and moral truths, which of

[23] Specially translated for *The London Tablet* by Msgr. Ronald A. Knox, Sept. 2, 1950.

their own nature lie within the scope of human reason, cannot be apprehended promptly, with full certainty, and without some alloy of error, in the present state of mankind (Con. Vatic. D.B. 1876, *Const. de Fide cath.* cap 2, *De revelatione*).

It is the same with the Catholic faith. It is, sometimes, not without difficulty that a man makes up his mind in favour of its credentials. True, God has provided us with an amazing wealth of external evidence by which the divine origin of the Christian religion can be brought home beyond question, even to the unaided light of reason. But a man may be so blinded by prejudice, so much at the mercy of his passions and his animosity, that he can shake his head and remain unmoved; not only the evidence of external proofs, which is plain to the view, but even the heavenly inspirations which God conveys to our minds, can go for nothing.

A glance at the world outside the Christian Fold will familiarize us, easily enough, with the false directions which the thought of the learned often takes. Some will contend that the theory of evolution, as it is called—a theory which has not yet been proved beyond contradiction even in the sphere of natural science—applies to the origin of all things whatsoever. Accepting it without caution, without reservation, they boldly give rein to monistic or pantheistic speculations which represent the whole universe as left at the mercy of a continual process of evolution. Such speculations are eagerly welcomed by the Communists, who find in them a powerful weapon for defending and popularizing their system of dialectical materialism; the whole idea of God is thus to be eradicated from men's minds.

These false evolutionary notions, with their denial of all that is absolute or fixed or abiding in human experience, have paved the way for a new philosophy of error. Idealism, immanentism, pragmatism, have now a rival in what is called "existentialism." Its method, as the name implies, is to leave the unchanging essences of things out of sight, and concentrate all its attention on particular existences.

There is, too, a false use of the historical method, which confines its observations to the actual happenings of human life, and in doing so contrives to undermine all absolute truth, all absolute laws, whether it is dealing with the problems of philosophy or with the doctrines of the Christian religion.

Amid all this welter of speculation, We find some comfort in the contemplation of a different school of thinkers. Not a few of the moderns, reacting from the dogmas of the rationalism in which they were brought up, are thirsting afresh for the wells of divine revelation. They recognize and proclaim the Word of God, preserved for us in Holy Scripture, as the foundation of Christian teaching. But many of them, alas, in their determination to hold fast by God's Word, banish the exercise of human reason. The more loudly they extol the authority of God revealing, the more bitter is their contempt for the teaching office of the Church, although our Lord Jesus Christ himself instituted it as the means by which the truths God has revealed should be safeguarded and interpreted. This attitude of theirs is flatly contradicted by Scripture itself, and its falsehood is further demonstrated by experience. How often it has happened that men who revolted against the Church fall out among themselves, and complain so openly of their divisions that they are forced, against their own wills, to admit the necessity of a Living Teacher!

All this, evidently, concerns our own Catholic theologians and philosophers. They have a grave responsibility for defending truth, both divine and human, and for installing it into men's minds; they must needs acquaint themselves with all these speculations, to a more or a less extent erroneous; they must needs take them into account. Nay, it is their duty to have a thorough understanding of them. There is no curing a disease unless you have made a study of its symptoms. Moreover, there is some truth underlying even the wrong-headed ideas; yes, and they spur the mind on to study and to weigh certain truths, philosophical and theological, more carefully than we otherwise should. . . .

Notoriously, the Church makes much of human reason, in the following connexions: when we establish beyond doubt the existence of one God, who is a personal Being; when we establish irrefutably, by proofs divinely granted to us, the basic facts on which the Christian faith itself rests; when we give just expression to the natural law which the Creator has implanted in men's hearts; and finally, when we would attain what knowledge we can—and it is a most fruitful kind of knowledge—about the divine mysteries (cf Conc. Vat. D.B. 1796). But if reason is to perform this office adequately and without fear of error, it must be trained on the right principles; it must be steeped in that sound philosophy which we have long possessed as an heirloom handed down to us by former ages of Christendom. Actually it enjoys a higher degree of credit; the principles on which it is based, and the chief assertions which it makes, have not only been laid bare and clearly set forth, century after century, by men of the highest gifts; the Teaching Authority of the Church has gone further, and brought them to the touchstone of divine revelation. What is the character of the philosophy which the Church thus recognizes and receives? It upholds the real, genuine validity of human thought-processes; it upholds the unassailable principles of metaphysics—sufficient reason, causality, and finality; it upholds the possibility of arriving at certain and unalterable truth.

There is much in the tenets of this philosophy which does not touch, either directly or indirectly, the provinces of faith and morals. All this the Church leaves open to free discussion among the learned. But this liberty cannot be claimed over a multitude of other points, and notably over the main principles it rests on, the main assertions it makes, as We have outlined them above. Where these all-important questions are concerned, what progress is possible? You may deck out philosophy in more elaborate garments, and such as are more becoming to it; you may fortify it with more telling terminology; you may relieve it of an ill-conceived argument, here and there, which schoolmen have brought forward in its defense; you may enrich it, if due caution be observed, with certain new elements which the progress of human thought has brought with it. But whatever you do, you must not uproot it, you must not adulterate it with false principles, you must not treat it as an interesting ruin. Truth, and the philosophic expression of truth, cannot change in a night. We are dealing with those principles of thought which impose themselves, in their own right, on the human mind; We are speaking of conclusions which are based on the wisdom of the ages, and for that matter on the coincident support of divine revelation. The mind of man, when it is engaged in a sincere search for truths, will never light on one which contradicts the truths it has already ascertained. God is truth itself; He it is who has created, and who directs, the human intellect. He does not mean it to be contrasting, each day that passes, some new point of view with one it has already solidly acquired. He means it to eliminate any error that may have entered into its calculations, and then to build up new truth on the foundation of the old; that is the order of nature's own architecture, and it is from nature that we derive our knowledge of truth. It is not for the Christian, be he theologian or philosopher, to give every latest fantasy of the day a thoughtless and hasty welcome. He will weigh it carefully, and with a just balance, making sure that he does not lose hold of the truth already in his possession, or contaminate it in any way, with great danger and perhaps great loss to the faith itself. . . .

. . . The Teaching of the Church leaves the doctrine of

Evolution an open question, as long as it confines its speculations to the development, from other living matter already in
existence, of the human body. (That souls are immediately
created by God, is a view which the Catholic faith imposes on
us.) In the present state of scientific and theological opinion,
this question may be legitimately canvassed by research, and
by discussion between experts on both sides. At the same time,
the reasons for and against either view must be weighed and
adjudged with all seriousness, fairness, and restraint; and
there must be a readiness on all sides to accept the arbitrament
of the Church, as being entrusted by Christ with the right to
interpret the Scriptures, and the duty of safeguarding the
doctrines of the faith (cf. Allocut. Pont. ad membra
Academiae Scientiarum, 30 novembris 1941; A.A.A. vol.
xxxiii, p. 506). There are some who take rash advantage of
this liberty of debate, by treating the subject as if the whole
matter were closed—as if the discoveries hitherto made, and
the arguments based on them, were sufficiently certain to
prove, beyond doubt, the development of the human body
from other living matter already in existence. They forget, too,
that there are certain references to the subject in the sources of
divine revelation, which call for the greatest caution and
prudence in discussing it.

There are other conjectures, about polygenism (as it is
called), which leave the faithful no such freedom of choice.
Christians cannot lend their support to a theory which involves
the existence, after Adam's time, of some earthly race of men,
truly so called, who were not descended ultimately from him,
or else supposes that Adam was the name given to some group
of our primordial ancestors. It does not appear how such
views can be reconciled with the doctrine of original sin, as
this is guaranteed to us by Scripture and tradition, and proposed to us by the Church. Original sin is the result of a sin
committed, in actual historical fact, by an individual man
named Adam, and it is a quality native to all of us, only
because it has been handed down by descent from him (cf.
Rom. v. 12-19; Conc. Trid, sess. v, ca. 1-4). . . .

[Since the encyclicals began to be frequently used, there
have only been two dogmas defined, and neither was defined
in an encyclical, although encyclicals prepared the way for the
definitions in both cases. The first definition was that of the
Immaculate Conception on December 8, 1854, by the Apostolic Letter *Ineffabilis Deus:* the second was the formal
definition of the dogma of the Assumption by the Apostolic

Constitution *Munificentissimus Deus* of November 2, 1950. The words of the actual definition are as follows:[24]]

Wherefore, after We have unceasingly offered Our most fervent prayers to God, and have called upon the Spirit of Truth, for the glory of Almighty God who has lavished His special affection upon the Virgin Mary, for the honor of her Son, the immortal King of the Ages and the Victor over sin and death, for the increase of the glory of that same august Mother, and for the joy and exultation of the entire Church; by the authority of our Lord Jesus Christ, of the blessed Apostles Peter and Paul, and by Our own authority, *We pronounce, declare, and define it to be a divinely revealed dogma: that the Immaculate Mother of God, the ever Virgin Mary, having completed the course of her earthly life, was assumed body and soul into heavenly glory.*

Hence if anyone, which God forbid, should dare wilfully to deny or to call into doubt that which we have defined, let him know that he has fallen away completely from the divine and Catholic Faith. . . . [D-2332]

[The importance and the sanctity of the Sacrament of Marriage must never lead Christians to think that, in itself, marriage is a higher state of life than holy virginity, or even as high a state. That is the message of the following encyclical.]

Sacra Virginitas, March 25, 1954

Holy virginity and that perfect chastity which is consecrated to the service of God is without doubt among the most precious treasures which the Founder of the Church has left in heritage to the society which He established. . . .

Innumerable is the multitude of those who from the beginning of the Church until our time have preserved their virginity unspoiled, others after the death of their spouse, have consecrated to God their remaining years in the unmarried state, and still others, after repenting their sins, have chosen to lead a life of perfect chastity; all of them at one in this common oblation, that is, for love of God to abstain for the rest of their lives from sexual pleasure. May then what the Fathers of the Church preached about the glory and merit of virginity be an invitation, a help, and a source of strength to those who have made the sacrifice to persevere with constancy,

[24] This and the following encyclical are from the Official English Versions, Vatican Polyglot Press.

and not take back or claim for themselves even the smallest part of the holocaust they have laid on the altar of God.

And while this perfect chastity is the subject of one of the three vows which constitute the religious state, and is also required by the Latin Church of clerics in major orders and demanded from members of Secular Institutes, it also flourishes among many who are lay people in the full sense: men and women who are not constituted in a public state of perfection and yet by private promise or vow completely abstain from marriage and sexual pleasures, in order to serve their neighbor more freely and to be united with God more easily and more closely. . . .

However, since there are some who, straying from the right path in this matter, so exalt marriage as to rank it ahead of virginity and thus depreciate chastity consecrated to God and clerical celibacy, Our apostolic duty demands that We now in a particular manner declare and uphold the Church's teaching on the sublime state of virginity, and so defend Catholic truth against these errors. . . .

Those therefore who do not marry because of exaggerated self-interest, or because, as Augustine says, they shun the burdens of marriage, or because like Pharisees they proudly flaunt their physical integrity, an attitude which has been condemned by the Council of Gangra, lest men and women renounce marriage as though it were something despicable instead of because virginity is something beautiful and holy,— none of these can claim for themselves the honour of Christian virginity. . . .

This then is the primary purpose, this the central idea of Christian virginity: to aim only at the divine, to turn thereto the whole mind and soul; to want to please God in everything, to think of Him continually, to consecrate body and soul completely to Him. . . .

. . . And certainly those who obligate themselves by perpetual vow to keep their virginity, put into practice in the most perfect way possible what Christ said about perpetual abstinence from marriage; nor can it justly be affirmed that the intention of those who wish to leave open a way of escape from this state of life is better and more perfect. . . .

And here We think it opportune, Venerable Brothers, to expose more fully and to explain more carefully why the love of Christ moves generous souls to abstain from marriage, and what is the mystical connection between virginity and the perfection of Christian charity. From our Lord's words referred to above, it has already been implied that this complete renunciation of marriage frees men from its grave duties and obligations. Writing by divine inspiration, the Apostle of the Gentiles proposes the reason for this freedom in these words: "And I would have you to be without solicitude. . . . But he that is with a wife, is solicitous for the things of the world, how he may please his wife; and he is divided." Here however it must be noted that the Apostle is not reproving men because they are concerned about their wives, nor does he reprehend wives because they seek to please their husbands; rather is he asserting clearly that their hearts are divided between love of God and love of their spouse, and beset by gnawing cares, and so by reason of the duties of their married state they can hardly be free to contemplate the divine. For the duty of the married life to which they are bound clearly demands: "They shall be two in one flesh." For spouses are to be bound to each other by mutual bonds both in joy and in sorrow. It is easy to see, therefore, why persons who desire to consecrate themselves to God's service embrace the state of virginity as a liberation, in order to be more entirely at God's disposition and devoted to the good of their neighbor. . . .

There is yet another reason why souls desirous of a total consecration to the service of God and neighbor embrace the state of virginity. It is, as the holy Fathers have abundantly illustrated, the numerous advantages for advancement in spiritual life which derive from a complete renouncement of all sexual pleasure. It is not to be thought that such pleasure, when it arises from lawful marriage, is reprehensible in itself; on the contrary, the chaste use of marriage is ennobled and sanctified by a special sacrament, as the Fathers themselves have clearly remarked. Nevertheless, it must be equally admitted that as a consequence of the fall of Adam the lower faculties of human nature are no longer obedient to right reason, and may involve man in dishonourable actions. As the Angelic Doctor has it, the use of marriage "keeps the soul from the full abandon to the service of God." . . .

Virginity is preferable to marriage then, as We have said, above all else because it has a higher aim: that is to say, it is a very efficacious means for devoting oneself wholly to the service of God, while the heart of married persons will always remain more or less "divided." . . .

Recent attacks on the traditional doctrine of the Church, the danger they constitute, and the harm they do to the souls of the faithful lead Us, in fulfillment of the duties of Our charge, to take up the matter once again in this Encyclical Letter, and to reprove these errors which are so often propounded under a specious appearance of truth.

First of all, it is against common sense, which the Church

always holds in esteem, to consider the sexual instinct as the most important and the deepest of human tendencies, and to conclude from this that man cannot restrain it for his whole life without danger to his vital nervous system, and consequently without injuring the harmony of his personality.

As St. Thomas very rightly observes, the deepest natural instinct is the instinct of conservation; the sexual instinct comes second. In addition, it is for the rational inclination, which is the distinguishing privilege of our nature, to regulate these fundamental instincts and by dominating to ennoble them. . . .

In order to acquire this perfect mastery of the spirit over the senses, it is not enough to refrain from acts directly contrary to chastity, but it is necessary also generously to renounce anything that may offend this virtue nearly or remotely; at such a price will the soul be able to reign fully over the body and lead its spiritual life in peace and liberty. Who then does not see, in the light of Catholic principles, that perfect chastity and virginity, far from harming the normal unfolding of man or woman, on the contrary endow them with the highest moral nobility?

We have recently with sorrow censured the opinion of those who contend that marriage is the only means of assuring the natural development and perfection of the human personality. For there are those who maintain that the grace of the sacrament, conferred *ex opere operato,* renders the use of marriage so holy as to be a fitter instrument than virginity for uniting souls with God; for marriage is a sacrament, but not virginity. We denounce this doctrine as a dangerous error. Certainly, the sacrament grants the married couple the grace to accomplish holily the duties of their married state, and it strengthens the bonds of mutual affection that unite them; but the purpose of its institution was not to make the employment of marriage the means, most suitable in itself, for uniting the souls of the husband and wife with God by the bonds of charity.

Or rather does not the Apostle Paul admit that they have the right of abstaining for a time from the use of marriage, so that they may be more free for prayer, precisely because such abstinence gives greater freedom to the soul which wishes to give itself over to spiritual thoughts and prayer to God? . . .

We think it necessary, moreover, to warn that it is altogether false to assert that those who are vowed to perfect chastity are practically outside the community of men. Are not consecrated virgins, who dedicate their lives to the service of the poor and the sick, without making any distinction as to race, social rank, or religion, are not these virgins united intimately with their miseries and sorrows, and affectionately drawn to them, as though they were their mothers? And does not the priest likewise, moved by the example of his Divine Master, perform the function of a good shepherd, who knows his flock and calls them by name? Indeed it is from that perfect chastity which they cultivate that priests and religious men and women find the motive for giving themselves to all, and love all men with the love of Christ. And they too, who live the contemplative life, precisely because they not only offer to God prayer and supplication but immolate themselves for the salvation of others, accomplish much for the good of the Church. . . .

[The following encyclical demonstrates the truly Catholic nature of the pope's concern. *Ad sinarum gentem* (October 7, 1954) was addressed to the people of China; it deals with the sufferings of the Church there.[25]]

. . . In recent years, however, the situation of the Catholic Church in your country has in no way improved; on the contrary, accusations and calumnies have been increasingly directed against this Apostolic See and against those who remain faithful to it; the Apostolic Nuncio, who represented Our Person among you, has been expelled; and snares, intended to deceive the less well instructed, have been multiplied.

Nevertheless, as we wrote to you before, "you are opposing with a firm will all forms of insidious attacks, whether subtle, hidden, or masked under a false appearance of truth." We are aware that those words of Ours were not able to reach you then; and therefore We gladly repeat them in this letter. We know also, to the great consolation of Our heart, that you have persevered in your resolution, so that no pressure whatever has succeeded in separating you from the unity of the Church; and for this We sincerely congratulate you and pay you worthy tribute of praise.

Since, however, we must deal with the eternal salvation of each, we cannot conceal the sadness and the distress of our spirit on learning that although the overwhelming majority of you Catholics remain steadfast in the Faith, there have not been lacking among you those who, either tricked in their good faith or because of fear, or misled by new and false doctrines, have given their support to dangerous "movements" sponsored by the enemies of all religion, especially of that divinely revealed by Jesus Christ. . . .

[25] Translation in *Unitas*, Spring, 1955. New York: The Graymoor Press.

In this our day, as in ancient times, those who persecute Christians accuse them falsely of not loving their fatherland and of not being good citizens. Therefore, first of all, we wish again to proclaim a fact that cannot be denied by anyone guided by right reason—that the Chinese Catholics are second to none in the ardent love and true fidelity towards their most noble country. . . .

Moreover, we esteem you to be worthy of praise in that you proceed rightly, during your continued daily difficulties, when, as Christians should, you give respectful submission to your public authorities in the sphere of their competence and, loving your country, you are prepared to fulfill all your duties as citizens. What, however, is of great consolation is to know that you have openly professed that in no way is it lawful for you to refrain from the fulfillment of the precepts of the Catholic religion and that in no way can you deny your Creator and Redeemer, for Whose love many of you have faced torments and prison. . . .

All must note moreover—as is already quite clear to you, Venerable Brothers and beloved sons—that it is our ardent desire that the time may soon come when the contributions made by the Chinese faithful themselves will be sufficient to meet the needs of the Church in China. However, as you well know, the offerings collected for this purpose in other countries have their origin in that Christian charity whereby all those redeemed by the Sacred Blood of Christ are of necessity bound to one another by a brotherly alliance, and are compelled by divine love to do their utmost to spread everywhere the Kingdom of our Redeemer. This is not done, therefore, for any political reasons or to further profane causes, but solely to put into practice in a useful manner that precept of charity which Christ gave to all of us and by which His true disciples are recognized (John XIII, 35). At every age of the Church, Christians have gladly and willingly done this, as the Apostle of the Gentiles testifies concerning the faithful of Macedonia and Achaia, who spontaneously sent their contributions to "the poor among the saints at Jerusalem" (Rom. XV, 26). And Saint Paul exhorted his children in Christ who lived in Corinth or in Galatia to do likewise (I Cor. XVI, 1-2).

Finally, there are some among you who would not only wish that your Church were completely independent, as we have said, in its government and economically, but who strive to claim for it furthermore a so-called "autonomy" even in the teaching of Christian doctrine and in sacred preaching.

We do not deny at all that the method of teaching and of preaching ought to vary from place to place and that, therefore, it should conform whenever possible to the nature and particular character of the Chinese people and to their ancient and traditional customs; in fact, it is certain that if this were done in the proper way, your country would yield more abundant fruits.

What, however, is absurd even to imagine is by what right men can, of their own choice, interpret differently the Gospel of Christ according to the different nations.

On the bishops, who are the successors of the Apostles, and upon priests, who in accordance with their proper office, are the co-operators of the bishops, has been conferred the task of announcing and teaching that Gospel which was first announced and taught by Jesus Christ and His Apostles and which this Apostolic See and all the bishops in communion with it have preserved and handed down pure and inviolate throughout the centuries. The sacred pastors are not the inventors and composers of this Gospel but merely the authorized guardians and preachers divinely established. Wherefore, we ourselves, and all Bishops with us, can and must repeat the words of Jesus Christ: "My teaching is not my own, but His who sent me" (John VII, 16). . . . Therefore, we are not teachers of a doctrine born of the human mind, but we are in conscience bound to embrace and follow the doctrine which Christ Our Lord taught and which He solemnly commanded His Apostles and their successors to teach (Matthew, XXVIII, 19-20). . . .

You can thus, brethren and dear children, easily see that a man cannot presume to be held and honored with the name of Catholic if he professes or teaches differently from what we have here briefly expounded, as do those who have supported those dangerous principles that inspire the movement of the "three autonomies" or other principles of the same kind.

The sponsors of such movements, with the greatest cunning, seek to deceive the simple or the fearful or to mislead them from the right path. To this end they falsely assert that the only true patriots are those who support the church of their design—that is to say, that which has the "three autonomies." In reality they are seeking to constitute eventually among you a "national" church which would not be Catholic because it would be the denial of that universality or catholicity by which the Society founded by Christ is above all nations and embraces them all. . . .

Fidei Donum, April 21, 1957
On the Condition of the Catholic Missions[26]
Especially in Africa

*   *   *   *   *

We deem it fitting at the present moment to direct your serious attention to Africa—the Africa that is at long last reaching out toward the higher civilization of our times and aspiring to civic maturity; the Africa that is involved in such grave upheavals as perhaps have never before been recorded in her ancient annals.

I

Considering the healthy progress made by the Church in Africa during recent decades, Christians have every right to rejoice and feel justly proud. Upon Our elevation to the Chair of Peter, We asserted that "We should spare no efforts in order that the Cross of Christ in which is our salvation and life might cast its shadow over even the most distant quarters of the universe." [27] Therefore We have striven to promote the cause of the Gospel in that continent with all Our might. This is evidenced by the great increase of ecclesiastical provinces there, by the widespread increase in the number of Catholics, who daily become more numerous, and especially by the Hierarchy which it has been Our consolation to establish in not a few districts, as well as by the considerable number of African priests who have been elevated to the Episcopate.

This last is, of course, in accordance with that final, as it were, goal of missionary efforts, namely, that "the Church should be solidly established among other peoples, and a Hierarchy given to them chosen from among their own sons." [28] In accordance with this policy the new Churches of Africa are taking their legitimate place in the great Catholic family, while the rest of the faithful who have preceded them in embracing the faith unite with them in brotherly love and welcome them enthusiastically.

Past Success and Present Cares. This plentiful harvest of souls has been gathered by hosts of missionaries—priests, religious (both men and women), catechists, and lay assistants —with an infinite toil and sacrifice whose value, unknown to men, is known only to God Himself. We are happy to offer Our congratulations to these good people, one and all, and to open Our grateful heart to them on this occasion; for the

[26] From *The Pope Speaks*, 1957, trans. Rt. Rev. Charles E. Spence.
[27] Allocution, May 1, 1939, *Discorsi e Radiomessaggi di S. S. Pio XII*, 1, 87.
[28] Encyclical, *Evangelii praecones, A. A. S.*, 43 (1951) p. 507.

Church has abundant reason for taking a holy pride in the achievements of her missionaries, who are doing their duty in Africa and wherever else they have an opportunity.

However, one must not allow the prodigious success of missionary effort, that We allude to here, to cause him to forget that "what still remains to be done demands an immense amount of work and countless workers." [29] And although some might rashly conclude that once a Hierarchy has been established there is no further need for the work of the missionaries, yet We Ourselves are greatly troubled by Our "solicitude for all the Churches" of that vast continent.

Can We be aught but deeply anxious as We behold from the heights of this Apostolic See the gravity of the questions that are being debated there with regard to the manner of spreading the Christian way of life and its deeper cultivation, as well as the great scarcity of apostolic laborers to undertake the many important tasks that are waiting to be done? These are the cares and anxieties that We have been wishing to share with you, Venerable Brethren. If your response is prompt and eager, it may happily come to pass that the hearts of the many hard-working apostles already in the field will be encouraged to hope anew for better things.

Africa and Europe. You cannot fail to be aware of the extraordinarily difficult circumstances under which the Church in Africa is striving nowadays to forward her work among the heathen multitudes. In fact the greater part of Africa is undergoing such speedy changes in social, economic, and political life that the entire future of that continent appears to depend upon their outcome.

No one must overlook the fact that current events, involving as they do the entire community of nations, have grave repercussions in individual countries and do not always afford an opportunity, even to the wisest rulers, to advance their people to that level of civilization demanded by the genuine prosperity of nations.

The Church, however, has seen in the course of her history the rise and growth of many nations, and therefore, cannot help directing her careful attention to those nations that she perceives to be now on the point of obtaining the rights of civil liberty. We Ourselves have on frequent occasions exhorted the nations concerned to take the proper course, impelled by their sincere desire for peace and a mutual recognition of their respective interests. "At any rate," We told one group, "let not those people be denied a fair and progressive political freedom or be hindered in its pursuit." We admonished another

[29] *Ibid.* p. 505.

"to give credit to Europe for their advancement: to that Europe without whose influence, extended to all fields, they might be drawn by a blind nationalism to plunge into chaos or slavery." [30]

As We now repeat these same admonitions, it is Our burning desire that in Africa men may attain to that concord of minds that begets every form of strength: a concord that will exclude prejudice and offence on either side, that will rise above the dangerous narrowness of excessive love of country, that will make it possible to communicate the outstanding benefits of Christian civilization to these peoples, whose natural resources are abundant and whose future prospects are bright. These benefits have already been accompanied by great advantages to the nations of the other continents. . . .

A New Social Order. The gravity of these statements is further increased by the too precipitate course of events—this can be observed everywhere—which has by no means escaped the notice of the Catholic bishops and the leading Catholics. While the peoples of this continent are striving to adopt new ways and new methods (and some of them appear to be only too eager to lend an ear to the fallacies of that species of civilization known as technological), it is the solemn duty of the Church to impart to these same peoples, so far as possible, the outstanding blessings of her life and her teaching, from which a new social order should be derived, based on Christian principles.

Any delay or hesitation is full of danger. For the people of Africa have made as much progress toward civilization during the past few decades as required many centuries among the nations of Western Europe. Thus they are more easily unsettled and confused by the introduction of theoretical and applied scientific methods, with the result that they tend to be unduly inclined to a materialistic outlook on life. Hence a condition of affairs is sometimes brought about that is difficult to correct and in the course of time may prove to be a great obstacle to the growth of faith, whether in individuals or in society at large. For this reason it is imperative that help should be given now to the shepherds of the Lord's flock in order that their apostolic labors may correspond to the ever-growing needs of the times.

Insufficiency of Means and Men. At the same time, the various forms of aid supplied at present to the sacred missions are everywhere far short of the amount required for a satisfactory prosecution of missionary effort. This insufficiency of means, which, unfortunately, is not confined to Africa, seems

[30] *A.A.S.* 48 (1956), p. 40. [Christmas Message, Dec. 24, 1955. English tr.: TPS (Winter 1955-56) v. 2, no. 4, p. 313.—Ed.]

to affect this continent more seriously than other missionary fields on account of Africa's peculiar situation at the present moment. For this reason, We deem it opportune, Venerable Brethren, to go into some detail with regard to the problems that are met in Africa.

For example, mission stations recently founded (i.e., within the last ten or twenty years) will have to wait a long time before they can enjoy the effective assistance of a native clergy. To this problem is added the small number of missionary workers, who are scattered widely throughout an immense population where not infrequently non-Catholic ministers are also active; they therefore cannot possibly perform all the tasks they are called upon to undertake. In one district some forty priests are working very hard among a million natives of whom only 25,000 profess the Catholic faith. In another locality fifty priests are stationed in the midst of a population of 2,000,000 persons, where the care of 60,000 Catholics in the area alone requires almost full-time service.

No true Catholic can fail to be concerned by these statistics. If twenty apostolic men were sent to the assistance of the local clergy in these regions, the standard of the Cross could be moved forward today, where tomorrow perhaps, after the activities of others who are not the followers of Christ have already cultivated the field, there will no longer be any opening for the true faith.

Moreover, it is not enough merely to preach the Gospel as if this were the whole of the missionary's task. The present situation in Africa, both social and political, requires that a carefully trained Catholic elite be formed at once from the multitudes already converted. How urgent it is then to increase the number of missionaries able to give a more adequate training to these native leaders!

The drawbacks experienced by the few apostolic workers in the field are increased by their want of material means, which often approaches real poverty. Who will furnish these recently established missions with the generous financial backing they so urgently need? For they are situated, for the most part, in poverty-stricken districts which are, nevertheless, promising fields for the spread of the Gospel. The apostolic laborer is deeply grieved by his lack of so many things while the performance of so many tasks rests upon him. He does not need our admiration so much as our assistance which if plentifully given will enable him to establish new mission stations and settlements. . . .

Native Clergy and Foreign Missionaries. Accordingly, missionaries are asked for with increasing urgency on all sides from the various missionary Institutes, but the latter are unable to meet all these demands on account of the dearth of new vocations. You are well aware, Venerable Brethren, that in Africa the increase in the number of clergy has not by any means kept pace with the growth of the body of the faithful. It is true that a native clergy is being developed there, but these priests will not be properly prepared to assume full responsibility for the people in their own dioceses for a considerable time. In the meanwhile they must be assisted by the foreign missionaries in their midst, the same missionaries who brought them to the light of faith. For the present these young Christian communities are not ready to cope with the extremely grave problems of this age. . . .

II

This state of the African apostolate, which We have summarily set before you, Venerable Brethren, makes it manifest that in Africa it is not a question of merely local problems that can eventually be solved without any reference to those that touch upon the entire Christian community.

Although formerly "the life of the Church in its visible aspects showed its vigor chiefly in the older parts of Europe from which it began to spread out to the shores that may be called the periphery of the world, now however there is a kind of mutual exchange of life and strength among all the members of the Mystical Body of Christ." [31]

What befalls the Church in Africa is not confined to that continent, but also affects those who dwell far beyond its borders. It follows then that, in accordance with the admonitions of the Apostolic See, fraternal assistance must be extended by all parts of the Church to meet the needs of Catholics anywhere. . . .

Asian and African Youth Studying in Other Lands. With the same affectionate interest that joins its efforts with those of others in fraternal harmony and excludes all selfish considerations, be especially careful to bestow spiritual care upon the youths from Africa and Asia, who perchance are resident in your dioceses for the purpose of continuing their studies.

These young men, uprooted by the social upheavals in their own countries, for many reasons often do not enjoy sufficient Catholic social contacts among the people who are giving them hospitality. Owing to this their Christian lives may be endangered, as the true values and excellences of the new culture they are seeking may escape them and they may be, in conse-

[31] *A. A. S.*, 38 (1946) p. 20.

quence, seduced by the doctrines of materialism and may succumb to the blandishments of atheistic coteries. You cannot ignore the impact of this on their present and future careers. It would be a good idea to appoint some devout and well-equipped members of the clergy to take charge of this apostolate, thus relieving the anxieties of their own bishops in the mission fields.

Priests on the Missions. Another form of assistance, which is more burdensome, has been undertaken by some bishops who, despite the difficulties attendant upon so doing, have permitted this or that priest of the diocese to go and spend some time in working for the bishops of Africa.

This procedure has the exceptional result of allowing the wise and well-planned establishment of specialized forms of the priestly ministry, such as taking charge of teaching the secular and sacred sciences for which the local clergy have not been trained. We are happy to encourage these timely and fruitful undertakings. If this course of action is taken with due preparation, very important advantages will accrue to the Catholic Church in present-day Africa, which has its full measure of both difficulties and hopes.

The Lay Apostolate. There is yet another and quite different form of assistance given nowadays to missionary dioceses, which affords Us intense pleasure and which is deserving of notice before We bring this Encyclical Letter to an end. This is the active work undertaken by laymen under the direction of the Church in behalf of the new Christian communities. It consists for the most part in cooperating with the various national and international Catholic Institutes. The application of this assistance surely requires the zeal, the moderation, and the prudence that are proper in working for the good of others; but it is of great benefit to dioceses harassed by insistent demands from fresh apostolic activities.

These laymen, thus enlisted under the banner of Christ and completely obedient to the bishop who properly reserves to himself the final authority in the apostolate, and being in complete accord with the Catholics of Africa who look favorably upon these fraternal recruits, usefully bring to bear upon the recently established dioceses the full weight of their experience in Catholic Action and other social programs and in any other particular activities required in the apostolate. Further—and this is extremely beneficial—they are able to effect a speedier and easier union of their own national Institutes with countless other agencies that are international in scope. We are happy to congratulate them on the excellent work they are doing for the good of the Church. . . .

Chapter 21

✠

John XXIII (1958-1963)

Angelo Roncalli was born on 25 November 1881 to a peasant family. He was ordained on 10 August 1904, and became secretary to the Bishop of Bergamo. His studies were interrupted for two years in World War I while he did his military service. In 1935 he was appointed apostolic delegate to Bulgaria, and on 19 March 1925 he was raised to the rank of archbishop. He was appointed apostolic delegate to Turkey and Greece in 1935, and Papal Nuncio to France in December 1944. He was made a Cardinal in 1953, and Patriarch of Venice in January 1953. He became Pope in 1958 and summoned the second Vatican Council which met in October 1962. He died on June 3, 1963.

Ad Petri Cathedram, May 29, 1959
On Peace, Truth, and Unity*

Since the time when despite our utter unworthiness, we were elevated to the Chair of Peter, we have been considering anew not without a suggestion of consolation the things which we saw and heard as almost everyone from every nation and every persuasion mourned the death of our immediate Predecessor. Later, when we were called to the dignity of the Supreme Pontificate, although the world was disturbed and unsettled by other events and circumstances of serious import, literally multitudes turned their minds and hearts toward us and looked to us with hope and expectation. This openly demonstrates that the Catholic Church flourishes with an everlasting youth, and is, as it were, "a standard lifted up among the nations." [1] From it is poured forth a light that pierces the darkness and a gentle love that reaches out to all the people.

Furthermore, when we announced that we intended to hold an Ecumenical Council and Roman Synod and that we in-

* Published in a pamphlet by the National Catholic Welfare Conference, Washington, D. C.
[1] Isaias. XI, 12.

tended to prepare a Code of Canon Law adapted to modern needs and to publish a new Code of the same type for the Eastern Churches, it was a source of great pleasure to us to have found so many in agreement with our plans. We were delighted to have fed the common hope that the minds of men be stirred with pleasure to a better and more thorough knowledge of the truth, to a profitable renewal of the Christian way of life, and to the restoration of unity, harmony, and peace.

At present, then, in this Encyclical Letter, the first we are issuing to the Universal Church, we are going to discuss these three topics, truth, unity and peace together with the necessity of acquiring and promoting them under the inspiration of love. The obligations of the Apostolic Office which we hold seem to demand this in a very particular way. May the guiding light of the Holy Spirit from on high be at our hand as we write and in your hearts as you read and may the grace of God which shapes the soul move all toward the acquisition of these things. They are actually the expression of a common desire despite the fact that prejudiced opinions, many difficulties and many obstacles stand in the way of their realization.

I: TRUTH

Knowledge of truth, especially revelation. Of all the evils which corrupt individuals, society and even whole nations and which upset the minds of many, the cause, or a better word might be, the root is this: the ignorance of truth or more correctly, not only an ignorance of it, but even at times, a contempt for and a rash betrayal of it. From this source, all kinds of errors spring, errors which like an evil disease penetrate into the deepest recesses of the soul and enter the blood stream of human society. They knock all values out of kilter and result in incalculable losses to the individual and the whole social structure. . . .

Press and obligation to truth. In this regard, then, those who willingly and rashly impugn the known truth and who employ the weapon of the lie in their writing, speaking or acting to attract and win over to themselves the unlearned poor people, and who strive in this way to mold the inexperienced and pliable minds of youth and to shape them to their way of thinking, are without a doubt abusing the guilelessness of the innocent and are engaged in a work worthy of the deepest scorn. Consequently, we cannot help but appeal to those who, through books, magazines and the daily paper (today their name is legion), play so large a part in teaching and forming the minds of their fellow men. Particularly in the case of the young, they are influential in forming opinions and in controlling the tone of moral life. We beg them to handle the truth with care, caution and prudence. They are bound under a very serious obligation not to publicize the lie, the half-truth and the moral evil of society. On the contrary, they should emphasize truth and especially those things which lead to lives of solid virtue rather than to lives of vice.

With sadness of heart, we see that our Predecessor of immortal memory, Leo XIII, used to complain of "the imperceptible but bold entrance of the lie through the ponderous tome or the slender pamphlet, through the ephemeral pages of the newspaper and the deliberate allurements of the theater." [2] We note that he also refers to "the books and magazines published for the sole purpose of making sport of virtue and of glorifying crime." [3]

Radio, motion pictures and television. In our modern age . . . there have been added to these the radio program, the motion picture and most especially, television. The last of these invades the very family circle. Yet from all of these, if they are devoted to the good and the true, attractive inducements to good living, even Christian living, can get their start. But, alas, they can all too frequently stir the minds, particularly of the young, to loose morals, to the seamy side of life, to the deceit of error and to the ever dangerous allurements of pleasure. For this reason, we must don the armor of goodness and truth to withstand these weapons of destruction so that the force of these evils so great, evils which grow almost imperceptibly stronger every day, might by our watchfulness and care be kept in check. To counteract the evil and deceitful writings, it becomes a matter of necessity to provide books that are morally sound. As an antidote to the type of radio program, motion picture and television show that makes error attractive and vice enticing, we should present those things which safeguard truth and which strive to preserve the blameless wholesomeness of sound moral living. This we must do that these new arts which can be such powerful allies of the forces of evil might be harnessed for the benefit and salvation of mankind without subtracting one bit from their entertainment value. Thus the remedy itself will be found in the very source from which the evil poisons flow in abundance.

Religious indifference. In addition, there is a certain group who, though they do not deliberately attack the truth, yet

[2] Letter *Saepenumero Considerantes* A. L., Vol. III, 1883, p. 262.
[3] Letter *Exeunte iam anno* A. L., Vol. VIII, 1888, p. 398.

by their want of respect for it war against it just as though God did not give us the faculty to seek after and discover it. Acting in this fashion leads to the untenable position that since there is no distinction between the true and the false, all religions are basically true. "This kind of reasoning," in the words of our Predecessor quoted above, "is pointed toward the destruction of all religion, and in particular of the Catholic Faith since, of all religions, this alone is true, and cannot be equated with others without serious injustice."[4] We would go even farther and state that a failure to distinguish between contraries has only this fatal outcome: an unwillingness to accept or practice any religion. For how can God who is truth have any patience with the carelessness, negligence or laziness of those who completely disregard their obligation of searching for and finding these essential truths, though such an obligation is concerned with the eternal salvation of all of us, and who in the end refuse to render to God the lawful worship due to Him alone.

If so much effort and industry are spent in adding to the store of human knowledge and to pushing back the horizons of natural science so that this, our age rejoices, and justly so, in the remarkable progress that has been made in scientific and philosophical knowledge, why should we not show the same ingenuity and assiduity, nay even greater, in acquiring in a safe and certain manner that knowledge that is concerned not with the passing things of this world but with the heavenly goal that is to come. Only when we accept that truth which flows from the pages of the Gospels and which should overflow into our daily actions, then only, we say, will our spirit rest in that peace and that joy which far exceeds in measure the pride in accomplishment from the findings of modern science and from the marvelous inventions which we enjoy today and which are extolled to the heavens in daily press notices.

II: UNITY, HARMONY, PEACE

Truth advances the cause of peace. From the wholehearted acceptance of full and complete truth, there should bubble forth a unity which will permeate our minds, our hearts, and all our actions. For all discord, all disagreements and all dissension flow as from a primal spring from this one source, from a failure to recognize truth or, what is worse, from a rejection of it even though it has been studied and understood, be this for the sake of the conveniences and benefits that are often expected to come from false hypotheses or because of that

---

[4] Encyclical Letter *Humanum genus* A. L., Vol. IV, 1884, p. 53.

willful blindness which men are all too prone to use as an excuse for vice and evil.

It is imperative, then, that everyone, the private citizen as well as those who handle the affairs of state, cherish the truth in their hearts if they wish to find that peace and harmony from which the well-being of the individual as well as of society can spring.

To this harmony and peace, we expressly exhort those who are active in political life. We who are placed above the disagreements between nations, we who embrace all people with equal affection, we who are not motivated by earthly benefits nor by desire of political ascendency, nor by any desires in this present life, seem to be able to be judged with fairness, heard with equanimity by all regardless of national background when we speak on matters of such importance.

Men created as brothers. God created men to be brothers, not enemies. He gave them the earth to be cultivated in the sweat of their brow that everyone might share in its fruits and take from it the necessities of daily existence. The various nations are nothing other than societies of men, that is, of brothers who ought to strive not only for their own individual prosperity, but, bound together in a bond of brotherly love, for the good of all human society.

Furthermore, this earthly life is not to be considered as an end in itself or even in the light of the pleasures it gives. The end of life is not complete destruction at death but rather an immortal life and a homeland that will endure forever. If this teaching, this hope so full of consolation is stripped from the lives of men, then the whole reason for existence collapses. There is left no check-rein strong enough to bridle the greed, dissension and discord that try to burst from our very souls. In place of the olive branch of peace shining forth in our hearts, the firebrands of discord will burst into flames. In short, our plight becomes synonymous with that of the beast who is devoid of reason. As a matter of fact, our lot is worse for, since we have been endowed with reason, we can sink to lower depths, by the abuse of it. Alas, as rather often happens, we can collapse into utter ruin and just like Cain, can stain the earth with the serious crime of spilling a brother's blood.

Our first task is then, to realign our thinking in accordance with right principles of action if we wish, as we ought, that our actions be firmly placed on the path of justice. For why if we are brothers in name and in fact, if we are sharers in a common destiny both in this life and in that to come, why, we repeat, can we act as adversaries, rivals and bitter foes toward each other? Why envy others? Why stir up hatred and prepare death-dealing weapons against our brothers? Alas, there is already enough strife among men! Already too many of our young men have poured out their blood in the flower of their youth! Already too many cemeteries, gorged with the victims of war, dot the earth and in solemn tones admonish all of us to return at long last to harmony, unity and a just peace! Let us therefore occupy our minds not with those thoughts that divide and sever one man from the other, but rather with those things by which men can be united in a mutual and equable respect for himself, his possessions and his goals.

Union and agreement among nations. If all, as they should be, are eager for peace and not for war, if they look forward with sincerity of heart toward the peace of brotherhood, then only can governments and the affairs of state be seen in their proper perspective and properly regulated. Herein lies the only possibility of a search for and the adoption of that co-operative planning from which will flow out to the whole family of mankind that unity so universally desired. In the enjoyment of this harmony, individual nations will then discover the proper limits of their freedom and will strive not to destroy others by stepping out of their prescribed limits. This is a unity which is foreign to the minds of those who try to oppress others or who strive to deprive them of their freedom. In accord with this is the opinion of our most wise Predecessor of happy memory, Leo XIII: "There is nothing better adapted to checking ambition, to curbing greed for another's goods, or to bridling envy, all of which are the firebrands of war, than Christian virtue and most especially justice."[5]

If, on the other hand, the people of the world do not seek this brotherly unity which ought to rest on the demands of justice and be fed by the fire of love, conditions will remain in a state of crisis. Because of this, prudent men everywhere sorrow and are sad that the uncertainty persists as to whether they are steering in the direction of a peace sound, sincere and true, or are rapidly slipping into a new and terrifying flare-up of war through their utter blindness. We repeat "utter blindness"; for if, and may God spare us this, a new war breaks out, the potential destructive power of the arms that have graced our age promises and holds out to all, the victor as well as the vanquished, nothing other than immeasurable destruction and complete ruin. . . .

Signs of lessening tensions. In regard to this point, we

[5] Letter *Praeclara gratulationis* A. L., Vol. XIV. 1894, p. 210.

must confess—and indeed this bears the hope of better things —that rather recently in some areas, the necessary relationships between classes are becoming less bitter and less strained. Our most recent Predecessor called attention to this in his words to the Catholics of Germany: "The extremely terrifying destruction of the last war which inflicted so much damage on you brought with it at least this advantage that among many classes of your people with the laying aside of prejudice and the love of personal advantage, conflicting class interest came closer to peaceful settlement. Adversity borne in common is a teacher of salutary albeit bitter lessons."[6]

In reality, class distinctions are today less pronounced than formerly for they cannot be limited to that between capital and labor but have become so numerous that they embrace all citizens. Then, too, those who are particularly industrious or skillful have an opportunity of climbing to a higher step in the ladder of social standing. In relation to the day-laborer, it is consoling to see all the recent advances made to provide a more human environment in the factories and other places where they ply their trades. As a result, these workmen have not only an economic value but one more in keeping with human dignity.

Labor problems. Yet, there still remains much to be done. Since there still remains too great a difference in the distribution of wealth, there are still too many causes for disagreement among the classes. This springs mainly from the concept of the right of private property, which is at times defective and downright unjust, held by those who are interested only in their own personal benefit and convenience. Added to this are those despicable lay-offs from work which affect so many and work such hardship upon them. Today, particularly, they work even greater hardships, for the human worker is so often replaced by some kind of supposedly more perfect machine. . . .

Consequently, we earnestly exhort all those who hold responsible positions in the field of labor and those into whose hands falls the fate, and at times the very existence, of the workingman not only to weigh carefully the wages given for their hire, not only to see that their rights in this regard are protected but also that they regard them as fellow men or more specifically as brothers. They should see to it that the workman shares more and more in the fruits of his labor and that he be made aware that he is, as it were, an integral part of the entire enterprise. We offer these suggestions that

[6] "Radio Message to the 73rd Congress of German Catholics," *op. cit.*, Vol. XI, p. 189.

the rights and obligations of the employer and employee be placd on a more equal basis and that the proper recognition be given them. Then, the various professional organizations in the field of industry "may seem to be not a weapon for inflicting or warding off wrongdoing which stirs up the resolute will and stubbornness of others, not as a dam bursting forth from its broken retaining wall, but rather as a bridge joining together the opposite banks of a river." [7]

Oh! let it never happen and for this we earnestly beseech God that this oneness so desirable, so agreeable, so necessary be ever shattered. If the sacrosanct customs of the family hearth are destroyed, if the teachings of the Divine Redeemer on this matter are passed over and allowed to collapse, then the immediate result will be the weakening of the very foundations of the public weal and the ultimate collapse of civil society with the consequent loss and damage to the individual.

III: THE UNITY OF THE CHURCH

Motives for hope. Now we want to speak of that unity which is closest to our heart and with which this pastoral office entrusted to us by God is most particularly concerned. We refer to the Unity of the Church.

It is a matter of record that our Divine Redeemer founded a society which was of such a nature that it alone would exist until the end of the world. This He promised in the words "Behold, I am with you all days even to the consummation of the world" [8] and for this he prayed ever so ardently to His heavenly Father. This prayer of Jesus, "That all may be one, even as thou, Father, in me and I in thee; that they also may be one in us" [9] was without a doubt accepted and heeded because of its deep reverence. [10] By this, we are given the most gratifying hope and assurance that, at some time, all the sheep that are not of this fold will earnestly desire to return to it. Thus, in accordance with the sentiment expressed by our Divine Redeemer, "there shall be one fold and one shepherd." [11]

The promise of this hope has already stirred us deeply to the action of announcing our intention of convening an Ecumenical Council to which Bishops from every corner of the globe will come to consider the serious problems confronting religion. Its special concerns will be the growth of the Catholic Church, the renewal of the spirit of the Gospel in the hearts

---

[7] "Toward a Sound Social Order." Discourses and Radio Addresses of His Holiness Pope Pius XII, Vol. VII, p. 350.
[8] Matthew xxviii, 20. [9] *See* Hebr. v, 7.
[10] John xvii, 21. [11] John x, 16.

of people everywhere and the adjustment of Christian discipline to the exigencies of modern day living. This will surely be a particularly remarkable display of truth, unity and love, a display which those who are cut off from this Apostolic See will observe. We sincerely hope that they will receive it as a gentle invitation to seek and acquire that unity which Jesus Christ prayed for so ardently to His heavenly Father.

Desires for unity by non-Catholics. In regard to this, we are aware, and this is a consolation to us, that the faith and teachings of the Catholic Church have struck a responsive chord in the souls of many among several communities separated from the Chair of Peter. Then, too, considerable respect toward this Apostolic See has arisen and has grown daily as the desire for truth has meant the downfall of prejudice. In addition, we have noticed that almost all those who are called Christians, even though they are separated from us, have again and again held congresses for finding a bond of unity among themselves and have established Councils for this purpose. What further proof do we need that they are experiencing a desire of coming to at least a basic unity?

Unity of the Church. Without a doubt, Our Divine Redeemer established His Church endowed with and buttressed by a very solid unity. If, on the other hand, He had not done so (and here we speak foolishly), He would have established something transitory and eventually at least self-contradictory in much the same way as almost all philosophical systems, springing from the ebb and flow of human opinion, are born one from the other, are transformed and finally disappear. Surely there is no one who cannot see that this is diametrically opposed to the Divine Teaching of Jesus Christ, "the Way, the Truth and the Life." [12]

This unity, Venerable Brethren and Beloved Children, as we have said, by its very nature can be nothing frail, wavering or transitory but on the contrary, solid strong and safe. [13] Though it may be lacking to other Christian communities, all who give it a moment's serious consideration can see that it is part of the warp and woof of the Catholic Church. It is a unity distinguished and embellished by one faith, one government, one worship. It is so immediately apparent to the eyes of all that they can recognize and follow it. It is, in short, patterned after the will of our Divine Founder, Himself, in that all the sheep are really gathered together in one fold under the leadership of one shepherd. It is so fashioned

[12] John xiv, 6.
[13] See Enc. Letter, Plus XI *Mortalium animos* "On Embracing the Unity of the True Religion." A. A. S., Vol. XX, 1928, p. 5 ffg.

that all children are called to the one paternal home which rests on the corner stone of Peter, and, thus, strive to unite all men by a bond of brotherly love into one kingdom of God. In this kingdom, all the members are joined together among themselves in unity of mind and affection with the hope of some day enjoying eternal happiness in heaven.

Unity of doctrine. In relation to doctrine, the Catholic Church expressly teaches that all the truths that have been divinely revealed must be believed faithfully and firmly. This includes all that is contained in Sacred Scripture and in oral or written tradition and all that from apostolic times down through the centuries has had the stamp of approval or the definition of either the Supreme Pontiff or of the lawfully constituted Ecumenical Councils. As often as anyone has strayed from this path, the Church in its motherly solicitude has never ceased to call him back to the path of truth. She knows indeed that there is only one truth and that "truth" opposed to it cannot be held. She clearly asserts and bears witness to the statement of the Apostle of the Gentiles as though it were her own: "We can do nothing against the truth but only for the truth." [14]

There are a few things that the Catholic Church leaves open to the discussion of theologians inasmuch as they are not completely certain. Besides, controversies of this type, as that bright light of the English Church, John Henry Cardinal Newman, has pointed out, do not destroy unity but rather add quite a bit to the deeper and better understanding of dogma. Such controversies throw new light on old truths and by the mere airing of opinions level the paths and straighten the way to a better unity. [15] It is well to keep in mind and give your approval to that old axiom attributed to many authors and even expressed at different times in different words "In essentials, unity; in doubt, freedom; in all things, charity."

Unity of government. Besides this unity of faith, it is perfectly obvious to everyone that there is a unity of government in the Catholic Church. For, indeed, just as the faithful are subject to their priests and their priests to their bishops, whom "the Holy Spirit has placed . . . to rule the Church of God" [16] so each and every bishop must be subject to the Roman Pontiff. He must be considered the successor of St. Peter whom Christ the Lord placed as the rock and foundation stone of His Church [17] and to whom He gave in a very particular way the full power of binding and loosing upon earth, [18]

[14] 2 Cor. xiii, 8.
[15] *See* Newman, J. H., *Difficulties of Anglicans,* Vol. I, Lecture X, p. 261 ffg.
[16] Acts xx, 28.　　[17] *See* Matthew xvi, 18.
[18] *See* Matthew xvi, 19.

of strengthening his brethren [19] and of feeding the entire flock. [20]

Unity of Worship. Finally, there is a unity of worship. No one can deny that the Catholic Church from its first beginnings down to the present has had seven sacraments, no more, no less. These were received as a sacred heritage from Jesus Christ Himself and from birth to death, contributing unceasingly to the nourishing and fostering of the supernatural life of the faithful. Who can deny that there is only one sacrifice, that of the Eucharist? In this sacrifice, in an unbloody manner Christ Himself our Salvation and our Redeemer, is really and truly immolated for us just as He once hung from a cross in the place called Calvary. In this way, He pours forth upon us in His mercy the vast riches of His grace. St. Cyprian rightly and meritoriously comments on this point in these words: "There can be no other priesthood and no other altar save the one altar and the one priesthood." [21] This does not, however, rule out the existence and the approval of different rites within the Church. In this way, this great sacrifice shines forth more beautifully, when like the daughter of the king of kings, it is seen dressed in various robes. [22]

That all might attain to this true and harmonious unity, the catholic priest in his celebration of Mass offers a spotless host to the most clement God with a prayer for "Your holy Catholic Church that You might deign to give her peace and protection, to unite and guide her the world over, together with Your servant our Pope, and all true believers who cherish the catholic and apostolic faith." [23]

Fatherly invitation to unity. We direct a plea to all you who are separated from this Apostolic See. May this wondrous manifestation of unity by which the Catholic Church shines forth for all to see, and may her prayers from the heart by which she begs this unity from God for all of you, move you in a deep and salutary way.

Do not object if we give in to the desire of our heart and call you brothers and children. Do not object if in the loving way of a father, we nourish the hope of your return. We long to address you with the same zeal with which Theophilus, the Bishop of Alexandria, addressed his brothers when faced with an unfortunate schism which rent the seamless robe of the Church. "Let us, beloved and heirs of a heavenly heritage, imitate for our mutual good the Leader and Accomplisher of our salvation, Jesus. Let us embrace that humility of soul

---

[19] *See* Luke xxii, 32.
[20] *See* John xxi, 15-17.   [21] Epist. XLII, 5 Corp Vind. III, 2, 594; *see* Epist. XL, apud Migne, PL IV, 345.
[22] *See* Psalm xliv, 15.   [23] *Canon Missae.*

which lifts us up, the love that joins us to God, the sincere faith toward the divine mysteries. Flee schism, avoid discord, embrace each other in mutual love. Heed the word of Christ as He says: 'By this shall all men know that you are my disciples, if you have love one for another.' " [24]

Please note that when we call you tenderly to the unity of the true Church, we are not inviting you to a strange home, but to your very own, the common home of our Father. In our longing, permit us to exhort all of you "in the heart of Jesus Christ" [25] to call to mind your fathers "who spoke to you the word of God. Consider how they ended their lives and imitate their faith." [26] The illustrious cohort of saints which every one of your nations has sent before you into heaven, and in particular, those who in their writings have handed down true and lucid explanations of the teachings of Jesus Christ, seem to invite you by the example of their lives toward that unity with this Apostolic See to which every Christian community was, for so many years, so strongly connected.

Again we address all of you who are separated from us as brothers on the strength of these words of St. Augustine: "Whether they wish it or not, they are our brothers. They will only cease to be our brothers if they cease to say 'Our Father.' " [27] "Let us love the Lord our God, let us love the Church; let us love Him as father, her as mother; the former as the Master, the latter as the maidservant for we are all children of that maidservant. This marriage is joined by bonds of great love; no one can offend the one and expect the approval of the other. What advantage is it to you not to have offended a Father who will not leave unrevenged an offended mother? Therefore, with one mind, regard God as a father, the Church as a mother." [28] . . .

Princeps Pastorum, November 28, 1959
On the Catholic Missions*

On the day when "the Prince of the Shepherds" [1] entrusted to Us His lambs and sheep,[2] God's flock, which dwells all over the earth, We responded to the sweet invitation of His love with a sense of Our unworthiness but with trust in His

[24] *See Hom. in mysticam caenam* PG, LXXVII, 1027.
[25] Philippians i, 8.
[26] Hebrews xiii, 7.
[27] St. Augustine In Ps. 32, Enarr. II, 29 Migne. PL XXXVI, 299.
[28] St. Augustine In Ps. 82, Enarr. II, 14 Migne, PL XXXVII, 1140.
* From *The Pope Speaks*, 1960, trans. Mrs. L. C. M. Rose.
[1] I Peter iv, 4.
[2] Cf. John xxi, 15-17.

all-powerful assistance. And the magnitude, the beauty, and the importance of the Catholic Missions have been constantly on Our mind.[3] For this reason, We have never ceased to devote to them Our greatest solicitude and attention. . . .

Also at that time Our predecessor Pius XII by word and example incited Us to give Our warmest support to missionary activities and projects. Just before the College of Cardinals was convened for the Conclave during which, by divine inspiration, he was chosen as the successor of St. Peter, he spoke the following words in Our presence: "We cannot expect anything greater or more beneficial from the new Vicar of Christ than these two most important things: that he will strive with all his might to propagate the doctrine of the Gospel among all men, and that he will bring peoples together in a spirit of true peace and strengthen them therein."[4]

Subject of this letter. With these and many other sweet memories in Our mind, and aware of the grave duties imposed upon the Supreme Shepherd of the flock of God, We would like, Venerable Brethren—seizing an occasion offered by that memorable Apostolic Letter, *Maximum illud,*[5] with which, forty years ago, Our predecessor Benedict XV furthered the cause of the Catholic missions by establishing new rules and enkindling the faithful with new zeal—We would like, We repeat, to speak to you with a fatherly heart, by means of this letter, on the necessity and hopes of extending God's kingdom to the many parts of the world where missionaries labor zealously, sparing no effort in order that new branches of the Church may grow and produce wholesome fruits.

Our predecessors Pius XI and Pius XII also issued decrees and exhortations to the furtherance of this cause,[6] which We confirmed with like authority and like charity when We issued Our first Encyclical Letter, *Ad Petri Cathedram.*[7] We think, however, and We feel sure that We will never do enough to carry out the wishes of the Divine Redeemer in this matter until all sheep are happily gathered in one fold under the leadership of one Shepherd.[8]

---

[3] Cf. *"Homilia in die Coronationis habita,"* AAS 50 (1958); 886, TPS (Spring 1959) v. 5, no. 2, 140.
[4] Cf. *"La propagazione della fede,"* Scritti di A. G. Roncalli, Rome, 1958, p. 103 ff.
[5] Cf. AAS 11 (1919) 440 ff.
[6] Cf. Pius XI's Encyclical *"Rerum Ecclesiae,"* AAS 18 (1926) 65 ff.; Pius XII's Encyclicals *"Evangelii praecones,"* AAS 43 (1951) 497ff., and *"Fidei donum,"* AAS 49 (1957) 225 ff. An English translation of the latter is in TPS (Winter 1957–58) v. 4, no. 3, 295–312.
[7] Encyclical *"Ad Petri Cathedram,"* AAS 51 (1959) 497 ff.; TPS (Autumn 1959) v. 5, no. 4, 359–383.
[8] Cf. John x, 16.

A cry for help. When We turn Our mind and Our heart to the supernatural blessings of the Church that are to be shared with those people whose souls have not yet been suffused with the light of the Gospel, there appear before Our eyes either regions of the world where bountiful crops grow, thrive, and ripen, or regions where the labors of the toilers in God's vineyard are very arduous, or regions where the enemies of God and Jesus Christ are harassing and threatening to destroy Christian communities by violence and persecutions, and are striving to smother and crush the seed of God's word.[9] We are everywhere confronted by appeals to Us to ensure the eternal salvation of souls in the best way We can, and a cry seems to reach Our ears: "Help us!"[10] Innumerable regions have already been made fruitful by the sweat and blood of messengers of the Gospel "from every nation under heaven,"[11] and native apostles, with the help of divine grace, are blossoming like new buds and are bringing forth saving fruits. We desire to reach those regions with Our words of praise and encouragement, and with Our affection. We also wish to give them Our instructions and admonitions, which are prompted by firm hope based on the infallible promise of Our Divine Master, that is contained in these words: "Behold I am with you all days, even unto the consummation of the world."[12] "Take courage, I have overcome the world."[13]

I

The First World War involved many countries all over the world and caused grievous losses to many individuals and nations. When it finally ended, Benedict XV's Apostolic Letter[14] (which We mentioned above), like the exalted invitation of a fatherly voice, enflamed the souls of all Catholics to expand peacefully the Kingdom of God, the only one, We say, which can give and secure permanent peace and prosperity to all men, children of their Heavenly Father. From that time, during forty very active years, the works and undertakings of the heralds of the Gospel have been flourishing and producing increasingly abundant fruits every day; and the most noteworthy result is the fact that a local hierarchy and clergy have been increasingly developed in the mission areas.

A local hierarchy. It is necessary that missionaries obey the words of Our immediate predecessor, Pius XII, to the

[9] Cf. Matt. xiii, 19.
[10] Acts xvi, 9.
[11] Acts ii, 5.
[12] Matt. xxviii, 20.
[13] John xvi, 33
[14] *AAS* 11 (1919) 440 ff.

effect that they "must constantly keep before their mind's eyes their ultimate goal, which is to establish the Church firmly in other countries, and subsequently to entrust it to a local hierarchy, chosen from their own people." [15] Therefore, this Apostolic See, abundantly and at the opportune time, has taken measures especially in recent times, to establish or re-establish a hierarchy in those areas in which local conditions favored the foundation of Episcopal Sees, and if possible, to place locally born prelates at their head. At any rate, it is well known that this has always been the principal and constant goal of the Sacred Congregation for the Propagation of the Faith. It was an Apostolic Letter, however, which highlighted the importance and immediacy of the matter as never before. In this letter Our predecessor, Benedict XV, urgently reminded the authorities in charge of the missions to nurture carefully the vocations of those who felt the divine call to the priest-hood in mission territories and to contribute to the quantitative and qualitative growth of that clergy which was called native. (Neither slight nor discrimination was intended by the word "native," or was ever expressed or implied by the language of the Roman Pontiffs and ecclesiastical documents.)

Growth of native clergy. This exhortation of Benedict XV, which was repeated by Our predecessors Pius XI and Pius XII, with the help of God's divine Providence has had visible and copious results. We want you to join Us in rendering thanks to God for the fact that a numerous and elect legion of bishops and priests has arisen in the Mission territories, Our brethren and beloved sons, who fill Our heart with great expectations. If We cast even a cursory glance on the ecclesi-astical situation in the areas which are entrusted to the Sacred Congregation for the Propagation of the Faith, with the exception of those at present under persecution, We note that the first bishop of east Asian origins was consecrated in 1923, and the first vicars apostolic of African Negro descent were named in 1939. By 1959, We count 68 Asian and 25 African bishops. The remaining native clergy grew in number from 919 in 1918 to 5553 in 1957 in Asia, and during the same period in Africa from 90 in 1918 to 1811 in 1957. With such an admirable increase in the numbers of the clergy did the Lord of the harvest [16] desire to reward adequately the labors and merits of those who zealously did mission work, either individually or in cooperation with many others, responding with a generous heart to the repeated exhortations of this Apostolic See.

---

[15] Encyclical *"Evangelii praecones," AAS* 43 (1951) 507.
[16] Cf. Matt. ix, 38.

Mutual exchange. It was, therefore, with good reason that Our predecessor Pius XII was able to affirm with satisfaction: "Once upon a time it seemed as though the life of the Church used to prosper and blossom chiefly in the regions of ancient Europe, whence it would flow, like a majestic river, through the remaining areas which, to use the Greek term, were considered almost the periphery of the world; today, however, the life of the Church is shared, as though by a mutual irradiation of energies, among all individual members of the Mystical Body of Christ. Not a few countries on other continents have long since outgrown the missionary stage, and are now governed by an ecclesiastical hierarchy of their own, have their own ecclesiastical organization, and are liberally offering to other Church communities those very gifts, spiritual and material, which they formerly used to receive." [17]

Encouraging vocations. We wish especially to exhort the bishops and clergy of the new Christian communities to pray to God, and to conduct themselves in such a way that the priestly gift they are enjoying may grow in spiritual fruitfulness; in their talks with the people, as often as feasible they should praise the dignity, the beauty, and the merits of the priesthood, and, by so doing, they will induce all those whom God has chosen for this exalted honor to respond to the call with an open and generous heart. They should also cause the faithful entrusted to their care to pray to God for this cause, in unity of spirit with the whole Church, which, in response to the Divine Redeemer's exhortations, prays "the Lord of the Harvest to send forth laborers into his harvest," [18] especially at the present time, when "the harvest indeed is great, but the laborers are few." [19]

Place of foreign missionaries. However, Christian communities to which missionaries still devote their zeal, although already governed by their own hierarchy, are still in need of the work of missionaries from other countries, either because of the vastness of the territory, or the increasing number of converts, or the multitude of those who have not yet benefited from the doctrine of the Gospel. To such missionaries, no doubt, apply these words of Our immediate predecessor: "These cannot be considered foreigners, for all Catholic priests who truly answer their vocation feel themselves native sons wherever they work, in order that the Kingdom of God may flourish and develop." [20] Let them therefore work united by

---

[17] Pius XII's Christmas Broadcast, *AAS* 38 (1946) 20.
[18] Luke x, 2.
[19] *Ibid.*
[20] Letter of Pius XII to Cardinal Adeodatus Piazza, *AAS* 47 (1955) 542; TPS (Autumn 1955) v. 2, no. 3, 253–4.

the bond of that loving, brotherly, and sincere charity which mirrors the love they must feel toward the Divine Redeemer and His Church; and, in prompt and filial obedience to their Bishops, whom "the Holy Spirit placed . . . to rule the Church of God," [21] they must be "of one heart and one soul," [22] grateful to each other for the mutual cooperation and help; indeed, if they act in this manner, it should be apparent to everyone's eyes that they are the disciples of Him Who, in His own and most distinctive "new" commandment, exhorted all to a mutual and always increasing love. [23]

II

Our predecessor Benedict XV, in his Apostolic Letter *Maximum illud*, especially exhorted Catholic mission authorities to mold and shape the minds and souls of the clergy selected from the local population, and to do so in such a way that their formation and education would turn out "perfect and complete in every respect." [24] "In fact," he wrote, "a native priest, having a place of birth, character, mentality, and emotional make-up in common with his countrymen, is in a privileged position for sowing the seeds of the Faith in their hearts: indeed, he knows much better than a stranger the ways of persuasion with them." [25] . . .

Native teachers in seminaries. Furthermore, Our fatherly soul harbors the happy hope that everywhere the local clergy will be able to select from among its ranks just and holy men capable of governing, forming, and educating their own seminarians. That is the reason why We are already instructing the bishops and the mission authorities to choose without hesitation from among the local clergy those priests who, for their exceptional virtue and wise actions, qualify as teachers in the local seminaries and are able to lead their students to sanctity.

Adaptation to locality. Furthermore, Venerable Brethren, as you well know, the Church has prescribed at all times that priests must prepare for their calling by means of a solid intellectual and spiritual education. Indeed, no one will doubt, especially in our time, that young people of all races and from all parts of the world are capable of absorbing such an education; this fact has already been clearly demonstrated.

---

[21] Acts xx, 28.
[22] Acts iv, 32.
[23] Cf. *John* 13, 34 and 15, 12.
[24] *AAS* 11 (1919) 445.
[25] *Ibid.*

Without doubt, the formation to be given to this clergy must take into account the circumstances which obtain in different areas and nations. This extremely wise norm applies to all students for the priesthood; it is advisable that young seminarians never be "educated in places too far removed from human society," [26] because "once they step out into the world, they will have problems in dealing both with simple people and with intellectuals; this will often cause them to assume the wrong attitude toward the Christian population, or to regard the formation they received as a bad one." [27] Indeed, it is necessary that youths not only conform to the ideal of priestly spiritual perfection in everything, but also that they "gradually and prudently penetrate the mentality and feelings of the people" [28]—of the people, We repeat, whom they must enlighten with the truth of the Gospel and lead to perfection of life, with the help of God's grace. Therefore it is necessary that seminary superiors conform to this plan of training and education while yet welcoming those material and technical facilities which the genius of mankind has made the patrimony, as it were, of every civilization in order to insure an easier and better life and to preserve the bodily health and safety of mankind.

Training for responsibility. The formation of the local clergy, as Our same predecessor, Benedict XV, wrote, must enable them, in compliance with the first requirement of their divine calling, "to assume rightly the rule of their people" [29] —to lead their people, by the influence of their teaching and their ministry, along the path to eternal salvation. To this end, We highly recommend that everyone, whether local or foreign, who contributes to the formation in question, do his conscientious best to develop in these students a sense of the importance and difficulty of their mission, and a capability for wisely and discreetly using the freedom allowed to them. This should be done so that they may be in a position to assume, quickly and progressively, all the functions, even the most important ones, pertaining to their calling, not only in harmonious cooperation with the foreign clergy, but also on an equal footing with them. [30] Indeed, this is the touchstone of the effectiveness of their formation, and will be the best reward for the efforts of all those who contributed to it. . . .

[26] Pius XII's Apostolic Letter *"Menti Nostrae," AAS* 42 (1950) 686.
[27] *Ibid.*
[28] *Ibid.,* p. 687.
[29] Apostolic Letter *"Maximum illud," AAS* 11 (1919) 445.
[30] Cf. Pius XII's Apostolic Letter *"Menti Nostrae," AAS* 42 (1950) 686.

The Church and cultures. "The Catholic Church," stated Our same predecessor, "has never fostered an attitude of contempt or outright rejection of pagan teachings but, rather, has completed and perfected them with Christian doctrine, after purifying them from all dross of error. So, too, the Church, to a certain extent, consecrated native art and culture . . ., as well as the special customs and traditional institutions of the people . . .; she has even transformed their feast days, leaving unchanged their methods of computation and their form, but dedicating them to the memory of the martyrs and to the celebration of the sacred Mysteries." [31] We Ourselves have already expressed Our thoughts on this matter as follows: "Wherever artistic and philosophical values exist which are capable of enriching the culture of the human race, the Church fosters and supports these labors of the spirit. On the other hand, the Church, as you know, does not identify itself with any one culture, not even with European and Western civilization, although the history of the Church is closely intertwined with it; for the mission entrusted to the Church pertains chiefly to other matters, that is, to matters which are concerned with religion and the eternal salvation of men. The Church, however, which is so full of youthful vigor and is constantly renewed by the breath of the Holy Spirit, is willing, at all times, to recognize, welcome, and even assimilate anything that redounds to the honor of the human mind and heart, whether or not it originates in parts of the world washed by the Mediterranean Sea, which, from the beginning of time, had been destined by God's Providence to be the cradle of the Church." [32]

Conversion of the learned. If native priests are well instructed in these practical matters and serious disciplines, and if they overcome difficulties and are equipped to take the right course of action, they will be able, under guidance of their bishops, to make highly valuable contributions. In particular, they will find a more sympathetic audience among the educated citizens of their own countries and will be able to attract them to the Christian truth, in the manner of the famous missionary, Matthew Ricci. This will happen especially in those countries which possess an ancient and highly-developed civilization of their own. Indeed, local priests are entrusted with the mission of "bringing every mind into captivity to the obedience of Christ," [33] as Paul, that incomparable missionary and apostle

[31] *Ibid.*, p. 522.
[32] Cf. "Address to Participants in Second World Congress of Negro Writers and Artists," *Osservatore Romano*, April 3, 1959. Brief summary in *TPS* (Summer 1959) v. 5, no. 3, 290–1.
[33] 2 Cor. x, 5.

of the people, affirmed; thus, they will also be "held in great honor by the members of the intellectual elite of their country." [34]

Study centers. Therefore, making use of their judgment and cooperation, bishops will take care to establish, at opportune moments, study centers to meet the needs of one or more regions in order to make basic doctrine known and understood. In these, both foreign and local priests can employ their learning and experience to benefit the particular countries in which they were born or in which they have chosen to spread the Christian truth. In this connection, We should also like to quote the teaching of Our immediate predecessor Pius XII, expressed in these words: there must be promoted "the publication and dissemination of Catholic books of every description"; [35] and care must be taken to advance "the use of modern means of communication in spreading Christian doctrine. No one can ignore the importance of gaining the good will of native peoples and making them favorable to Catholicism." [36] Certainly, all methods cannot be employed in all places; all opportunities must be taken, however, to fulfill different needs, whenever they arise, even though, sometimes, "one sows, another reaps." [37]

Social welfare work. To propagate the truth of Jesus Christ is the truest function of the Church. Indeed, "it is the solemn duty of the Church to impart to . . . peoples, so far as possible, the outstanding blessings of her life and her teaching, from which a new social order should be derived, based on Christian principles." [38] Therefore, in mission territories, the Church takes the most generous measures to encourage social welfare projects, to support welfare work for the poor, and to assist Christian communities and the peoples concerned. Care must be taken, however, not to clutter and obstruct the apostolic work of the missions with an excessive quantity of secular projects. Economic assistance must be limited to necessary undertakings which can be easily maintained and utilized, and to projects whose organization and administration can be easily transferred to the lay men and women of the particular nation, thus allowing the missionaries to devote themselves to their task of propagating the faith, and to other

[34] Pius XI's encyclical *"Rerum Ecclesiae," AAS* 18 (1926) 77.
[35] Encyclical *"Fidei donum," AAS* 49 (1957) 233; *TPS* (Winter 1957–58) v. 4, no. 3, 301.
[36] *Ibid.*
[37] John iv, 37.
[38] Encyclical *"Fidei donum," AAS* 49 (1957) 231; *TPS* (Winter 1957–58) v. 4, no. 3, 300.

pursuits aimed directly at personal sanctification and eternal salvation.

Universality. If it is true, as We said, that in order for the apostolate to bear abundant fruits, the most important requirement the native priests must meet is that they should know, and carefully evaluate, everything connected with the institutions peculiar to their countries, what Our predecessor said of the whole world will remain even truer: "the prospects and plans of the Church, which embrace the whole world, will be the prospects and plans of their daily Christian lives." [39] To this end, the native clergy not only will be bound to know the affairs and developments of the universal Church, but must also be guided by, and filled with, that charity which embraces all the faithful. This is the reason why St. John Chrysostom said of Christian liturgical celebrations: "When we approach the altar, we pray, above all, for the whole universe and the common good"; [40] and St. Augustine uttered a beautiful sentence: "Extend your charity to the whole world, if you want to love Christ, because the members of Christ's body cover the whole world." [41]

Ultra-nationalism. Indeed, it was in this spirit that Our predecessor Benedict XV, in order to preserve the integrity of the concept of Catholic unity, which must inspire all missionary work, sternly warned of a danger which he did not hesitate to define in these words, and which must be avoided by missionaries in their thoughts, lest it jeopardize the effectiveness of their actions: "It would be a sad thing if any missionary should appear to be so oblivious of his dignity as to think of his country on earth rather than of his fatherland in heaven, and be excessively concerned with increasing the power and the glory of his own nation above all other nations. Such conduct would greatly impair the cause of the apostolate, and would cut the sinews of charity in his heart, while lowering his prestige in the eyes of the public." [42]

This danger, in different ways and forms, could arise again in our time, especially since several countries already enlightened by the light of the Gospel have been aroused to seek freedom and self-government. The acquisition of political freedom can sometimes be accompanied by disorders and excesses which are detrimental to the common good and are the opposite of the spirit of Christian charity.

We feel perfectly confident, however, that the native clergy

[39] *Ibid.,* p. 238; English translation *op. cit.,* p. 305.
[40] *Hom. 11 in 2 Cor.,* Migne, *PG* 61, 398.
[41] *In Ep. Ioan. ad Parthos.* Tr. X. c. 5, Migne, *PL* 35, 2060.
[42] Apostolic Letter *"Maximum illud,"* AAS 11 (1919) 446.

is animated by lofty purposes and sentiments which conform to the general principles of the Christian religion and entirely correspond with the teachings of the Catholic Church, which embraces all men with the same love; We are also certain that they contribute their share to the real interests of their own nations. In this connection, Our Predecessor very aptly uttered the following words of warning: "The Catholic Church is not a stranger among any people or nation." [43] No Christian community anywhere will ever achieve unity with the Universal Church, from which emanates the supernatural life of Jesus Christ, if the local clergy and population succumb to the influence of a particularist spirit, if they arouse enmity in other nations, and if they are misled and perturbed by an ultra-nationalism which can destroy the spirit of universal charity—that charity upon which the Church of God is built and is called "Catholic." . . .

Adaptation to local conditions. However, it is necessary —and We can never warn sufficiently of this—that this form of apostolate be carefully adapted to local conditions and needs. What has been done in one country cannot be carried over indiscriminately to another. The people concerned, submitting in all things to the directives of the ecclesiastical hierarchy and willingly obeying their pastors, must beware of defeating the purposes of the apostolate by carrying the burden of an excessive number of activities. For thus they thwart valuable efforts and dissipate valuable energy through compartmentalized and overly specialized projects, which, while satisfactory elsewhere, may be less useful where different conditions and needs prevail. In Our first encyclical, We also promised to deal with the subject of Catholic Action in more detail and at greater length; when We do, We trust that the mission territories will receive additional support and a new incentive. In the meantime, let everyone work in perfect harmony and with supernatural inspiration, in the certainty that only thus will they be able to say that they are serving the divine cause and the common good of their people.

Training for leadership. Catholic Action is an association of laymen "who are entrusted with certain duties, which involve executive responsibilities, to be carried out in submission to the hierarchy"; [44] thus laymen do hold executive offices therein. For this reason it is necessary to train men who are capable of enkindling different organizations with apostolic zeal and insuring their most efficient operation; men and

[43] *Ibid.*, p. 445.
[44] Cf. Pius XII's *"Epistola de Actione Catholica,"* October 11, 1946, *Discorsi e Radiomessaggi di S.S. Pio XII,* v. VIII, p. 468.

women, We say, who in order to be worthy of managerial and executive roles in these organizations, entrusted to them by the ecclesiastical hierarchy, must furnish convincing proof that they possess a solid Christian formation, both intellectual and moral, in order that "they may impart to others what, with the help of God's grace, they have won for themselves." [45] . . .

Problems in public life. The "good fight" [46] in the cause of the Faith is fought not only in the secrecy of the individual conscience or in the privacy of the home, but also in public life in all of its forms. In all the different parts of the world there exist nowadays problems of various kinds. There is no solution to these problems in exclusively human advice nor in principles which are often in contrast with the precepts of Christian law. Several mission countries are now "undergoing such speedy changes in social, economic, and political life that their entire future appears to depend on the outcome of those changes." [47] Indeed, problems which some countries have already solved or are solving with the help of their experience and traditions, are urgently in need of solution in other countries. There the problems are beset by serious dangers, inasmuch as they could be approached with deplorable levity, by resorting to certain doctrines which disregard, or even oppose, the religious values of individuals and nations. In order to safeguard both their private interests and those of the Church, Catholics must not ignore such problems, or wait until they are given the wrong solutions, which would thereafter require a much greater expenditure of energy in order to correct them and would place further obstacles in the path of the propagation of the Christian religion in the world.

Christians in public life. The laymen of mission countries exert their most direct and effective influence in the field of public activity, and it is necessary that Christian communities take urgent, timely measures to bring laymen into the public life of their countries for the common good—men who not only acquit themselves creditably in their professions and trades, but are also an asset to the Church which re-created them in her grace. Thus may their pastors praise them with the words which we read in the writings of St. Basil: "I thanked the Most Holy God for the fact that, even though busily attending to public affairs, you did not neglect the interests of the Church: on the contrary, each one of you has been solicitous of her affairs just as though they had

---

[45] Encyclical *"Ad Petri Cathedran," AAS* 51 (1959) 524; *TPS* (Autumn 1959) v. 5, no. 4, 378.
[46] 2 Tim. iv, 7.
[47] Pius XII's Encyclical *"Fidei donum," AAS* 49 (1957) 229; *TPS* (Winter 1957–58) v. 4, no. 3, 298.

been your own private affairs, and, indeed, as though your life depended on it." [48]

Particularly in the field of education, in organized public welfare, in trade unions, and in public administration, will the talents of local Catholic experts play a paramount role, if they, following the duty imposed by their consciences—a duty whose neglect would be traitorous—base their thinking and action on Christian principles. These, as we learn from experience acquired in the course of many centuries, possess the highest power and influence for the pursuit of the common good.

Aid to missions from Catholic groups. Everybody knows how the mutual assistance which is exchanged among Catholic organizations established all over the world can be—as Our predecessor Pius XII has pointed out—of great use and much value to the apostolate of the laity in mission territories. On the educational plane, these organizations can help by devising Christian solutions to current problems, especially social problems, in the newly established nations; on the apostolic plane, they can help by recruiting and organizing a body of laymen, willing to serve under Christ's banner. We know that this has been done, and is being done, by lay missionaries who chose to leave their countries, either temporarily or for life, in order to contribute, by manifold activities, to the social and religious welfare of mission countries. Let us pray fervently to God that the numbers of these generous Christians be multiplied, and that God's support will never be absent in their difficulties and labors, which they are meeting with truly apostolic spirit. The Secular Institutes will be able to give the local laity in mission territories generous and loyal help, if, by their example, they attract imitators, and if they place their talents and work, promptly and willingly, at the disposal of the local ordinaries, in order to speed the growing-up process of the new Christian communities.

Lay help from afar. We appeal especially to all Catholic laymen everywhere who are distinguishing themselves in their professions and in public life to consider seriously how they can help their newly acquired brethren in the Faith, even without leaving their countries. They can do this by giving them the benefit of their advice, their experience, and their technical assistance; they can, without too much labor or grave inconvenience, sometimes give them help that will be decisive. Good men will surely find a way to fulfill this fatherly desire of Ours. They will make Our wish known to those

[48] *Ep. 288,* Migne, *PG* 32, 855.

whom they find favorably disposed, in order first to arouse good will, and then to channel it into the most suitable work.

Students from abroad. Our immediate predecessor exhorted the bishops "with the same affectionate interest that shares work with others in fraternal harmony and excludes all selfish considerations" to provide for the spiritual assistance of young Catholics who come to their dioceses from mission countries to study and to acquire the necessary experience for assuming leadership in their own nations. [49] All of you, Venerable Brethren, are aware of the intellectual and moral dangers to which they will be exposed in a society which is not only different from their own but also, alas, may be unfavorable ground for the growth of their Faith, and not capable of attracting them to the practice of Christian virtue. Each one of you, moved by the missionary spirit which is a conscientious duty of all pastors, will meet this situation with the greatest charity and zeal, using the most suitable means. It will not be difficult for you to find these students and entrust them to the care of priests and laymen who are equipped for this task. It should not be difficult to assuage their spiritual needs, and, last but not least, to have them experience the sweet consolations of Christian charity in which we are all brothers, ministering to one another's welfare. Therefore, to the many kinds of help which you are now giving the missions, add this particular one, which brings close to your hearts those regions of the world which, although far away, are entrusted to your care.

To these students We would like not only to reveal the affection We feel for them, but also to exhort them, urgently and lovingly, to carry their heads high and proud, marked with the sign of Jesus' blood and with the sacred chrism; We would like to exhort them during their stay abroad never to bypass an opportunity not only to acquire the right professional training but also to achieve perfection in their religious education. Although they will be exposed to dangers and evils, they will nevertheless have a wonderful opportunity to share in many spiritual advantages while living in Catholic countries, if all the faithful remember that, whoever and wherever they are, they must be a good example to others and bring mutual edification to one another. . . .

[49] Encyclical *"Fidei donum,"* AAS 49 (1957) 245; TPS (Winter 1957–58) v. 4, no. 3, 310.

Mater et Magistra, May 15, 1961
Christianity and Social Progress*

The Catholic Church has been established by Jesus Christ as MOTHER AND TEACHER of nations, so that all who in the course of centuries come to her loving embrace, may find salvation as well as the fullness of a more excellent life. To this Church, "the pillar and mainstay of the truth," [1] her most holy Founder has entrusted the double task of begetting sons unto herself, and of educating and governing those whom she begets, guiding with maternal providence the life both of individuals and of peoples. The lofty dignity of this life, she has always held in the highest respect and guarded with watchful care.

2. For the teaching of Christ joins, as it were, earth with heaven, in that it embraces the whole man, namely his soul and body, intellect and will, and bids him to lift up his mind from the changing conditions of human existence to that heavenly country where he will one day enjoy unending happiness and peace.

3. Hence, although Holy Church has the special task of sanctifying souls and of making them sharers of heavenly blessings, she is also solicitous for the requirements of men in their daily lives, not merely those relating to food and sustenance, but also to their comfort and advancement in various kinds of goods and in varying circumstances of time.

4. Realizing all this, Holy Church implements the commands of her Founder, Christ, who refers primarily to man's eternal salvation when He says, "I am the Way, and the Truth, and the Life" [2] and elsewhere "I am the Light of the World." [3] On other occasions, however, seeing the hungry crowd, He was moved to exclaim sorrowfully. "I have compassion on the crowd," [4] thereby indicating that He was also concerned about the earthly needs of mankind. The divine Redeemer shows this care not only by His words but also by the actions of His life, as when, to alleviate the hunger of the crowds, He more than once miraculously multiplied bread.

5. By this bread, given for the nourishment of the body, He wished to foreshadow that heavenly food of the soul which He was to give to men on *the day before He suffered.*

* Text of "Mater et Magistra," translated by William J. Gibbons, S. J., is reprinted with the permission of The Paulist Press, 401 West 59th Street, New York 19, N. Y., copyright, 1961, 1962, by The Missionary Society of St. Paul the Apostle in the State of New York.

[1] Cf. 1 Tim. 3, 15.
[2] John 14, 6.
[3] John 8, 12.
[4] Mark 8, 2.

6. It is no wonder, then, that the Catholic Church, instructed by Christ and fulfilling His commands, has for two thousand years, from the ministry of the early deacons to the present time, tenaciously held aloft the torch of charity not only by her teaching but also by her widespread example—that charity which, by combining in a fitting manner the precepts and the practice of mutual love, puts into effect in a wonderful way this twofold commandment of *giving,* wherein is contained the full social teaching and action of the Church.

7. By far the most notable evidence of this social teaching and action, which the Church has set forth through the centuries, undoubtedly is the very distinguished Encyclical Letter *Rerum Novarum,*[5] issued seventy years ago by our predecessor of immortal memory, Leo XIII. Therein he put forward teachings whereby the question of the workers' condition would be resolved in conformity with Christian principles.

8. Seldom have the admonitions of a Pontiff been received with such universal approbation, as was that Encyclical of Leo XIII, rivaled by few in the depth and scope of its reasoning and in the forcefulness of its expression. Indeed, the norms and recommendations contained therein were so momentous that their memory will never fall into oblivion. As a result, the action of the Catholic Church became more widely known. For its Supreme Pastor, making his own the problems of weak and harassed men, their complaints and aspirations, had devoted himself especially to the defense and restoration of their rights.

9. Even today, in spite of the long lapse of time since the Letter was published, much of its effectiveness is still evident. It is indeed evident in the documents of the Popes who succeeded Leo XIII, and who, when they discussed economic and social affairs, have always borrowed something from it, either to clarify its application or to stimulate further activity on the part of Catholics. The efficacy of the document also is evident in the laws and institutions of many nations. Thus does it become abundantly clear that the solidly grounded principles, the norms of action, and the paternal admonitions found in the masterly Letter of our predecessor, even today retain their original worth. Moreover, from it can be drawn new and vital criteria, whereby men may judge the nature and extent of the social question, and determine what their responsibilities are in this regard.

RADIO BROADCAST OF PENTECOST, 1941

41. In specifying social rights and obligations, our predecessor of immortal memory, Pius XII, made a significant contri-

[5] *Acta Leonis* XIII, XI (1891), pp. 97–144.

bution, when on the feast of Pentecost, June 1, 1941, he broadcast to the world community a message: "in order to call to the attention of the Catholic world the memory of an event worthy of being written in letters of gold on the Calendar of the Church: namely, the fiftieth anniversary of the publication of the epoch-making Encyclical of Leo XIII, *Rerum Novarum*." [6] He broadcast this message, moreover, "to render special thanks to Almighty God that His Vicar on earth, in a Letter such as this, gave to the Church so great a gift, and also to render praise to the eternal Spirit that through this same Letter, He enkindled a fire calculated to rouse the whole human race to new and better effort." [7]

42. In the message, the great Pontiff claimed for the Church "the indisputable competence" to "decide whether the bases of a given social system are in accord with the unchangeable order which God our Creator and Redeemer has fixed both in the natural law and revelation." [8] He noted that the Letter of Leo XIII is of permanent value and has rich and abiding usefulness. He takes the occasion "to explain in greater detail what the Catholic Church teaches regarding the three principal issues of social life in economic affairs, which are mutually related and connected one with the other, and thus interdependent: namely, the use of material goods, labor, and the family." [9]

43. Concerning the use of material goods, our predecessor declared that the right of every man to use them for his own sustenance is prior to all other rights in economic life, and hence is prior even to the right of private ownership. It is certain, however, as our predecessor noted, that the right of private property is from the natural law itself. Nevertheless, it is the will of God the Creator that this right to own property should in no wise obstruct the flow of "material goods created by God to meet the needs of all men, to all equitably, as justice and charity require." [10]

44. As regards labor, Pius XII repeating what appeared in Leo XIII's Letter, declared it to be both a duty and a right of every human being. Consequently, it is in the first place the responsibility of men themselves to regulate mutual labor relations. Only in the event that the interested parties are unwilling or unable to fulfill their functions, does it "devolve upon the State to intervene and to assign labor equitably, safeguard-

[6] Cf. *Acta Apostolicae Sedis*, XXXIII (1941), p. 196.
[7] Cf. *Ibid.*, p. 197.
[8] Cf. *Ibid.*, p. 196.
[9] Cf. *Ibid.*, p. 198f.
[10] Cf. *Ibid.*, p. 199.

ing the standards and aims that the common good properly understood demands." [11]

45. Turning to the family, the Supreme Pontiff stresses that private ownership of material goods helps to safeguard and develop family life. Such goods are an apt means "to secure for the father of a family the healthy liberty he needs in order to fulfill the duties assigned him by the Creator, regarding the physical, spiritual, and religious welfare of the family." [12] From this arises the right of the family to migrate. Accordingly, our predecessor reminds governments, both those permitting emigration and those accepting immigrants, that "they never permit anything whereby mutual and sincere understanding between States is diminished or destroyed." [13] If this be mutually accomplished, it will come to pass that benefits are equalized and diffused widely among peoples, as the supply of goods and the arts and crafts are increased and fostered.

FURTHER CHANGES

46. But just as contemporary circumstances seemed to Pius XII quite dissimilar from those of the earlier period, so they have changed greatly over the past twenty years. This can be seen not only in the internal situation of each individual country, but also in the mutual relations of countries.

47. In the fields of science, technology, and economics, these developments are especially worthy of note: the discovery of atomic energy, employed first for military purposes and later increasingly for peaceful ends; the almost limitless possibilities opened up by chemistry in synthetic products; the growth of automation in the sectors of industry and services; the modernization of agriculture; the nearly complete conquest, especially through radio and television, of the distance separating peoples; the greatly increased speed of all manner of transportation; the initial conquests of outer space.

48. Turning to the social field, the following contemporary trends are evident: development of systems for social insurance; the introduction of social security systems in some more affluent countries; greater awareness among workers, as members of unions, of the principal issues in economic and social life; a progressive improvement of basic education; wider diffusion among the citizenry of the conveniences of life; increased social mobility and a resulting decline in divisions among the classes: greater interest than heretofore in world affairs on the

[11] Cf. *Ibid.*, p. 201.
[12] Cf. *Ibid.*, p. 202.
[13] Cf. *Ibid.*, p. 203.

part of those with average education. Meanwhile, if one considers the social and economic advances made in a growing number of countries, he will quickly discern increasingly pronounced imbalances: first, between agriculture on the one hand and industry and the services on the other; between the more and the less developed regions within countries; and, finally, on a worldwide scale, between countries with differing economic resources and development.

49. Turning now to political affairs, it is evident that there, too, a number of innovations have occurred. Today, in many communities, citizens from almost all social strata participate in public life. Public authorities intervene more and more in economic and social affairs. The peoples of Asia and Africa, having set aside colonial systems, now govern themselves according to their own laws and institutions. As the mutual relationships of peoples increase, they become daily more dependent one upon the other. Throughout the world, assemblies and councils have become more common, which, being supranational in character, take into account the interests of all peoples. Such bodies are concerned with economic life, or with social affairs, or with culture and education, or, finally, with the mutual relationships of peoples.

REASONS FOR THE NEW ENCYCLICAL

50. Now, reflecting on all these things, we feel it our duty to keep alive the torch lighted by our great predecessors and to exhort all to draw from their writings light and inspiration, if they wish to resolve the social question in ways more in accord with the needs of the present time. Therefore, we are issuing this present Letter not merely to commemorate appropriately the Encyclical Letter of Leo XIII, but also, in the light of changed conditions, both to confirm and explain more fully what our predecessors taught, and to set forth the Church's teaching regarding the new and serious problems of our day.

Part II

Explanation and Development
of the Teachings of "Rerum Novarum"

PRIVATE INITIATIVE AND STATE INTERVENTION
IN ECONOMIC LIFE

51. At the outset it should be affirmed that in economic affairs first place is to be given to the private initiative of individual men who, either working by themselves, or with others in one fashion or another, pursue their common interests.

52. But in this matter, for reasons pointed out by our predecessors, it is necessary that public authorities take active interest, the better to increase output of goods and to further social progress for the benefit of all citizens.

53. This intervention of public authorities that encourages, stimulates, regulates, supplements, and complements, is based on the *principle of subsidiarity* [14] as set forth by Pius XI in his Encyclical *Quadragesimo Anno:* "It is a fundamental principle of social philosophy, fixed and unchangeable, that one should not withdraw from individuals and commit to the community what they can accomplish by their own enterprise and industry. So, too, it is an injustice and at the same time a grave evil and a disturbance of right order, to transfer to the larger and higher collectivity functions which can be performed and provided for by lesser and subordinate bodies. Inasmuch as every social activity should, by its very nature, prove a help to members of the body social, it should never destroy or absorb them." [15]

54. Indeed, as is easily perceived, recent developments of science and technology provide additional reasons why, to a greater extent than heretofore, it is within the power of public authorities to reduce imbalances, whether these be between various sectors of economic life, or between different regions of the same nation, or even between different peoples of the world as a whole. These same developments make it possible to keep fluctuations in the economy within bounds, and to provide effective measures for avoiding mass unemployment. Consequently, it is requested again and again of public authorities responsible for the common good, that they intervene in a wide variety of economic affairs, and that, in a more extensive and organized way than heretofore, they adapt institutions, tasks, means, and procedures to this end.

[14] *Acta Apostolicae Sedis*, XXIII (1931), p. 203.
[15] *Ibid.*, p. 203.

55. Nevertheless, it remains true that precautionary activities of public authorities in the economic field, although widespread and penetrating, should be such that they not only avoid restricting the freedom of private citizens, but also increase it, so long as the basic rights of each individual person are preserved inviolate. Included among these is the right and duty of each individual normally to provide the necessities of life for himself and his dependents. This implies that whatever be the economic system, it allow and facilitate for every individual the opportunity to engage in productive activity.

56. Furthermore, the course of events thus far makes it clear that there cannot be a prosperous and well-ordered society unless both private citizens and public authorities work together in economic affairs. Their activity should be characterized by mutual and amicable efforts, so that the roles assigned to each fit in with requirements of the common good, as changing times and customs suggest.

57. Experience, in fact, shows that where private initiative of individuals is lacking, political tyranny prevails. Moreover, much stagnation occurs in various sectors of the economy, and hence all sorts of consumer goods and services, closely connected with needs of the body and more especially of the spirit, are in short supply. Beyond doubt, the attainment of such goods and services provides remarkable opportunity and stimulus for individuals to exercise initiative and industry.

58. Where, on the other hand, appropriate activity of the State is lacking or defective, commonwealths are apt to experience incurable disorders, and there occurs exploitation of the weak by the unscrupulous strong, who flourish, unfortunately, like cockle among the wheat, in all times and places.

COMPLEXITY OF SOCIAL STRUCTURE

DIRECTION OF THE TREND

59. One of the principal characteristics of our time is the multiplication of social relationships, that is, a daily more complex interdependence of citizens, introducing into their lives and activities many and varied forms of association, recognized for the most part in private and even in public law. This tendency seemingly stems from a number of factors operative in the present era, among which are technical and scientific progress, greater productive efficiency, and a higher standard of living among citizens.

60. These developments in social living are at once both a symptom and a cause of the growing intervention of public

authorities in matters which, since they pertain to the more intimate aspects of personal life, are of serious moment and not without danger. Such, for example, are the care of health, the instruction and education of youth, the choice of a personal career, the ways and means of rehabilitating or assisting those handicapped mentally or physically. But this trend also indicates and in part follows from that human and natural inclination, scarcely resistible, where men are impelled voluntarily to enter into association in order to attain objectives which each one desires, but which exceed the capacity of single individuals. This tendency has given rise, especially in recent years, to organizations and institutes on both national and international levels, which relate to economic and social goals, to cultural and recreational activities, to athletics, to various professions, and to political affairs.

EVALUATION

61. Such an advance in social relationships definitely brings numerous services and advantages. It makes possible, in fact, the satisfaction of many personal rights, especially those of economic and social life; these relate, for example, to the minimum necessities of human life, to health services, to the broadening and deepening of elementary education, to a more fitting training in skills, to housing, to labor, to suitable leisure and recreation. In addition, through the ever more perfect organization of modern means for the diffusion of thought—press, cinema, radio, television—individuals are enabled to take part in human events on a world-wide scale.

62. But as these various forms of association are multiplied and daily extended, it also happens that in many areas of activity, rules and laws controlling and determining relationships of citizens are multiplied. As a consequence, opportunity for free action by individuals is restricted within narrower limits. Methods are often used, procedures are adopted, and such an atmosphere develops wherein it becomes difficult for one to make decisions independently of outside influences, to do anything on his own initiative, to carry out in a fitting way his rights and duties, and to fully develop and perfect his personality. Will men perhaps, then become automatons, and cease to be personally responsible, as these social relationships multiply more and more? It is a question which must be answered negatively.

63. Actually, increased complexity of social life by no means results from a blind drive of natural forces. Indeed, as stated above, it is the creation of free men who are so disposed to act

by nature as to be responsible for what they do. They must, of course, recognize the laws of human progress and the development of economic life and take these into account. Furthermore, men are not altogether free of their milieu.

64. Accordingly, advances in social organization can and should be so brought about that maximum advantages accrue to citizens while at the same time disadvantages are averted or at least minimized.

65. That these desired objectives be more readily obtained, it is necessary that public authorities have a correct understanding of the common good. This embraces the sum total of those conditions of social living, whereby men are enabled more fully and more readily to achieve their own perfection. Hence, we regard it as necessary that the various intermediary bodies and the numerous social undertakings wherein an expanded social structure primarily finds expression, be ruled by their own laws, and as the common good itself progresses, pursue this objective in a spirit of sincere concord among themselves. Nor is it less necessary that the above mentioned groups present the form and substance of a true community. This they will do, only if individual members are considered and treated as persons, and are encouraged to participate in the affairs of the group.

66. Accordingly, as relationships multiply between men, binding them more closely together, commonwealths will more readily and appropriately order their affairs to the extent these two factors are kept in balance: (1) the freedom of individual citizens and groups of citizens to act autonomously, while cooperating one with the other; (2) the activity of the State whereby the undertakings of private individuals and groups are suitably regulated and fostered.

67. Now if social systems are organized in accordance with the above norms and moral laws, their extension does not necessarily mean that individual citizens will be gravely discriminated against or excessively burdened. Rather, we can hope that this will enable man not only to develop and perfect his natural talents, but also will lead to an appropriate structuring of the human community. Such a structure, as our predecessor of happy memory, Pius XI, warned in his Encyclical Letter *Quadragesimo Anno,*[16] is absolutely necessary for the adequate fulfillment of the rights and duties of social life.

[16] Cf. *Ibid.,* p. 222f.

REMUNERATION FOR WORK

STANDARDS OF JUSTICE AND EQUITY

68. Our heart is filled with profound sadness when we observe, as it were, with our own eyes a wretched spectacle indeed —great masses of workers who, in not a few nations, and even in whole continents, receive too small a return from their labor. Hence, they and their families must live in conditions completely out of accord with human dignity. This can be traced, for example, to the fact that in these regions, modern industrial techniques either have only recently been introduced or have made less than satisfactory progress.

69. It happens in some of these nations that, as compared with the extreme need of the majority, the wealth and conspicuous consumption of a few stand out, and are in open and bold contrast with the lot of the needy. It happens in other places that excessive burdens are placed upon men in order that the commonwealth may achieve within a brief span, an increase of wealth such as can by no means be achieved without violating the laws of justice and equity. Finally, it happens elsewhere that a disproportionate share of the revenue goes toward the building up of national prestige, and that large sums of money are devoted to armaments.

70. Moreover, in the economically developed countries, it frequently happens that great, or sometimes very great, remuneration is had for the performance of some task of lesser importance or doubtful utility. Meanwhile, the diligent and profitable work that whole classes of decent and hard-working citizens perform, receives too low a payment and one insufficient for the necessities of life, or else, one that does not correspond to the contribution made to the community, or to the revenues of the undertakings in which they are engaged, or to the national income.

71. Wherefore, we judge it to be our duty to reaffirm once again that just as remuneration for work cannot be left entirely to unregulated competition, neither may it be decided arbitrarily at the will of the more powerful. Rather, in this matter, the norms of justice and equity should be strictly observed. This requires that workers receive a wage sufficient to lead a life worthy of man and to fulfill family responsibilities properly. But in determining what constitutes an appropriate wage, the following must necessarily be taken into account: first of all, the contribution of individuals to the economic effort; the economic state of the enterprises within which they work; the

requirements of each community, especially as regards over-all employment; finally, what concerns the common good of all peoples, namely, of the various States associated among themselves, but differing in character and extent.

72. It is clear that the standards of judgment set forth above are binding always and everywhere. However, the measure in which they are to be applied in concrete cases cannot be established unless account is taken of the resources at hand. These resources can and in fact do vary in quantity and quality among different peoples, and may even change within the same country with the passing of time.

Balancing Economic Developments and Social Progress

73. Whereas in our era the economics of various countries are evolving very rapidly, more especially since the last great war, we take this opportunity to draw the attention of all to a strict demand of social justice, which explicitly requires that, with the growth of the economy, there occur a corresponding social development. Thus, all classes of citizens will benefit equitably from an increase in national wealth. Toward this end vigilance should be exercised and effective steps taken that class differences arising from disparity of wealth not be increased, but lessened so far as possible.

74. "National wealth"—as our predecessor of happy memory, Pius XII, rightfully observed—"inasmuch as it is produced by the common efforts of the citizenry, has no other purpose than to secure without interruption those material conditions in which individuals are enabled to lead a full and perfect life. Where this is consistently the case, then such a people is to be judged truly rich. For the system whereby both the common prosperity is achieved and individuals exercise their right to the material goods, conforms fully to norms laid down by God the Creator.[17] From this it follows that the economic prosperity of any people is to be assessed not so much from the sum total of goods and wealth possessed as from the distribution of goods according to norms of justice, so that everyone in the community can develop and perfect himself. For this, after all, is the end toward which all economic activity of a community is by nature ordered.

75. We must here call attention to the fact that in many countries today, the economic system is such that large and medium size productive enterprises achieve rapid growth precisely because they finance replacement and plant expansion

---

[17] Cf. *Acta Apostolicae Sedis*, XXXIII (1941), p. 200.

from their own revenues. Where this is the case, we believe that such companies should grant to workers some share in the enterprise, especially where they are paid no more than the minimum wage.

76. In this matter, the principle laid down by our predecessor of happy memory, Pius XI, in the Encyclical Letter *Quadragesimo Anno,* should be borne in mind: "It is totally false to ascribe to a single factor of production what is in fact produced by joint activity; and it is completely unjust for one factor to arrogate to itself what is produced, ignoring what has been contributed by other factors." [18]

77. The demands of justice referred to, can be met in various ways, as experience shows. Not to mention other ways, it is very desirable that workers gradually acquire some share in the enterprise by such methods as seem more appropriate. For today, more than in the times of our predecessor, "every effort should be made that at least in the future, only an equitable share of the fruits of production accumulate in the hands of the wealthy, and a sufficient and ample portion go to the workingmen." [19]

78. But we should remember that adjustments between remuneration for work and revenues are to be brought about in conformity with the requirements of the common good, both of one's own community and of the entire human family.

79. Considering the common good on the national level, the following points are relevant and should not be overlooked: to provide employment for as many workers as possible; to take care lest privileged groups arise even among the workers themselves; to maintain a balance between wages and prices; to make accessible the goods and services for a better life to as many persons as possible; either to eliminate or to keep within bounds the inequalities that exist between different sectors of the economy—that is, between agriculture, industry and services; to balance properly any increases in output with advances in services provided to citizens, especially by public authority; to adjust, as far as possible, the means of production to the progress of science and technology; finally, to ensure that the advantages of a more humane way of existence not merely subserve the present generation but have regard for future generations as well.

80. As regards the common good of human society as a whole, the following conditions should be fulfilled: that the competitive striving of peoples to increase output be free of

[18] *Acta Apostolicae Sedis,* XXIII (1931), p. 195.
[19] *Ibid.,* p. 198.

bad faith; that harmony in economic affairs and a friendly and beneficial cooperation be fostered; and, finally, that effective aid be given in developing the economically underdeveloped nations.

81. It is evident from what has been said that these demands of the common good, on both the national and world levels, should be borne in mind, when there is question of determining the share of earnings assigned to those responsible for directing the productive enterprise, or as interest and dividends to those who have invested capital.

DEMANDS OF JUSTICE AS REGARDS PRODUCTIVE INSTITUTIONS

INSTITUTIONS CONFORMING TO THE DIGNITY OF MAN

82. Justice is to be observed not merely in the distribution of wealth, but also in regard to the conditions under which men engage in productive activity. There is, in fact, an innate need of human nature requiring that men engaged in productive activity have an opportunity to assume responsibility and to perfect themselves by their efforts.

83. Consequently, if the organization and structure of economic life be such that the human dignity of workers is compromised, or their sense of responsibility is weakened, or their freedom of action is removed, then we judge such an economic order to be unjust, even though it produces a vast amount of goods, whose distribution conforms to the norms of justice and equity.

REAFFIRMATION OF A DIRECTIVE

84. Nor is it possible in economic affairs to determine in one formula all the measures that are more conformable to the dignity of man, or are more suitable in developing in him a sense of responsibility. Nevertheless, our predecessor of happy memory, Pius XII, appropriately laid down certain norms of action: "Small and medium-sized holdings in agriculture, in the arts and crafts, in commerce and industry, should be safeguarded and fostered. Such enterprises should join together in mutual-aid societies in order that the services and benefits of large-scale enterprises will be available to them. So far as these larger enterprises are concerned, work agreements should in some way be modified by partnership arrangements." [20]

[20] Radio Broadcast, September 1, 1944; cf. *A.A.S.*, XXXVI (1944), p. 254.

ARTISAN ENTERPRISES AND COOPERATIVE ASSOCIATIONS

85. Wherefore, conformably to requirements of the common good and the state of technology, artisan and farm enterprises of family type should be safeguarded and fostered, as should also cooperatives that aim to complement and perfect such enterprises.

86. We shall return shortly to the subject of farm enterprises. Here, we think it appropriate to say something about artisan enterprises and cooperative associations.

87. Above all, it must be emphasized that enterprises and bodies of this sort, in order that they may survive and flourish, should be continuously adapted—both in their productive structure and in their operating methods—to new conditions of the times. These new conditions constantly arise from advances in science and technology, or from changing consumer needs and preferences. It is especially appropriate that all this be done by the craftsmen themselves and by the associates in the cooperatives.

88. Hence, it is most fitting not only that both these groups be suitably formed in technical and in spiritual and intellectual matters, but also that they be joined together professionally. Nor is it less fitting that the State make special provision for them in regard to instruction, taxes, credit facilities, social security and insurance.

89. Moreover, the measures taken by the State on behalf of the craftsmen and members of cooperatives are also justified by the fact that these two categories of citizens are producers of genuine wealth, and contribute to the advance of civilization.

90. Accordingly, we paternally exhort our beloved sons, craftsmen and members of cooperatives throughout the world, that they fully realize the dignity of their role in society, since, by their work, the sense of responsibility and spirit of mutual aid can be daily more intensified among the citizenry, and the desire to work with dedication and originality be kept alive.

PARTICIPATION OF WORKERS IN MEDIUM-SIZE AND LARGE ENTERPRISES

91. Furthermore, as did our predecessors, we regard as justifiable the desire of employees to be partners in enterprises with which they are associated and wherein they work. We do not think it possible, however, to decide with certain and explicit norms the manner and degree of such partnerships, since this must be determined according to the state of the individual

productive enterprises. For the situation is not everywhere the same, and, in fact, it can change suddenly within one and the same enterprise. Nevertheless, we do not doubt that employees should have an active part in the affairs of the enterprise wherein they work, whether these be private or public. But it is of the utmost importance that productive enterprises assume the character of a true human fellowship whose spirit suffuses the dealings, activities, and standing of all its members.

92. This requires that mutual relations between employers and directors on the one hand and the employees of the enterprise on the other, be marked by mutual respect, esteem, and good will. It also demands that all collaborate sincerely and harmoniously in their joint undertaking, and that they perform their work not merely with the objective of deriving an income, but also of carrying out the role assigned them and of performing a service that results in benefit to others. This means that the workers may have a say in, and may make a contribution toward, the efficient running and development of the enterprise. Thus, our predecessor of happy memory, Pius XII, clearly indicated: "The economic and social functions which everyone aspires to fulfill, require that efforts of individuals be not wholly subjected to the will of others." [21] Beyond doubt, an enterprise truly in accord with human dignity should safeguard the necessary and efficient unity of administration. But it by no means follows that those who work daily in such an enterprise are to be considered merely as servants, whose sole function is to execute orders silently, and who are not allowed to interject their desires and interests, but must conduct themselves as idle standbys when it comes to assignment and direction of their tasks.

93. Finally, attention is drawn to the fact that the greater amount of responsibility desired today by workers in productive enterprises, not merely accords with the nature of man, but also is in conformity with historical developments in the economic, social, and political fields.

94. Unfortunately, in our day, there occur in economic and social affairs many imbalances that militate against justice and humanity. Meanwhile, throughout all of economic life, errors are spread that seriously impair its operation, purposes, organization, and the fulfillment of responsibilities. Nevertheless, it is an undeniable fact that the more recent productive systems, thanks to the impulse deriving from advances in technology and science, are becoming more modern and efficient, and are expanding at a faster rate than in the past. This demands of workers greater abilities and professional qualifications. Ac-

cordingly, workers should be provided with additional aids and time to achieve a suitable and more rounded formation, and to carry out more fittingly their duties as regards studies, morals, and religion.

95. Thus it happens that in our day youths can be allotted additional years to acquire a basic education and necessary skills.

96. Now if these things be done, a situation will emerge wherein workers are enabled to assume greater responsibilities even within their own enterprises. As regards the commonwealth as such, it is of great importance that all ranks of citizens feel themselves daily more obligated to safeguard the common good.

PARTICIPATION OF WORKERS AT ALL LEVELS

97. Now, as is evident to all, in our day associations of workers have become widespread, and for the most part have been given legal status within individual countries and even across national boundaries. These bodies no longer recruit workers for purposes of strife, but rather for pursuing a common aim. And this is achieved especially by collective bargaining between associations of workers and those of management. But it should be emphasized how necessary, or at least very appropriate, it is to give workers an opportunity to exert influence outside the limits of the individual productive unit, and indeed within all ranks of the commonwealth.

98. The reason is that individual productive units, whatever their size, efficiency, or importance within the commonwealth, are closely connected with the over-all economic and social situation in each country, whereon their own prosperity ultimately depends.

99. Nevertheless, to decide what is more helpful to the overall economic situation is not the prerogative of individual productive enterprises, but pertains to the public authorities and to those institutions which, established either nationally or among a number of countries, function in various sectors of economic life. From this is evident the propriety or necessity of ensuring that not only managers or agents of management are represented before such authorities and institutions, but also workers or those who have the responsibility of safeguarding the rights, needs, and aspirations of workers.

100. It is fitting, therefore, that our thoughts and paternal affection be directed toward the various professional groups and associations of workers which, in accord with principles of Christian teaching, carry on their activities on several continents. We are aware of the many and great difficulties expe-

rienced by these beloved sons of ours, as they effectively worked in the past and continue to strive, both within their national boundaries and throughout the world, to vindicate the rights of workingmen and to improve their lot and conduct.

101. Furthermore, we wish to give deserved praise to the work of these our sons. Their accomplishments are not always immediately evident, but nevertheless permeate practically the entire field of labor, spreading correct norms of action and thought, and the beneficial influence of the Christian religion.

102. And we wish also to praise paternally those dear sons of ours who, imbued with Christian principles, give their special attention to other labor associations and those groups of workingmen that follow the laws of nature and respect the religious and moral liberty of individuals.

103. Nor can we at this point neglect to congratulate and to express our esteem for the International Labor Organization— variously signified popularly by the letters O.I.L. or I.L.O. or O.I.T.—which, for many years, has done effective and valuable work in adapting the economic and social order everywhere to the norms of justice and humanity. In such an order, the legitimate rights of workers are recognized and preserved.

PRIVATE PROPERTY

CHANGED CONDITIONS

104. In recent years, as we are well aware, the role played by the owners of capital in very large productive enterprises has been separated more and more from the role of management. This has occasioned great difficulties for governments, whose duty it is to make certain that directors of the principal enterprises, especially those of greatest influence in the economic life of the entire country, do not depart from the requirements of the common good. These difficulties, as we know from experience, are by no means less, whether it be private citizens or public bodies that make the capital investments requisite for large-scale enterprises.

105. It is also quite clear that today the number of persons is increasing who, because of recent advances in insurance programs and various systems of social security, are able to look to the future with tranquillity. This sort of tranquillity once was rooted in the ownership of property, albeit modest.

106. It sometimes happens in our day that men are more inclined to seek some professional skill than possession of goods. Moreover, such men have greater esteem for income from labor or rights arising from labor, than for that deriving from capital investment or rights associated therewith.

107. This clearly accords with the inherent characteristics of labor, inasmuch as it proceeds directly from the human person, and hence is to be thought more of than wealth in external goods. These latter, by their very nature, must be regarded as instruments. This trend indicates an advance in civilization.

108. Economic conditions of this kind have occasioned popular doubt as to whether, under present circumstances, a principle of economic and social life, firmly enunciated and defended by our predecessors, has lost its force or is to be regarded as of lesser moment: namely, the principle whereby it is established that men have from nature a right of privately owning goods, including those of a productive kind.

CONFIRMATION OF THE RIGHT OF PRIVATE PROPERTY

109. Such a doubt has no foundation. For the right of private property, including that pertaining to goods devoted to productive enterprises, is permanently valid. Indeed, it is rooted in the very nature of things, whereby we learn that individual men are prior to civil society, and hence, that civil society is to be directed toward man as its end. Indeed, the right of private individuals to act freely in economic affairs is recognized in vain, unless they are at the same time given an opportunity of freely selecting and using things necessary for the exercise of this right. Moreover, experience and history testify that where political regimes do not allow to private individuals the possession also of productive goods, the exercise of human liberty is violated or completely destroyed in matters of primary importance. Thus it becomes clear that in the right of property, the exercise of liberty finds both a safeguard and a stimulus.

110. This explains the fact that socio-political groups and associations which endeavor to reconcile freedom with justice within society, and which until recently did not uphold the right of private property in productive goods, have now, enlightened by the course of social events, modified their views and are disposed actually to approve this right.

111. Accordingly, we make our own the insistence of our predecessor of happy memory, Pius XII: "In defending the right of private property, the Church has in mind a very important ethical aim in social matters. She does not, of course, strive to uphold the present state of affairs as if it were an expression of the divine will. And even less does she accept the patronage of the affluent and wealthy, while neglecting the rights of the poor and needy. . . . The Church rather does

intend that the institution of private property be such as is required by the plan of divine wisdom and the law of nature." [22] Private ownership should safeguard the rights of the human person, and at the same time make its necessary contribution to the establishment of right order in society.

112. While recent developments in economic life progress rapidly in a number of countries, as we have noted, and produce goods ever more efficiently, justice and equity require that remuneration for work also be increased within limits allowed by the common good. This enables workers to save more readily and hence to achieve some property status of their own. Wherefore, it is indeed surprising that some reject the natural role of private ownership. For it is a right which continually draws its force and vigor from the fruitfulness of labor, and which, accordingly, is an effective aid in safeguarding the dignity of the human person and the free exercise of responsibility in all fields of endeavor. Finally, it strengthens the stability and tranquillity of family life, thus contributing to the peace and prosperity of the commonwealth.

Effective Distribution

113. It is not enough, then, to assert that man has from nature the right of privately possessing goods as his own, including those of productive character, unless, at the same time, a continuing effort is made to spread the use of this right through all ranks of the citizenry.

114. Our predecessor of happy memory, Pius XII, clearly reminded us that on the one hand the dignity of the human person necessarily "requires the right of using external goods in order to live according to the right norm of nature. And to this right corresponds a most serious obligation, which requires that, so far as possible, there be given to all an opportunity of possessing private property." [23] On the other hand, the nobility inherent in work, besides other requirements, demands "the conservation and perfection of a social order that makes possible a secure, although modest, property to all classes of people." [24]

115. It is especially appropriate that today, more than heretofore, widespread private ownership should prevail, since, as noted above, the number of nations increases wherein the economic systems experience daily growth. Therefore, by prudent

---

[22] Radio Broadcast, September 1, 1944; cf. *A.A.S.*, XXXVI (1944), p. 253.
[23] Radio Broadcast, December 24, 1942; cf. *A.A.S.*, XXXV (1943), p. 17.
[24] Cf. *Ibid.*, p. 20.

use of various devices already proven effective, it will not be difficult for the body politic to modify economic and social life so that the way is made easier for widespread private possession of such things as durable goods, homes, gardens, tools requisite for artisan enterprises and family-type farms, investments in enterprises of medium or large size. All of this has occurred satisfactorily in some nations with developed social and economic systems.

PUBLIC PROPERTY

116. Obviously, what we have said above does not preclude ownership of goods pertaining to production of wealth by States and public agencies, especially "if these carry with them power too great to be left in private hands, without injury to the community at large." [25]

117. It seems characteristic of our times to vest more and more ownership of goods in the State and in other public bodies. This is partially explained by the fact that the common good requires public authorities to exercise ever greater responsibilities. However, in this matter, the *principle of subsidiarity,* already mentioned above, is to be strictly observed. For it is lawful for States and public corporations to expand their domain of ownership only when manifest and genuine requirements of the common good so require, and then with safeguards, lest the possession of private citizens be diminished beyond measure, or, what is worse, destroyed.

118. Finally, we cannot pass over in silence the fact that economic enterprises undertaken by the State or by public corporations should be entrusted to citizens outstanding in skill and integrity, who will carry out their responsibilities to the commonwealth with a deep sense of devotion. Moreover, the activity of these men should be subjected to careful and continuing supervision, lest, in the administration of the State itself, there develop an economic imperialism in the hands of a few. For such a development is in conflict with the highest good of the commonwealth.

SOCIAL FUNCTION OF PROPERTY

119. Our predecessors have always taught that in the right of private property there is rooted a social responsibility. In-

[25] Encyclical Letter *Quadragesimo Anno; A.A.S.,* XXIII (1931), p. 214.

deed, in the wisdom of God the Creator, the over-all supply of goods is assigned, first of all, that all men may lead a decent life. As our predecessor of happy memory, Leo XIII, clearly reminded us in the Encyclical Letter *Rerum Novarum,* "This is the heart of the matter: whoever has received from the divine bounty a larger share of blessings, whether these be corporal or external or gifts of the mind, has received them to use for his own perfection, and, at the same time, as the minister of God's providence, for the benefit of others. 'He who has a talent' [says St. Gregory the Great], 'let him take care that he hides it not; he who has abundance, let him arouse himself to mercy and generosity; he who has skill in managing affairs, let him make special effort to share the use and utility thereof with his neighbor.' " [26]

120. Although in our day, the role assigned the State and public bodies has increased more and more, it by no means follows that the social function of private ownership is obsolescent, as some seem to think. For social responsibility in this matter derives its force from the very right of private property. Furthermore, it is quite clear that there always will be a wide range of difficult situations, as well as hidden and grave needs, which the manifold providence of the State leaves untouched, and of which it can in no way take account. Wherefore, there is always wide scope for humane action by private citizens and for Christian charity. Finally, it is evident that in stimulating efforts relating to spiritual welfare, the work done by individual men or by private civic groups has more value than what is done by public authorities.

121. Moreover, it is well to recall here that the right of private ownership is clearly evident in the Gospels, which reveal Jesus Christ ordering the rich to share their goods with the poor so as to turn them into spiritual possessions: "Do not lay up for yourselves treasures on earth, where rust and moth consume, and where thieves break in and steal; but lay up for yourselves treasures in heaven, where neither rust nor moth consumes nor thieves break in and steal." [27] And the divine Master states that whatever is done for the poor is done for Him: "Amen I say to you, as long as you did it for one of these, the least of My brethren, you did it for Me." [28]

[26] *Acta Leonis* XIII, XI (1891), p. 114.
[27] Matt. 6, 19-20.
[28] Matt. 25, 40.

Part III

New Aspects
of the
Social Question

122. The progress of events and of time have made it increasingly evident that the relationships between workers and management in productive enterprises must be readjusted according to norms of justice and charity. But the same is also true of the systems whereby various types of economic activity and the differently endowed regions within a country ought to be linked together. Meanwhile, within the over-all human community, many nations with varied endowments have not made identical progress in their economic and social affairs.

JUST REQUIREMENTS IN THE MATTER OF
INTERRELATED PRODUCTIVE SECTORS

AGRICULTURE: A DEPRESSED SECTOR

123. First of all, to lay down some norms in regard to agriculture, we would note that the over-all number of rural dwellers seemingly has not diminished. Beyond doubt, however, many farmers have abandoned their rural birthplace, and seek out either the more populous centers or the cities themselves. Now since this is the case in almost all countries, and since it affects large numbers of human beings, problems concerning life and dignity of citizens arise, which are indeed difficult to overcome.

124. Thus, as economic life progresses and expands, the percentage of rural dwellers diminishes, while the great number of industrial and service workers increases. Yet, we feel that those who transfer from rural activities to other productive enterprises often are motivated by reasons arising from the very evolution of economic affairs. Very often, however, they are caught up by various enticements of which the following are noteworthy: a desire to escape from a confined environment offering no prospect of a more comfortable life; the wish, so common in our age, to undertake new activities and to acquire new experiences; the attraction of quickly acquired ~~ds and fortunes; a longing after a freer life, with the advan- ~~ larger towns and cities usually provide. But there is

no doubt about this point: rural dwellers leave the fields because nearly everywhere they see their affairs in a state of
depression, both as regards labor productivity and the level of
living of farm populations.

125. Accordingly, in this grave matter, about which enquir-
ies are made in nearly all countries, we should first of all ask
what is to be done to prevent so great imbalances between
agriculture, industry, and the services in the matter of productive efficiency? Likewise, what can be done to minimize differences between the rural standard of living and that of city
dwellers whose money income is derived from industry or some
service or other? Finally, how can it be brought about that
those engaged in agricultural pursuits no longer regard themselves as inferior to others? Indeed, rural dwellers should be
convinced not only that they can strengthen and develop their
personalities by their toil, but also that they can look forward
to the future vicissitudes with confidence.

126. Accordingly, we judge it opportune in this connection
to lay down some norms of permanent validity; although, as is
evident, these must be adapted as various circumstances of
time and place permit, or suggest, or absolutely require.

Provision for Essential Public Services

127. First, it is necessary that everyone, and especially
public authorities, strive to effect improvements in rural areas
as regards the principal services needed by all. Such are, for
example: highway construction; transport services; marketing
facilities; pure drinking water; housing; medical services; elementary, trade, and professional schools; things requisite for
religion and for recreation; finally, furnishings and equipment
needed in the modern farm home. Where these requirements
for a dignified farm life are lacking to rural dwellers, economic
and social progress does not occur at all, or else very slowly.
Under such conditions, nothing can be done to keep men from
deserting the fields, nor can anyone readily estimate their
number.

Gradual and Orderly Development of the Economic System

128. It is desirable, moreover, that economic development
of commonwealths proceed in orderly fashion, meanwhile preserving appropriate balance between the various sectors of the
economy. In particular, care must be had that within the agricultural sector innovations are introduced as regards productive
technology, whether these relate to productive methods, or to

cultivation of the fields, or to equipment for the rural enterprise, as far as the over-all economy allows or requires. And all this should be done as far as possible, in accordance with technical advances in industry and in the various services.

129. In this way, agriculture not only absorbs a larger share of industrial output, but also demands a higher quality of services. In its turn, agriculture offers to the industrial and service sectors of the economy, as well as to the community as a whole, those products which in kind and in quantity better meet consumer needs. Thus, agriculture contributes to stability of the purchasing power of money, a very positive factor for the orderly development of the entire economic system.

130. By proceeding in this manner, the following advantages, among others, arise: first of all, it is easier to know the origins and destinations of rural dwellers displaced by modernization of agriculture. Thereupon, they can be instructed in skills needed for other types of work. Finally, economic aids and helps will not be lacking for their intellectual and cultural development, so that they can fit into new social groups.

APPROPRIATE ECONOMIC POLICY

131. To achieve orderly progress in various sectors of economic life, it is absolutely necessary that as regards agriculture, public authorities give heed and take action in the following matters: taxes and duties, credit, insurance, prices, the fostering of requisite skills, and, finally, improved equipment for rural enterprises.

TAXATION

132. As regards taxation, assessment according to ability to pay is fundamental to a just and equitable system.

133. But in determining taxes for rural dwellers, the general welfare requires public authorities to bear in mind that income in a rural economy is both delayed and subject to greater risk. Moreover, there is difficulty in finding capital so as to increase returns.

CAPITAL AT SUITABLE INTEREST

134. Accordingly, those with money to invest are more inclined to invest it in enterprises other than in the rural economy. And for the same reason, rural dwellers cannot pay high rates of interest. Nor are they generally able to pay prevailing market rates for capital wherewith to carry on and expand their

operations. Wherefore, the general welfare requires that public authorities not merely make special provision for agricultural financing, but also for establishment of banks that provide capital to farmers at reasonable rates of interest.

Social Insurance and Social Security

135. It also seems necessary to make provision for a twofold insurance, one covering agricultural output, the other covering farmers and their families. Because, as experience shows, the income of individual farmers is, on the average, less than that of workers in industry and the services, it does not seem to be fully in accord with the norms of social justice and equity to provide farmers with insurance or social security benefits that are inferior to those of other classes of citizens. For those insurance plans or provisions that are established generally should not differ markedly one from the other, whatever be the economic sector wherein the citizens work, or from which they derive their income.

136. Moreover, since social security and insurance can help appreciably in distributing national income among the citizens according to justice and equity, these systems can be regarded as means whereby imbalances among various classes of citizens are reduced.

Price Protection

137. Since agricultural products have special characteristics, it is fitting that their price be protected by methods worked out by economic experts. In this matter, although it is quite helpful that those whose interests are involved take steps to safeguard themselves, setting up, as it were, appropriate goals, public authorities cannot stand entirely aloof from the stabilization procedure.

138. Nor should this be overlooked, that, generally speaking, the price of rural products is more a recompense for farmers' labor than for capital investment.

139. Thus, our predecessor of happy memory, Pius XI, touching on the welfare of the human community, appropriately notes in his Encyclical Letter *Quadragesimo Anno,* that "a reasonable relationship between different wages here enters into consideration." But he immediately adds, "Intimately connected with this is a reasonable relationship between the prices obtained for the products of the various economic groups: agrarian, industrial, and so forth." [29]

---

[29] Cf. *Acta Apostolicae Sedis,* XXIII (1931), p. 202.

140. Inasmuch as agricultural products are destined especially to satisfy the basic needs of men, it is necessary that their price be such that all can afford to buy them. Nevertheless, there is manifest injustice in placing a whole group of citizens, namely, the farmers, in an inferior economic and social status, with less purchasing power than required for a decent livelihood. This, indeed, is clearly contrary to the common good of the country.

STRENGTHENING FARM INCOME

141. In rural areas it is fitting that industries be fostered and common services be developed that are useful in preserving, processing, and finally, in transporting farm products. There is need, moreover, to establish councils and activities relating to various sectors of economic and professional affairs. By such means, suitable opportunity is given farm families to supplement their incomes, and that within the milieu wherein they live and work.

APPROPRIATE ORGANIZATION OF FARMING ENTERPRISES

142. Finally, no one person can lay down a universal rule regarding the way in which rural affairs should be definitely organized, since in these matters there exists considerable variation within each country, and the difference is even greater when we consider the various regions of the world. However, those who hold man and the family in proper esteem, whether this be based upon nature alone, or also upon Christian principles, surely look toward some form of agricultural enterprise, and particularly of the family type, which is modeled upon the community of men wherein mutual relationships of members and the organization of the enterprise itself are conformed to norms of justice and Christian teaching. And these men strive mightily that such organization of rural life be realized as far as circumstances permit.

143. The family farm will be firm and stable only when it yields money income sufficient for decent and humane family living. To bring this about, it is very necessary that farmers generally receive instruction, be kept informed of new developments, and be technically assisted by trained men. It is also necessary that farmers form among themselves mutual-aid societies; that they establish professional associations; that they function efficiently in public life, that is, in various administrative bodies and in political affairs.

RURAL WORKERS: PARTICIPANTS IN
  IMPROVING CONDITIONS

144. We are of the opinion that in rural affairs, the principal agents and protagonists of economic improvement, of cultural betterment, or of social advance, should be the men personally involved, namely, the farmers themselves. To them it
should be quite evident that their work is most noble, because
it is undertaken, as it were, in the majestic temple of creation;
because it often concerns the life of plants and animals, a life
inexhaustible in its expression, inflexible in its laws, rich in allu-
sions to God, Creator and Provider. Moreover, labor in the
fields not only produces various foodstuffs wherewith human-
kind is nourished, but also furnishes an increasing supply of raw
materials for industry.

145. Furthermore, this is a work endowed with a dignity of
its own, for it bears a manifold relationship to the mechanical
arts, chemistry, and biology: these must be continually adapted
to the requirements of emerging situations because scientific
and technological advance is of great importance in rural life.
Work of this kind, moreover, possesses a special nobility because it requires farmers to understand well the course of the
seasons and to adapt themselves to the same; that they await
patiently what the future will bring; that they appreciate the
importance and seriousness of their duties; that they constantly
remain alert and ready for new developments.

Solidarity and Cooperation

146. Nor may it be overlooked that in rural areas, as indeed
in every productive sector, farmers should join together in fellowships, especially when the family itself works the farm.
Indeed, it is proper for rural workers to have a sense of solidarity. They should strive jointly to set up mutual-aid societies and
professional associations. All these are very necessary either to
keep rural dwellers abreast of scientific and technical progress,
or to protect the prices of goods produced by their labor. Besides, acting in this manner, farmers are put on the same footing as other classes of workers who, for the most part, join
together in such fellowships. Finally, by acting thus, farmers
will achieve an importance and influence in public affairs proportionate to their own role. For today it is unquestionably
true that the solitary voice speaks, as they say, to the winds.

Recognizing Demands of the Common Good

147. But when rural dwellers, just as other classes of workers, wish to make their influence and importance felt, they should never disregard moral duties or civil law. Rather they should strive to bring their rights and interests into line with the rights and needs of other classes, and to refer the same to the common good. In this connection, farmers who strive vigorously to improve the yield of their farm may rightly demand that their efforts be aided and complemented by public authorities, provided they themselves keep in mind the common needs of all and also relate their own efforts to the fulfillment of these needs.

148. Wherefore, we wish to honor appropriately those sons of ours who everywhere in the world, either by founding and fostering mutual-aid societies or some other type of association, watchfully strive that in all civic affairs farmers enjoy not merely economic prosperity but also a status in keeping with justice.

Vocation and Mission

149. Since everything that makes for man's dignity, perfection, and development seems to be invoked in agricultural labor, it is proper that man regard such work as an assignment from God with a sublime purpose. It is fitting, therefore, that man dedicate work of this kind to the most provident God who directs all events for the salvation of men. Finally, the farmer should take upon himself, in some measure, the task of educating himself and others for the advancement of civilization.

AID TO LESS DEVELOPED AREAS

150. It often happens that in one and the same country citizens enjoy different degrees of wealth and social advancement. This especially happens because they dwell in areas which, economically speaking, have grown at different rates. Where such is the case, justice and equity demand that the government make efforts either to remove or to minimize imbalances of this sort. Toward this end, efforts should be made, in areas where there has been less economic progress, to supply the principal public services, as indicated by circumstances of time and place and in accord with the general level of living. But in bringing this about, it is necessary to have very competent administration and organization to take careful account of the

following: labor supply, internal migration, wages, taxes, interest rates, and investments in industries that foster other skills and developments—all of which will further not merely the useful employment of workers and the stimulation of initiative, but also the exploitation of resources locally available.

151. But it is precisely the measures for advancement of the general welfare which civil authorities must undertake. Hence, they should take steps, having regard for the needs of the whole community, that progress in agriculture, industry, and services be made at the same time and in a balanced manner so far as possible. They should have this goal in mind, that citizens in less developed countries—in giving attention to economic and social affairs, as well as to cultural matters—feel themselves to be the ones chiefly responsible for their own progress. For a citizen has a sense of his own dignity when he contributes the major share to progress in his own affairs.

152. Hence, those also who rely on their own resources and initiative should contribute as best they can to the equitable adjustment of economic life in their own community. Nay, more, those in authority should favor and help private enterprise in accordance with the *principle of subsidiarity*, in order to allow private citizens themselves to accomplish as much as is feasible.

IMBALANCES BETWEEN LAND AND POPULATION

153. It is appropriate to recall at this point that in a number of nations there exists a discrepancy between available agricultural land and the number of rural dwellers. Some nations experience a shortage of citizens, but have rich land resources; others have many citizens but an insufficiency of agricultural land.

154. Nor are there lacking nations wherein, despite their great resource potential, farmers use such primitive and obsolete methods of cultivation that they are unable to produce what is needed for the entire population. On the other hand, in certain countries, agriculture has so adapted itself to recent advances that farmers produce surpluses which to some extent harm the economy of the entire nation.

155. It is evident that both the solidarity of the human race and the sense of brotherhood which accords with Christian principles, require that some peoples lend others energetic help in many ways. Not merely would this result in a freer movement of goods, of capital, and of men, but it also would lessen imbalances between nations. We shall treat of this point in more detail below.

156. Here, however, we cannot fail to express our approval of the efforts of the Institute knowns as F.A.O. which concerns itself with the feeding of peoples and the improvement of agriculture. This Institute has the special goal of promoting mutual accord among peoples, of bringing it about that rural life is modernized in less developed nations, and finally, that help is brought to people experiencing food shortages.

REQUIREMENTS OF JUSTICE AS BETWEEN NATIONS DIFFERING IN ECONOMIC DEVELOPMENT

PROBLEM OF THE MODERN WORLD

157. Perhaps the most pressing question of our day concerns the relationship between economically advanced commonwealths and those that are in process of development. The former enjoy the conveniences of life; the latter experience dire poverty. Yet, today men are so intimately associated in all parts of the world that they feel, as it were, as if they are members of one and the same household. Therefore, the nations that enjoy a sufficiency and abundance of everything may not overlook the plight of other nations whose citizens experience such domestic problems that they are all but overcome by poverty and hunger, and are not able to enjoy basic human rights. This is all the more so, inasmuch as countries each day seem to become more dependent on each other. Consequently, it is not easy for them to keep the peace advantageously if excessive imbalances exist in their economic and social conditions.

158. Mindful of our role of universal father, we think it opportune to stress here what we have stated in another connection: "We all share responsibility for the fact that populations are undernourished.[80] [Therefore], it is necessary to arouse a sense of responsibility in individuals and generally, especially among those more blessed with this world's goods." [81]

159. As can be readily deduced, and as the Church has always seriously warned, it is proper that the duty of helping the poor and unfortunate should especially stir Catholics, since they are members of the Mystical Body of Christ. "In this we have come to know the love of God," said John the Apostle, "that He laid down His life for us; and we likewise ought to lay down our life for the brethren. He who has the goods of this world and sees his brother in need and closes his heart to him, how does the love of God abide in him?" [82]

[80] *Allocution.* May 3, 1960; cf. *A.A.S.*, LII (1960), p. 465.
[81] Cf. *Ibid.*
[82] 1 John 3, 16-17.

160. Wherefore, we not with pleasure that countries with advanced productive systems are lending aid to less privileged countries, so that these latter may the more readily improve their condition.

EMERGENCY ASSISTANCE

161. It is clear to everyone that some nations have surpluses in foodstuffs, particularly of farm products, while elsewhere large masses of people experience want and hunger. Now justice and humanity require that these richer countries come to the aid of those in need. Accordingly, to destroy entirely or to waste goods necessary for the lives of men, runs counter to our obligations in justice and humanity.

162. We are quite well aware that to produce surpluses, especially of farm products, in excess of the needs of a country, can occasion harm to various classes of citizens. Nevertheless, it does not therefore follow that nations with surpluses have no obligation to aid the poor and hungry where some particular emergency arises. Rather, diligent efforts should be made that inconveniences arising from surplus goods be minimized and borne by every citizen on a fair basis.

SCIENTIFIC, TECHNICAL, AND FINANCIAL COOPERATION

163. However, the underlying causes of poverty and hunger will not be removed in a number of countries by these means alone. For the most part, the causes are to be found in the primitive state of the economy. To effect a remedy, all available avenues should be explored with a view, on the one hand, to instruct citizens fully in necessary skills and in carrying out their responsibilities, and, on the other hand, to enable them to acquire the capital wherewith to promote economic growth by ways and means adapted to our times.

164. It has not escaped our attention that in recent years there has grown in many minds a deep awareness of their duty to aid poorer countries still lacking suitable economic development, in order that these may more readily make economic and social progress.

165. Toward this end, we look to councils, either of a number of nations, or within individual nations; we look to private enterprises and societies to exert daily more generous efforts on behalf of such countries, transmitting to them requisite productive skills. For the same reason help is given to as many youths as possible that they may study in the great universities of more developed countries, thus acquiring a knowledge of the arts and sciences in line with the standards of

our time. Moreover, international banks, single nations, or private citizens often make loans to these countries that they may initiate various programs calculated to increase production. We gladly take this opportunity to give due praise to such generous activity. It is hoped that in the future the richer countries will make greater and greater efforts to provide developing countries with aid designed to promote sciences, technology, and economic life.

AVOIDANCE OF PAST ERRORS

166. In this matter we consider it our duty to offer some warnings.

167. First of all, it seems only prudent for nations which thus far have made little or no progress, to weigh well the principal factor in the advance of nations that enjoy abundance.

168. Prudent foresight and common need demand that not only more goods be produced, but that this be done more efficiently. Likewise, necessity and justice require that wealth produced be distributed equitably among all citizens of the commonwealth. Accordingly, efforts should be made to ensure that improved social conditions accompany economic advancement. And it is very important that such advances occur simultaneously in the agricultural, industrial, and various service sectors.

RESPECT FOR INDIVIDUAL CHARACTERISTICS OF COUNTRIES

169. It is indeed clear to all that countries in process of development often have their own individual characteristics, and that these arise from the nature of the locale, or from cultural tradition, or from some special trait of the citizens.

170. Now when economically developed countries assist the poorer ones, they not only should have regard for these characteristics and respect them, but also should take special care lest, in aiding these nations, they seek to impose their own way of life upon them.

DISINTERESTED AID

171. Moreover, economically developed countries should take particular care lest, in giving aid to poorer countries, they endeavor to turn the prevailing political situation to their own advantage, and seek to dominate them.

172. Should perchance such attempts be made, this clearly would be but another form of colonialism, which, although

disguised in name, merely reflects their earlier but outdated dominion, now abandoned by many countries. When international relations are thus obstructed, the orderly progress of all peoples is endangered.

173. Genuine necessity, as well as justice, require that whenever countries give attention to the fostering of skills or commerce, they should aid the less developed nations without thought of domination, so that these latter eventually will be in a position to progress economically and socially on their own initiative.

174. If this be done, it will help much toward shaping a community of all nations, wherein each one, aware of its rights and duties, will have regard for the prosperity of all.

RESPECT FOR A HIERARCHY OF VALUES

175. There is no doubt that when a nation makes progress in science, technology, economic life, and the prosperity of its citizens, a great contribution is made to civilization. But all should realize that these things are not the highest goods, but only instruments for pursuing such goods.

176. Accordingly, we note with sorrow that in some nations economic life indeed progresses, but that not a few men are there to be found, who have no concern at all for the just ordering of goods. No doubt, these men either completely ignore spiritual values, or put these out of their mind, or else deny they exist. Nevertheless, while they pursue progress in science, technology, and economic life, they make so much of external benefits that for the most part they regard these as the highest goods of life. Accordingly, there are not lacking grave dangers in the help provided by more affluent nations for development of the poorer ones. For among the citizens of these latter nations, there is operative a general awareness of the higher values on which moral teaching rests—an awareness derived from ancient traditional custom which provides them with motivation.

177. Thus, those who seek to undermine in some measure the right instincts of these peoples, assuredly do something immoral. Rather, those attitudes, besides being held in honor, should be perfected and refined, since upon them true civilization depends.

CONTRIBUTION OF THE CHURCH

178. Moreover, the Church by divine right pertains to all nations. This is confirmed by the fact that she already is everywhere on earth and strives to embrace all peoples.

179. Now, those peoples whom the Church has joined to Christ have always reaped some benefits, whether in economic affairs or in social organization, as history and contemporary events clearly record. For everyone who professes Christianity promises and gives assurance that he will contribute as far as he can to the advancement of civil institutions. He must also strive with all his might not only that human dignity suffer no dishonor, but also, by the removal of every kind of obstacle, that all those forces be promoted which are conducive to moral living and contribute to it.

180. Moreover, when the Church infuses her energy into the life of a people, she neither is, nor feels herself to be, an alien institution imposed upon that people from without. This follows from the fact that wherever the Church is present, there individual men are reborn or resurrected in Christ. Those who are thus reborn or who have risen again in Christ feel themselves oppressed by no external force. Rather, realizing they have achieved perfect liberty, they freely move toward God. Hence, whatever is seen by them as good and morally right, that they approve and put into effect.

181. "The Church of Jesus Christ," as our predecessor Pius XII clearly stated, "is the faithful guardian of God's gracious wisdom. Hence, she makes no effort to discourage or belittle those characteristics and traits which are proper to particular nations, and which peoples religiously and tenaciously guard, quite justly, as a sacred heritage. She aims indeed at a unity which is profound and in conformity with that heavenly love whereby all are moved in their innermost being. She does not seek a uniformity which is merely external in its effects and calculated to weaken the fibre of the peoples concerned. And all careful rules that contribute to the wise development and growth within bounds of these capacities and forces, which indeed have their deeply rooted ethnic traits, have the Church's approval and maternal prayers, provided they are not in opposition to those duties which spring from the common origin and destiny of all mortal men." [38]

182. We note with deep satisfaction that Catholic men, citizens of the less developed nations, are for the most part second to no other citizens in furthering efforts of their countries to make progress economically and socially according to their capacity.

183. Furthermore, we note that Catholic citizens of the richer nations are making extensive efforts to ensure that aid given by their own countries to needy countries is directed

increasingly toward economic and social progress. In this connection, it seems specially praiseworthy that appreciable aid in various forms is provided increasingly each year to young people from Africa and Asia, so that they may pursue literary and professional studies in the great universities of Europe and America. The same applies to the great care that has been taken in training for every responsibility of their office men prepared to go to less developed areas, there to carry out their profession and duties.

184. To those sons of ours who, by promoting solicitously the progress of peoples and by spreading, as it were, a wholesome civilizing influence, everywhere demonstrate the perennial vitality of Holy Church and her effectiveness, we wish to express our paternal praise and gratitude.

POPULATION INCREASE AND ECONOMIC DEVELOPMENT

185. More recently, the question often is raised how economic organization and the means of subsistence can be balanced with population increase, whether in the world as a whole or within the needy nations.

IMBALANCE BETWEEN POPULATION AND MEANS OF SUBSISTENCE

186. As regards the world as a whole, some, consequent to statistical reasoning, observe that within a matter of decades mankind will become very numerous, whereas economic growth will proceed much more slowly. From this some conclude that unless procreation is kept within limits, there subsequently will develop an even greater imbalance between the number of inhabitants and the necessities of life.

187. It is clearly evident from statistical records of less developed countries that, because recent advances in public health and in medicine are there widely diffused, the citizens have a longer life expectancy consequent to lowered rates of infant mortality. The birth rate, where it has traditionally been high, tends to remain at such levels, at least for the immediate future. Thus the birth rate in a given year exceeds the death rate. Meanwhile the productive systems in such countries do not expand as rapidly as the number of inhabitants. Hence, in poorer countries of this sort, the standard of living does not advance and may even deteriorate. Wherefore, lest a serious crisis occur, some are of the opinion that the conception or birth of humans should be avoided or curbed by every possible means.

THE TERMS OF THE PROBLEM

188. Now to tell the truth, the interrelationships on a global scale between the number of births and available resources are such that we can infer grave difficulties in this matter do not arise at present, nor will in the immediate future. The arguments advanced in this connection are so inconclusive and controversial that nothing certain can be drawn from them.

189. Besides, God in His goodness and wisdom has, on the one hand, provided nature with almost inexhaustible productive capacity; and, on the other hand, has endowed man with such ingenuity that, by using suitable means, he can apply nature's resources to the needs and requirements of existence. Accordingly, that the question posed may be clearly resolved, a course of action is not indeed to be followed whereby, contrary to the moral law laid down by God, procreative function also is violated. Rather, man should, by the use of his skills and science of every kind, acquire an intimate knowledge of the forces of nature and control them ever more extensively. Moreover, the advances hitherto made in science and technology give almost limitless promise for the future in this matter.

190. When it comes to questions of this kind, we are not unaware that in certain locales and also in poorer countries, it is often argued that in such an economic and social order, difficulties arise because citizens, each year more numerous, are unable to acquire sufficient food or sustenance where they live, and peoples do not show amicable cooperation to the extent they should.

191. But whatever be the situation, we clearly affirm these problems should be posed and resolved in such a way that man does not have recourse to methods and means contrary to his dignity, which are proposed by those persons who think of man and his life solely in material terms.

192. We judge that this question can be resolved only if economic and social advances preserve and augment the genuine welfare of individual citizens and of human society as a whole. Indeed, in a matter of this kind, first place must be accorded everything that pertains to the dignity of man as such, or to the life of individual men, than which nothing can be more precious. Moreover, in this matter, international cooperation is necessary, so that conformably with the welfare of all, information, capital, and men themselves may move about among the peoples in orderly fashion.

RESPECT FOR THE LAWS OF LIFE

193. In this connection, we strongly affirm that human life is transmitted and propagated through the instrumentality of the family which rests on marriage, one and indissoluble, and, so far as Christians are concerned, elevated to the dignity of a sacrament. Because the life of man is passed on to other men deliberately and knowingly, it therefore follows that this should be done in accord with the most sacred, permanent, inviolate prescriptions of God. Everyone without exception is bound to recognize and observe these laws. Wherefore, in this matter, no one is permitted to use methods and procedures which may indeed be permissible to check the life of plants and animals.

194. Indeed, all must regard the life of man as sacred, since from its inception, it requires the action of God the Creator. Those who depart from this plan of God not only offend His divine majesty and dishonor themselves and the human race, but they also weaken the inner fibre of the commonwealth.

EDUCATION TOWARD A SENSE OF RESPONSIBILITY

195. In these matters it is of great importance that new off-spring, in addition to being very carefully educated in human culture and in religion—which indeed is the right and duty of parents—should also show themselves very conscious of their duties in every action of life. This is especially true when it is a question of establishing a family and of procreating and educating children. Such children should be imbued not only with a firm confidence in the providence of God, but also with a strong and ready will to bear the labors and inconveniences which cannot be lawfully avoided by anyone who undertakes the worthy and serious obligation of associating his own activity with God in transmitting life and in educating off-spring. In this most important matter certainly nothing is more relevant than the teachings and supernatural aids provided by the Church. We refer to the Church whose right of freely carrying out her function must be recognized also in this connection.

CREATION FOR MAN'S BENEFIT

196. When God, as we read in the book of Genesis, imparted human nature to our first parents, He assigned them two tasks, one of which complements the other. For He first

directed: "Be fruitful and multiply," [34] and then immediately added: "Fill the earth and subdue it." [35]

197. The second of these tasks, far from anticipating a destruction of goods, rather assigns them to the service of human life.

198. Accordingly, with great sadness we note two conflicting trends: on the one hand, the scarcity of goods is vaguely described as such that the life of men reportedly is in danger of perishing from misery and hunger; on the other hand, the recent discoveries of science, technical advances, and economic productivity are transformed into means whereby the human race is led toward ruin and a horrible death.

199. Now the provident God has bestowed upon humanity sufficient goods wherewith to bear with dignity the burdens associated with procreation of children. But this task will be difficult or even impossible if men, straying from the right road and with a perverse outlook, use the means mentioned above in a manner contrary to human reason or to their social nature, and hence, contrary to the directives of God Himself.

INTERNATIONAL COOPERATION

WORLD DIMENSIONS OF IMPORTANT HUMAN PROBLEMS

200. Since the relationships between countries today are closer in every region of the world, by reason of science and technology, it is proper that peoples become more and more interdependent.

201. Accordingly, contemporary problems of moment— whether in the fields of science and technology, or of economic and social affairs, or of public administration, or of cultural advancement—these, because they may exceed the capacities of individual States, very often affect a number of nations and at times all the nations of the earth.

202. As a result, individual countries, although advanced in culture and civilization, in number and industry of citizens, in wealth, in geographical extent, are not able by themselves to resolve satisfactorily their basic problems. Accordingly, because States must on occasion complement or perfect one another, they really consult their own interests only when they take into account at the same time the interests of others. Hence, dire necessity warns commonwealths to cooperate among themselves and provide mutual assistance.

[34] Gen., 1, 28.
[35] Ibid.

MUTUAL DISTRUST

203. Although this becomes more and more evident each day to individuals and even to all peoples, men, and especially those with high responsibility in public life, for the most part seem unable to accomplish the two things toward which people aspire. This does not happen because peoples lack scientific, technical, or economic means, but rather because they distrust one another. Indeed, men, and hence States, stand in fear of one another. One country fears lest another is contemplating aggression and lest the other seize an opportunity to put such plans into effect. Accordingly, countries customarily prepare defenses for their cities and homeland, namely, armaments designed to deter other countries from aggression.

204. Consequently, the energies of man and the resources of nature are very widely directed by peoples to destruction rather than to the advantage of the human family, and both individual men and entire peoples become so deeply solicitous that they are prevented from undertaking more important works.

FAILURE TO ACKNOWLEDGE THE MORAL ORDER

205. The cause of this state of affairs seems to be that men, more especially leaders of States, have differing philosophies of life. Some even dare to assert that there exists no law of truth and right which transcends external affairs and man himself, which of necessity pertains to everyone, and, finally, which is equitable for all men. Hence, man can agree fully and surely about nothing, since one and the same law of justice is not accepted by all.

206. Although the word *justice* and the related term *demands of justice* are on everyone's lips, such verbalizations do not have the same meaning for all. Indeed, the opposite frequently is the case. Hence, when leaders invoke *justice* or the *demands of justice*, not only do they disagree as to the meaning of the words, but frequently find in them an occasion of serious contention. And so they conclude that there is no way of achieving their rights or advantages, unless they resort to force, the root of very serious evils.

GOD, THE FOUNDATION OF THE MORAL ORDER

207. That mutual faith may develop among rulers and nations and may abide more deeply in their minds, the laws

of truth and justice first must be acknowledged and preserved on all sides.

208. However, the guiding principles of morality and virtue can be based only on God; apart from Him, they necessarily collapse. For man is composed not merely of body, but of soul as well, and is endowed with reason and freedom. Now such a composite being absolutely requires a moral law rooted in religion, which, far better than any external force or advantage, can contribute to the resolution of problems affecting the lives of individual citizens or groups of citizens, or with a bearing upon single States or all States together.

209. Yet, there are today those who assert that, in view of the flourishing state of science and technology, men can achieve the highest civilization even apart from God and by their own unaided powers. Nevertheless, it is because of this very progress in science and technology that men often find themselves involved in difficulties which affect all peoples, and which can be overcome only if they duly recognize the authority of God, author and ruler of man and of all nature.

210. That this is true, the advances of science seem to indicate, opening up, as they do, almost limitless horizons. Thus, an opinion is implanted in many minds that inasmuch as mathematical sciences are unable to discern the innermost nature of things and their changes, or express them in suitable terms, they can scarcely draw inferences about them. And when terrified men see with their own eyes that the vast forces deriving from technology and machines can be used for destruction as well as for the advantage of peoples, they rightly conclude that things pertaining to the spirit and to moral life are to be preferred to all else, so that progress in science and technology does not result in destruction of the human race, but prove useful as instruments of civilization.

211. Meanwhile it comes to pass that in more affluent countries men, less and less satisfied with external goods, put out of their mind the deceptive image of a happy life to be lived here forever. Likewise, not only do men grow daily more conscious that they are fully endowed with all the rights of the human person, but they also strive mightily that relations among themselves become more equitable and more conformed to human dignity. Consequently men are beginning to recognize that their own capacities are limited, and they seek spiritual things more intensively than heretofore. All of which seems to give some promise that not only individuals, but even peoples may come to an understanding for extensive and extremely useful collaboration.

Part IV

Reconstruction of Social Relationships in Truth, Justice and Love

INCOMPLETE AND ERRONEOUS PHILOSOPHIES OF LIFE

212. As in the past, so too in our day, advances in science and technology have greatly multiplied relationships between citizens; it seems necessary, therefore, that the relationships themselves, whether within a single country or between all countries, be brought into more humane balance.

213. In this connection many systems of thought have been developed and committed to writing: some of these already have been dissipated as mist by the sun; others remain basically unchanged today; still others now elicit less and less response from men. The reason for this is that these popularized fancies neither encompass man, whole and entire, nor do they affect his inner being. Moreover, they fail to take into account the weaknesses of human nature, such as sickness and suffering: weaknesses that no economic or social system, no matter how advanced, can completely eliminate. Besides, men everywhere are moved by a profound and unconquerable sense of religion, which no force can ever destroy nor shrewdness suppress.

214. In our day, a very false opinion is popularized which holds that the sense of religion implanted in men by nature is to be regarded as something adventitious or imaginary, and hence, is to be rooted completely from the mind as altogether inconsistent with the spirit of our age and the progress of civilization. Yet, this inward proclivity of man to religion confirms the fact that man himself was created by God, and irrevocably tends to Him. Thus we read in Augustine: "Thou hast made us for Thyself, O Lord, and our hearts are restless until they rest in Thee." [36]

215. Wherefore, whatever the progress in technology and economic life, there can be neither justice nor peace in the world, so long as men fail to realize how great is their dignity; for they have been created by God and are His children. We speak of God, who must be regarded as the first and final cause

[36] *Confessions*, I, 1.

of all things He has created. Separated from God, man becomes monstrous to himself and others. Consequently, mutual relationships between men absolutely require a right ordering of the human conscience in relation to God, the source of all truth, justice, and love.

216. It is well known and recognized by everyone that in a number of countries, some of ancient Christian culture, many of our very dear brothers and sons have been savagely persecuted for a number of years. Now this situation, since it reveals the great dignity of the persecuted, and the refined cruelty of their persecutors, leads many to reflect on the matter, though it has not yet healed the wounds of the persecuted.

217. However, no folly seems more characteristic of our time than the desire to establish a firm and meaningful temporal order, but without God, its necessary foundation. Likewise, some wish to proclaim the greatness of man, but with the source dried up from which such greatness flows and receives nourishment: that is, by impeding and, if it were possible, stopping the yearning of souls for God. But the turn of events in our times, whereby the hopes of many are shattered and not a few have come to grief, unquestionably confirm the words of Scripture: "Unless the Lord build the house, they labor in vain who built it." [87]

THE CHURCH'S TRADITIONAL TEACHING
REGARDING MAN'S SOCIAL LIFE

218. What the Catholic Church teaches and declares regarding the social life and relationships of men is beyond question for all time valid.

219. The cardinal point of this teaching is that individual men are necessarily the foundation, cause, and end of all social institutions. We are referring to human beings, insofar as they are social by nature, and raised to an order of existence that transcends and subdues nature.

220. Beginning with this very basic principle whereby the dignity of the human person is affirmed and defended, Holy Church—especially during the last century and with the assistance of learned priests and laymen, specialists in the field—has arrived at clear social teachings whereby the mutual relationships of men are ordered. Taking general norms into account, these principles are in accord with the nature of things and the changed conditions of man's social life, or with the special genius of our day. Moreover, these norms can be approved by all.

87 Ps. 126, 1.

221. But today, more than ever, principles of this kind must not only be known and understood, but also applied to those systems and methods, which the various situations of time or place either suggest or require. This is indeed a difficult, though lofty, task. Toward its fulfillment we exhort not only our brothers and sons everywhere, but all men of good will.

STUDY OF SOCIAL MATTERS

222. Above all, we affirm that the social teaching proclaimed by the Catholic Church cannot be separated from her traditional teaching regarding man's life.

223. Wherefore, it is our earnest wish that more and more attention be given to this branch of learning. First of all, we urge that attention be given to such studies in Catholic schools on all levels, and especially in seminaries, although we are not unaware that in some of these latter institutions this is already being done admirably. Moreover, we desire that social study of this sort be included among the religious materials used to instruct and inspire the lay apostolate, either in parishes or in associations. Let this diffusion of knowledge be accomplished by every modern means: that is, in journals, whether daily or periodical; in doctrinal books, both for the learned and the general reader; and finally, by means of radio and television.

224. We judge that our sons among the laity have much to contribute through their work and effort, that this teaching of the Catholic Church regarding the social question be more and more widely diffused. This they can do, not merely by learning it themselves and governing their actions accordingly, but also by taking special care that others also come to know its relevance.

225. Let them be fully persuaded that in no better way can they know this teaching to be correct and effective, than by demonstrating that present day social difficulties will yield to its application. In this way they will win minds today antagonistic to the teaching because they do not know it. Perhaps it will also happen that such men will find some enlightenment in the teaching.

APPLICATION OF SOCIAL TEACHING

226. But social norms of whatever kind are not only to be explained but also applied. This is especially true of the Church's teaching on social matters, which has truth as its guide, justice as its end, and love as its driving force.

227. We consider it, therefore, of the greatest importance that our sons, in addition to knowing these social norms, be reared according to them.

228. To be complete, the education of Christians must relate to the duties of every class. It is therefore necessary that Christians thus inspired conform their behavior in economic and social affairs to the teaching of the Church.

229. If it is indeed difficult to apply teaching of any sort to concrete situations, it is even more so when one tries to put into practice the teaching of the Catholic Church regarding social affairs. This is especially true for the following reasons: there is deeply rooted in each man an instinctive and immoderate love of his own interests; today there is widely diffused in society a materialistic philosophy of life; it is difficult at times to discern the demands of justice in a given situation.

230. Consequently, it is not enough for men to be instructed, according to the teachings of the Church, on their obligation to act in a Christian manner in economic and social affairs. They must also be shown ways in which they can properly fulfill their duty in this regard.

231. We do not regard such instructions as sufficient, unless there be added to the work of instruction that of the formation of man, and unless some action follow upon the teaching, by way of experience.

232. Just as, proverbially, no one really enjoys liberty unless he uses it, so no one really knows how to act according to Catholic teaching in the economic and social fields, unless he acts according to this teaching in the same area.

A TASK FOR LAY APOSTOLATE

233. Accordingly, in popular instruction of this kind, it seems proper that considerable attention be paid to groups promoting the lay apostolate, especially those whose aim is to ensure that efforts in our present concern draw their inspiration wholly from Christian law. Seeing that members of such groups can first train themselves by daily practice in these matters, they subsequently will be able the better to instruct young people in fulfilling obligations of this kind.

234. It is not inappropriate in this connection to remind all, the great no less than the lowly, that the will to preserve moderation and to bear difficulties, by God's grace, can in no wise be separated from the meaning of life handed down to us by Christian wisdom.

235. But today, unfortunately, very many souls are preoccupied with an inordinate desire for pleasure. Such persons

see nothing more important in the whole of life than to seek pleasure, to quench the thirst for pleasure. Beyond doubt, grave ills to both soul and body proceed therefrom. Now in this matter, it must be admitted that one who judges even with the aid of human nature alone, concludes that it is the part of the wise and prudent man to preserve balance and moderation in everything, and to restrain the lower appetites. He who judges matters in the light of divine revelation, assuredly will not overlook the fact that the Gospel of Christ and the Catholic Church, as well as the ascetical tradition handed down to us, all demand that Christians steadfastly mortify themselves and bear the inconveniences of life with singular patience. These virtues, in addition to fostering a firm and moderate rule of mind over body, also present an opportunity of satisfying the punishment due to sin, from which, except for Jesus Christ and His Immaculate Mother, no one is exempt.

PRACTICAL SUGGESTIONS

236. The teachings in regard to social matters for the most part are put into effect in the following three stages: first, the actual situation is examined; then, the situation is evaluated carefully in relation to these teachings; then only is it decided what can and should be done in order that the traditional norms may be adapted to circumstances of time and place. These three steps are at times expressed by the three words: *observe, judge, act.*

237. Hence, it seems particularly fitting that youth not merely reflect upon this order of procedure, but also, in the present connection, follow it to the extent feasible, lest what they have learned be regarded merely as something to be thought about but not acted upon.

238. However, when it comes to reducing these teachings to action, it sometimes happens that even sincere Catholic men have differing views. When this occurs they should take care to have and to show mutual esteem and regard, and to explore the extent to which they can work in cooperation among themselves. Thus they can in good time accomplish what necessity requires. Let them also take great care not to weaken their efforts in constant controversies. Nor should they, under pretext of seeking what they think best, meanwhile, fail to do what they can and hence should do.

239. But in the exercise of economic and social functions, Catholics often come in contact with men who do not share their view of life. On such occasions, those who profess Catholicism must take special care to be consistent and not com-

promise in matters wherein the integrity of religion or morals
would suffer harm. Likewise, in their conduct they should
weigh the opinions of others with fitting courtesy and not
measure everything in the light of their own interests. They
should be prepared to join sincerely in doing whatever is naturally good or conducive to good. If, indeed, it happens that
in these matters sacred authorities have prescribed or decreed
anything, it is evident that this judgment is to be obeyed
promptly by Catholics. For it is the Church's right and duty
not only to safeguard principles relating to the integrity of
religion and morals, but also to pronounce authoritatively when
it is a matter of putting these principles into effect.

MANIFOLD ACTION AND RESPONSIBILITY

240. But what we have said about the norms of instruction
should indeed be put into practice. This has special relevance
for those beloved sons of ours who are in the ranks of the laity
inasmuch as their activity ordinarily centers around temporal
affairs and making plans for the same.

241. To carry out this noble task, it is necessary that laymen
not only should be qualified, each in his own profession, and
direct their energies in accordance with rules suited to the
objective aimed at, but also should conform their activity to
the teachings and norms of the Church in social matters. Let
them put sincere trust in her wisdom; let them accept her admonitions as sons. Let them reflect that, when in the conduct
of life they do not carefully observe principles and norms laid
down by the Church in social matters, and which we ourselves
reaffirm, then they are negligent in their duty and often injure
the rights of others. At times, matters can come to a point
where confidence in this teaching is diminished, as if it were
indeed excellent but really lacks the force which the conduct
of life requires.

A GRAVE DANGER

242. As we have already noted, in this present age men have
searched widely and deeply into the laws of nature. Then they
invented instruments whereby they can control the forces of
nature; they have perfected and continue to perfect remarkable
works worthy of deep admiration. Nevertheless, while they endeavor to master and transform the external world, they are
also in danger, lest they become neglectful and weaken the
powers of body and mind. This is what our predecessor of
happy memory, Pius XI, noted with sorrow of spirit in his

Encyclical Letter *Quadragesimo Anno*: "And so bodily labor, which was decreed by divine providence for the good of man's body and soul even after original sin, has too often been changed into an instrument of perversion: for dead matter leaves the factory ennobled and transformed whereas men are there corrupted and degraded." [38]

243. And our predecessor of happy memory, Pius XII, rightly asserted that our age is distinguished from others precisely by the fact that science and technology have made incalculable progress, while men themselves have departed correspondingly from a sense of dignity. It is a "monstrous masterpiece" of this age "to have transformed man, as it were, into a giant as regards the order of nature, yet in the order of the supernatural and the eternal, to have changed him into a pygmy." [39]

244. Too often in our day is verified the testimony of the Psalmist concerning worshipers of false gods, namely, human beings in their activity very frequently neglect themselves, but admire their own works as if these were gods: "Their idols are silver and gold; the handiwork of men." [40]

Respect for the Hierarchy of Values

245. Wherefore, aroused by the pastoral zeal wherewith we embrace all men, we strongly urge our sons that, in fulfilling their duties and in pursuing their goals, they do not allow their consciousness of responsibilities to grow cool, nor neglect the order of the more important goods.

246. For it is indeed clear that the Church has always taught and continues to teach that advances in science and technology and the prosperity resulting therefrom, are truly to be counted as good things and regarded as signs of the progress of civilization. But the Church likewise teaches that goods of this kind are to be judged properly in accordance with their natures: they are always to be considered as instruments for man's use, the better to achieve his highest end: that he can the more easily improve himself, in both the natural and supernatural orders.

247. Wherefore, we ardently desire that our sons should at all times heed the words of the divine Master: "For what does it profit a man, if he gain the whole world, but suffer the loss of his own soul? Or what will a man give in exchange for his soul?" [41]

[38] *Acta Apostolicae Sedis*, XXIII (1931), p. 221f.
[39] Radio Broadcast, Christmas Eve, 1953; cf. *A.A.S.*, XLVI (1954), p. 10.
[40] Ps. 113, 4.
[41] Matt. 16, 26.

SANCTIFICATION OF HOLY DAYS

248. Not unrelated to the above admonitions is the one having to do with rest to be taken on feast days.

249. In order that the Church may defend the dignity with which man is endowed, because he is created by God and because God has breathed into him a soul to His own image, she has never failed to insist that the third commandment: "Remember to keep holy the Sabbath day," [42] be carefully observed by all. It is the right of God, and within His power, to order that man put aside a day each week for proper and due worship of the divinity. He should direct his mind to heavenly things, setting aside daily business. He should explore the depths of his conscience in order to know how necessary and inviolable are his relations with God.

250. In addition, it is right and necessary for man to cease for a time from labor, not merely to relax his body from daily hard work and likewise to refresh himself with decent recreation, but also to foster family unity, for this requires that all its members preserve a community of life and peaceful harmony.

251. Accordingly, religion, moral teaching, and care of health in turn require that relaxation be had at regular times. The Catholic Church has decreed for many centuries that Christians observe this day of rest on Sunday, and that they be present on the same day at the Eucharistic Sacrifice because it renews the memory of the divine Redemption and at the same time imparts its fruits to the souls of men.

252. But we note with deep sorrow, and we cannot but reprove the many who, though they perhaps do not deliberately despise this holy law, yet more and more frequently disregard it. Whence it is that our very dear workingmen almost necessarily suffer harm, both as to the salvation of their souls and to the health of their bodies.

253. And so, taking into account the needs of soul and body, we exhort, as it were, with the words of God Himself, all men, whether public officials or representatives of management and labor, that they observe this command of God Himself and of the Catholic Church, and judge in their souls that they have a responsibility to God and society in this regard.

RENEWED DEDICATION

254. From what we have briefly touched upon above, let none of our sons conclude, and especially the laity, that they

[42] Exod. 20, 8.

act prudently if, in regard to the transitory affairs of this life, they become quite remiss in their specific Christian contributions. On the contrary, we reaffirm that they should be daily more zealous in carrying out this role.

255. Indeed, when Christ our Lord made that solemn prayer for the unity of His Church, He asked this from the Father on behalf of His disciples: "I do not pray that Thou take them out of the world, but that Thou keep them from evil." [43] Let no one imagine that there is any opposition between these two things so that they cannot be properly reconciled: namely, the perfection of one's own soul and the business of this life, as if one had no choice but to abandon the activities of this world in order to strive for Christian perfection, or as if one could not attend to these pursuits without endangering his own dignity as a man and as a Christian.

256. However, it is in full accord with the designs of God's providence that men develop and perfect themselves by exercise of their daily tasks, for this is the lot of practically everyone in the affairs of this mortal life. Accordingly, the role of the Church in our day is very difficult: to reconcile this modern respect for progress with the norms of humanity and of the Gospel teaching. Yet, the times call the Church to this role; indeed, we may say, earnestly beseech her, not merely to pursue the higher goals, but also to safeguard her accomplishments without harm to herself. To achieve this, as we have already said, the Church especially asks the cooperation of the laity. For this reason, in their dealings with men, they are bound to exert effort in such a way that while fulfilling their duties to others, they do so in union with God through Christ, for the increase of God's glory. Thus the Apostle Paul asserts: "Whether you eat or drink, or do anything else, do all for the glory of God." [44] And elsewhere: "Whatever you do in word or in work, do all in the name of the Lord Jesus Christ, giving thanks to God the Father through Him." [45]

GREATER EFFECTIVENESS IN TEMPORAL AFFAIRS

257. As often, therefore, as human activity and institutions having to do with the affairs of this life, help toward spiritual perfection and everlasting beatitude, the more they are to be regarded as an efficacious way of obtaining the immediate end to which they are directed by their very nature. Thus, valid for all times is that noteworthy sentence of the divine Master:

[43] John 17, 15.
[44] I Cor. 10, 31.
[45] Col. 3, 17.

"Seek first the kingdom of God and His justice, and all these things shall be given you besides." [46] For he who is, as it were a *light in the Lord*, [47] and walks as a *son of light*, [48] perceives more clearly what the requirements of justice are, in the various sectors of human zeal, even in those that involve greater difficulties because of the excessive love which many have for their own interests, or those of their country, or race. It must be added that when one is motivated by Christian charity, he cannot but love others, and regard the needs, sufferings and joys of others as his own. His work, wherever it be, is constant, adaptable, humane, and has concern for the needs of others: For "Charity is patient, is kind; charity does not envy, is not pretentious, is not puffed up, is not ambitious, is not self seeking, is not provoked; thinks no evil, does not rejoice over wickedness, but rejoices with the truth; bears with all things, believes all things, hopes all things, endures all things." [49]

LIVING MEMBERS OF THE MYSTICAL BODY OF CHRIST

258. But we do not wish to bring this letter of ours to a close, Venerable Brothers, without recalling to your minds that most fundamental and true element of Catholic teaching, whereby we learn that we are living members of His Mystical Body, which is the Church: "For as the body is one and has many members, and all the members of the body, many as they are, form one body, so also is it with Christ." [50]

259. Wherefore, we urgently exhort all our sons in every part of the world, whether clergy or laity, that they fully understand how great is the nobility and dignity they derive from being joined to Christ, as branches to the vine, as He Himself said: "I am the vine, you are the branches," [51] and that they are sharers of His divine life. Whence it is, that if Christians are also joined in mind and heart with the most Holy Redeemer, when they apply themselves to temporal affairs, their work in a way is a continuation of the labor of Jesus Christ Himself, drawing from it strength and redemptive power: "He who abides in Me, and I in him, he bears much fruit." [52] Human labor of this kind is so exalted and ennobled that it leads men engaged in it to spiritual perfection, and can likewise contribute to the diffusion and propagation of the fruits of the Redemption

[46] Matt. 6, 33.
[47] Eph. 5, 8.
[48] Cf. *Ibid.*
[49] I Cor. 13, 4-7.
[50] I Cor. 12, 12.
[51] John 15, 5.
[52] *Ibid.*

to others. So also it results in the flow of that Gospel leaven, as it were, through the veins of civil society wherein we live and work.

260. Although it must be admitted that the times in which we live are torn by increasingly serious errors, and are troubled by violent disturbances, yet, it happens that the Church's laborers in this age of ours have access to enormous fields of apostolic endeavor. This inspires us with uncommon hope.

261. Venerable Brothers and beloved sons, beginning with that marvelous letter of Leo, we have thus far considered with you the varied and serious issues which pertain to the social condition of our time. From them we have drawn norms and teachings, upon which we especially exhort you not merely to meditate deeply, but also to do what you can to put them into effect. If each one of you does his best courageously, it will necessarily help in no small measure to establish the kingdom of Christ on earth. This is indeed: "A kingdom of truth and of life; a kingdom of holiness and grace; a kingdom of justice, of love and of peace." [53] And this we shall some day leave to go to that heavenly beatitude, for which we were made by God, and which we ask for with most ardent prayers.

262. For it is a question here of the teaching of the Catholic and Apostolic Church, mother and teacher of all nations, whose light illumines, sets on fire, inflames. Her warning voice, filled with heavenly wisdom, reaches out to every age. Her power always provides efficacious and appropriate remedies for the growing needs of men, for the cares and solicitudes of this mortal life. With this voice, the age-old song of the Psalmist is in marvelous accord, to strengthen at all times and to uplift our souls: "I will hear what God proclaims; the Lord —for He proclaims peace to His people, and to His faithful ones, and to those who put in Him their hope. Near indeed is His salvation to those who fear Him, glory dwelling in our land. Kindness and truth shall meet; justice and peace shall kiss. Truth shall spring out of the earth, and justice shall look down from heaven. The Lord Himself will give His benefits; our land shall yield its increase. Justice shall walk before Him, and salvation, along the way of His steps." [54] . . .

JOHN XXIII, Pope

[53] *Preface of Jesus Christ the King.*
[54] Ps. 84, 9ff.

Aeterna Dei Sapientia, November 11, 1961
On Pope Leo the Great*

* * * * *

The Bishop of Rome, Center of Visible Unity. The center and fulcrum of all visible unity of the Catholic Church, then, is the Bishop of Rome as successor of St. Peter and Vicar of Jesus Christ. The statements of St. Leo are only the faithful echo of the Gospel texts and constant Catholic tradition, as the following passage reveals: "In all the world only Peter is placed over the evangelization of all people, over all apostles and over all the Fathers of the Church, so that, although there are many pastors and priests in the midst of God's people, all are governed properly by Peter, as all are governed principally by Christ. In a great and marvelous way, oh beloved, the Lord deigned to make this man partaker of His power; and if He wishes that others also should have something in common with him, He grants all to the others always by means of him." [1]

St. Leo believes it is fitting to insist on this truth which is fundamental to Catholic unity, that is, the divine and indissoluble bond between the power of Peter and that of the other apostles: "This power (to bind and to loose: cf. *Matt.* 14, 91) was certainly extended also to the other apostles, and it was transmitted to all the heads of the Church, but it was not without purpose that that which was to be communicated to all the others was recommended to one person alone. In fact, this power was entrusted to Peter particularly, exactly because the figure of Peter stands above all those who govern the Church." [2]

The Prerogative of Magisterium of St. Peter and His Successors. But the Holy Pontiff does not forget the other essential bond of the visible unity of the Church, that is, the supreme and infallible *magisterium* reserved by the Lord to Peter personally and to his successors: "The Lord took care of Peter in a special way; He prayed for the faith of Peter in particular, almost as though the perseverance of the others would have been better guaranteed if the soul of their chief would not be overcome. In Peter, therefore, the strength of all is protected, and the assistance of divine grace follows this

---

* From a pamphlet published by the National Catholic Welfare Conference.
[1] Serm. 4, 2, *de natali ipsius, PL* 54, 149–150.
[2] *Ibid.* col. 151; cf. Serm. 83, 2, *in natali s. petri Apost., PL* 54, 430.

order: the strength which was given to Peter through Christ, is conferred on the other apostles through Peter."[3]

Wishes for the Return of the Separated Brothers. We wish to repeat, Venerable Brothers, that the chorus of praises singing the sanctity of the Supreme Pontiff, St. Leo the Great was in ancient times agreed upon both in the East and the West. Oh, may he once more receive the plaudits of all the representatives of the ecclesiastical learning of the Churches who are not in communion with Rome.

With the painful differences of opinion about the doctrine and pastoral action of the immortal Pontiff thus overcome, the doctrine which they also profess to believe will shine with greater brilliance: "There is one God and one Mediator between God and men, Himself man, Christ Jesus."[4]

We, having succeeded St. Leo in the episcopal See of St. Peter, as We profess with him faith in the divine origin of the mandate of universal evangelization and salvation entrusted by Jesus Christ to the Apostles and to their successors, so We likewise cherish the great desire to see all peoples enter on the way of truth, charity and peace.

And it is precisely for the purpose of rendering the Church more capable of accomplishing in our times this great mission that We decided to convene the Second Vatican Ecumenical Council. We did so, confident that the impressive gathering of the Catholic hierarchy would not only strengthen the bonds of unity in faith, worship and government, which are the prerogatives of the true Church, [5] but would also attract the attention of numberless believers in Christ and would invite them to gather about "the great pastor of the sheep," [6] who entrusted their perennial custody to Peter and his successors. [7]

Our warm appeal for unity is intended to be, therefore, the echo of that which was made many times by St. Leo in the fifth century, and which was reminiscent of that addressed to the faithful of all the Churches by St. Ireneus, whom Divine Providence called from Asia to govern the See of Lyons and to confirm it with his marytrdom. After having recognized the uninterrupted succession of the Bishops of Rome, heirs of the very power of the two Princes of the Apostles, [8] he (Ireneus) concluded, exhorting: "Because of its pre-eminent superiority, it is with this Church that every Church, that is, all the faithful in the universe, must agree; and it is through communion with it

[3] Serm. 4, 3, *PL* 54, 151–152; cf. Serm. 83, 2, *PL* 54, 451.
[4] I Tim. ii, 5.
[5] Cf. Conc. Vat I, Sess. III, *cap. 3 de fide.*
[6] Heb. xiii, 20.
[7] Cf. John xxi, 15–17.
[8] Cf. *Advers. haeres* 1, III, c. 2, *PG* 7, 848.

that all these faithful (or, all the heads of the Churches) have preserved apostolic tradition." [9]

But Our appeal for unity is intended to be, above all, an echo of the prayer which Our Saviour addressed to His Divine Father at the Last Supper: "That all may be one, even as Thou, Father, in Me and I in Thee; that they also may be one in Us." [10] There is no doubt about the fulfillment of this prayer, just as the cruel Sacrifice of Golgotha was fulfilled. Did the Lord not say that His Father always hears him? [11] We then believe that the Church for which He prayed and for which He sacrificed Himself on the cross, and to which He promised His abiding presence, has always been and remains one, holy, catholic and apostolic, just as it was instituted.

Unfortunately, as in the past, We must record with sorrow that also in these times the unity of the Church does not really correspond to the communion of all believers in one single profession of faith and in the same practice of worship and of obedience. However, it is a cause of comfort and of gentle hope to Us to see those generous and growing efforts done in various parts of the world for the purpose of reconstructing even the visible unity of all Christians. . . .

Venerable Brothers, the 15th centenary of the death of St. Leo the Great finds the Catholic Church in sorrowful conditions which are similar in part to those which it knew in the fifth century. How many sufferings truly afflict the Church in these times and resound in Our paternal heart, as the Divine Redeemer clearly predicted!

We see that in many regions the "faith of the Gospel" [12] is in danger, and that there are not wanting attempts—which, thank God, for the most part are doomed to failure—to separate bishops, priests and faithful from the center of Catholic unity, that is, the Roman See.

Therefore, to check these grave dangers, We confidently invoke upon the Church militant the patronage of the holy Pontiff who wrote, suffered and did so much for the cause of Catholic unity. And to those who patiently cry after truth and justice, We address the comforting words which St. Leo spoke to the clergy, to the authorities and to the people of Constantinople: "Persevere, therefore, in the spirit of Catholic truth, and through Us receive the apostolic exhortation: 'For you have been given the favor on Christ's behalf—not only to believe in Him but also to suffer for Him.'" (Phil. 1, 29) [13]

[9] Ibid.
[10] John xvii, 21.
[11] Cf. Io. xi, 42.
[12] Cf. Phil. i, 27.
[13] Ep. 50, 2 ad Constantinopolitanos, PL 54, 843.

For all those, finally, who live in the Catholic Faith, We who, though unworthily, hold the place of the Divine Saviour on earth, make Ours the prayer which He made for His beloved disciples and for all those who would have believed in Him: "Holy Father . . . I pray that they may be perfected in unity." [14]

We, therefore, ask for all the sons of the Church the perfection of unity, that perfection which only charity, "the bond of perfection," [15] can give. It is from a burning love for God and the ever ready, cheerful and generous practice of all the works of mercy toward one's neighbor that the Church, "temple of the living God," [16] is clothed in each and all of its children with supernatural beauty.

Therefore, with St. Leo We exhort you: "Since, therefore, all the faithful together and separately constitute the one and the same temple of God, it is necessary that it be perfect in each one as it must be perfect in the whole; because, even if the beauty is not equal in all the members, nor the merits equal in such a great diversity of parts, the bond of charity produces the communion in beauty. Those whom a holy love unites, even though they do not share the same gifts of grace, enjoy their benefits mutually, however, and that which they love together cannot be foreign to them, for to find joy in the progress of others increases their own riches." [17]

At the end of this Apostolic Letter of Ours, may We be permitted to renew the ardent wish that came forth from the mind of St. Leo, that is, to see all those redeemed by the Most Precious Blood of Jesus Christ, reunited in the same Church militant, to see them resist, united and fearless, the powers of evil which continue to threaten the Christian faith, from so many parts.

Because "the people of God become very powerful when, in the union of holy obedience, the hearts of all the faithful are in agreement, when in the camps of the Christian legions the preparation is the same in all parts and the defenses are the same everywhere." [18]

The prince of darkness shall not prevail as long as love reigns in the Church of Christ: "For the works of the demon will be destroyed with greater power when the hearts of men are burning with love for God and for neighbor." [19]

[14] Cf. John xvii, 20, 23.
[15] Col. iii, 14.
[16] Cf. 2 Cor. vi, 16.
[17] Serm. 48, 1, *de Quadrag.* PL 54, 298–299.
[18] *Ep.* xxii, 2, PL 54, 441–442.
[19] *Ep.* xcv, 2, *ad Pulcheriam august,* PL 54, 943.

Pacem in Terris, April 10, 1963
Peace on Earth*

Introduction

ORDER IN THE UNIVERSE

Peace on earth, which men of every era have most eagerly yearned for, can be firmly established only if the order laid down by God be dutifully observed. The progress of learning and the inventions of technology clearly show that, both in living things and in the forces of nature, an astonishing order reigns, and they also bear witness to the greatness of man, who can understand that order and create suitable instruments to harness those forces of nature and use them to his benefit.

But the progress of science and the inventions of technology show above all the infinite greatness of God, who created the universe and man himself. . . .

ORDER IN HUMAN BEINGS

How strongly does the turmoil of individual men and peoples contrast with the perfect order of the universe! It is as if the relationships which bind them together could be controlled only by force. But the creator of the world has imprinted in man's heart an order which his conscience reveals to him and enjoins him to obey: This shows that the obligations of the law are written in their hearts, their conscience utters its own testimony.[1] And how could it be otherwise? For whatever God has made shows forth His infinite wisdom, and it is manifested more clearly in the things which have greater perfection.[2]

But fickleness of opinion often produces this error, that many think that the relationships between men and states can be governed by the same laws as the forces and irrational elements of the universe, whereas the laws governing them are of quite a different kind and are to be sought elsewhere, namely, where the Father of all things wrote them, that is, in the nature of man. By these laws men are most admirably taught, first of all how they should conduct their mutual deal-

---

* Official translation provided by the Vatican Press Office, as published in *The New York Times*, April 11, 1963.
[1] Romans ii, 15.
[2] Cf. Psalms xviii, 3-11.

ings among themselves, then how the relationships between the citizens and the public authorities of each state should be regulated, then how states should deal with one another, and finally how, on the one hand, individual men and states, and on the other hand, the community of all peoples, should act towards each other, the establishment of such a world community of peoples being urgently demanded today by the requirements of universal common good.

Part I

ORDER BETWEEN MEN

EVERY MAN IS A PERSON WITH RIGHTS AND DUTIES

First of all, it is necessary to speak of the order which should exist between men. Any human society, if it is to be well-ordered and productive, must lay down as a foundation this principle, namely, that every human being is a person, that is, his nature is endowed with intelligence and free will. By virtue of this, he has rights and duties of his own, flowing directly and simultaneously from his very nature, which are therefore universal, inviolable and inalienable.[3]

If we look upon the dignity of the human person in the light of divinely revealed truth, we cannot help but esteem it far more highly. For men are redeemed by the blood of Jesus Christ, they are by grace the children and friends of God and heirs of eternal glory.

RIGHTS

THE RIGHT TO LIFE AND A WORTHY STANDARD OF LIVING

Beginning our discussion of the rights of man, we see that every man has the right to life, to bodily integrity and to the means which are necessary and suitable for the proper development of life. These are primarily food, clothing, shelter, rest, medical care and, finally, the necessary social services. Therefore, a human being also has the right to security in cases of sickness, inability to work, widowhood, old age, unemployment, or in any other case in which he is deprived of the means of subsistence through no fault of his own.[4]

---

[3] Cf. Pius XII's radio message on Christmas Eve, 1942. Acta Apostolicae Sedis, Vol. 35, pp. 9–24, and John XXIII's sermon Jan. 4, 1963. Acta Apostolicae Sedis, Vol. 55, pp. 89–91.

[4] Cf. Pius XI's encyclical letter "Divini Redemptoris" ("Of the Divine Redeemer"). Acta Apostolicae Sedis, Vol. 29, p. 78, and radio message by Pius XII on the Feast of Pentecost, 1941, Acta Apostolicae Sedis, Vol. 33, pp. 195–205.

RIGHT PERTAINING TO MORAL AND CULTURAL VALUES

By the natural law every human being has the right to respect for his person, to his good reputation, the right to freedom in searching for truth and in expressing and communicating his opinions, and in pursuit of art, within the limits laid down by the moral order and the common good. And he has the right to be informed truthfully about public events.

The natural law also gives man the right to share in the benefits of culture, and therefore the right to a basic education and to technical and professional training in keeping with the stage of educational development in the country to which he belongs. Every effort should be made to insure that persons be enabled, on the basis of merit, to go on to higher studies, so that, as far as possible, they may occupy posts and take on responsibilities in human society in accordance with their natural gifts and the skills they have acquired.[5]

THE RIGHT TO WORSHIP GOD ACCORDING TO ONE'S CONSCIENCE

Every human being has the right to honor God according to the dictates of an upright conscience, and therefore the right to worship God privately and publicly. For, as Lactantius so clearly taught: We were created for the purpose of showing to the God who bore us the submission we owe Him, or recognizing Him alone, and of serving Him. We are obliged and bound by this duty to God. From this religion itself receives its name.[6] And on this point our predecessor of immortal memory, Leo XIII, declared: "This genuine, this honorable freedom of the sons of God, which most nobly protects the dignity of the human person, is greater than any violence or injustice. It has always been sought by the church, and always most dear to her. This was the freedom which the apologists claimed with intrepid constancy, which the apologists defended with their writings, and which the martyrs in such numbers consecrated with their blood." [7]

THE RIGHT TO CHOOSE FREELY ONE'S STATE OF LIFE

Human beings have the right to choose freely the state of life which they prefer, and therefore the right to set up a family, with equal rights and duties for man and woman, and

[5] Cf. Pius XII's radio message on Christmas Eve, 1942, op. cit., pp. 9–24.
[6] Divinae Institutiones, Vol. 4, Chap. 28, Subheading 2, editions P. L. 6, 535.
[7] Encyclical letter "Libertas praestantissimum" ("freedom of the most excellent"), Acts of Leo XIII, Vol. 8, pp. 237–38.

also the right to follow a vocation to the priesthood or the religious life.[8]

The family, grounded on marriage freely contracted, monogamous and indissoluble, is and must be considered the first and essential cell of human society. To it must be given every consideration of an economic, social, cultural and moral nature which will strengthen its stability and facilitate the fulfillment of its specific mission.

Parents, however, have a prior right in the support and education of their children.[9]

ECONOMIC RIGHTS

Human beings have the natural right to free initiative in the economic field, and the right to work.[10]

Indissolubly linked with those rights is the right to working conditions in which physical health is not endangered, morals are safeguarded and young people's normal development is not impaired. Women have the right to working conditions in accordance with their requirements and their duties as wives and mothers.[11]

From the dignity of the human person, there also arises the right to carry on economic activities according to the degree of responsibility of which one is capable. [12] Furthermore —and this must be specially emphasized—there is the right to a working wage, determined according to criterions of justice and sufficient, therefore, in proportion to the available resources to give the worker and his family a standard of living in keeping with the dignity of the human person. In this regard, our predecessor Pius XII said: "To the personal duty to work imposed by nature, there corresponds and follows the natural right of each individual to make of his work the means to provide for his own life and the lives of his children. So profoundly is the empire of nature ordained for the preservation of man." [13]

The right to private property, even of productive goods, also derives from the nature of man. This right, as we have elsewhere declared, is a suitable means for safeguarding the dig-

[8] Cf. Pius XII radio message on Christmas Eve, 1942, loc. cit.

[9] Cf. Pius XI's encyclical letter "Casti Connubii" ("Of Chaste Marriage") Acta Apostolicae Sedis, Vol. 22, pp. 539–92, and Pius XII's radio message on Christmas Eve, 1942, loc. cit.

[10] Cf. Pius XII's radio message on the Feast of Pentecost, 1941, loc. cit., p. 201.

[11] Cf. Leo XIII's encyclical letter "Rerum Novarum" ("Of New Things"), Acts of Leo XIII, Vol. 11, pp. 128–29.

[12] Cf. John XXIII's encyclical letter "Mater et Magistra" ("Mother and Teacher"), Acta Apostolicae Sedis, Vol. 53, p. 422.

[13] Cf. Pope Pius XII, loc. cit.

nity of the human person and for the exercise of responsibility in all fields; it strengthens and gives serenity to family life, thereby increasing the peace and prosperity of the state.[14]

However, it is opportune to point out that there is a social duty essentially inherent in the right of private property.[15]

THE RIGHT OF MEETING AND ASSOCIATION

From the fact that human beings are by nature social, there arises the right of assembly and association. They have also the right to give the societies of which they are members the form they consider most suitable for the aim they have in view, and to act within such societies on their own initiative and on their own responsibility in order to achieve their desired objectives.[16]

We ourselves stated in the encyclical "Mater et Magistra" that, for the achievement of ends which individual human beings cannot attain except by association, it is necessary and indispensable to set up a great variety of such intermediate groups and societies in order to guarantee for the human person a sufficient sphere of freedom and responsibility.[17]

THE RIGHT TO EMIGRATE AND IMMIGRATE

Every human being has the right to freedom of movement and of residence within the confines of his own country; and, when there are just reasons for it, the right to emigrate to other countries and take up residence there.[18] The fact that one is a citizen of a particular state does not detract in any way from his membership of the human family as a whole, nor from his citizenship of the world community.

POLITICAL RIGHTS

The dignity of the human person involves the right to take an active part in public affairs and to contribute one's part to the common good of the citizenry. For, as our predecessor of happy memory, Pius XII, pointed out: The human individual,

---

[14] "Mater et Magistra," p. 428.
[15] Cf. Ibid., p. 430.
[16] Cf. "Rerum Novarum," pp. 134–42; Pius XI's encyclical "Quadragesimo Anno" ("in the fortieth year"), Acta Apostolicae Sedis, Vol. 23, pp. 199–200, and Pius XII's encyclical letter "Sertum Laetitiae" ("A Garland of Joy"), Acta Apostolicae Sedis, Vol. 31, pp. 635–44.
[17] Cf. Acta Apostolicae Sedis, Vol. 53, p. 430.
[18] Cf. Pius XII's radio message on Christmas Eve, 1942, op. cit., pp. 33–46.

far from being an object and, as it were, a merely passive element in the social order, is in fact, must be and must continue to be, its subject, its foundation and its end.[19]

The human person is also entitled to a juridical protection of his rights, a protection that should be efficacious, impartial and inspired by the true norms of justice.

As our predecessor Pius XII teaches: That perpetual privilege proper to man, by which every individual has a claim to the protection of his rights, and by which there is assigned to each a definite and particular sphere of rights, immune from all arbitrary attacks, is the logical consequence of the order of justice willed by God.[20]

Duties

RIGHTS AND DUTIES NECESSARILY LINKED IN THE ONE PERSON

The natural rights with which we have been dealing are, however, inseparably connected, in the very person who is their subject, with just as many respective duties; and rights as well as duties find their source, their sustenance and their inviolability in the natural law which grants or enjoins them.

For example, the right of every man to life is correlative with the duty to preserve it; his right to a decent standard of living with the duty of living it becomingly; and his right to investigate the truth freely, with the duty of seeking it and of possessing it ever more completely and profoundly.

RECIPROCITY OF RIGHTS AND DUTIES BETWEEN PERSONS

Once this is admitted, it is also clear that in human society to one man's right there corresponds a duty in all other persons: the duty, namely, of acknowledging and respecting the right in question. For every fundamental human right draws its indestructible moral force from the natural law, which, in granting it, imposes a corresponding obligation. Those, therefore, who claim their own rights, yet altogether forget or neglect to carry out their respective duties, are people who build with one hand and destroy with the other. . . .

[19] Cf. Pius XII's radio message on Christmas Eve, 1944, Acta Apostolicae Sedis, Vol. 37, p. 12.
[20] Cf. Pius XII's radio message on Christmas Eve, 1942, op. cit., p. 21.

SOCIAL LIFE IN TRUTH, JUSTICE, CHARITY AND FREEDOM

A political society is to be considered well-ordered, beneficial and in keeping with human dignity if it is grounded on truth. As the Apostle Paul exhorts us: "Away with falsehood then: let everyone speak out the truth to his neighbor; membership of the body binds us to one another." [21] This demands that reciprocal rights and duties be sincerely recognized. Furthermore, human society will be such as we have just described it, if the citizens, guided by justice, apply themselves seriously to respecting the rights of others and discharging their own duties; if they are moved by such fervor of charity as to make their own the needs of others and share with others their own goods: If, finally, they work for a progressively closer fellowship in the world of spiritual values. Human society is realized in freedom, that is to say, in ways and means in keeping with the dignity of its citizens, who accept the responsibility of their actions, precisely because they are by nature rational beings.

Human society, venerable brothers and beloved children, ought to be regarded above all as a spiritual reality: in which men communicate knowledge to each other in the light of truth; in which they can enjoy their rights and fulfil their duties, and are inspired to strive for moral good. Society should enable men to share in and enjoy every legitimate expression of beauty, and encourage them constantly to pass on to others all that is best in themselves, while they strive to make their own the spiritual achievements of others. These are the spiritual values which continually give life and basic orientation to cultural expressions, economic and social institutions, political movements and forms, laws, and all other structures by which society is outwardly established and constantly developed.

GOD AND THE MORAL ORDER

The order which prevails in society is by nature moral. Grounded as it is in truth, it must function according to the norms of justice, it should be inspired and perfected by mutual love, and finally it should be brought to an ever more refined and human balance in freedom.

Now an order of this kind, whose principles are universal, absolute and unchangeable, has its ultimate source in the one

---

[21] Ephesians, iv, 25.

true God, who is personal and transcends human nature. Inasmuch as God is the first truth and the highest good, He alone is that deepest source from which human society can draw its vitality, if that society is to be well-ordered, beneficial, and in keeping with human dignity.[22] As St. Thomas Aquinas says: "Human reason is the norm of the human will, according to which its goodness is measured, because reason derives from the eternal law which is the divine reason itself. It is evident then that the goodness of the human will depends much more on the eternal law than on human reason." [23]

CHARACTERISTICS OF THE PRESENT

Our age has three distinctive characteristics. First of all, the working classes have gradually gained ground in economic and public affairs. They began by claiming their rights in the socioeconomic sphere; they extended their action then to claims on the political level; and finally applied themselves to the acquisition of the benefits of a more refined culture. Today, therefore, workers all over the world refuse to be treated as if they were irrational objects without freedom, to be used at the arbitrary disposition of others. They insist that they be always regarded as men with a share in every sector of human society: in the social and economic sphere, in the fields of learning and culture, and in public life.

Secondly, it is obvious to everyone that women are now taking a part in public life. This is happening more rapidly, perhaps, in nations of Christian civilization, and, more slowly but broadly, among peoples who have inherited other traditions or cultures. Since women are becoming ever more conscious of their human dignity, they will not tolerate being treated as mere material instruments, but demand rights befitting a human person both in domestic and in public life.

Finally, the modern world, as compared with the recent past, has taken on an entirely new appearance in the field of social and political life. For since all nations have either achieved or are on the way to achieving independence, there will soon no longer exist a world divided into nations that rule others and nations that are subject to others.

Men all over the world have today—or will soon have—the rank of citizens in independent nations. No one wants to feel subject to political powers located outside his own country

[22] Cf. Pius XII's 1942 radio message op. cit., p. 14.
[23] St. Thomas Aquinas, "Summa Theologica," I/A-II/AE, quest. 19, para. 4, cf. para. 9.

or ethnic group. Thus in very many human beings the inferiority complex which endured for hundreds and thousands of years is disappearing, while in others there is an attenuation and gradual fading of the corresponding superiority complex which had its roots in social-economic privileges, sex or political standing.

On the contrary, the conviction that all men are equal by reason of their natural dignity has been generally accepted. Hence racial discrimination can no longer be justified, at least doctrinally or in theory. And this is of fundamental importance and significance for the formation of human society according to those principles which we have outlined above. For, if a man becomes conscious of his rights, he must become equally aware of his duties. Thus he who possesses certain rights has likewise the duty to claim those rights as marks of his dignity, while all others have the obligation to acknowledge those rights and respect them.

When the relations of human society are expressed in terms of rights and duties, men become conscious of spiritual values, understand the meaning and significance of truth, justice, charity and freedom, and become deeply aware that they belong to this world of values. Moreover, when moved by such concerns, they are brought to a better knowledge of the true God who is personal and transcendent, and thus they make the ties that bind them to God the solid foundations and supreme criterion of their lives, both of that life which they live interiorly in the depths of their own souls and of that in which they are united to other men in society.

Part II

Relations Between Individuals and the Public Authorities

NECESSITY AND DIVINE ORIGIN OF AUTHORITY

Human society can be neither well-ordered nor prosperous unless it has some people invested with legitimate authority to preserve its institutions and to devote themselves as far as is necessary to work and care for the good of all. These, however, derive their authority from God, as St. Paul teaches in the words, "Authority comes from God alone." [24] These words of St. Paul are explained thus by St. John Chrysostom: What

[24] St. Paul's Epistle to the Romans, xiii, 1–6.

are you saying? Is every ruler appointed by God? I do not say that, he replies, for I am not dealing now with individual rulers, but with authority itself. What I say is, that it is the divine wisdom and not mere chance that has ordained that there should be government, that some should command and others obey.[25] Moreover, since God made men social by nature, and since no society can hold together uness some one be over all, directing all to strive earnestly for the common good, every civilized community must have a ruling authority, and this authority, no less than society itself, has its source in nature, and has, consequently, God for its authority.[26]

But authority is not to be thought of as a force lacking all control. Indeed, since it is the power to command according to right reason, authority must derive its obligatory force from the moral order, which in turn has God for its first source and final end. Wherefore our predecessor of happy memory, Pius XII, said: "That same absolute order of beings and their ends which presents man as an autonomous person, that is, as the subject of inviolable duties and rights, and as at once the basis of society and the purpose for which it exists, also includes the state as necessary society invested with the authority without which it could not come into being or live. . . . And since this absolute order, as we learn from sound reason, especially from the Christian faith, can have no origin save in a personal God who is our Creator, it follows that the dignity of the state's authority is due to its sharing to some extent in the authority of God himself.[27]

Where the civil authority uses as its only or its chief means either threats and fear of punishment or promises of rewards, it cannot effectively move men to promote the common good of all. Even if it did so move them, this would be altogether opposed to their dignity as men, endowed with reason and free will. As authority is chiefly concerned with moral force, it follows that civil authority must appeal primarily to the conscience of individual citizens, that is, to each one's duty to collaborate readily for the common good of all. Since by nature all men are equal in human dignity, it follows that no one may be coerced to perform inferior acts. That is in the power of God alone, who sees and judges the hidden designs of men's hearts. Those therefore who have authority in the state may oblige men in conscience only if their authority is

[25] Op. cit., xiii, 1–2; Homily 23, Edition P. G. 60, 615.
[26] Leo XIII's encyclical letter "Immortale Dei" ("Of Immortal God"), Acts of Leo XIII, Vol. 5, p. 120.
[27] Cf. Pius XII's 1944 radio message, op. cit., p. 15.

intrinsically related with the authority of God and shares in it.[28]

By this principle the dignity of the citizens is protected. When, in fact, men obey their rulers, it is not all as men that they obey them, but through their obedience it is God, the provident Creator of all things, whom they reverence, since he has decreed that men's dealings with one another should be regulated by an order which he himself has established. Moreover, in showing this due reverence to God, men not only do not debase themselves but rather perfect and ennoble themselves. For to serve God is to rule.[29]

Since the right to command is required by the moral order and has its source in God, it follows that, if civil authorities legislate for or allow anything that is contrary to that order and therefore contrary to the will of God, neither the laws made nor the authorizations granted can be binding on the consciences of the citizens, since God has more right to be obeyed than men.[30] Otherwise, authority breaks down completely and results in shameful abuse. As St. Thomas Aquinas teaches: Human law has the true nature of law only in so far as it corresponds to right reason, and therefore is derived from the eternal law. In so far as it falls short of right reason, a law is said to be a wicked law. And so, lacking the true nature of law, it is rather a kind of violence.[31]

It must not be concluded, however, because authority comes from God, that therefore men have no right to choose those who are to rule the state, to decide the form of government and to determine both the way in which authority is to be exercised and its limits. It is thus clear that the doctrine which we have set forth is fully consonant with any truly democratic regime.[32]

ATTAINMENT OF THE COMMON GOOD

PURPOSES OF THE PUBLIC AUTHORITY

Individual citizens and intermediate groups are obliged to make their specific contributions to the common welfare.

[28] Cf. Encyclical Letter "Diuturnum Illud" ("That Longlived"), Acts of Leo XIII, Vol. 2, p. 274.

[29] Cf. Ibid, p. 278, and encyclical "Immortale Dei," op. cit., p. 130.

[30] Acts of the Apostles, v, 29.

[31] St. Thomas Aquinas, op. cit., quest., 93, para. 3; Cf. Pius XII's 1944 radio message, op. cit., pp. 5–23.

[32] Cf. "Diuturnum Illud," op. cit., pp. 271–72; and Pius XII's 1944 radio message, op. cit., pp. 9–23.

One of the chief consequences of this is that they must bring their own interests into harmony with the needs of the community, and must dispose of their goods and their services as civil authorities have prescribed, in accord with the norms of justice, in due form and within the limits of their competence. This they must do by means of formally perfect actions, the content of which must be morally good, or at least capable of being directed towards good.

Indeed, since the whole reason for the existence of civil authorities is the realization of the common good, it is clearly necessary that, in pursuing this objective, they should respect its essential elements, and at the same time conform their laws to the needs of a given historical situation.[83]

Assuredly, the ethnic characteristics of the various human groups are to be respected as constituent elements of the common good,[84] but these values and characteristics by no means exhaust the content of the common good. For the common good is intimately bound up with human nature. It can never exist fully and completely unless, its intimate nature and realization being what they are, the human person is taken into account.[85]

In the second place, the very nature of the common good requires that all members of the political community be entitled to share in it, although in different ways according to each one's tasks, merits and circumstances. For this reason, every civil authority must take pains to promote the common good of all, without preference for any single citizen or civil group. As our predecessor of immortal memory, Leo XIII, has said: The civil power must not serve the advantage of any one individual or of some few persons, inasmuch as it was established for the common good of all.[86] Considerations of justice and equity, however, can at times demand that those involved in civil government give more attention to the less fortunate members of the community, since they are less able to defend their rights and to assert their legitimate claims.[87]

In this context, we judge that attention should be called to the fact that the common good touches the whole man, the needs both of his body and of his soul. Hence it follows that

---

[83] Cf. Pius XII's 1942 radio message, op. cit., p. 13, and Leo XIII's "Immortale Dei," op. cit., p. 120.

[84] Cf. Pius XII's encyclical letter "Summi Pontificatus" ("Of the Supreme Pontificate"), Acta Apostolicae Sedis, Vol. 31, pp. 412–53.

[85] Cf. Pius XI's encyclical letter "Mit Brennender Sorge" ("For With Burning Sorrow"), Acta Apostolicae Sedis, Vol. 29, p. 159, and encyclical letter "Divini Redemptoris," Acta Apostolicae Sedis, Vol. 29, pp. 65–106.

[86] "Immortale Dei," op. cit., p. 121.

[87] Cf. "Rerum Novarum," op. cit., pp. 133–34.

the civil authorities must undertake to effect the common good by ways and means that are proper to them. That is, while respecting the hierarchy of values, they should promote simultaneously both the material and the spiritual welfare of the citizens.[38]

These principles are clearly contained in the doctrine stated in our encyclical, "Mater et Magistra," where we emphasized that the common good of all embraces the sum total of those conditions of social living whereby men are enabled to achieve their own integral perfection more fully and more easily.[39]

Men, however, composed as they are of bodies and immortal souls, can never in this mortal life succeed in satisfying all their needs or in attaining perfect happiness. Therefore, all efforts made to promote the common good, far from endangering the eternal salvation of men, ought rather to serve to promote it.[40]

RESPONSIBILITIES OF THE PUBLIC AUTHORITY, AND RIGHTS AND DUTIES OF INDIVIDUALS

It is agreed that in our time the common good is chiefly guaranteed when personal rights and duties are maintained. The chief concern of civil authorities must therefore be to insure that these rights are acknowledged, respected, coordinated with other rights, defended and promoted, so that in this way each one may more easily carry out his duties. For to safeguard the inviolable rights of the human person, and to facilitate the fulfillment of its duties, should be the essential office of every public authority.[41]

This means that, if any government does not acknowledge the rights of man or violates them, it not only fails its duty, but its orders completely lack juridical force.[42]

RECONCILIATION AND PROTECTION OF RIGHTS AND DUTIES OF INDIVIDUALS

One of the fundamental duties of civil authorities, therefore, is to coordinate social relations in such fashion that the exercise of one man's rights does not threaten others in the exer-

---

[38] Cf. "Summi Pontificatus," op. cit., p. 433.

[39] Acta Apostolicae Sedis, Vol. 53, p. 19.

[40] Cf. "Quadragesimo Anno," Vol. 23, p. 215.

[41] Cf. Pius XII's 1941 Feast of Pentecost radio message, op. cit., p. 200.

[42] Cf. "Mit Brennender Sorge," op. cit., p. 159; "Divini Redemptoris," op. cit., p. 79, and Pius XII's 1942 radio message, op. cit., pp. 9–24.

cise of their own rights nor hinder them in the fulfillment of
their duties. Finally, the rights of all should be effectively safeguarded and, if they have been violated, completely restored.[43]

DUTY OF PROMOTING THE RIGHTS OF INDIVIDUALS

It is also demanded by the common good that civil authorities should make earnest efforts to bring about a situation in
which individual citizens can easily exercise their rights and
fulfill their duties as well. For experience has taught us that,
unless these authorities take suitable action with regard to
economic, political and cultural matters, inequalities between
the citizens tend to become more and more widespread, especially in the modern world, and as a result human rights are
rendered totally ineffective, and the fulfillment of duties is
compromised.

It is therefore necessary that the Administration give wholehearted and careful attention to the social as well as to the
economic progress of the citizens, and to the development,
in keeping with the development of the productive system,
of such essential services as the building of roads, transportation, communications, water supply, housing, public health,
education, facilitation of the practice of religion and recreational facilities. It is necessary also that governments make
efforts to see that insurance systems are made available to the
citizens, so that, in case of misfortune or increased family
responsibilities, no person will be without the necessary means
to maintain a decent standard of living. The government should
make similarly effective efforts to see that those who are able
to work can find employment in keeping with their aptitudes,
and that each worker receives a wage in keeping with the
laws of justice and equity. It should be equally the concern
of civil authorities to insure that workers be allowed their
proper responsibility in the work undertaken in industrial
organization, and to facilitate the establishment of intermediate
groups which will make social life richer and more effective.
Finally, it should be possible for all the citizens to share as
far as they are able in their country's cultural advantages.

HARMONIOUS RELATION BETWEEN PUBLIC AUTHORITY'S TWO FORMS OF INTERVENTION

The common good requires that civil authorities maintain
a careful balance between coordinating and protecting the

[43] Cf. "Divini Redemptoris," op. cit., p. 81, and 1942 radio message, loc. cit.

rights of the citizens, on the one hand, and promoting them, on the other. It should not happen that certain individuals or social groups derive special advantage from the fact that their rights have received preferential protection. Nor should it happen that governments, in seeking to protect these rights, become obstacles to their full expression and free use. For this principle must always be retained: that state activity in the economic field, no matter what its breadth or depth may be, ought not to be exercised in such a way as to curtail an individual's freedom of personal initiative. Rather it should work to expand that freedom as much as possible by the effective protection of the essential personal rights of each and every individual."[44]

The same principle should inspire the various steps which governments take in order to make it possible for the citizens more easily to exercise their rights and fulfill their duties in every sector of social life.

STRUCTURE AND OPERATION OF PUBLIC AUTHORITY

It is impossible to determine, once and for all, what is the most suitable form of government, or how civil authorities can most effectively fulfill their respective functions, i.e., the legislative, judicial and executive functions of the state. In determining the structure and operation of government which a state is to have, great weight has to be given to the historical background and circumstances of given political communities, circumstances which will vary at different times and in different places. We consider, however, that it is in keeping with the innate demands of human nature that the state should take a form which embodies the three-fold division of powers corresponding to the three principal functions of public authority. In that type of state, not only the official functions of government but also the mutual relations between citizens and public officials are set down according to law, which in itself affords protection to the citizens both in the enjoyment of their rights and in the fulfillment of their duties.

If, however, this political and juridical structure is to produce the advantages which may be expected of it, public officials must strive to meet the problems which arise in a way that conforms both to the complexities of the situation and the proper exercise of their function. This requires that, in constantly changing conditions, legislators never forget the norms of morality, or constitutional provisions, or the objec-

44 "Mater et Magistra," op. cit., p. 415.

tive requirements of the common good. Moreover, executive authorities must coordinate the activities of society with discretion, with a full knowledge of the law and after a careful consideration of circumstances, and the courts must administer justice impartially and without being influenced by favoritism or pressure. The good order of society also demands that individual citizens and intermediate organizations should be effectively protected by law whenever they have rights to be exercised or obligations to be fulfilled. This protection should be granted to citizens both in their dealings with each other and in their relations with governmental agencies.[45]

Law and Conscience

It is unquestionable that a legal structure in conformity with the moral order and corresponding to the level of development of the political community is of great advantage to achievement of the common good.

And yet, social life in the modern world is so varied, complex and dynamic that even a juridical structure which has been prudently and thoughtfully established is always inadequate for the needs of society.

It is also true that the relations of the citizens with each other, of citizens and intermediate groups with public authorities, and finally of the public authorities with one another are often so complex and so sensitive that they cannot be regulated by inflexible legal provisions. Such a situation therefore demands that the civil authorities have clear ideas about the nature and extent of their official duties if they wish to maintain the existing juridical structure in its basic elements and principles, and at the same time meet the exigencies of social life, adapting their legislation to the changing social scene and solving new problems. They must be men of great equilibrium and integrity, competent and courageous enough to see at once what the situation requires and to take necessary action quickly and effectively.[46]

[45] Cf. Pius XII's 1942 radio message, op. cit., p. 21.
[46] Op. cit., pp. 15–16.

Part III

Relations Between States

SUBJECTS OF RIGHTS AND DUTIES

Our predecessors have constantly maintained, and we join them in reasserting, that political communities are reciprocally subjects of rights and duties. This means that their relationships also must be harmonized in truth, in justice, in a working solidarity, in liberty. The same moral law which governs relations between individual human beings serves also to regulate the relations of political communities with one another. This will be readily understood when one reflects that the individual representatives of political communities cannot put aside their personal dignity while they are acting in the name and interest of their countries. And that they cannot therefore violate the very law of their being, which is the moral law.

It would be absurd, moreover, even to imagine that men could surrender their own human attributes, or be compelled to do so, by the very fact of their appointment to public office, whereas they have been given that noble assignment precisely because the wealth of their human endowments has earned them their reputation as outstanding members of the body politic. Furthermore, authority is a necessary requirement of the moral order in human society. It may not therefore be used against that order. And the very instant such an attempt were made, it would cease to be authority. . . .

Lastly, it is to be borne in mind that also in the regulating of relations between political communities, authority is to be exercised for the achievement of the common good, which constitutes the reason for its existence.

But a fundamental factor of the common good is acknowledgment of the moral order and respect for its prescriptions. Order between the political communities must be built upon the unshakable and unchangeable rock of the moral law, made manifest in the order of nature by the Creator himself and by Him engraved on the hearts of men with letters that may never be effaced. . . .

IN TRUTH

First among the rules governing the relations between states is that of truth. This calls, above all, for the elimination of every trace of racism, and the consequent recognition of the principle that all states are by nature equal in dignity. Each of them, accordingly, is vested with the right to existence, to self-development, to the means fitting to its attainment and to be the one primarily responsible for this self-development. Add to that the right of each to its good name, and to the respect which is its due. Very often, experience has taught us, individuals will be found to differ considerably, in knowledge, virtue, talent and wealth. Yet these inequalities must never be held to excuse any man's attempt to lord it over his neighbors unjustly. They constitute rather a source of greater responsibility in the contribution which each and everyone must make towards mutual improvement.

Similarly, political communities may have reached different levels of culture, civilization or economic development. Neither is that a sufficient reason for some to take unjust advantage of their superiority over others. Rather should they see in it an added motive for more serious commitment to the common cause of social progress.

It is not true that some human beings are by nature superior and others inferior. All men are equal in their natural dignity. Consequently, there are no political communities which are superior by nature and none which are inferior by nature. All political communities are of equal natural dignity, since they are bodies whose membership is made up of these same human beings. Nor must it be forgotten, in this connection, that peoples can be highly sensitive, and with good reason, in matters touching their dignity and honor.

Truth further demands that the various media of social communications made available by modern progress, which enable the nations to know each other better, be used with serene objectivity. That need not, of course, rule out any legitimate emphasis on the positive aspects of their way of life. But methods of information which fall short of the truth, and by the same token impair the reputation of this people or that, must be discarded. [47]

[47] Cf. Pius XII's radio message on Christmas Eve, 1940, Acta Apostolicae Sedis, Vol. 33, pp. 5–14.

IN JUSTICE

Relations between political communities are to be further regulated by justice. This implies, over and above recognition of their mutual rights, the fulfillment of their respective duties.

Political communities have the right to existence, to self-development and to the means necessary for this. They have the right to play the leading part in the process of their own development and the right to their good name and due honors. From which it follows as a simultaneous consequence that they have also the corresponding duty of respecting these rights in others and of avoiding any act of violation. Just as an individual man may not pursue his own interests to the detriment of other men, so, on the international level, one state may not develop itself by restricting or oppressing other states. St. Augustine rightly says, "What are kingdoms without justice but bands of robbers?" [48] . . .

THE TREATMENT OF MINORITIES

From the 19th century there has been a rather widespread tendency in historical evolution that political communities equate themselves to national communities. However, for various reasons, it has not always been possible to make geographical boundaries coincide with ethnic ones. This gives rise to the phenomenon of minorities and to the relative complex problems.

In the first place, it must be made clear that justice is seriously violated by whatever is done to limit the strength and numerical increase of these lesser peoples. The injustice is even more serious if such sinful projects are aimed at the very extinction of these groups.

On the other hand, the demands of justice are admirably observed by those civil authorities who promote the natural betterment of those citizens belonging to a smaller ethnic group, particularly when that betterment concerns their language, the development of their natural gifts, their ancestral customs, and their accomplishments and endeavors in the economic order. [49]

[48] St. Augustine's "De Civitate Dei," book IV, chapt. 4, edition P. L. 41, p. 115; cf. Pius XII's radio message on Christmas Eve, 1939, Acta Apostolicae Sedis, Vol. 32, pp. 5–13.

[49] Cf. Pius XII's 1941 radio message, op. cit., pp. 10–21.

It should be noted, however, that these minority groups, either because of a reaction to their present situation or because of their historical difficulties are often inclined to exalt beyond due measure anything proper to their own people, so as to place them even above human values, as if that which is proper to humanity were to be at the service of that which is proper to the nation. Reason rather demands that these very people recognize also the advantages that accrue to them from their peculiar circumstances. For instance, no small contribution is made towards the development of their particular talents and spirit by their daily dealings with people who have grown up in a different culture. This, however, will be true only if they will know how to act as a bridge, which facilitates the circulation of life in its various expressions among different traditions or civilizations, and not a zone of discord which can cause great damage and choke natural development.

ACTIVE SOLIDARITY

Certainly relations between states must be regulated by the norms of truth and justice, but they also derive great benefits from active solidarity, through mutual cooperation on various levels, such as, in our own times, has already taken place with laudable results in the economic, social, political, educational, health and sport spheres. We must remember that, of its very nature, civil authority exists, not to confine its people within the boundaries of their nation, but rather to protect, above all else, the common good of that particular civil society, which certainly cannot be divorced from the common good of the entire human family.

This entails not only that civil societies should pursue their particular interests without hurting others, but also that they should join forces and plans whenever the efforts of an individual government cannot achieve its desired goals. But in the execution of such common efforts, great care must be taken lest what helps some nations should injure others.

Furthermore, the universal common good requires that in every nation friendly relations be fostered in all fields between the citizens and their intermediate societies.

There are groupings of people of more or less different racial backgrounds. However, the elements which characterize an ethnic group must not be transformed into a watertight compartment in which human beings are prevented from communicating with their fellowmen belonging to different ethnic groups. That would contrast with our contemporary situation, in which the distances separating peoples have been almost wiped out. Nor can one overlook the fact that, even though human beings differ from one another by virtue of their ethnic peculiarities, they all possess certain essential common elements, and are inclined by nature to meet each other in the world of spiritual values, whose progressive assimilation opens to them the possibility of perfection without limits. They have the right and duty therefore to live in communion with one another.

PROPER BALANCES BETWEEN POPULATION, LAND AND CAPITAL

As everybody knows, there are countries with an abundance of arable land and a scarcity of manpower, while in other countries there is no proportion between natural resources and the capital available. This demands that peoples should set up relationships of mutual collaboration, facilitating the circulation from one to the other of capital, goods and manpower. [50]

Here we deem it opportune to remark that, whenever possible, the work to be done should be taken to the workers, not vice versa.

In this way a possibility of a better future is offered to many persons without being forced to leave their own environment in order to seek residence elsewhere, which almost always entails the heartache of separation and difficult periods of adjustment and social integration.

THE PROBLEM OF POLITICAL REFUGEES

The sentiment of universal fatherhood which the Lord has placed in our heart makes us feel profound sadness in considering the phenomenon of political refugees: a phenomenon which has assumed large proportions and which always hides numberless and acute sufferings.

Such expatriations show that there are some political regimes which do not guarantee for individual citizens a sufficient sphere of freedom within which their souls are allowed to breathe humanly. In fact, under those regimes even the lawful existence of such a sphere of freedom is either called into question or denied. This undoubtedly is a radical inversion of the order of human society, because the reason for the existence of public authority is to promote the common good, a fundamental element of which is the recognition of that sphere of freedom and the safeguarding of it.

At this point it will not be superfluous to recall that such

[50] Cf. "Mater et Magistra," op. cit., p. 439.

exiles are persons, and that all their rights as persons must be recognized, since they do not lose those rights on losing the citizenship of lands of which they are former members.

Now among the rights of a human person there must be included that by which a man may enter a political community where he hopes he can more fittingly provide a future for himself and his dependents. Wherefore, as far as the common good rightly understood permits, it is the duty of that state to accept such immigrants and to help to integrate them into itself as new members.

Wherefore, on this occasion, we publicly approve and commend every undertaking, founded on the principles of human solidarity and Christian charity, which aims at making migration of persons from one country to another less painful.

And we will be permitted to signal for the attention and gratitude of all right-minded persons the manifold work which specialized international agencies are carrying out in this very delicate field.

DISARMAMENT

On the other hand, it is with deep sorrow that we note the enormous stocks of armaments that have been and still are being made in more economically developed countries, with a vast outlay of intellectual and economic resources. And so it happens that, while the people of these countries are loaded with heavy burdens, other countries as a result are deprived of the collaboration they need in order to make economic and social progress.

The production of arms is allegedly justified on the grounds that in present-day conditions peace cannot be preserved without an equal balance of armaments. And so, if one country increases its armaments, others feel the need to do the same; and if one country is equipped with nuclear weapons, other countries must produce their own, equally destructive.

Consequently, people live in constant fear lest the storm that every moment threatens should break upon them with dreadful violence. And with good reason, for the arms of war are ready at hand. Even though it is difficult to believe that anyone would deliberately take the responsibility for the appalling destruction and sorrow that war would bring in its train, it cannot be denied that the conflagration may be set off by some uncontrollable and unexpected chance. And one must bear in mind that, even though the monstrous power of modern weapons acts as a deterrent, it is to be feared that the mere continuance of nuclear tests, undertaken with war in mind, will have fatal consequences for life on the earth.

Justice, then, right reason and humanity urgently demand that the arms race should cease. That the stockpiles which exist in various countries should be reduced equally and simultaneously by the parties concerned. That nuclear weapons should be banned. And that a general agreement should eventually be reached about progressive disarmament and an effective method of control. In the words of Pius XII, our predecessor of happy memory: "The calamity of a world war, with the economic and social ruin and the moral excesses and dissolution that accompany it, must not be permitted to envelop the human race for a third time." [51]

All must realize that there is no hope of putting an end to the building up of armaments, nor of reducing the present stocks, nor, still less, of abolishing them altogether, unless the process is complete and thorough and unless it proceeds from inner convictions: unless, that is, everyone sincerely cooperates to banish the fear and anxious expectation of war with which men are oppressed. If this is to come about, the fundamental principle on which our present peace depends must be replaced by another, which declares that the true and solid peace of nations consists not in equality of arms, but in mutual trust alone. We believe that this can be brought to pass, and we consider that it is something which reason requires, that it is eminently desirable in itself and that it will prove to be the source of many benefits.

In the first place, it is an objective demanded by reason. There can be, or at least there should be, no doubt that relations between states, as between individuals, should be regulated not by the force of arms, but by the light of reason, by the rule, that is, of truth, of justice and of active and sincere cooperation.

Secondly, we say that it is an objective earnestly to be desired in itself. Is there anyone who does not ardently yearn to see war banished, to see peace preserved and daily more firmly established?

And finally, it is an objective which will be a fruitful source of many benefits, for its advantages will be felt everywhere, by individuals, by families, by nations, by the whole human family. The warning of Pius XII still rings in our ears: "Nothing is lost by peace. Everything may be lost by war." [52]

[51] Cf. Pius XII's 1941 radio message, op. cit., p. 17, and Benedict XV's exhortation Aug. 1, 1917, Acta Apostolicae Sedis, Vol. 9, p. 418.

[52] Cf. Pius XII's radio message on Aug. 24, 1939, Acta Apostolicae Sedis, Vol. 31, p. 334.

Since this is so, we, the vicar on earth of Jesus Christ, Saviour of the world and author of peace, and as interpreter of the very profound longing of the entire human family, following the impulse of our heart, seized by anxiety for the good of all, we feel it our duty to beseech men, especially those who have the responsibility of public affairs, to spare no labor in order to insure that the world events follow a reasonable and human course.

In the highest and most authoritative assemblies, let men give serious thought to the problem of a peaceful adjustment of relations between political communities on a world level: an adjustment founded on mutual trust, on sincerity in negotiations, on faithful fulfillment of obligations assumed. Let them study the problem until they find that point of agreement from which it will be possible to commence to go forward towards accords that will be sincere, lasting and fruitful.

We, for our part, will not cease to pray God to bless these labors so that they may lead to fruitful results.

In Liberty

It has also to be borne in mind that relations between states should be based on freedom, that is to say, that no country may unjustly oppress others or unduly meddle in their affairs. On the contrary, all should help to develop in others a sense of responsibility, a spirit of enterprise and an earnest desire to be the first to promote their own advancement in every field.

The Evolution of Economically Underdeveloped Countries

Because all men are joined together by reason of their common origin, their redemption by Christ and their supernatural destiny, and are called to form one single family, we appealed in the encyclical "Mater et Magistra" to economically developed nations to come to the aid of those which were in the process of development. [53]

We are greatly consoled to see how widely that appeal has been favorably received. And we are confident that even more so in the future it will contribute to the end that the poorer countries, in as short a time as possible, will arrive at that degree of economic development which will enable every citizen to live in conditions in keeping with his human dignity.

But it is never sufficiently repeated that the cooperation, to which reference has been made, should be effected with the

[53] Cf. Acta Apostolicae Sedis, Vol. 53, pp. 440–41.

greatest respect for the liberty of the countries being developed, for these must realize that they are primarily responsible, and that they are the principal artisans in the promotion of their own economic development and social progress.

Our predecessor Pius XII already proclaimed that in the field of a new order founded on moral principles, there is no room for violation of freedom, integrity and security of other nations, no matter what may be their territorial extension or their capacity for defense. It is inevitable that the powerful states, by reason of their greater potential and their power, should pave the way in the establishment of economic groups comprising not only themselves but also smaller and weaker states as well. It is nevertheless indispensable that in the interests of the common good they, as all others, should respect the rights of those smaller states to political freedom, to economic development and to the adequate protection, in the case of conflicts between nations, of that neutrality which is theirs according to the natural, as well as international, law. In this way, and in this way only, will they be able to obtain a fitting share of the common good, and assure the material and spiritual welfare of their people. [54]

It is vitally important, therefore, that the wealthier states, in providing varied forms of assistance to the poorer, should respect the moral values and ethnic characteristics peculiar to each, and also that they should avoid any intention of political domination. If this is done, a precious contribution will be made towards the formation of a world community, a community in which each member, whilst conscious of its own individual right and duties, will work in a relationship of equality towards the attainment of the universal common good. [55]

SIGNS OF THE TIMES

Men are becoming more and more convinced that disputes which arise between states should not be resolved by recourse to arms, but rather by negotiation.

It is true that on historical grounds this conviction is based chiefly on the terrible destructive force of modern arms. And it is nourished by the horror aroused in the mind by the very thought of the cruel destruction and the immense suffering which the use of those armaments would bring to the human family. And for this reason it is hardly possible to imagine

[54] Cf. Pius XII's 1941 radio message, op. cit., pp. 16–17.
[55] "Mater et Magistra," op. cit., p. 443.

that in the atomic era war could be used as an instrument of justice.

Nevertheless, unfortunately, the law of fear still reigns among peoples, and it forces them to spend fabulous sums for armaments: not for aggression, they affirm—and there is no reason for not believing them—but to dissuade others from aggression.

There is reason to hope, however, that by meeting and negotiating, men may come to discover better the bonds that unite them together, deriving from the human nature which they have in common. And that they may also come to discover that one of the most profound requirements of their common nature is this: that between them and their respective peoples it is not fear which should reign but love, a love which tends to express itself in a collaboration that is loyal, manifold in form and productive of many benefits.

Part IV

Relationship of Men and of Political Communities with the World Community

INTERDEPENDENCE BETWEEN POLITICAL COMMUNITIES

Recent progress of science and technology has profoundly affected human beings and influenced men to work together and live as one family. There has been a great increase in the circulation of ideas, of persons and of goods from one country to another, so that relations have become closer between individuals, families and intermediate associations belonging to different political communities, and between the public authorities of those communities. At the same time the interdependence of national economies has grown deeper, one becoming progressively more closely related to the other, so that they become, as it were, integral parts of the one world economy. Likewise the social progress, order, security and peace of each country are necessarily connected with the social progress, order, security and peace of all other countries.

At the present day no political community is able to pursue its own interests and develop itself in isolation, because the degree of its prosperity and development is a reflection and a component part of the degree of prosperity and development of all the other political communities.

INSUFFICIENCY OF MODERN STATES TO ENSURE THE UNIVERSAL COMMON GOOD

The unity of the human family has always existed, because its members were human beings all equal by virtue of their natural dignity. Hence there will always exist the objective need to promote, in sufficient measure, the universal common good, that is, the common good of the entire human family.

In times past, one would be justified in feeling that the public authorities of the different political communities might be in a position to provide for the universal common good, either through normal diplomatic channels or through top-level meetings, by making use of juridical instruments such as conventions and treaties, for example: juridical instruments suggested by the natural law and regulated by the law of nations and international law.

As a result of the far-reaching changes which have taken place in the relations between the human family, the universal common good gives rise to problems which are complex, very grave and extremely urgent, especially as regards security and world peace.

On the other hand, the public authorities of the individual political communities—placed as they are on a footing of equality one with the other—no matter how much they multiply their meetings or sharpen their wits in efforts to draw up new juridical instruments, they are no longer capable of facing the task of finding an adequate solution to the problems mentioned above. And this is not due to a lack of good will or of a spirit of enterprise, but because of a structural defect which hinders them.

It can be said, therefore, that at this historical moment the present system of organization and the way its principle of authority operates on a world basis no longer correspond to the objective requirements of the universal common good.

There exists an intrinsic connection between the common good on the one hand and the structure and function of public authority on the other. The moral order, which needs public authority in order to promote the common good in human society, requires also that the authority be effective in attaining that end. This demands that the organs through which the authority is formed, becomes operative and pursues its ends, must be composed and act in such a manner as to be capable of bringing to realization the new meaning which the common good is taking on in the historical evolution of the human family.

Today the universal common good poses problems of worldwide dimensions, which cannot be adequately tackled or solved except by the efforts of public authorities endowed with a wideness of powers, structure and means of the same proportions: that is, of public authorities which are in a position to operate in an effective manner on a worldwide basis. The moral order itself, therefore, demands that such a form of public authority be established.

PUBLIC AUTHORITY INSTITUTED BY COMMON CONSENT AND NOT IMPOSED BY FORCE

A public authority, having worldwide power and endowed with the proper means for the efficacious pursuit of its objective, which is the universal common good in concrete form, must be set up by common accord and not imposed by force. The reason is that such an authority must be in a position to operate effectively yet, at the same time, its action must be inspired by sincere and real impartiality: in other words, it must be an action aimed at satisfying the objective requirements of the universal common good. The difficulty is that there would be reason to fear that a supernational or worldwide public authority, imposed by force by the more powerful political communities, might be or might become an instrument of one-sided interests and even should this not happen, it would be difficult for it to avoid all suspicion of partiality in its actions, and this would take from the efficaciousness of its activity.

Even though there may be pronounced differences between political communities as regards the degree of their economic development and their military power, they are all very sensitive as regards their juridical equality and their moral dignity. For that reason, they are right in not easily yielding in obedience to an authority imposed by force, or to an authority in whose creation they had no part, or to which they themselves did not decide to submit by conscious and free choice.

THE UNIVERSAL COMMON GOOD AND PERSONAL RIGHTS

Like the common good of individual political communities, so too the universal common good cannot be determined except by having regard to the human person. Therefore, the public authority of the world community, too, must have as its fundamental objective the recognition, respect, safeguarding and promotion of the rights of the human person; this can be done by direct action when required, or by creating on a world scale an environment in which the public authorities of the individual political communities can more easily carry out their specific functions.

THE PRINCIPLE OF SUBSIDIARITY

Just as within each political community the relations between individuals are governed by the principle of subsidiarity, so too the relations between the public authority of each political community and the public authority of the world community must be regulated by the light of the same principle. This means that the public authority of the world community must tackle and solve problems of an economic, social, political and cultural character which are posed by the universal common good. For, because of the vastness, complexity and urgency of those problems, the public authorities of the individual states are not in a position to tackle them with any hope of a positive solution.

The public authority of the world community is not intended to limit the sphere of action of the public authority of the individual political community, much less to take its place. On the contrary, its purpose is to create, on a world basis, an environment in which the public authorities of each political community, its citizens and intermediate associations, can carry out their tasks, fulfil their duties and exercise their rights with greater security.[56]

MODERN DEVELOPMENTS

As is known, the United Nations Organization (U.N.O.) was established on June 26, 1945, and to it there were subsequently added intergovernmental agencies with extensive international tasks in the economic, social, cultural, educational and health fields. The United Nations Organization had as its essential purpose the maintenance and consolidation of peace between peoples, fostering between them friendly relations, based on the principles of equality, mutual respect, and varied forms of cooperation in every sector of human society.

An act of the highest importance performed by the United Nations Organization was the Universal Declaration of Human Rights, approved in the General Assembly of December 10, 1948. In the preamble of that declaration, the recognition and respect of those rights and respective liberties is proclaimed as an ideal to be pursued by all peoples and all countries.

[56] Cf. Pius XII's allocution on Sept. 19, 1948, Acta Apostolicae Sedis, Vol. 40, p. 412.

Some objections and reservations were raised regarding certain points in the declaration. There is no doubt, however, that the document represents an important step on the path towards the juridical-political organization of the world community. For in it, in most solemn form, the dignity of a person is acknowledged to all human beings. And as a consequence there is proclaimed as a fundamental right, the right of free movement in the search for truth and in the attainment of moral good and justice, and also the right to a dignified life, while other rights connected with those mentioned are likewise proclaimed.

It is our earnest wish that the United Nations Organization —in its structure and in its means—may become ever more equal to the magnitude and nobility of its tasks, and that the day may come when every human being will find therein an effective safeguard for the rights which derive directly from his dignity as a person, and which are therefore universal, inviolable and inalienable rights. This is all the more to be hoped for since all human beings, as they take an ever more active part in the public life of their own political communities, are showing an increasing interest in the affairs of all peoples, and are becoming more consciously aware that they are living members of a world community.

Part V

Pastoral Exhortations

DUTY OF TAKING PART IN PUBLIC LIFE

Once again we deem it opportune to remind our children of their duty to take an active part in public life, and to contribute toward the attainment of the common good of the entire human family as well as to that of their own political community. They should endeavor, therefore, in the light of the faith and with the strength of love, to insure that the various institutions—whether economic, social, cultural or political in purpose—should be such as not to create obstacles, but rather to facilitate or render less arduous man's perfections of himself both in the natural order as well as in the supernatural.

SCIENTIFIC COMPETENCE, TECHNICAL CAPACITY AND PROFESSIONAL EXPERIENCE

Nevertheless, in order to imbue civilization with sound principles and enliven it with the spirit of the gospel, it is not enough to be illumined with the gift of faith and enkindled with the desire of forwarding a good cause. For this end it is necessary to take an active part in the various organizations and influence them from within. And since our present age is one of outstanding scientific and technical progress and excellence, one will not be able to enter these organizations and work effectively from within unless he is scientifically competent, technically capable and skilled in the practice of his own profession. . . .

RELATIONS BETWEEN CATHOLICS AND NON-CATHOLICS IN SOCIAL AND ECONOMIC AFFAIRS

The doctrinal principles outlined in this document derive from or are suggested by requirements inherent in human nature itself, and are, for the most part, dictates of the natural law. They provide Catholics, therefore, with a vast field in which they can meet and come to an understanding both with Christians separated from this Apostolic See, and also with human beings who are not enlightened by faith in Jesus Christ, but who are endowed with the light of reason and with a natural and operative honesty. In such relations let the faithful be careful to be always consistent in their actions, so that they may never come to any compromise in matters of religion and morals.

At the same time, however, let them be, and show themselves to be animated by a spirit of understanding and detachment, and disposed to work loyally in the pursuit of objectives which are of their nature good, or conducive to good.[67]

However, one must never confuse error and the person who errs, not even when there is question of error or inadequate knowledge of truth in the moral or religious field. The person who errs is always and above all a human being, and he retains in every case his dignity as a human person, and he must be always regarded and treated in accordance with that lofty dignity. Besides, in every human being, there is a need that is congenital to his nature and never becomes extinguished, compelling him to break through the web of error and open his mind to the knowledge of truth. And God will never fail to act on his interior being, with the result that a person, who at a given moment of his life lacks the clarity of faith or even adheres to erroneous doctrines, can at a future date be enlightened and believe the truth. Meetings and agreements, in the various sectors of daily life, between believers and those who do not believe or believe insufficiently because they adhere to error, can be occasions for discovering truth and paying homage to it.

It must be borne in mind, furthermore, that neither can false philosophical teachings regarding the nature, origin and destiny of the universe and of man, be identified with historical movements that have economic, social, cultural or political ends, not even when these movements have originated from those teachings and have drawn and still draw inspiration therefrom. Because the teachings, once they are drawn up and defined, remain always the same, while the movements, working on historical situations in constant evolution, cannot but be influenced by these latter and cannot avoid, therefore, being subject to changes, even of a profound nature. Besides, who can deny that those movements, in so far as they conform to the dictates of right reason and are interpreters of the lawful aspirations of the human person, contain elements that are positive and deserving of approval?

It can happen, then, that a drawing nearer together or a meeting for the attainment of some practical end, which was formerly deemed inopportune or unproductive, might now or in the future be considered opportune and useful. But to decide whether this moment has arrived, and also to lay down the ways and degrees in which work in common might be possible for the achievement of economic, social, cultural and political ends which are honorable and useful: these are the problems which can only be solved with the virtue of prudence, which is the guiding light of the virtues that regulate the moral life, both individual and social. Therefore, as far as Catholics are concerned, this decision rests primarily with those who live and work in the specific sectors of human society in which those problems arise, always, however, in accordance with the principles of the natural law, with the social doctrine of the church, and with the directives of ecclesiastical authority. For it must not be forgotten that the church has the right and the duty not only to safeguard the principles of ethics and religion, but also to intervene authoritatively with her children in the temporal sphere, when there is a question of judging about the application of those principles to concrete cases.[58]

---

[58] Ibid; cf. "Immortale Dei Actas," op. cit., p. 100; Pius XI's encyclical "Ubi Arcano" ("Where in the Inscrutable Design"), Acta Apostolicae Sedis, Vol. 14, p. 698, and Pius XII's allocution on Sept. 11, 1947, Acta Apostolicae Sedis, Vol. 39, p. 486.

LITTLE BY LITTLE

There are some souls, particularly endowed with generosity, who, on finding situations where the requirements of justice are not satisfied or not satisfied in full, feel enkindled with the desire to change the state of things, as if they wished to have recourse to something like a revolution.

It must be borne in mind that to proceed gradually is the law of life in all its expressions, therefore in human institutions, too, it is not possible to renovate for the better except by working from within them, gradually. Pius XII proclaimed: Salvation and justice are not to be found in revolution, but in evolution through concord. Violence has always achieved only destruction, not construction, the kindling of passions, not their pacification, the accumulation of hate and ruin, not the reconciliation of the contending parties. And it has reduced men and parties to the difficult task of rebuilding, after sad experience, on the ruins of discord.[59] . . .

[59] Cf. Pius XII's allocution on June 13, 1943, Acta Apostolicae Sedis, Vol. 35, p. 175.

Complete List of Encyclicals Since 1740

Encyclicals of Pope Benedict XIV (1740-58)

DATE	NAME OF ENCYCLICAL	TO WHOM ADDRESSED	SUBJECT
Dec. 3, 1740	*Ubi primum*	all archbishops, bishops, etc.	on exercise of their ministry
April 11, 1741	*Matrimonii*	Polish episcopate	marriage
Aug. 4, 1741	*Con quanta consolatione*	all bishops, etc.	exhorting obedience to Constitution *Unigenitus*
June 30, 1741	*Quanta cura*	all	forbidding traffic in alms under pain of censure, absolution from which is reserved to the sovereign pontiff
Nov. 17, 1741	*Satis vobis*	all	marriages to be publicly performed
Nov. 13, 1742	*Certiores effecti*	archbishops and bishops of Italy	frequent communion
Mar. 23, 1743	*Quemadmodum preces*	all	liturgical prayer
1744	*In suprema*	all	priests not obliged to administer Holy Communion to all
Feb. 2, 1744	*Inter omnigenas*	Serbian episcopate	marriage by Moslem rites forbidden; divorce forbidden
Aug. 19, 1744	*Cum semper*	Italian episcopate	Mass on feast days to be celebrated for the parishioners
1745	*Cum multorum*	all	on fasting

June 10, 1745	*Libentissime quidem*	all	on fasting
Nov. 1, 1745	*Vix pervenit*	all	on usury
Nov. 5, 1745	*Ab eo tempore*	bishops of Papal States	trading on Sundays forbidden
July 16, 1746	*Accepimus*	ordinaries of the Papal States	vestments
Jan. 1, 1748	*Inter caetera*	all	profane festivals
June 29, 1748	*Magnae nobis*	Polish episcopate	mixed marriages
1749	*Apostolica constitutio*	all	Constitution *Unigenitus*
Feb. 19, 1749	*Annus qui hunc*	bishops of Papal States	sacred music
Jan. 8, 1750	*Benedictus Deus*	all	Jubilee year
Jan. 1, 1751	*Celebrationem magni*	all	Jubilee year
Feb. 20, 1751	*Elapso proximo anno*	all	Holy Inquisition
June 2, 1751	*Magno cum*	episcopate of Poland	abuses in private oratories
June 14, 1751	*A quo primum*	all	on prohibitions to Jews living in same localities as Christians
June 26, 1754	*Cum religiosi aeque*	episcopate of Papal States	teaching catechism
Aug. 10, 1754	*Quod provinciale*	episcopate of Albania	Christians subject to Turks not to take Moslem names
1755	*Allatea sunt Quam ex sublimi*		
Oct. 16, 1756	*Ex omnibus*	French episcopate	*Unigenitus*
Aug. 2, 1757	*Quam grave*	all	priests not properly ordained

ENCYCLICALS OF POPE CLEMENT XIII (1758-69)

DATE	NAME OF ENCYCLICAL	TO WHOM ADDRESSED	SUBJECT
Sept. 11, 1758	*Venimus in altitudinem*	all	jubilee proclaimed
Sept. 13, 1758	*A quo die nobis*	all	on charity necessary among Christians

1759	*Pastoralis officii*	clergy of Sardinia	duties of priests
	Cum primum	all	observation of canonical sanctions
	Appetente sacro	all	merits of fasting
1761	*In dominico*	all	uniformity of instruction in Catholic faith
1762	*Quanto in dolore*	French clergy	local tribulations
1765	*Ubi primum accepimus*	Archduke Joseph of Austria	"Josephism"
1765	*Quanta auxilii*	clergy of Paris	Constitution *Unigenitus*
June 25, 1766	*Quam graviter*	clergy of Paris	
1766	*Christianae reipublicae*	episcopate of Austria	
1768	*Summa quae*	clergy of Poland	
	Accedamus cum	all	jubilee

ENCYCLICALS OF POPE CLEMENT XIV (1769-74)

DATE	NAME OF ENCYCLICAL	TO WHOM ADDRESSED	SUBJECT
Dec. 12, 1769	*Inscrutabili divini*	all	jubilee
1769	*Cum summi*	all	program for the pope's reign
1771	*Magna atque*	all	jubilee
July 21, 1773	*Dominus ac Redemptor Noster*	all	dissolving Jesuit Order
1774	*Salutis nostrae*	all	jubilee

ENCYCLICALS OF POPE PIUS VI (1775-99)

DATE	NAME OF ENCYCLICAL	TO WHOM ADDRESSED	SUBJECT
Dec. 9, 1775	*Inscrutabile divinae*	all	choice of clergy; respect for house of God
1775	*Summa Dei*	all	Jubilee
Mar. 10, 1791	*Quod aliquantulum*	French episcopate	civil constitution of France

427

April 13, 1791	*Caritas quae*	French episcopate	French Revolution
April 23, 1791	*Adeo nota*	bishop of Aleria	protest against Avignon defection
1792	*In gravissimis*	all	France
June 13, 1792	*Ubi Lutetiam*	all	schismatic French clergy
1792	*Ignotae nemini*	all	France
1792	*Quae causa*	all	jubilee
July 31, 1793	*Ad nostros*	French clergy	condemnation of French manifesto
1794	*Auctorem fidei*	clergy of Papal States	condemnation of an Italian book
1799	*Quoties animo*	S. American clergy	grants right to sequester goods to pay public debt

ENCYCLICALS OF POPE PIUS VII (1800-23)

DATE	NAME OF ENCYCLICAL	TO WHOM ADDRESSED	SUBJECT
May 15, 1800	*Diu Satis*	French episcopate	contemporary troubles
1801	*Tam multa*	French episcopate	new arrangements in French hierarchy
1801	*La Chiesa di Gesu Cristo*	French episcopate	new distribution of dioceses in France
Feb. 27, 1809	*Vix nova a Nobis*	French episcopate	new concessions
June 22, 1817	*Vineam quam plantavi*	French episcopate	new bishoprics in France
1820	*Praeclara quam*	French episcopate	withdrawal of faculties from French bishoprics

Encyclicals of Pope Leo XII (1823-29)

DATE	NAME OF ENCYCLICAL	TO WHOM ADDRESSED	SUBJECT
1824	*Ubi Primum*	all	dignity of papacy
May 24, 1824	*Quod hoc ineunte*	all	jubilee
1825	*Ad plurimas easque gravissimas*	all	basilica of St. Peter
Dec. 25, 1825	*Caritate Christi urgente nos*	all	santification of Sunday
Mar 13, 1826	*Quo graviora*	all	secret societies

Encyclicals of Pope Pius VIII (1829-30)

DATE	NAME OF ENCYCLICAL	TO WHOM ADDRESSED	SUBJECT
May 21, 1829	*Traditi humilitati*	all	asks prayers of his bishops
1829	*In supremi apostolatus*	all	jubilee
Mar. 25, 1830	*Litteris alto*	German bishops	mixed marriages

Encyclicals of Pope Gregory XVI (1831-46)

DATE	NAME OF ENCYCLICAL	TO WHOM ADDRESSED	SUBJECT
1831	*Chiamati della Divina Providenza*	bishops of Italy	cultural reforms
1831	*Alli dilettissimi sudditi*	bishops of Italy	cultural reforms
Feb. 3, 1832	*Inter gravissimas*	the Armenians of Constantinople	cultural reforms
May 27, 1832	*Summo jugiter*	bishops of Bavaria	mixed marriages
June 9, 1832	*Cum primum ad aures*	Polish episcopate	insurrections in Poland
1832	*Plura post*	all	jubilee

DATE	NAME OF ENCYCLICAL	TO WHOM ADDRESSED	SUBJECT
Aug. 15, 1832	*Mirari vos*	all	indifferentism in religion
Oct. 4, 1833	*Quo graviora*	bishops of Rhineland	pragmatic
June 25, 1834	*Singulari nos*	all	Abbé de Lamennais condemned
May 17, 1835	*Commissum divinitus*	clergy of Switzerland	German state interference in Church affairs
Dec. 21, 1840	*Augustissimam*	all	appeal for funds
May 8, 1844	*Fra le principali*	all	condemns non-Catholic Bible societies

ENCYCLICALS OF POPE PIUS IX (1846-78)

DATE	NAME OF ENCYCLICAL	TO WHOM ADDRESSED	SUBJECT
Nov. 9, 1846	*Qui pluribus*	all	Communism
1847	*Predecessores nostros*	all	Ireland
Feb. 2, 1849	*Ubi primum*	all	Immaculate Conception
Dec. 8, 1849	*Nostis et nobiscum*	all	attempts to undermine religion in Italy
1851	*Exultavit cor nostrum*	all	jubilee
1851	*Ex aliis nostris*	all	jubilee
1852	*Nemo certe ignorat*	all	Irish
1852	*Probe noscitis Venerabiles*	Spanish episcopate	Spanish problems
1853	*Inter multiplices angustias*	all	praise of French clergy
1854	*Neminem vestrum latet*	all	clergy of Constantinople
1854	*Optime noscitis*	Irish episcopate	license for Catholic University
1854	*Apostolicae nostrae*	all	jubilee
1855	*Optime noscitis*	Austrian episcopate	

Date	Title	Addressed to	Subject
March 17, 1856	*Singulari quidem*	Austrian episcopate	concordat; provincial councils
May 3, 1858	*Amantissimi*	all	The Mass and its fruits
June 18, 1859	*Qui nuper*	all	necessity of temporal power of the Church
1860	*Nullis certe verbis*	all	amplification of above
March 18, 1861	*Jamdudum cernimus*	all	Italian revolutionaries
April 7, 1862	*Amantissimus*	all	Unity of the Church and diversity of rites
Aug. 10, 1863	*Quanto conficiamur*	all	clerico-liberals
Sept. 17, 1863	*Incredibili*	all	Chilean attack on the Church
July 30, 1864	*Ubi urbaniano*	all	Russian persecution of Catholics in Poland
Dec. 8, 1864	*Quantacura*	all	accompanies *Syllabus of Errors*
Oct. 17, 1867	*Venerabilis*	all	the Church in Russia
Dec. 8, 1869	*Aeterni patris*	all	convocation of Vatican council
Nov. 1, 1870	*Respiciantes ea omnia*	all	protests against the tone of Italian press
1871	*Ubi nos arcano Dei*	all	Church-state relations in Italy
June 1871	*Beneficia Dei*	all	25th anniversary
June 1871	*Saepe, Venerabiles*	all	same
1872	*Quae in Patriarchatu*	episcopate of Chaldea and Babylonia	local matters
1873	*Quantus supra*	Armenians	local problems
Nov. 21, 1873	*Etsi multa*	all	invasion of Papal States
1874	*Vix dum a vobis*	Austrian Catholics	
1874	*Gravibus Ecclesiae*	all	the current misfortunes of the Church

431

| May 13, 1874 | *Omnem sollicitudinem* | Ruthenians | care of the Holy See for Oriental rites |
| Feb. 5, 1875 | *Quod nunquam* | Prussian episcopate | *Kulturkampf* |

Encyclicals of Pope Leo XIII (1878-1903)

DATE	NAME OF ENCYCLICAL	TO WHOM ADDRESSED	SUBJECT
April 21, 1878	*Inscrutabili Dei*	all	of the evils that afflict human society
Dec. 28, 1878	*Quod Apostolici muneris*	all	on Socialism
Aug. 4, 1879	*Aeterni Patris*	all	on philosophy of St. Thomas
Feb. 10, 1880	*Arcanum*	all	Christian marriage
Sept. 30, 1880	*Grande munus*	all	SS Cyril and Methodius
Dec. 3, 1880	*Sancta Dei civitas*	French episcopate	propagation of the Faith
June 29, 1881	*Diuturnum*	all	origin of civil power
Aug. 3, 1881	*Licet multa*	Belgian episcopate	local controversies
Feb. 15, 1882	*Etsi nos*	Italian episcopate	Italian conditions
Sept. 17, 1882	*Auspicato concessum*	all	Third Order of St. Francis
Dec. 8, 1882	*Cum multa*	Spanish episcopate	conditions in Spain
Sept. 1, 1883	*Supremi Apostolatus officio*	all	Rosary
Feb. 8, 1884	*Nobilissima Gallorum gens*	French episcopate	religious question
April 20, 1884	*Humanum Genus*	all	freemasonry
Aug. 30, 1884	*Superiore anno*	all	Rosary
Nov. 1, 1885	*Immortale Dei*	all	Christian constitution of states
Nov. 27, 1885	*Spectata fides*	British episcopate	maintenance of denominational schools

Dec. 22, 1885	*Quod auctoritate*	all	jubilee
Jan. 6, 1886	*Jampridem*	German episcopate	anti-Church laws in Germany
Aug. 22, 1886	*Quod multum*	Hungarian episcopate	liberty of the Church
Sept. 14, 1886	*Pergrata*	Portuguese episcopate	local needs of the Church
Sept. 20, 1887	*Vi è ben noto*	Italian bishops	Rosary
Dec. 22, 1887	*Officio sanctissimo*	Bavarian episcopate	church conditions in Bavaria
April 1, 1888	*Quod anniversarius*	all	sacerdotal jubilee
May 5, 1888	*In plurimis*	Brazilian episcopate	slavery of Africans
June 20, 1888	*Libertas*	all	human liberty
June 24, 1888	*Sape Nos*	Irish episcopate	disapproval of boycotting
July 25, 1888	*Paterna caritas*	Armenian episcopate	recalling dissidents to unity
Dec. 10, 1888	*Quam aerumnosa*	American episcopate	Italo-Americans
Dec. 21, 1888	*Etsi cunctas*	Irish bishops	Holy See's program for Ireland
Dec. 25, 1888	*Exeunte jam anno*	all	right ordering of Christian life
March 7, 1889	*Magni nobis*	South American bishops	Catholic university
Aug. 15, 1889	*Quanquam pluries*	all	patronage of St. Joseph
Jan. 10, 1890	*Sapientiae christianae*	all	duties of Christian citizens
Oct. 15, 1890	*Dall' alto dell' Apostolico seggio*	Italian bishops	sects in Italy
Nov. 20, 1890	*Catholicae Ecclesiae*	all	African slavery
March 3, 1891	*In ipso*	Austrian bishops	episcopal reunions
May 15, 1891	*Rerum novarum*	all	condition of the working class
June 25, 1891	*Pastoralis*	Portuguese hierarchy	religious union
Sept. 12, 1891	*Pastoralis officii*	German and Austro-Hungarian bishops	dueling

Sept. 22, 1891	*Octobri mense*	all	Rosary
Feb. 16, 1892	*Au milieu des sollicitudes*	French bishops	Church-state relations
July 16, 1892	*Quarto abeunte saeculo*	Spanish, Italian, American bishops	Columbus
Sept. 8, 1892	*Magnae Dei Matris*	all	Rosary
Dec. 8, 1892	*Inimica vis*	Italian bishops	freemasons
Dec. 8, 1892	*Custodi di quella fede*	Italian bishops	freemasons
Dec. 8, 1892	*Ad extremas*	all	Indian seminaries
Sept. 2, 1893	*Constanti Hungarorum*	Hungarian episcopate	conditions
Sept. 8, 1893	*Laetitiae sanctae*	all	Rosary
Oct. 25, 1893	*Non mediocri*	Spanish hierarchy	Spanish college in Rome
Nov. 18, 1893	*Providentissimus Deus*	all	study of Scripture
March 19, 1894	*Caritatis*	Polish bishops	conditions in Poland
May 1, 1894	*Inter greges*	Peruvian bishops	Catholic Church in Peru
July 2, 1894	*Litteras a vobis*	Brazilian bishops	formation of clergy
Sept. 8, 1894	*Jucunda semper*	all	Rosary
Dec. 24, 1894	*Christi nomen*	all	Society for the Propagation of the Faith
Jan. 6, 1895	*Longinqua*	U. S. Bishops	Catholicism in U. S.
July 10, 1895	*Permoti Nos*	Belgian bishops	social problems
Sept. 5, 1895	*Adjutricem*	all	Rosary
May 1, 1896	*Insignes*	Hungarian bishops	millennium in Hungary
June 29, 1896	*Satis cognitum*	all	Church unity
Sept. 13, 1896	*Apostolicae Curae*	all	Anglican orders
Sept. 20, 1896	*Fidentem piumque annum*	all	Rosary
May 9, 1897	*Divinum illud munus*	all	Holy Ghost
Aug. 1, 1897	*Militantis Ecclesias*	German, Austrian and Swiss bishops	tercentenary of St. Peter Canisius

Sept. 12, 1897	*Affari vos*	Canadian bishops	schools in Manitoba
July 25, 1898	*Caritatis studium*	Scottish bishops	
Aug. 5, 1898	*Spesse volto*	Italian bishops	Catholic Action in Italy
Sept. 5, 1898	*Diuturni temporis*	all	Rosary
Dec. 25, 1898	*Quum diuturnum*	Latin-American bishops	convoking them to Rome
May 25, 1899	*Annum Sacrum*	all	consecration of mankind to the Sacred Heart
Sept. 8, 1899	*Depuis le jour*	French bishops	clerical education in France
Sept. 18, 1899	*Paternae*	Brazilian bishops	ecclesiastical education in Brazil
July 21, 1900	*Omnibus compertum*	Byzantine bishops	union among Greek Melchites
Nov. 1, 1900	*Tametsi*	all	Jesus Christ our Redeemer
Jan. 18, 1901	*Graves de communi*	all	Christian democracy
May 16, 1901	*Gravissimas*	Portuguese bishops	religious Orders in Portugal
Aug. 20, 1901	*Reputantibus*	Bohemian and Moravian bishops	language problems
Nov. 20, 1901	*Urbanitatis veteris*	Greek bishops	foundation of a seminary in Athens
April 15, 1902	*In amplissimo*	U.S. bishops	Church in the U.S.
April 30, 1902	*Quod votis*	Austrian bishops	Catholic University in Austria
May 28, 1902	*Mirae caritatis*	all	Holy Eucharist
Nov. 22, 1902	*Quae ad Nos*	Bohemian and Moravian bishops	church matters locally
Dec. 8,1902	*Fin dal principio*	Italian bishops	ecclesiastical education
Dec. 24, 1902	*Dum multa*	Ecuadorean bishops	marriage

ENCYCLICALS OF POPE ST. PIUS X (1903-14)

DATE	NAME OF ENCYCLICAL	TO WHOM ADDRESSED	SUBJECT
Oct. 4, 1903	*E Supremi*	all	restoration of all things in Christ
Feb. 3, 1904	*Ad diem illum*	all	50th anniversary of definition of Immaculate Conception
March 12, 1904	*Jacunda sane*	all	13th centenary of the death of St. Gregory
April 15, 1905	*Acerbo nimis*	all	catechetical instruction
June 11, 1905	*Il fermo proposito*	Italian bishops	Catholic action
Feb. 11, 1906	*Vehementer Nos*	French bishops	French separation law
April 5, 1906	*Tribus circiter*	bishops of Poland	condemnation of the Mariavites
July 28, 1906	*Pieni l'animo*	Italian bishops	clergy in Italy
Aug. 10, 1906	*Gravissimo officii*	French bishops	forbidding *Associations culturelles*
Jan. 6, 1907	*Une fois encore*	French bishops	separation of church and state
Sept. 8, 1907	*Pascendi Dominici gregis*	all	Modernism condemned
April 21, 1909	*Communium rerum*	all	8th centenary of death of St. Anselm
May 26, 1910	*Editae semper*	all	3rd centenary of St. Charles Borromeo
May 24, 1911	*Jamdudum*	all	separation law in Portugal
June 7, 1912	*Lacrimabili statu*	S. American bishops	condition of Indians
Sept. 24, 1912	*Singulari quadam*	German bishops	labor organizations

ENCYCLICALS OF POPE BENEDICT XV (1914-22)

DATE	NAME OF ENCYCLICAL	TO WHOM ADDRESSED	SUBJECT
Nov. 1, 1914	*Ad beatissimi*	all apostolorum	appeal for peace
June 15, 1917	*Humani generis*	all	preaching
Dec. 1, 1918	*Quod jam diu*	all	Peace Congress, Paris
May 14, 1919	*In hac tanta*	all	12th centenary of St. Boniface
Nov. 24, 1919	*Paterno jam diu*	all	charity to children of central Europe
May 23, 1920	*Pacem, Dei munus*	all	peace
Sept. 15, 1920	*Spiritus Paraclitus*	all	Holy Scripture
Oct. 5, 1920	*Principi apostolorum Petro*	all	St. Ephrem the Syrian
Dec. 1, 1920	*Annus jam plenus*	all	child war victims
Jan. 6, 1921	*Sacra propediem*	all	7th centenary of the Third Order of St. Francis
April 30, 1921	*In praeclara summorum*	all	6th centenary of Dante's death
June 29, 1921	*Fausto appetente die*	all	7th centenary of death of St. Dominic

ENCYCLICALS OF POPE PIUS XI (1922-39)

DATE	NAME OF ENCYCLICAL	TO WHOM ADDRESSED	SUBJECT
Dec. 23, 1922	*Ubi arcano Dei*	all	peace of Christ in the Kingdom of Christ
Jan. 26, 1923	*Rerum omnium*	all	3rd centenary of death of St. Francis de Sales
June 29, 1923	*Studiorem ducem*	all	6th centenary of canonization of St. Thomas Aquinas

Date	Title	Recipients	Subject
Nov. 12, 1923	*Ecclesiam Dei*	all	3rd centenary of death of St. Josaphat
Jan. 18, 1924	*Maximam gravissimamque*	French bishops	diocesan associations
Dec. 11, 1925	*Quas primas*	all	Feast of Christ the King
Feb. 28, 1926	*Rerum ecclesiae*	all	missions
April 30, 1926	*Rite expiatis*	all	7th centenary of death of St. Francis of Assisi
Nov. 18, 1926	*Iniquis aflictisque*	all	persecution of the Church in Mexico
Jan. 6, 1928	*Mortalium animos*	all	promotion of true religious unity
May 8, 1928	*Miserentissumus Redemptor*	all	reparation due to the Sacred Heart
Sept. 8, 1928	*Rerum Orientalium*	all	reunion with the Eastern Churches
Dec. 20, 1929	*Mens Nostra*	all	promotion of spiritual exercises
Dec. 23, 1929	*Quinquagesimo ante*	all	sacerdotal jubilee
Dec. 31, 1929	*Rappresentanti in terra*	Italian bishops	Christian education of youth
April 30, 1930	*Ad salutem*	all	15th centenary of St. Augustine
Dec. 31, 1930	*Casti connubii*	all	Christian marriage
May 15, 1931	*Quadragesimo anno*	all	40th anniversary of *Rerum Novarum*
June 29, 1931	*Non abbiamo bisogno*	Italian bishops	Fascism (Catholic Action)
Oct. 2, 1931	*Nova impendet*	all	economic crisis
Dec. 25, 1931	*Lux veritatis*	all	15th centenary of Council of Ephesus
May 3, 1932	*Caritate Christi compulsi*	all	economic depression
Sept. 29, 1932	*Acerba animi*	S. American bishops	persecution of Church in Mexico

June 3, 1933	*Dilectissima Nobis*	Spanish bishops	conditions in Spain
Dec. 20, 1935	*Ad catholici sacerdotii*	all	Catholic priesthood
June 29, 1936	*Vigilanti cura*	all	motion pictures
March 14, 1937	*Mit brennender Sorge*	German bishops	Naziism
March 19, 1937	*Divini Redemptoris*	all	atheistic communism
March 28, 1937	*Firmissimam constantiam*	S. American clergy	conditions in Mexico
Sept. 29, 1937	*Ingravescentibus malis*	all	rosary

ENCYCLICALS OF POPE PIUS XII (1939-58)

DATE	NAME OF ENCYCLICAL	TO WHOM ADDRESSED	SUBJECT
Oct. 20, 1939	*Summi Pontificatus*	all	Function of the state in the modern world
Nov. 1, 1939	*Sertum laetitiae*	Episcopate of USA	150th anniversary of establishment of hierarchy
June 13, 1940	*Saeculo exeunto octavo*	Portuguese Episcopate	8th centenary of Portuguese independence
June 29, 1943	*Mystici Corporis*	all	Mystical Body of Christ
Sept. 30, 1943	*Divino afflante Spiritu*	all	promotion of Biblical studies
April 9, 1944	*Orientalis Ecclesiae*	all	15th centenary of St. Cyril of Alexandria
April 15, 1944	*Communium interpretes dolorum*	all	For prayers for peace during May
Dec. 23, 1945	*Orientales omnes Eccelesias*	Ruthenian Hierarchy	350th anniversary of reunion with Holy See
Jan. 6, 1946	*Quemadmodum*	all	appeal for world's destitute children
March 21, 1947	*Fulgens radiatur*	all	14th centenary of St. Benedict
Nov. 20, 1947	*Mediator Dei*	all	Sacred Liturgy
Dec. 18, 1947	*Optatissima pax*	all	prescribing prayers for world peace

Date	Title	Audience	Subject
May 1, 1948	*Auspicia quaedam*	all	asking prayers for solution of Paletsine problem
Oct. 24, 1948	*In multiplicibus curis*	all	same
April 15, 1949	*Redemptoris nostri*	all	Holy places of Palestine
March 12, 1950	*Anni sacri*	all	combating atheistic propaganda
July 19, 1950	*Summi maeroris*	all	peace
Aug. 12, 1950	*Humani generis*	all	concerning false opinions
Dec. 6, 1950	*Mirabile illud*	all	peace
June 2, 1951	*Evangeli praecones*	all	missions
Oct. 8, 1951	*Sempiternus Rex*	all	15th centenary of Council of Chalcedon
Oct. 15, 1951	*Ingruentium malorum*	all	Rosary
Dec. 15, 1952	*Orientales Ecclesias*	Eastern bishops	persecution of the Church in the East
May 24, 1953	*Doctor mellifluus*	all	12th centenary of St. Bernard
Oct. 8, 1953	*Fulgens corona*	all	Marian year
March 25, 1954	*Sacra virginitas*	all	consecrated virginity
June 5, 1954	*Ecclesiae fastos*	all	12th centenary of St. Boniface
Oct. 7, 1954	*Ad sinarum gentem*	all	sufferings of the Church in China
Oct. 11, 1954	*Ad caeli reginum*	all	Coronation of Our Lady
Dec. 25, 1955	*Musicae sacrae*	all	sacred music
May 15, 1956	*Haurietus aquas*	all	devotion to the sacred heart
Oct. 28, 1956	*Luctuosissimi eventus*	all	prayers for peace and justice in Eastern Europe

Nov. 1, 1956	*Laetamur admodum*	all	prayers for peace
Nov. 5, 1956	*Datis nuperrime*	all	repression of Hungarian revolt
April 21, 1957	*Fidei donum*	all	African missions
May 16, 1957	*Invicti athletae*	all	3rd centenary of death of St. Andrew Bobola
July 2, 1957	*Le pèlerinage de Lourdes*	all	centenary of apparitions at Lourdes
Sept. 8, 1957	*Miranda prorsus*	all	modern mass communications
Sept. 8, 1958	*Ad apostolorum principus*	all	ex-communication of pro-communist Chinese prelates

ENCYCLICALS OF POPE JOHN XXIII (1958-63)

June 29, 1959	*Ad Petri Cathedram*	all	truth, unity, peace
Aug. 1, 1959	*Sacerdotii nostri primordia*	all	1st centenary of death of St. Jean-Marie-Baptiste Vianney
Sept. 26, 1959	*Grata recordio*	all	Rosary
Nov. 28, 1959	*Princeps pastorum*	all	missions; native clergy
May 15, 1961	*Mater et Magistra*	all	social justice
Dec. 9, 1961	*Aeterna dei sapienta*	all	15th centenary of death of Leo the Great
June 14, 1962	*Paenitentiam agere*	all	penance
April 10, 1963	*Pacem in terris*	all	hopes for peace

Bibliography

Acta Sancta sedis. Rome: 1865-1908. Latin texts of the encyclicals; published periodically. Known since 1909 as *Acta Apostolicae sedis*.

Ayer, J. C. *Source Book for Ancient Church History*. New York: Charles Scribner's Sons, 1926.

Batiffol, P. *Le Siège Apostolique*. Paris: 1898.

Bencini, Dominic. *De litteris encyclicis*. Turin: 1728.

Butler, B. C. *The Church and Infallibility*. New York: Sheed and Ward, 1954.

Carlen, Sister M. Claudia. *Guide to the Documents of Pius XII (1939-1949)*. Westminster, Maryland: The Newman Press, 1951.

————. *Guide to the Encyclicals*. New York: H. W. Wilson Company, 1939.

Chevalier, E. J. and E. Marmy. *La Communauté humaine selon l'esprit Chrétien*. Fribourg, 1944.

Denzinger, Heinrich. *Enchiridion Symbolorum*. Friburgi Brisgoviae: Herder & Co., 1947.

Dogmatic Canons and Decrees. New York: The Devin-Adair Company, 1912.

Doheny, W. F. and J. P. Kelly. *Papal Documents on Mary*. Milwaukee: The Bruce Publishing Co., 1954.

Ehler, Sidney and John B. Morrall. *Church and State Through the Centuries*. Westminster, Maryland: The Newman Press, 1954.

Giles, E. *Documents Illustrating Papal Authority*. London: S.P.C.K., 1952.

Gilson, E. *The Church Speaks to the Modern World*. New York: Doubleday & Company (Image Books), 1954.

Hales, E. E. Y. *Pio Nono*. New York: P. J. Kenedy, 1954.

Hertling, Ludwig. *Geschichte des katolischen Kirche*, 1953.

Hughes, Philip. *A Popular History of the Catholic Church*. New York: Doubleday & Company (Image Books), 1954.

————. *The Reformation in England*. New York: The Macmillan Company, 1951-54 (3 vols.).

Knox, Ronald A. *The New Testament*. New York: Sheed & Ward, 1944.

Koenig, Harry. *Principles for Peace*. National Catholic Welfare Conference, 1943.

Les enseignements pontificaux: presentation et tables par les Moines de Solesmes. Desclée et Cie., 1954.

Lilley, A. Leslie. *The Programme of Modernism*. London: T. Fisher Unwin, 1908.

Michon, Georges. *Les documents pontificaux sur la démocratie et la société moderne*. Paris: Rieder, 1928.

Mirbt, C. *Quellen zur Geschichte des Papsttums*. Berlin, 1878.

National Catholic Almanac 1950. Paterson, New Jersey: St. Anthony's Guild.

Receuil des allocutions consistoriales encycliques citées dans le Syllabus. Paris, 1866.

Robinson, J. H. *Readings in European History*. Chicago: Ginn & Co., 1904.

Rouët de Journel, M. J. *Enchiridion Patristicum*. Friburgi Brisgoviae: Herder & Co., 1929.

Sanctissimi Domini Nostri Benedicti XIV Litterae Encyclicae. Rome, 1761.

Shotwell, James T. and Louise R. Loomis. *The See of Peter*. New York: Columbia University Press, 1927.

Tutti le Encicliche Dei Sommi Pontifici. Milano: Edizioni Corbaccio, 1940.

Whatley, Stephen. *A Parallel of the Doctrine of the Pagans with the Doctrine of the Jesuits*. London: J. Pemberton, 1726.

Wynne, John. *The Great Encyclical Letters of Leo XIII*. New York: Benziger, 1903.

Articles:

Bastnagel, C. "Authority of Papal Encyclicals," in *Catholic Educational Review*, March, 1930, pp. 166-69.

Connell, Francis J. "Does Catholic Doctrine Change?" in *American Ecclesiastical Review*, November, 1947, pp. 321-31.

Fenton, Joseph C. "The Doctrinal Authority of Papal Encyclicals," in *American Ecclesiastical Review*, August-September, 1949, pp. 136-50; 210-20.

Pegues, T. M. "L'autorité des encycliques d'aprés St. Thomas," in *Revue Thomiste 12*, pp. 513-32.

Index

Abortions, 240-41
Acerbo nimis, 28; cited, 207-11
Action Française, 220
Acton, Lord, cited, 85, 103, 221
Ad Beatissimi, 214; cited, 215
Ad caeli reginam, 29
Ad nostros, cited, 117-18
Ad Petri Cathedram, cited, 312-23, 324
Ad sinarum gentem, cited 303-05
Africa, Catholic Church in, 306-311, 371
African students abroad, 310-311, 371
Agnosticism, 198, 264
Agra, bishop of, 118
Agriculture, 340, 349, 350, 357-66
Aid to underdeveloped countries, 367-69
Alaric the Goth, 47
Alexander VI, cited, 77-80
Allorchè Focili, cited, 215-17
Ambrose, St., 59, 63; cited, 46, 63
America, discovery of, 77-78
Anastasius I, Emperor, 53, 62
Annus qui hunc, cited, 108
Antonelli, Cardinal, 129-30, 134
Apollinarian heresy, 44
Apostasy, 36-37
Apostolic letters, 21, 24-25, 29
Aquinas, St. Thomas, 224; cited, 28, 172, 176, 181, 189, 236, 283, 301, 399, 402
Arcano Divinae Providentiae concilio, 142
Arian heresy, 41-43, 45, 56, 60
Ariminum council, 45
Arles, Council of, 41
Art, modern, 293
Asian students abroad, 310-11, 371
Assumption, dogma of the, 104, 298-99
Athanasius, St., cited, 41-42
Atomic energy, 340
Augustine, St., cited, 64, 164, 237-38, 272, 279, 289, 323, 332, 377
Augustine of Canterbury, St., 54
Automation, 340
Avenir, l', 127-28
Avignon, 65, 118
Ayer, J. C., 36

Baptism, Sacrament of, 106-7, 205, 225
Basil, St., cited, 334
Beatification, procedure of, 106
"Belligerent Peoples and to Their Leaders, To," cited, 215-19

Benedict I, 54
Benedict XIV, 29, 105-6, 139; cited, 106-9
Benedict XV, 214, 324, 325; cited, 215-19, 326, 328, 329, 332, 333
Bergamo, Bishop of, 312
Bernetti, Cardinal, 126
Berthier, General, 119
"Biblical Studies, On Promotion of," cited, 275-86
Birth control, 239-40, 371-74
Bismarck, 154, 157
Boethius, 60
Bonaparte, Jerome, 120
Boniface, St., 250; cited, 49
Boniface VIII, 151; cited, 71-74
Bulgars, Council of the, 59
Butler, Dom B. C., 41, 60

Caritas quae, cited, 117
Caritate Christi, cited, 122
Carlen, Sister Mary Claudia, cited, 21
Casti Connubi, cited, 235-43
"Catechism, On the," cited, 207-11
Catholic Action, 311, 333
"Catholic Action, Concerning," cited, 234-49
"Catholic Action in Italy, On the," cited, 211-13
Catholic Emancipation in England, 123
Catholic Institutes, 311
"Catholic Missions, On the," cited, 323-36
"Catholic Missions Especially in Africa, On the Condition of," cited, 306-11
Cavour, Camillo Benso, 130
Celestine I, St., cited, 50
Celestius, 49
Celibacy, 151, 171, 299-303
Chalcedon, Council of, 51-52, 55-56, 132, 204
Charity, 180
Charlemagne, 60, 76
Charles I (of England), 34
Charles I (of Spain), 80-81
Charles III (of Spain), 110
China, Catholic Church in, 303-05
"Christian Constitution of the State, The," 181
"Christian Education of Youth," cited, 224-27
"Christianity and Social Progress," cited, 337-87
Civil Constitution of the Clergy, 117
Class war, 222, 228-29, 256, 318, 341, 347, 355

444

Clement, St., 34
Clement XI, 106, cited, 85-103
Clement XII, 105, 139
Clement XIII, 110-13; cited, 111-12
Clement XIV, 113, 121; cited, 114-15
Clericis laicos, cited, 71-72
Clermont, Council of, 67
Code of Canon Law, 313
Collectivism, 231
College of Cardinals, 324
Columbus, Christopher, 77-78
Communion of the Church, 21-23, 66, 130, 138
Communism, atheistic, 14, 103-4, 145, 166, 220 295; encyclical on, cited, 255-62
Concordat of 1801, 120
Concordat of 1933, 250
Confirmation, Sacrament of, 205, 211
Constance, Council of, 74
Constans II, 112
Constantine the Great, 41
Constantinople, Council of, 56
Conversion, 330
Cornelius, St., cited, 37-39
Crusades, 67
Cyprian, St., 11, cited, 37-40, 322

Damascus I, St., cited, 43-45
Dawson, Christopher, cited, 103, 113-14
Decian persecution, 37
Deism, 85
Democracy, 402
Dès le début, 214; cited, 217-19
Dialectical materialism, 103, 256, 295
Dionysius, St., 73
Dioscurus, patriarch of Alexandria, 51-52, 56
Disarmament, 346, 375, 413-14, 416
Divini Redemptoris, 14, 104, 220; cited, 255-62
Divino afflante Spiritu, cited, 275
Divinum Illud, cited, 157-61
Divorce, 106, 242. See also Marriage, Sacrament of
Docetists, 41
Dominus ac Redemptor noster, 113, 121; cited, 114-15
Donation of Pepin, 76
Donatus, bishop of, 41, 60
Ducatus Romanus, 76

Ecumenical Council, 312-23
Ecumenical Council, Fourth, 52
Elizabeth I (of England), 82-84
Encyclicals, papal, 11-12, 26-29, 106; authority of, 27-28; defined, 21-25; since 1740, listed, 425-41
Enlightenment, 103, 127

Ephesus, council of, 51, 56, 204
Etsi multa luctuosa, cited, 152-54
Eucharist, Sacrament of the, 22-23, 28, 161-66, 196, 205, 286, 287, 289, 290, 291, 322
Eugene III, cited, 67-69
Eugenics, 241-42
Eusebius of Caesarea, 41; cited, 36
Eusebius of Constantinople, 42
Eutyches, 51, 53, 56
Evolution, 295, 297, 298
Execrabilis, cited, 74-76
Existentialism, 294

F.A.O., 366
Fabian, St., 37
"False Opinions, Concerning Certain," cited, 294-99
Family life, 340, 395
Fascism, 103-4, 220, 243-55
Felicissimus, 39
Felix I, St., 141; cited, 40
Fenton, Monsignor Joseph, cited, 27-28
Ferdinand and Isabella, 77
Fidei donum, cited, 306-11
Fideism, 199
Flacillus, bisop of Antioch, 42
Fortunatus, bishop of Carthage, 39-40
Franco-Prussian War, 152
Frederick II (of Prussia), 105
French Revolution, 103, 113, 116, 127

Gangra, Council of, 300
Gasparri, Cardinal, 214, 220, 263
Gelasius I, St., 62; cited, 53-54
"German Empire, On the Present Position of the Catholic Church in," cited, 250-55
Gilson, Etienne, 29, 166
Gizzi, Cardinal, 129
Gnostics, 41
Gore, Charles, cited, 34
Government and Catholics, 316, 317, 334, 335, 341, 342-72, 402-24
Gregorian plain chant, 196, 293
Gregory the Great, St., cited, 54-59, 177, 357
Gregory VII, St., cited, 60-66
Gregory XIII, 111
Gregory XIV, 111
Gregory XVI, 126-28, 132, 137; cited, 127-28
Günther, Anthony, 145

Hartel, W., 38
Henry VIII (of England), 83
Henry IV (of the Holy Roman Empire), 60-61, 65-66
Hermann, Bishop of Metz, 60-61
Hermas, Shepherd of, 21; cited, 36-37

Hertling, Dr., cited, 21-22
Hilary, St., 42
Hitler, 154, 250
Holy Ghost, 157-61, 272, 275
Hughes, Father Philip, cited, 47, 60, 69-70, 113, 156
Hugon de Basseville, Nicholas Jean, 116
Humani generis, cited, 294-99

Idealism, 295
Il Fermo Proposito, cited, 211-13
Immaculate Conception, dogma of, 104, 130, 132-34, 298-99
Immanentism, 295
Immensa aeterni, 24
Immortale Dei, 156
Incarnate Word of God, doctrine on the, 158-59, 164, 272, 290, 292
Index, Congregation of the, 123
Indians, slavery of, 80-81
Indifferentism, 145
Individualism, 231, 233-35, 259
Indulgences, Plenary, 67, 142
Ineffabilis Deus, 298, cited, 134
Infallibility of the Pope, doctrine of, 28-28, 85, 152
Innocent I, St., 63; cited, 22, 47-49
Innocent III, 114; cited, 69-70
Innocent XII, 158
Inquisition, 80
Intellectualism, 198
Inter Caetera Divinae, cited, 77-80
Inter omnigenas, cited, 106
International Labor Organization, 353
Irenaeus, St., cited, 36

Jamdudum Cernimus, 130
James, St., 206
Jansenism, 85-103, 116
Jeremiah, 73
Jerome, St., cited, 43-44, 279
Jesuits, 110-15, 120-21, 154
Jews, 107, 129
Joel, 160
John, St., 34, 159, 203, 204
John II (of Portugal), 77
John Chrysostom, St., 63, 283, 332, 400-01
John VIII, 59
John XXIII, 312; cited, 312-424
John of Falkenberg, 74
Joseph II (of Austria), 116
Josephine, Empress, 120
Julian the Apostate, 23
Julius I, St., cited, 41-43
Julius III, 111

Kapital, Das, 166
Knox, Monsignor Ronald A., 30
Konsequenzmacherei, 14
Kulturkampf, 154, 157

Labor, 318, 335, 340, 346, 348, 352, 354, 365, 399, 405
Lactantius, cited, 394
Lainez, Jaime, 107
Lambruschini, Cardinal, 126, 129
Lamennais, Abbé de, 127-28
Lamentabili Sane, 196; cited, 202-7
Last Supper, 291
Lateran, General Councils: First, 67; Fourth, 114
Lateran, Treaty of the, 77, 220
Latin, ecclesiastical use of, 12-13, 280
Latitudinarianism, 145
Lay Apostolate, the, 311
League of Nations, 224
Leo the Great, St., 338; cited, 51-53, 388-91
Leo III, St., 60
Leo XII, 122, 124, 139; cited, 122
Leo XIII, 29, 156-57, 166, 214, 220, 228-32, 234, 338, 339, 341; cited, 157-95, 236, 271, 275, 276, 278, 280, 284, 314, 317, 339-40, 357, 387, 394, 403
Leys, Leonard (Lessius), 107
Liberalism, 103-4, 126, 129, 145, 152, 156, 229-30, 259-60
Libertae praestantissimum, 156
Linus, St., 34
Litteris, alto, cited, 124
"Liturgy, On the Sacred," cited, 286-93
London, Treaty of, 214
Louis XVI, 116
Luther, Martin, 85, 201

Macedonius, 56
Manichaean heresy, 74
Mansi, G. D., 40
Maria Theresa (of Austria), 110
Mark, St., 34
Marriage: mixed, 121, 124-25; Sacrament of, 106, 150-51, 171, 206, 235-43, 257, 299-303
"Marriage, On Christian," cited, 235-43
Martin V, 74
Marx, Karl, 166, 256
Mary I (of England), 83
Mary the Virgin Mother of God, 290
Mater et Magistra, cited, 337-87, 396, 404, 415
Matilda (of Tuscany), 76
Maurice, Emperor, 54
Maximum illud, cited, 324-26
Maximus, bishop, 37-40
Mazzini, Giuseppi, 129
Mediator Dei, cited, 286-93
Melchiades, St., 41
Messalians, 23
Metternich, Prince, cited, 129
Migne, J. P., 41

Minorities, 410, 411
Mirae caritatis, cited, 161-66
Mirari vos, cited, 127-28
Missionary policy, 77-78, 80, 306-11, 323-36
Mit brennender Sorge, 104, 220; cited, 250-55
Modernist heresy, 103-4, 196-207, 231
Montor, Artaud, Chevalier de, cited, 124
Motion pictures, 314, 344
Munificentissimus Deus, cited, 298-99
Muratori, Lodovico Antonio, 105
Muratorian Fragment, cited, 36
Muslims, 66-67, 106-7
"Mystical Body of Christ, On the," cited, 270-75
Mystici Corporis, 104, 263; cited, 270-75
Mysticism, 271

Napoleon, 76, 103, 118, 120, 129
Nationalism, 85, 103, 220, 283
Native clergy, 306, 326, 329, 330, 332
Natural law, 130, 231-32, 264, 418
Naturalism, 137, 143-44, 271
Nazis. *See* Facism
Negroes, 269
Nestorius, bishop of Constantinople, 50-51, 53, 56
Newman, Cardinal, 15, 321
Nicea, Council of, 15, 41, 52, 56, 204
Nicholas I, St., cited, 59
Nicholas V, 77
Non abbiamo bisogno, 220; cited, 243-49
Novatian heresy, 37, 39, 45

Original sin, doctrine of, 298
Osius, Bishop of Cordova, cited, 112
Osservatore Romano, 245

Pacelli, Eugenio Cardinal. *See* Pius XII
Pacem Dei manus, 214
Pacem in terris, cited, 392-424
Pantheism, 143-44, 295
Papal States, 118, 120, 126-27, 129
Papias, St., 21
Pascendi Dominici Gregis, 28, 196; cited, 197-201
Pastor aeternus (Constitution), 152
Pastorale officium, cited, 80-81
Paul, St., 34, 35, 195, 204, 222, 274, 289, 301, 304, 330, 332, 400
Paul III, 111, 115; cited, 80-81
Paul V, 111
"Peace of Christ in the Kingdom of Christ, On the," cited, 221-24

"Peace on Earth," cited, 392-424
"Peace, Truth, and Unity, On," cited, 312-23
Peguès, Father Thomas, cited, 28
Pelagius, 49
Pelagius II, 54
Penance, Sacrament of, 205-6, 211, 290
Pentecost, Feast of, 158, 160
Pepin, 63, 76
Perón, Juan, 72
Peter, St., 35, 47-49, 72-74, 206, 288; First Epistle of, 21, 30-34
Philip IV (of France), 71-72, 74
Photius, schism of, 131
Pistoia, synod of, 116
Pius II, cited, 74-76
Pius V, St., cited, 82-85
Pius VI, 116-19, 138; cited, 117-18
Pius VII, 129, 139; cited, 120-21
Pius VIII, 123; cited, 123-25
Pius IX, 104, 129-55, 157; cited, 130-55
Pius X, St., 104, 196, 215; cited, 197-213
Pius XI, 14, 220-21; cited, 221-62, 324, 326, 342, 345, 348, 382
Pius XII, 29, 214, 263; cited, 263-311, 317, 319, 324, 325, 326, 327, 331, 333, 335, 339, 340, 347, 349, 351, 354, 355, 370, 383, 395, 396, 397, 401, 414, 416, 424
Political refugees, 412
Polygenism, 298
Pombal, Marquês de, 110
Pontifical Institute of Sacred Music, 196
Pragmatic: of 1821, 123-24; of 1830, 124
Pragmatism, 295
Princeps pastorum, cited, 323-36
Property, right of private, 167-72, 187-88, 230-31, 257, 318, 339, 355-57
Protestantism, 10, 17-18, 66, 82-104
Providentissimus Deus, 276, 277, 278; cited, 280
Pyrrhus, 15-16

Quadragessimo Anno, 104, 220, 261; cited, 228-35, 342, 345, 348, 383
Quanto Conficiamur, 131
Quanta Cura, 29, 134; cited, 135-43
Quesnel, Pasquier, 85
Qui pluribus, cited, 130
Quod numquam, cited, 154-55
Quod provinciale, cited, 106-7
Quran, cited, 66-67

Race hatred, 215, 400, 409
Radet, General, 120
Radio, 314, 339, 340, 344, 379

Rampolla, Cardinal, 214
Rappresentanti in terra, cited, 224-27
Rationalism, 127, 143-45, 271, 294, 295
"Reconstructing the Social Order, On," cited, 228-35
Reformation, Protestant, 66, 82-104
Regnans in excelsis, cited, 82-85
Rerum Novarum, 104, 156, 220, 228, 339; cited, 166-95, 338, 339-40, 357
Ricci, Matthew, 330
Rights of man, 393-97
Risorgimento, 129
Rochefoucauld, Cardinal de la, 117, 138
Roman Curia, reform of, 196
Romanus Pontifex, 77
Rome, Republic of, 130
Roncalli, Angelo. *See* John XXIII
Rossi, Count Pellegrino, 130

Sacra Virginitas, cited, 299-303
Sacred Heart of Jesus, worship of, 112, 270
St. Stephen's, Jerusalem, 276
Sapientiae Christianae, 156
Satis Cognitum, cited, 271
Science and technology, 314, 340, 342, 344, 368
Scriptures, 10-11; translation of, 86-88, 123
Secret societies, 139, 145
Secularism, 103, 260
Sertum Lactitiae, cited, 269-70
Shotwell, Dr., cited, 37
Sicut Universitatis conditor, cited, 70
Simoniacal heresy, 57
Singulari nos, 127; cited, 128
Siricius, St., cited, 45-46
Sixtus V, 24
Slavery, 80-81
Social mobility, 341
Social welfare, 331, 335, 343-45, 350, 353, 361, 377, 398, 402-03
Socialism, 103, 138, 145, 166-68, 172-73, 228-30, 260
"State in the Modern World, On the Function of the," cited, 263-69
Stephen II, 76
Studiorum Decem, cited, 224
Subsidiarity, principle of, 342, 365, 420
Summi Pontificatus, cited, 263-69
Sutri, Council of, 59
"Syllabus Condemning the Errors of the Modernists," cited, 202-7
"Syllabus of Errors," 134-35; cited, 143-52
Sylvester, St., 41

Taxation of clergy, 71-72
Television, 314, 340, 344, 379
Tertullian, cited, 180
Textual criticism, 279
Theodoret of Cyprus, 44; cited, 51
Theodosius I, the Great, 63
Theodosius II, 51
Theophilus, the Bishop of Alexandria, 322
Tolentino, treaty of, 118
Traditi humilitati, cited, 123
Trent, Council of, 17, 123, 125, 139, 150-51, 205, 209, 236
Trinitarian heresies, 41
Trinity, dogma of the Blessed, 157-59
Twenty-eighth Canon, 52

Ubi Arcano Dei, cited, 221-24
Ubi primum, 29, 106; cited, 132-34
Ultra-nationalism, 332
Unam Sanctam, 29; cited, 72-74, 131
Unigenitus, 29; cited, 85-103
Union Review, The, 130
United Nations, 420-21
"United States, Encyclical Letter to the Church in the," cited, 269-70
Unity of the Catholic Church, 312-23
Universal Declaration of Human Rights, 420
Urban II, 67-68
Usury, 107-8, 175

Vatican Council I, 104, 152; cited, 26-27
Vatican Council II, 312
Vienna, Congress of, 76
Victor I, St., 36
Vigilantiae, 277
Virginity, 151, 171, 299-303
Vital immanence, 198-200
Vix nova a Nobis, cited, 121
Vix pervenit, cited, 107-8
Voltaire, 103, 105
Vulgate, 278

Wiseman, Cardinal, cited, 25
Women, rights of, 399
"Working Classes, On the Condition of the," 228-30; cited, 166-95
Workingmen's unions, 188-93, 232-34, 335, 339-40, 352, 353
World War I, 214-19, 222, 263, 294, 325
World War II, 263, 269, 294
Worms, Concordat of, 67
Wynne, Father John, cited, 156

Zacharias, St., 63
Zelanti, 126
Zeno, Emperor, 141